W9-ATB-192

Winner of the 1989 National Book Critics Circle Award
and the 1989 Christopher Award—
Named as a notable book of 1989 by the American
Library Association, *Booklist*, and *Library Journal*

THE
BROKEN
CORD

MICHAEL DORRIS

With a foreword by LOUISE ERDRICH

 HarperPerennial
A Division of HarperCollins*Publishers*

A portion of Chapter Five appeared in somewhat different form in *Working Mother* magazine.

PHOTO CREDITS

Photo 1:   Sterling Clarren et al. "The Fetal Alcohol Syndrome." *The New England Journal of Medicine* 298 (19), 1978.

Photo 2:   K. L. Jones and D. W. Smith. "Recognition of the Fetal Alcohol Syndrome in Early Infancy," *Lancet* 2: 999–1001, 1973.

Photos 3 and 4:   A. P. Streissguth, C. S. Herman, and D. W. Smith. "Stability of Intelligence in the Fetal Alcohol Syndrome: A Preliminary Report," *Alcoholism: Clinical and Experimental Research* 2 (2): 165–170, 1978.

Photos 5, 6, and 7:   K. L. Jones, D. W. Smith, C. N. Ulleland, and A. P. Streissguth. "Patterns of Malformation in the Offspring of Chronic Alcoholic Mothers." *Lancet* 1: 1267–1271, 1973.

A hardcover edition of this book was published in 1989 by Harper & Row, Publishers.

First HarperPerennial edition published 1990.

The Library of Congress has catalogued the hardcover edition as follows:

Dorris, Michael.
    The broken cord/by Michael Dorris; with a foreword by Louise Erdrich.—1st ed.
      p.   cm.
    ISBN 0-06-016071-3
    1. Fetal alcohol syndrome—Patients—Family relationships.
    I. Title.
    RG629.F45D67   1989
    362.29'2'0880542—dc20   88-45893

ISBN 0-06-091682-6 (pbk.)

98 RRD 25 24 23 22

For Louise,
who shares this story
who joined me in its living and telling
who made us whole

For our brave son

ACKNOWLEDGMENTS

I thank the many people who talked to me with honesty and candor in the course of the years during which this book was written, especially Jeaneen and Robert Grey Eagle, Brenda Demery, Elaine Beaudreau, the late Mona Richards, Sharon Cuny, Melvin Brewer, Stan Shepard, Susan Lindsay, Philip May, Ann Streissguth, Sterling Clarren, Theda New Breast, Eva Smith, Ernest Abel, and Luis Escobar. I thank the Rockefeller Foundation and Dartmouth College for the time and funding they provided. Deep appreciation also goes to Charles Rembar and to my editor, Hugh Van Dusen, for valuable editorial suggestions.

The rest of the list of grateful acknowledgments is unending, for it embodies our son's history. Thanks go: to the chain of doctors, social workers, and dedicated teachers, among them Colleen Nooney, Denis Daigle, Robert Storrs, Edward Hart, Robert Lanzer, Alice Hendrick, the late Livia Alexion, Caroline Storrs, Richard Nordgren, Ken Kramberg—people who broke the rules of normal practice and worked for Adam's triumphs as if they were their own; to Eileen Cowin, Bea Medicine, Nina Sazer, and the late Jack Stokely, who have each in their own way been particularly close to Adam, instructing him by their example in friendship and kindness; to the circle of immediate family—Mary Besy Dorris, Marion Burkhardt, Virginia Burkhardt, the late Katherine Smith, Ralph and Rita Erdrich—who have unstintingly supplied all that love and hope can bring; to Adam's brother and sisters—Sava, Madeline, Persia, Pallas, and Aza—for their strengths and understandings; and always to Louise Erdrich, Adam's mother, who chose far better than I: she knew what she was doing and did it, beautifully, anyway. Finally, I thank Adam, who gave me permission to write this story, read or listened to every word, and is, at last, its true and ongoing creator.

This experience we did not choose, which we would have given anything to avoid, has made us different, has made us better. Through it we have learned the lesson that no one studies willingly, the hard, slow lesson of Sophocles and Shakespeare—that one grows by suffering. And that too is Jessy's gift. I write now what fifteen years past I would still not have thought possible to write: that if today I were given the choice, to accept the experience, with everything that it entails, or to refuse the bitter largesse, I would have to stretch out my hands—because out of it has come, for all of us, an unimagined life. And I will not change the last word of the story. It is still love.

—CLARA CLAIBORNE PARK
The Siege

FOREWORD

The snow fell deep today. February 4, 1988, two days before Michael and I are to leave for our first trip abroad together, ten days before Saint Valentine's holiday, which we will spend in Paris, fifteen days after Adam's twentieth birthday. This is no special day, it marks no breakthrough in Adam's life or in mine, it is a day held in suspension by the depth of snow, the silence, school closing, our seclusion in the country along a steep gravel road which no cars will dare use until the town plow goes through.

It is just a day when Adam had a seizure. His grandmother called and said that she could see, from out the window, Adam lying in the snow, having a seizure. He had fallen while shoveling the mailbox clear. Michael was at the door too, but I got out first because I had on sneakers. Jumping into the snow I felt a moment of obscure gratitude to Michael for letting me go to Adam's rescue. Though unacknowledged between us, these are the times when it is easy to be a parent to Adam. His seizures are increasingly grand mal now. And yet, unless he hurts himself in the fall there is nothing to do but be a comforting presence, make sure he's turned on his side, breathing. I ran to Adam and I held him, spoke his name, told him I was there, used my most soothing tone. When he came back to consciousness I rose, propped him against me, and we stood to shake out his sleeves and the neck of his jacket.

A lone snowmobiler passed, then circled to make sure we were all right. I suppose we made a picture that could cause mild concern. We stood, propped together, hugging and breathing hard. Adam is taller than me, and usually much stronger. I held him around the waist with both arms and looked past his shoulder. The snow was still coming, drifting through the deep-branched pines. All around us there was such purity, a wet and electric silence. The air was warm and the snow already melting in my shoes.

It is easy to give the absolute, dramatic love that a definite physical problem requires, easy to stagger back, slipping, to take off Adam's boots and make sure he gets the right amount of medicine into his system.

It is easy to be the occasional, ministering angel. But it is not easy to live day in and day out with a child disabled by Fetal Alcohol Syndrome or Fetal Alcohol Effect. This set of preventable birth defects is manifested in a variety of ways, but caused solely by alcohol in an unborn baby's developing body and brain. The U.S. Surgeon General's report for 1988 warned about the hazards of drinking while pregnant, and many doctors now say that since no level of alcohol has been established as safe for the fetus, the best policy to follow for nine months, longer if a mother nurses, is complete abstinence. As you will read, every woman reacts differently to alcohol, depending on age, diet, and metabolism. However, drinking at the wrong time of development can cause facial and bodily abnormalities, as well as lower intelligence, and may also impair certain types of judgment, or alter behavior. Adam suffers all the symptoms that I've mentioned, to some degree. It's a lot of fate to play with for the sake of a moment's relaxation.

I never intended to be the mother of a child with problems. Who does? But when, after a year of marriage to their father I legally adopted Adam, Sava, and Madeline—the three children *he* had adopted, years before, as a single parent—it simply happened. I've got less than the ordinary amount of patience, and for that reason I save all my admiration for those like Ken Kramberg, Adam's teacher, and others like Faith and Bob Annis, who work day in and day out with disability. I save it for my husband, Michael, who spent months of his life teaching Adam to tie his shoes. Living with Adam touches on my occupation only in the most peripheral ways; this is the first time I've ever written about him. I've never disguised him as a fictional character or consciously drawn on our experience together. It is, in fact, painful for a writer of fiction to write about actual events in one's personal life.

I have seen Michael, an anthropologist and novelist, struggle with this manuscript for six years. The work was a journey from the world of professional objectivity to a confusing realm where boundaries could no longer be so easily drawn. It has been wrenching for Michael to relive this story, but in the end, I think he felt compelled to do so after realizing the scope of the problem, after receiving so many desperate and generous stories from other people, and, in the end, out of that most frail of human motives—hope. If one story of FAS could be made accessible and real, it might just stop someone, somewhere, from producing another alcohol-stunted child.

Adam does not read with great ease, but he has pressed himself to read this story. He has reacted to it with fascination, and he has agreed to its publication. Although he has no concern about us as professionals, neither pride nor the slightest trace of resentment, Adam takes pleasure when, as a family, our pictures have occasionally appeared in the paper. He sees Michael and me primarily in the roles to which we've assigned ourselves around the house. Michael is the laundryman, I am the cook. And beyond that, most important, we are the people who respond to him. In that way, though an adult, he is at the stage of a very young child who sees the world only as an extension of his or her will. Adam is the world, at least his version of it, and he knows us only as who we are when we enter his purview.

Because of this, there are ways Adam knows us better than we know ourselves, though it would be difficult for him to describe this knowledge. He knows our limits, and I, at least, hide my limits from myself, especially when I go beyond them, especially when it comes to anger. Sometimes it seems to me that from the beginning, in living with Adam, anger has been inextricable from love, and I've been as helpless before the one as before the other.

We were married, Michael, his three children, and I, on a slightly overcast October day in 1981. Adam was thirteen, and because he had not yet gone through puberty, he was small, about the size of a ten-year-old. He was not, and is not, a charming person, but he is generous, invariably kind-hearted, and therefore lovable. He had then, and still possesses, the gift—which is also a curse, given the realities of the world—of absolute, serene trust. He took our ceremony, in which we exchanged vows, literally. At the end of it we were pronounced husband, wife, and family by the same friend, a local judge, who would later formally petition for me to become the adoptive mother of Adam, Sava, and Madeline; then still later, as we painfully came to terms with certain truths, he helped us set up a lifelong provision for Adam in our wills. As Judge Daschbach pronounced the magic words, Adam turned to me with delight and said, "Mom!" not Louise. Now it was official. I melted. That trust was not to change a whit, until I changed it.

Ten months pass. We're at the dinner table. I've eaten, so have our other children. It's a good dinner, one of their favorites. Michael's gone. Adam eats a bite then puts down his fork and sits before his plate. When I ask him to finish, he says, "But, Mom, I don't like this food."

"Yes, you do," I tell him. I'm used to a test or two from Adam when Michael is away, and these challenges are wearying, sometimes even maddening. But Adam has to know that I have the same rules as his father. He has to know, over and over and over. And Adam *does* like the food. I made it because he gobbled it down the week before and said he liked it, and I was happy.

"You have to eat or else you'll have a seizure in the morning," I tell him. This has proved to be true time and again. I am reasonable, firm, even patient at first, although I've said the same thing many times before. This is normal, Adam's way, just a test. I tell him again to finish.

"I don't like this food," he says again.

"Adam," I say, "you have to eat or you'll have a seizure."

He stares at me. Nothing.

Our younger children take their empty dishes to the sink. I wash them. Adam sits. Sava and Madeline go upstairs to play, and Adam sits. I check his forehead, think perhaps he's ill, but he is cool, and rather pleased with himself. He has now turned fourteen years old. But he still doesn't understand that, in addition to his medication, he must absorb so many calories every day or else he'll suffer an attack. The electricity in his brain will lash out, the impulses scattered and random.

"Eat up. I'm not kidding."

"I did," he says, the plate still full before him.

I simply point.

"I don't like this food," he says to me again.

I walk back to the cupboard. I slap a peanut butter sandwich together. He likes those. Maybe a concession on my part will satisfy him, maybe he'll eat, but when I put it on his plate he just looks at it.

I go into the next room. It is eight o'clock and I am in the middle of a book by Bruce Chatwin. There is more to life . . . but I'm responsible. I have to make him see that he's not just driving me crazy.

"Eat the sandwich . . ."

"I did." The sandwich is untouched.

"Eat the dinner . . ."

"I don't like this food."

"Okay then. Eat half."

He won't. He sits there. In his eyes there is an expression of stubborn triumph that boils me with the suddenness of frustration, dammed and suppressed, surfacing all at once.

"EAT!" I yell at him.

Histrionics, stamping feet, loud voices, usually impress him with the serious nature of our feelings much more than the use of reason. But not this time. There is no ordering, begging, or pleading that will make him eat, even for his own good. And he is thin, so thin. His face is gaunt, his ribs arch out of his sternum, his knees are big, bony, and his calves and thighs straight as sticks. I don't want him to fall, to seize, to hurt himself.

"Please . . . for me. Just do it."

He looks at me calmly.

"Just for me, okay?"

"I don't like this food."

The lid blows off. Nothing is left. If I can't help him to survive in the simplest way, how can I be his mother?

"Don't eat then. And don't call me Mom!"

Then I walk away, shaken. I leave him sitting and he does not eat, and the next morning he does have a seizure. He falls next to the aquarium, manages to grasp the table, and as his head bobs and his mouth twists, I hold him, wait it out. It's still two days before Michael will arrive home and I don't believe that I can handle it and I don't know how Michael has, but that is only a momentary surge of panic. Adam finally rights himself. He changes his pants. He goes on with his day. He does not connect the seizure with the lack of food: he won't. But he does connect my words, I begin to notice. He does remember. From that night on he starts calling me Louise, and I don't care. I'm glad of it at first, and think it will blow over when we forgive and grow close again. After all, he forgets most things.

But of all that I've told Adam, all the words of love, all the encouragements, the orders that I gave, assurances, explanations, and instructions, the only one he remembers with perfect, fixed, comprehension, even when I try to contradict it, even after months, is "Don't call me Mom."

Adam calls me "Mother" or "Mom" now, but it took years of patience, of backsliding, and of self-control, it took Adam's father explaining and me explaining and rewarding with hugs when he made me feel good, to get back to mother and son again. It took a long trip out west, just the two of us. It took a summer of side-by-side work. We planted thirty-five trees and one whole garden and a flower bed. We thinned the strawberries, pruned the lilacs and forsythia. We played tic-tac-toe, then Sorry. We lived together. And I gave up making him eat, or distanced myself enough to put the medicine in his hand and walk away, and realize I can't protect him.

That's why I say it takes a certain fiber I don't truly possess to live and work with a person obstinate to the core, yet a victim. Constant, nagging insults to good sense eventually wear on the steel of the soul. Logic that flies in the face of logic can madden one. In the years I've spent with Adam, I have learned more about my limits than I ever wanted to know. And yet, in spite of the ridiculous arguments, the life-and-death battles over medication and the puny and wearying orders one must give every day, in spite of pulling gloves onto the chapped, frost-bitten hands of a nearly grown man and knowing he will shed them, once out of sight, in the minus-thirty windchill of January, something mysterious has flourished between us, a bond of absolute simplicity, love. That is, unquestionably, the alpha and omega of our relationship, even now that Adam has graduated to a somewhat more independent life.

But as I said, that love is inextricable from anger, and in loving Adam, the anger is mostly directed elsewhere, for it is impossible to love the sweetness, the inner light, the qualities that I trust in Adam, without hating the fact that he will always be kept from fully expressing those aspects of himself because of his biological mother's drinking. He is a Fetal Alcohol Effect victim. He'll always, all his life, be a lonely person.

I drank hard in my twenties, and eventually got hepatitis. I was lucky. Beyond an occasional glass of wine, I can't tolerate liquor anymore. But from those early days, I understand the urge for alcohol, its physical pull. I had formed an emotional bond with a special configuration of chemicals, and I realize to this day the attraction of the relationship and the immense difficulty in abandoning it.

Adam's mother never did let go. She died of alcohol poisoning, and I'd feel sorrier for her, if we didn't have Adam. As it is, I only hope that she died before she had a chance to produce another child with his problems. I can't help but wish, too, that during her pregnancy, if she couldn't be counseled or helped, she had been forced to abstain for those crucial nine months. On some American Indian reservations, due to Reagan-era slashing of alcohol and drug treatment and prenatal care programs, the situation has grown so desperate that a jail internment during pregnancy has been the only answer possible in some cases. Some people, whose views you will read in these pages, have taken more drastic stands and even called for the forced sterilization of women who, after having previously blunted the lives of several children like Adam, refuse to stop drinking while they're pregnant. This will outrage some women, and men, good people who believe that it is the right of individuals to put themselves in harm's way, that drinking is a choice we make, that a person's liberty to court either happiness or despair is sacrosanct. I believed this, too, and yet the poignancy and frustration of Adam's life has fed my doubts, has convinced me that some of my principles were smug, untested. After all, where is the measure of responsibility here? Where, exactly, is the demarcation between self-harm and child abuse? Gross negligence is nearly equal to intentional wrong, goes a legal maxim. Where do we draw the line?

The people who advocate forcing pregnant women to abstain from drinking come from within the communities dealing with a problem of nightmarish proportions. Everyone agrees that the best answer is not to lock up pregnant women, but to treat them. However, this problem is now generations in the making. Women who themselves suffer from Fetal Alcohol Syndrome or Effect are extremely difficult to counsel because one of the most damaging aspects of FAS is the inability to make cause–effect connections, or to "think ahead." In addition, many alcohol and drug treatment programs are closed to pregnant women and, therefore, also to unborn children—the most crucial patients of all. It is obvious that the much-ballyhooed war on drugs is not being won with guns, but requires the concerted efforts of a compassionate society. Alcohol rehabilitation programs should be as easy to get into as liquor stores, and they should be free, paid for by the revenues from state liquor stores in some areas, and liquor taxes in others.

Since we the people are the government, we are all in some way to blame for allowing a problem of this magnitude to occur. Still, it is to devalue the worth of the individual not to hold one person, in some measure, responsible for his or her behavior. Once a woman decides to carry a child to term, to produce another human being, has she also the right to inflict on that person Adam's life? And isn't it also a father's responsibility to support and try to ensure an alcohol-free pregnancy? Because his mother drank, Adam is one of the earth's damaged. Did his mother have the right to take away Adam's curiosity, the right to take away the joy he could have felt at receiving a high math score, in reading a book, in wondering at the complexity and quirks of nature? Did she and his absent father have the right to make him an outcast among children, to make him friendless, to make of his sexuality a problem more than a pleasure, to slit his brain, to give him violent seizures?

It seems to me, in the end, that no one has the right to inflict such harm, even from the depth of ignorance. Roman Catholicism defines two kinds of ignorance, vincible and invincible. Invincible ignorance is that state in which a person is unexposed to certain forms of knowledge. The other type of ignorance, vincible, is willed. It is a conscious turning away from truth. In either case, I don't think Adam's mother had the right to harm her, and our, son.

Knowing what I know now, I am sure that even when I drank hard, I would rather have been incarcerated for nine months and produce a normal child than bear a human being who would, for the rest of his or her life, be imprisoned by what I had done. I would certainly go to jail for nine months now if it would make Adam whole. For those still outraged at this position, those so sure, so secure in opposition, I say the same thing I say to those who would not allow a poor woman a safe abortion and yet have not themselves gone to adoption agencies and taken in the unplaceable children, the troubled, the unwanted:

If you don't agree with me, then please, go and sit beside the alcohol-affected while they try to learn how to add. My mother, Rita Erdrich, who works with disabled children at the Wahpeton Indian

School, does this every day. Dry their frustrated tears. Fight for them in the society they don't understand. Tell them every simple thing they must know for survival, one million, two million, three million times. Hold their heads when they have unnecessary seizures and wipe the blood from their bitten lips. Force them to take medicine. Keep the damaged of the earth safe. Love them. Watch them grow up to sink into the easy mud of alcoholism. Suffer a crime they won't understand committing. Try to understand lack of remorse. As taxpayers, you are already paying for their jail terms, and footing the bills for expensive treatment and education. Be a victim yourself, beat your head against a world of brick, fail constantly. Then go back to the mother, face to face, and say again: *"It was your right."*

When I am angriest, I mentally tear into Adam's mother because, in the end, it was her hand that lifted the bottle. When I am saddest, I wish her, exhaustedly . . . but there is nowhere to wish her worse than the probable hell of her life and death. If I ever met her, I don't know what I'd do. Perhaps we'd both be resigned before this enormous lesson. It is almost impossible to hold another person responsible for so much hurt. Even though I know our son was half-starved, tied to the bars of his crib, removed by a welfare agency, I still think it must have been "society's fault." In public, when asked to comment on Native American issues, I am defensive. Yes, I say, there are terrible problems. It takes a long, long time to heal communities beaten by waves of conquest and disease. It takes a long time for people to heal themselves. Sometimes, it seems hopeless. Yet in places, it is happening. Tribal communities, most notably the Alkali Lake Band in Canada, are coming together, rejecting alcohol, reembracing their own humanity, their own culture. These are tough people and they teach a valuable lesson: to whatever extent we can, we must take charge of our lives.

Yet, in loving Adam, we bow to fate. Few of his problems can be solved or ultimately changed. So instead, Michael and I concentrate on only what we can control—our own reactions. If we can muster grace, joy, happiness in helping him confront and conquer the difficulties life presents . . . then we have received gifts. Adam has been deprived of giving so much else.

What I know my husband hopes for, in offering *The Broken Cord*, is a future in which this particular and preventable tragedy will not exist. I feel the same way. I would rather that FAS and FAE were eradicated through enlightenment, through education and a new commitment to treatment. That is the hope in which this book was written. But if that isn't possible, I would eliminate them any way I could.

Michael and I have a picture of our son. For some reason, in this photograph, taken on my grandfather's land in the Turtle Mountains of North Dakota, no defect is evident in Adam's stance or face. Although perhaps a knowing doctor could make the fetal alcohol diagnosis from his features, Adam's expression is intelligent and serene. He is smiling, his eyes are brilliant, and his brows are dark, sleek. There is no sign in this portrait that anything is lacking.

I look at this picture and think, "Here is the other Adam. The one our son would be if not for alcohol." Sometimes Michael and I imagine that we greet him, that we look into his eyes, and he into ours, for a long time and in that gaze we not only understand our son, but he also understands us. He has grown up to be a colleague, a peer, not a person who needs pity, protection, or special breaks. By the old reservation cabin where my mother was born, in front of the swirled wheat fields and woods of ancestral land, Adam stands expectantly, the full-hearted man he was meant to be. The world opens before him—so many doors, so much light. In this picture, he is ready to go forward with his life.

—LOUISE ERDRICH

CHAPTER ONE

I sat in the lobby of the Pierre airport, waiting. The terminal resembled an oversized department store display case, the kind in which jewelry or cosmetics are arranged—a glass front, neutral colors, brightly lit—except that this one existed in isolation, a rectangular box on the flat, wind-scoured plain of central South Dakota. A draft of air had lifted the wings of the small commuter plane just before we landed, releasing first a collective moan of dread and then the embarrassed laughter of survival among my fellow passengers.

On the ground I got a better look at them: three bureaucrats, dressed in wrinkle-free suits, with business in the state capital; two ranchers sporting their go-to-town buckles—large silver and turquoise affairs that divided barrel chests from thin, booted legs; a harried mother trying to convince a small child with pressure-stopped ears to yawn or swallow; a visiting in-law, met loudly by a woman in curlers and Bermuda shorts.

I felt exhilarated and out of place, a stranger on a mission no one would suspect: within the hour, I was due to become an unmarried father.

The year was 1971 and I was twenty-six years old, ex-would-be hippie, candidate for a Yale doctorate in anthropology, a first-year instructor at a small experimental college in New England. This cloudy afternoon in Pierre was the culmination of a journey I had begun nine months before when, while doing fieldwork in rural Alaska, it occurred to me that I wanted a child, I wanted to be a parent.

I remember precisely the context of this realization. I was living then in a cabin in Tyonek, an Athapaskan-speaking Indian community on the west coast of Cook Inlet, collecting information about the impact of modernization and oil revenues on the life of this remote fishing village. Much of my time was spent in the study of the local language, linguistically related to Navajo and Apache but distinctly adapted to the subarctic environment. One of its most difficult features for an outsider to grasp was the practice of almost always speaking, and thinking, in a collective plural voice. The word for people, "*dene*," was used as a kind of "we"—the subject for virtually every predicate requiring a personal pronoun—and therefore any act became, at least in conception, a group experience.

It was my second autumn in Tyonek. I had spent the morning interviewing an elderly woman, Mrs. Nickefor Alexan, the respected expert on subjects ranging from traditional herbal medicine to the do's and don'ts of appropriate courting behavior. In the course of our conversations, I consumed too much tea and my mouth was dry with the acidic taste.

I returned to my house in the afternoon and was uninterrupted as I organized my notes; most adults in the community were busy in their smokehouses, preserving and canning August's catch of fish, and the children, my frequent summer visitors, had returned to school. In a world of "we," I was an "I," with no essential responsibilities or links outside myself.

Periodically, I glanced from my window at the darkening sky. The twenty-four-hour circuit of day and night, upon which most of Western time is based, expands to a full twelve months in the far north. There is light enough to fish any time in the summer, and so the arbitrary schedules of passing salmon runs rather than a wrist-watch dictate when dories should put to sea. The darkness is absolute in winter, underlined by forbidding temperatures that sometimes dip fifty degrees below zero. The short fall season, therefore, is a blend of both fatigue and melancholy, of final consolidation of the summer's gains and of preparation for the severity of approaching weather. It is a bridge of contemplation, of taking stock, and there is no occasion more appropriate for that practice than when the turning of the tide corresponds to the setting or rising of the low sun. Then, on the best days, the usually ferocious water is tamed into the stillness of a mirror that reflects the red and violet light of the clouds. Immersed in this experience, renowned among Native peoples of the region as a moment out of ordinary time, the only possible response is surrender.

I rose from the table I used for a desk, and stood at the open front door. My cabin perched on a bank above the beach, high enough so that I seemed entirely surrounded by improbable light, awhirl in the energy of star and sea. The colors above and below merged incoherently, washed into each other and into me. It was not that I had a vision of any sort, but rather that my mind was temporarily cleansed, made ready for new writing; and on that board I read with no ambiguity that I wanted a baby. The message was so certain, so unwavering, that I did not once question it. Instead, when I shut the door, I put aside my work and composed four letters to social welfare agencies, asking if adoption were possible for a single man, and if so, how and when.

Single-parenthood had, for generations, been the practical norm in my family. My grandfathers and father had all died young, leaving widows to raise children alone and through extended family networks. My role models were strong, capable mothers, aunts, and grandmothers, and I saw no compelling reason not to continue the tradition. I imagined vaguely that I would someday marry, but there were no immediate prospects. For some women, especially in the 1960s, babies preceded husbands. Why couldn't a child come for me before a wife?

The only reply I received to my inquiries came from Alaska Catholic Social Services, and I arranged an interview for the next time I went to Anchorage to buy supplies. A few weeks later, when I rang the bell of the small brick building, I was no less sure of my goal, but I was terrified that I would somehow jeopardize my chances by making a bad first impression. I had dressed carefully in a dark suit and wore a tie for the first time in years. In the reception room I behaved as though I were being observed through one-way mirrors, and resolutely read three articles—not one word of which lodged in my brain—in the Catholic magazine I found in the rack. I refused a second cup of coffee, lest my unseen evaluator think I had an addictive personality, crossed my legs, then in order to look more manly, quickly uncrossed them and didn't even consider smoking the cigarette I craved.

At last my name was called, and I entered a blue-carpeted office. The nun who faced me was, if anything, even more ill-at-ease than I.

She averted her eyes behind rimless glasses, offered more coffee which I strenuously rejected, and finally stared hard at the lone piece of paper on her blotter—a piece of paper I recognized as my letter.

"Yours is an unusual request, Mr. Dorris," Sister Clare said. "Does it perhaps have something to do with your interest in anthropology?"

This was one question for which I had not been prepared, and so I simply looked at her, waiting for clarification. She seemed embarrassed.

"We thought, you know, it might be a kind of experiment you had in mind."

I tried to explain, but it wasn't easy. I had spent less time in analyzing my intentions than in devising strategies to accomplish them, but I did assure her of my sincerity. This was not some fly-by-night whim; I would not ring a bell and graph the results every time I fed my child. I was dependable, a solid citizen despite my longish hair and current lack of salaried employment; I had good prospects and no secrets. And, oh yes, I was an American Indian and preferred, if possible, an Indian baby.

She asked questions about my background and I answered copiously anything she wanted to know. I was an only child, yes, but I wasn't looking now for a little brother or sister but for a son or a daughter. I had never been engaged, but I certainly did enjoy the company of women though of course she shouldn't think I was promiscuous. I was not without complexities of the normal, interesting variety, but I was absolutely not seeking a child to fill a pathological void in my life. I was eminently capable of committed adult relationships—just ask anyone on this list of references I had conveniently prepared and happened to bring along—but there was no "special person" in my life just now.

She wrote all these facts on a yellow legal pad, filling the margin with a code of stars and check marks, which, reading upside down, I found impossible to predict or decipher. After an hour she said she'd discuss this matter with her board. The next step, should it occur, would entail a protracted visit to my residence by one of the agency's case workers. "Don't get your hopes up," she warned me as I rose to leave. She had heard of single women wanting to adopt, but never of an unmarried man. She wasn't at all sure how her people might react.

Disappointment must have crossed my face because, as Sister

Clare walked me to the door, she confided in a soft voice, "I'm on your side."

In the following weeks, I didn't write to my family about my plan, nor did I mention it to people in the village. It was as though I were awaiting the results of a pregnancy test and afraid to jinx the outcome by premature celebration. But I thought about fatherhood. I imagined a scattershot of vignettes of the coming years: my child learning to walk, riding a first bicycle, blowing out birthday candles, going to school, discovering the world, growing into a friend as well as a son or daughter. I mail-ordered books on parenting, on toilet training, on the possible special problems of a single-parent or an adopted child. By the time the Catholic Charities' letter arrived informing me that I could progress to the next plateau, I was so enmeshed in the surety of my impending fatherhood that I was relieved rather than surprised.

In preparation for my home visitation interview, I cleaned and straightened my one-room cabin, both intrigued and intimidated at the prospect of fielding more penetrating personal questions about my motivations and aspirations. I was, in fact, curious to hear what I'd say.

A social worker named Janet Lindeman arrived on the mail plane one brisk morning in early spring, and we walked from the landing strip to the beach to wait for the letters to be sorted. She was a tall, dark-haired woman in a beige pants suit and brown low-heeled shoes, distinctly out of place in a bush Native community, but straining to be oblivious to the curious glances of the people who passed by. She was serious, a bit skeptical, and extremely professional in her manner. Within minutes of our introduction she produced a notebook and a ballpoint pen, and began to record my words with disconcerting thoroughness. As a person used to conducting interviews, it was not long before I caught the direction she was heading in: *why,* if I wanted children, didn't I get married and father them biologically? Did I harbor some unspoken hostility toward women, matrimony, or long-term adult relationships? Was a child my ill-considered solution to a secretly miserable life?

"Describe two marriages that you would call 'happy,'" Janet suggested tellingly, and poised her pen.

I thought for a moment, then enthused about two sets of friends. I had met Barbara and Marty in Paris when I worked there as a bank intern several years previously. Both were American graduate students—bright, exuberant, Bohemian. I was hooked when, one evening, they served a meal of chilled three-bean salad, which seemed to me the epitome of casual sophistication. The other couple, whom I barely knew, were Shelly and Frederick, fellow anthropologists a few years my senior. They had done fieldwork in New Guinea and ever since had spoken privately to each other in the exotic, whispering language they had learned there. Any overheard conversation between them sounded romantic and intensely connubial.

In sketching these marriages to Janet, I felt wistful: they seemed so preordained, so impossible to achieve from scratch. I was determined to settle for nothing less, however, which was the reason, if I wanted a child immediately, adoption was the logical route. And why, Janet wanted to know, *did* I want children? A good question, but hard to answer without coming across as either maudlin or rhapsodic. The truth was, the words to define my emotions weren't available in standard male vocabulary.

My desire for a child was as clear and basic to me as instinct, and as undeniable and undissectable. It was pure *want*, not the short-cut to some other gratification or the tonic to a personal disappointment. It struck me that in retrospect everything that had ever happened to me had led to this juncture, but I kept this insight to myself. I worried that I would alienate Janet with an ingenuousness bound to sound false. I prided myself on being practical, level-headed. There was nothing bizarre about my feelings—as far as I was concerned they were as old as time—but even nonchalance might appear flighty.

I regarded Janet, willing myself to observe her not as an impediment in any way, not as an antagonist who could leave me dead in the water, but as a person who, despite her pads and pencils and hidden agenda, despite her power over the future direction of my life, *had* to feel awkward when dropped fresh into the sights and sounds of a village more remote from urban Anchorage than a mere hour's air transit. I admired her bravado, her refusal to acknowledge her minority status, and I surprised her by saying so. We made eye contact, then quickly looked away. Yet I realized that for the first time she had seen me, not as a strange anecdote for the file but as a rational client with a fairly simple idea.

I traded her question for question and learned as much as I yielded. Coincidentally, she and her husband were themselves contemplating the adoption of a child and had talked about many of the same issues we were now discussing. We spoke as equals who understood and respected each other, who sympathized. We relaxed into mutual encouragement, and by the time we walked up to check for mail at the house that served as a post office, Janet and I were in full accord. It was now simply a matter of filling in the details. We discussed strategies for the presentation of her home study, how best to portray me, how best to make my case. We became friends so quickly that, when I opened my post box and discovered, of all things, a letter from Shelly, I did not hesitate in sharing it aloud, unscreened.

"Dear Michael," I read, "Frederick and I have decided to separate."

The report that Janet submitted to Sister Clare apparently emphasized her positive assessment of my ability to be a parent rather than my bad nose for stable marriages. Before two younger friends and I left Alaska to drive six thousand miles to my new college teaching job in northern New England, I was informed that as far as the agency was concerned, I was approved. The case now rested with ARENA, a national adoption service that attempted to match would-be parents with available children. My records had been forwarded to the Catholic Charities office in Littleton, New Hampshire, and the staff there would contact me when and if there was any news.

As I bounced over the hundreds of unpaved miles of the Al-Can Highway, I daydreamed my upcoming life as a parent. Everything about my hypothetical child was vague except for his or her existence. I mentally placed us in various scenarios, and always our relationship was enlightened, companionable. I was a patient role model, a pal, a gentle guide. Our relationship was, above all, candid and honest, with no topic taboo, no problem undiscussable.

The scenery on this route was spectacular and empty, with immense, marshy lakes spreading beneath white-capped mountains. There were times while my traveling companions slept when I drove for seventy miles at a stretch without encountering another motorist, without hearing sounds other than the hum of my car's engine or the break of my own voice, whispering combinations of possible first names to see how they'd go with Dorris. It was on such a stretch, near Kluane Lake, that I finally settled upon my choice: if a boy, he would be Adam; if a girl, Hannah. Someday, I promised, the two of us would return to this place together.

The trip lasted over a week. At Dawson Creek, British Columbia, the road turned back into asphalt, and soon the topography changed to the Canadian high plains. The radio picked up stations filled with Russian language programs, the legacy of recent Ukrainian immigrants, and burnished fields of wheat extended in all directions. There was plenty of space to think, plenty of time to plan. At nights, in motels, I kept a record of all the day's ideas, complete with shopping lists of the books and toys and furniture I would need to acquire. In many ways, this was the first trip I took as a father. It was certainly the least complicated.

Once in New Hampshire, I enjoyed the role of house-hunting for two, but my minimum requirements didn't make the process easy. Any place I would rent had to have a yard for my child to play in, more than one bedroom, and permission for pets. Finally, after a week I found an apartment in the basement of a large, renovated Colonial house in Sugar Hill, about eight miles from Franconia College. My entrance was in the rear, and all windows faced northeast, revealing a long meadow that was bordered by a line of mountains. Practically the first thing I did upon moving in was to recover the beige walls of the smaller bedroom in a yellow paper sprinkled with red and blue rocking horses. There was no retreating from that.

In my two beginner-level anthropology classes, the self-consciously counterculture students dressed in army fatigues, wore their hair long, and preferred to talk about their "feelings" rather than ethnographic theory. Franconia College existed as a "community," I was often reminded. There were no departments, and the only distinctions between the "co-learners" of faculty and of students were those pertaining to advanced academic degree and chronological age. Learning was an "affective" process, impossible to grade. The worst crime was to "head-trip," that is, to be in touch with one's ideas at the expense of one's emotions. When I announced to students in the morning course that a term paper would be required, they recoiled as if I had proclaimed "Nixon's the One!"

Housed primarily in a former resort hotel, Franconia was a picturesque, if inefficiently designed institution. All faculty offices and classrooms had sinks, but instead of telephones they sported a kind of buzzer intercom through which the front desk, also known as the Dean's Office, could transmit either a wake-up call or a summons that a message was waiting. Thinking back, I can almost hear the shrill sound that marked a new boundary in my life on that noon of a late September day. I intuited, in the way one sometimes presciently does, what this signal must mean, and I flumped down the ballroom stairway to the partial privacy of the house–phone box.

Denis Daigle, a social worker with New Hampshire Catholic Charities, introduced himself and said that he had heard from ARENA, and that South Dakota *might,* might have an American Indian three-year-old for me—at least there was a response to my application. Could I drop by his office to discuss it? There was a slight edge to his voice; was he uncomfortable with my single status, or was there a problem with the child that he wasn't mentioning? I refused to worry, however. Nothing would interfere with my becoming a father.

Two hours later, sitting behind his desk, Denis explained that the little boy—*little boy*—in question was currently placed in a foster home near Pierre and was a child whose start in life had not been easy. Born almost seven weeks premature, he had been neglected to the point of malnutrition by his biological mother, a heavy drinker whose two older children were living temporarily with foster families. Adam—the name to which I remained committed for my first son—had been removed from her custody after contracting pneumonia, and had resided during the two years since that time in hospitals and with state-appointed guardians. The boy was small for his age and had not been toilet-trained or taught to speak more than a few words. He was diagnosed as mentally retarded. Was I still interested?

Denis was a sandy-haired man with a face that wanted to smile but was restrained by the serious information he had to impart. His eyes were kind, nonjudgmental. He didn't say that the reason I was being considered as the adoptive parent for this boy was because it might be difficult to find a couple who would not be put off by such a case history. He didn't say that this might be my only chance, the one-in-a-million shot in which some midwestern social worker had looked behind the drawbacks of my application and seen possibilities.

"Do you have a photograph?" I asked.

"Yes." Denis hesitated. "Sometimes it's not a good idea to see a picture until you weigh all sides. A photograph makes the child real, makes your decision harder if the answer is no."

"The answer is yes."

He was doubtful.

"Look," I said, "who knows whether that prognosis is correct? What chance has this kid had to develop? I believe in the positive impact of environment, and with me he'll catch up. I've been waiting a long time. There's no way I would refuse."

Denis sighed, glanced down to his desk, back up at me, finally smiled, and handed over a Polaroid snapshot. I saw a little boy, painfully thin, with black hair in a bowl-shaped cut, an oversized tank top, and no shoes. He leaned against the hood of a green car that was taller than he was, with an expression that looked at once forced and forlorn. I would have recognized him anywhere: my dream come true.

A week later, I was in Pierre, waiting in the airport lounge for Rita Duffy of the South Dakota State Welfare Office. My bag was at my feet, and under my arm I carried a stuffed toy dog which would serve both to identify me to Ms. Duffy and to provide a first gift to my son, "Adam" after all. I was disoriented from travel and anticipation.

"Mr. Dorris?" Rita was tall, blonde, and friendly. Before I could object she hefted my bag and carried it to her car while I hurried to keep pace.

"I'm sorry to be late," she said, "but I stopped by the office to make sure that everything was straight with the little boy. He's waiting for you."

"Now? We're going directly there?" After months of no action, after a day of long connections in airports, events were suddenly moving awfully fast.

Rita halted with the car keys poised at the lock on the driver's side of her car. "Unless you'd rather not," she said. "I thought you'd be anxious, so I went out to his foster home this morning and got him. Did you want to check into your motel first?"

"No way," I said. "It's just kind of a big moment, you know. I guess I'll never feel completely prepared."

"Relax." Rita slipped behind the wheel and leaned to open my door. When I got in, she turned toward me and grinned. "It's going to be great. We've shown him your picture, told him you were coming this afternoon. He's really psyched."

❋

I don't remember much of the drive into Pierre, though Rita did point out the sights. I have the impression of dampness, of fields scraped clean of crops and pooled with the crusts of standing, frozen water, of a landscape waiting to be covered by snow. We circled the state capitol, passed a three-block downtown shopping street bounded on either end by used-car lots, and finally stopped at a low-slung concrete building with designated parking spaces. Inside, Rita's headquarters consisted of a glass-partitioned corner decorated with bumper stickers bearing peppy admonitions and slogans: THANK YOU FOR NOT SMOKING, THE BUCK STOPS HERE (with a picture of a deer staring in cross-eyed frustration at a blank wall), IT'S IN THE MAIL, and SOMEDAY I'M GOING TO GET ORGANIZED.

"I'll just check on him." She left me to sit on a folding chair and hurried down the hall. I surveyed the almost deserted office—it was lunchtime—and then glanced back to Rita's desk. On it lay a Manila folder with my name typed on a preglued tab, and I had a strong impulse to sneak a look. What, after all the questions, all the answers, had been concluded about me? What did Janet Lindeman and the others to whom I had talked or whom I had asked to write letters of support have to say about my desire and fitness to become a parent? It had to be affirmative, encouraging, or else I wouldn't be here, but in my last few seconds—emotionally, if not legally—as a single man, I wanted reassurance. There was no sign of Rita, so I inched closer and, with false casualness, lifted one side of the folder and let it fall open. What I saw was not some annotated resume, not some condensed version of my life, not my past at all, but my future: on page one of my file was a duplicate of Adam's photograph, identical to the picture I had carried in my wallet for a month.

"We're all set," Rita announced, patted me on the back, then stepped aside. I turned the knob and the door swung inward. I raised my eyes, steeled not to anticipate too much, prepared to be initially rejected, ready for disappointment. The room had a green shag carpet, and strewn across it were toy trucks and blocks. A small boy, dressed from head to foot in a red zipped-up snowsuit, bent over them. He was not at first aware of my presence and went on with his play, but then he seemed to catch some unexpected echo. He looked up and met my eyes. His face was perfect, deeply etched with dark, narrow eyes, bright beneath thick, straight lashes and brows. Black hair feathered under the ruff of his snowsuit. His mouth was wide, his expression measuring. And then he lit with recognition.

"Hi, Daddy," he said, and without a beat of strangeness or doubt, went back to his trucks. I stood—stunned, blessed, transported, forever changed—listening with rapt attention to his sounds of screeching brakes and revving engines.

It was that simple. All that I had read about the process of "bonding," about the slow, erratic development of trust, about the complications of adopting an "older" child, went the way of fog at sunrise. I was politely deaf to the technicalities Rita, and later her superiors, threw at me: I should spend time with Adam in Pierre, they cautioned, and then have some time apart from him. Perhaps he could visit my hotel tomorrow for an hour. To gain perspective, I should travel back to New Hampshire alone and think about all this, and when—and if—I decided to assume temporary custody, Rita would bring Adam on a plane at the state's expense. I shouldn't rush into anything. I should take my time.

I thought they were out of their minds.

Adam and I spent our first night together at the Holiday Inn. He was not yet toilet-trained and had command, I was told, of only twenty words of vocabulary. He had been designated as mildly retarded because of his performance on a battery of tests, and I was warned that he probably could never attend a public school.

I didn't believe a word.

He was pure affection, totally at ease. When I bathed him I discovered the marks of IVs and catheters, souvenirs of his bouts with chronic pneumonia. His wrists and ankles were also scored with thin white scars—evidence of that time when, as an infant, he had been tied into a crib by his abusive, neglectful birth mother. Though chronologically three years old, he had the slight frame and demeanor of a much younger child. His limbs and fingers and toes were long and delicate, with fine nails. Strangely, his palms were almost entirely unlined, as though his past and future had yet to be determined. Occasionally, in answer to some inner voice, he hugged himself in a posture I interpreted as deep thought. He was without the emotion of fear, without regret, without encumbrance.

The next morning I talked to Rita in private.

"You know I'm not going to leave without him," I said. "There's no question of changing my mind, of thinking anything over."

"I know. I knew yesterday."

"So what do we do?"

"Leave it to me."

Holding tightly to Adam's small hand, I walked two blocks north from the Holiday Inn and found a musty-smelling variety store where I bought him a wardrobe: pants, a sweater, pajamas with trains on them, undershirts, diapers, socks. He carried the stuffed dog I had brought, and everywhere I went I made a point of introducing him—to salesclerks and waitresses and bellhops and bank tellers—as my son.

As it turned out, Adam and I flew out of South Dakota without official permission while Rita and her colleagues generously looked the other way. We violated procedures, took the law into our own hands, made a getaway. The illicit nature of our departure added a note of drama, a kind of thriller ending to this chapter of our story. We lurked like fugitives in the one-room airport, ducking behind cigarette machines and postcard racks whenever the outside door opened. We were Ingrid and Paul escaping Casablanca, with Rita as our Bogart. Once we were airborne, I unstrapped Adam's safety belt and set him on my lap for a view of the gray fields far below. His eyes were excited; instinctively, he was my co-conspirator.

While we waited in Minneapolis for our connecting plane, I let Adam race the length of the corridor. I checked our tickets to make sure of the time, and when I looked, he was gone. I ran to the spot I had last seen him, called his name, but realized he might not even recognize it. And then I saw him, happily riding a luggage belt between two suitcases, about to disappear into the loading dock through the flaps of a curtain.

In relief, I scooped him up and held his squirming body close against my chest.

"Poop," Adam proclaimed, proud of his accomplishment.

I took him to an empty waiting area, lay him on the floor, and pulled open the snaps of his pants. Then, while he contemplated the ceiling, I wiped and powdered. It was impossible to see his thin legs, dominated by the thick balls of his knee joints, without making resolutions. He needed nourishment, care, encouragement, stability.

I was determined that his development in every area would match his age before another year had passed.

Somewhere over the Great Lakes he fell asleep in my lap, and in wonder and absolute contentment I watched the ebb and flow of his breath, the movement beneath his lids as he dreamed, the sudden flutter of his fingertips. For the space of that flight, the world was in my arms.

The evening we arrived in Sugar Hill was like the climax of a G-rated movie. Some of my fellow faculty members had decorated the basement apartment with crepe-paper streamers and congratulatory posters. There was ice cream in the freezer, and even a Siberian Husky puppy named Skahota, with a bow around his neck. Adam was dazed from travel and excitement, but anxious to jump on every bed, to pull out every drawer, to open every wrapped gift. He teetered off-balance from one room to the next, smiling and periodically returning to hold onto my leg, and made a great hit with everyone. Finally, by ten o'clock, the guests had departed and we were alone.

"Do you want to sleep with me tonight?" I asked, thinking that amid all the strange surroundings he would feel lonely in the room with the rocking horse wallpaper.

"Okay, Daddy," he said, so I put on his sleepers, lined pillows on the floor in case he rolled in his sleep, and turned off the light.

"Do you want a story?"

"Yes, Daddy."

So I began "The Three Bears," but in an adapted version.

"There was Daddy Bear, Adam Bear, and Skahota Bear," I whispered, snuggling his small body close. "They lived together in a little house half under the ground but near the mountains. They were very happy."

It had been a long day for me as well, and before Goldilocks broke so much as a single chair, I had put myself to sleep. I woke in the dark some time later, and lay still for a moment while the realization of my changed circumstances sunk in. I reached out my hand to pat Adam's back, but encountered an empty bed. Instantly alert, I switched on the lamp and checked the floor. He was gone. I flung back the blankets and went through the kitchen to his bedroom, but nothing had been touched. The main door was chain-locked and bolted so he couldn't have wandered outside. He was not in a cabinet, not in the puppy's box, not in the closet. It was 3:12 A.M.

The thought occurred to me that perhaps I was still asleep. Perhaps I was experiencing some primal fear of loss that was common for new parents, but then I reasoned that if I had the presence of mind to have such an idea, I must be awake. Then another, even more disturbing thought crept into my consciousness: perhaps *Adam* was the dream. Perhaps I had not yet gone to South Dakota. But instantly, I was saved by the tangible evidence of his sneaker, abandoned near the stove. There had to be some explanation.

I returned to my bedroom, armed with the conviction that a disappearance was *impossible*, and began a systematic investigation of every conceivable hiding place. It was several moments, however, before I noticed that the blankets seemed to be piled especially high at the foot on one side of the bed, and when I lifted them, there was Adam. He slept in the classic fetal position, knees beneath his chest, occupying as small a physical space as possible.

How often in a four-day period can one person fall in love with another, each time as if it is the first? Gently, I drew my little boy to the pillows, settled myself at his side, and covered us. As I reached for the light he woke, blinked, and peered into my face.

"Three Bears?" he asked, and made himself at home.

CHAPTER TWO

That was November, just before Thanksgiving, and our idyll of familyhood continued without a hitch through Christmas. I remember in particular the day that Denis was scheduled for his first official "home visit," a hurdle I was determined to clear with distinction. The apartment was spotless, Adam was napping with a new suit of clothes laid out and ready to wear, and, with only hours to go, I confronted my refrigerator. The previous night I had scanned cookbooks for inspiration; I wanted to have on hand some casual yet telling bite to eat, some morsel that would subtly proclaim "good parent" or "domestic flair" in nonverbal but emphatic metalanguage.

I could not go wrong, I reasoned, with apple pie—*real* apple pie, of course, not some imitation bought from a bakery or some dairy counter redi-crust filled with canned fruit. No indeed. *My* child would grow up with the smell of steaming pastry in his nostrils, would play with the rounds of peeled apple skins while I stewed slices of Macintosh on the stove. So, with no lack of bravado I hauled out my implements, blended and rolled dough, crimped, sprinkled, scooped and covered, then cut an elaborate air vent in the shape of a capital "A."

While the pie baked, however, a dark thought occurred to me. What if Denis despised apples? What if he regarded my masterpiece as a cheap cliché, a homey camouflage for unseen parental inadequacy? I needed options, fallbacks, foods that carried alternative messages. As soon as the pie was done, I roasted a chicken on the theory that social service might work up a large appetite. Chocolate mousse could be made on top of the stove, and was. I arranged a platter of raw vegetables and creamy dill dip and set it to chill. Fortunately I happened to have all the ingredients I needed for a delicious-sounding tomato-bacon soup that I discovered in a cookbook; it could be prepared in no time at all. I unfroze a braided loaf of bread—a gift to me from a friend, but who would tell? I squeezed lemons for lemonade, ran to the store for a six-pack of beer, brewed coffee, and checked my supply of tea and milk. Just as I was about to sift flour as the first step to a double-Dutch chocolate cake, I heard Adam stir. There was barely time to bathe him, wash his hair, and feed him a bowl of the soup so that he would not appear too eager to eat, suggesting neglect.

The knock sounded and, casting a quick and approving eye around the wiped-down kitchen, I opened the door. Denis was all smiles and had even brought a bath toy for Adam, a large blue sailboat. He hoisted my son, who was anything but shy, and carried him while I ushered a tour of our four rooms. While we were standing in my bedroom, however, Denis's expression seemed to change, become mildly disturbed, even disapproving. Had I forgotten something? Was he expecting a color photograph of some bride-to-be on my bureau? Had my striped sheets conveyed decadence, a prison past? Was my closet too full or too empty?

"Michael," Denis began, as though he regretted the comment that was coming.

I swallowed, awaiting the blow.

"I think Adam could use a change."

That was an understatement. The new outfit went into a plastic garbage bag which, when sealed, went into another. Adam howled under the shower and insisted on dressing in a torn pair of overalls with a fresh tomato stain. He was still sobbing when at last I brought him back into the kitchen, where Denis was waiting.

"He's actually getting better," I said. "I'm sure he'll be toilet trained by spring."

Denis nodded. "He looks fine, happy."

I followed the direction of his eyes. Tears rolled down Adam's cheeks. His wet hair was unbrushed, and one shoe had come off.

I changed the subject. "Let me offer you something to eat."

Denis looked at his watch and scooted back his chair. "Don't bother," he said. "I'm late for a meeting at the office. It's clear you've got things under control."

He must have seen something in my face, some storm of distress, of madness, for he didn't rise.

"You must be hungry," I continued as though he had not spoken. My words fell slowly, one by one. They were pure command.

"Oh, well," Denis surrendered. "If it's no trouble, of course."

"It's no trouble. What do you want?"

"What do you have?"

"Everything."

I never did find out what Denis thought that afternoon. He had the tact and good manners to behave as though it were the most natural thing in the world to enter a strange kitchen and find a chalkboard with "Specials of the Day" written upon it. He ate some of each dish and, at my insistence, even took a slice of the pie home for his wife's dessert. But when he came for his next visit a few weeks later, he made a point of telling me that he would be eating lunch immediately before. That time I only made the cake.

I had no basis for comparing Adam with other children his age, and the idea to do so never occurred to me. I was so busy adjusting to my new self-image and circumstances, to the odds and ends of fatherhood and teaching and balancing the budget—high salary was not one of the plusses of an early 1970s experimental college—that I thought that Adam's physical and mental development was, all things considered, right on schedule. I didn't worry that he seemed vague about the names of others in his play group, that he continued to require diapers, that his level of activity was very high, that, when left alone, he preferred above all else to rock back and forth as if soothing himself. Despite having a good appetite, he continued to weigh so little that people passing us on the street would give a double take when they saw him, but the elderly, rural pediatrician assured me that Adam was healthy and strong, if small.

"He was a preemie," the man reminded me. "He has to catch up. Besides, his people were probably short."

Adam was terrified of the shower, so, since the bathroom in our apartment afforded little more than the room to turn around, a friend sent money to buy a tin washtub. Every morning before work I would fill it with warm water, Mr. Bubble, Adam, and his toy sailboat, and let him play. Outdoors our meadow was covered with snow, and the mountains reflected the rays of the sun. Usually, while he splashed, I played records—Elton John, Cat Stevens, the Beatles, Roberta Flack—and, seated at the kitchen table, I prepared my classes. There was no place else I wanted to be, nothing else I wished to be doing.

In late January, shortly after Adam's fourth birthday, I had an interview for a job at McGill University in Montreal, potentially a big step in my career from Franconia. It was only a four-hour drive through a Currier and Ives winter landscape, and Adam seemed to enjoy the journey as much as I did. After we arrived, he slept curled in an easy chair while I gave my presentation to the Anthropology Department, and was uncomplaining about the frigid blasts of air that swept in from the St. Lawrence as we toured the campus. As one does in such situations, I measured the city with a proprietary air: what would it be like to live here with Adam? How rusty was my French? Did I want to make the transition to a large academic department where publishing apparently counted far more than teaching? McGill and Franconia were poles apart in every respect, and I was preoccupied with the weighing of pros and cons.

My distraction persisted as in the gathering darkness we drove south toward the international border. Slowly I realized that I was lost, with snow forecast, in a foreign country, responsible for a hungry child, and had no local currency. I doubled back, asked directions as best I could. I was anxious to negotiate the road through the mountains before the weather worsened, so once I regained the right highway, I told Adam to stretch out in the backseat. I would fix him something to eat when we got home. I drove steadily, my defroster turned on high, my wipers sweeping the snow from the windshield, squinting to see, and finally, around midnight, we pulled into our driveway.

Adam was unrouseable, so I changed his diaper and put him to bed and then, exhausted myself, fell onto my mattress fully clothed. I slept without interruption for eight hours, and when I finally awoke I was struck by the quiet that seemed to have descended over the apartment. There were not even the sounds of traffic on the street; the ground had been covered by a fresh seven inches of snow, and the plowing crews had not yet made it up our hill.

I called Adam's name but received no answer. Normally, he rose at 5:30 A.M. regardless of what time he went to sleep, and as I walked toward his room I felt a twinge of worry.

He lay facedown on the floor, unconscious, his body hot to the touch. I rolled him on his back, shook his shoulders, but he gave no response. A trail of saliva extended from the corner of his mouth across his cheek and down to his pajama top. When I raised his eyelid I saw only white. I lifted him onto the bed, aware of the lightness of his bones, the frailty of his long limbs. His head lolled to one side, and his breathing was fast and shallow.

"Don't move." I raced to the kitchen for a pan of water and a dish towel, and returned to sponge at his fever. Still no reaction. I sank to that of panic that brings a low, persistent hum, an alarm to the brain, the kind that makes you calm, uncharacteristically capable. I was still dressed from the previous night, so all I needed to do was throw on my coat, wrap Adam in his blanket, grab the car keys, and leave. I willed the car to start, willed the new snow to yield a path, and drove at a steady, determined rate to the hospital, ten miles away. Adam slumped in the seat beside me, oblivious to everything, but I talked to him the entire way.

"Hang on. We'll be there soon. Look at the mountain. Be all right. Say something. Later you can pick out a new truck. You rest now, it's okay. Please. Please."

At the emergency room entrance I stopped the car, leaned on the horn, and in a moment two orderlies appeared.

"My son is sick," I shouted, and they followed the direction of my eyes. His lips were a pale, bruised blue and the wrist of his right hand had begun to tremble. One of the men opened the car door while the other went back inside and returned with a wheeled stretcher. I watched, a bystander paralyzed by my inability to help, as they pushed him up a ramp and through a set of swinging double doors. On the brick wall immediately in front of me, a sign read ABSOLUTELY NO PARKING, and I thought: I can't stay here. I put the gears in reverse and looked over my shoulder to back out, and then I stopped, took my foot off the gas. The car jolted into a stall. The generator light flashed a blood red signal, but when I ran toward the hospital I didn't take my keys from the ignition. I didn't shut the door behind me.

The emergency room was charged with activity, with nurses rushing, pushing IV racks and carrying trays of medicine. Adam's stretcher was partially concealed by cloth curtains that had been pulled to make a temporary partition, and a bearded, sandy-haired man in a white coat bent forward with a stethoscope. I went to stand beside him. Adam's body was convulsing, rising and thrashing against restraining straps with a strength that looked impossible. His lower lip bled from where he'd bitten it, his eyes were half open but unfocused.

"Will he be all right?"

The doctor either couldn't hear or ignored me. I touched his arm.

"What is it? What's the matter with him?"

This time he glanced in my direction.

"Who are you?" His accent was vaguely southern.

"I'm his father."

"How long has he been like this?"

I told him what I knew, my vocabulary automatically reaching for the jargon of medical shows on TV. I wanted to sound credible, wanted to speak professional-to-professional, wanted to conspire with this man in the news that the attack was minor, was somehow normal, was nothing to be unduly concerned about.

"We'll run tests," the doctor said. "But first we have to get this fever under control. What is this boy's normal weight?"

"Twenty-seven pounds at his last physical."

"He's fallen below twenty. If we don't stabilize him . . . Has he had previous epileptic episodes? Is he on Phenobarb?"

"He's been fine. Yesterday wore him out . . ." The doctor's words penetrated my consciousness. "No one's ever mentioned epilepsy. How could he lose so much weight?"

"That's what I need to find out. I'm moving him to ICU. You can wait in the lobby. As soon as I know something, I'll let you know."

Clearly in the way, I retreated to the empty waiting room. Littleton was a small hospital and apparently this was a slow morning. To pass the time I leafed through the outdated issues of *McCalls* and the *Tufts University Alumni Bulletin* that covered the coffee table, and watched the clock. Occasionally, I would hear approaching footsteps and straighten my back, move to the edge of my seat, expecting to be summoned, but for over an hour no one came for me. Finally I could bear it no longer and walked down the hall to the admitting office. A nurse and a clerical worker were chatting, and looked up at my knock.

"Excuse me," I said. "I brought my son in here sick over an hour ago and I wondered what was happening."

They stared at me with no comprehension.

"He's just over four years old and I couldn't rouse him this morning."

"Oh," said the nurse to her friend. "He means that Vietnamese child upstairs."

"American Indian," I corrected. "We're Indians."

"Whatever." They surveyed my appearance with curiosity. It was an expression I recognized, a reaction, familiar to most people of mixed-blood ancestry, that said, "You don't *look* like an Indian." No matter how often it happened, no matter how frequently I was blamed by strangers for not resembling their image of some Hollywood Sitting Bull, I was still defensive and vulnerable.

"I'm part Indian," I explained. From experience I knew they would not leave this topic until they were satisfied. "He's a full-blood. Adopted."

Now they got it, and exchanged a knowing glance. "He's pretty sick, I guess," the nurse volunteered. "He had a spinal, I know. They'll notify you when they find something."

I nodded and turned to go back to the lobby, but the other woman had a question.

"Did that adoption go through already?"

"No." I was surprised. "I've got temporary custody for another six months, then it becomes final."

"Oh, well, that's good. You can give him back if this turns out to be serious."

There was no answer to that, so I kept walking. I was too frightened for rage, too preoccupied to deal with such ignorance. Instead I mentally filed her remark, conscious of it as something to tell later to friends, a vignette of inhumane bureaucracy. Her words were so within the context of the day that they seemed almost appropriate.

I sat in a red vinyl-and-chrome chair with one uneven leg and attempted to slow my thoughts. I recited the words to what songs I could remember. I concentrated on biting the nail of my ring finger into an even line. I listened to the tide of my own breath as it was drawn in, then expelled.

Finally the doctor, tired and noncommittal, stood in the doorway. "You can see him for a minute."

We walked up a flight of stairs and down a long, quiet hall until we arrived at the glass walls of the intensive care unit. In the adjoining alcove was a bed, and on it was Adam. Brightly colored wires connected his naked body to a bank of machines that monitored his vital signs. The only noise was the "beep" of his heart register. The overhead light was dim, but I could tell he had not regained consciousness. His abdomen was concave, his arms and legs slim, jointed poles that swelled into hands and feet at their extremities. He seemed impossibly helpless.

"At least we've gotten him to stop seizing," the doctor's voice intruded. "But as to what caused this crisis . . ." He hunched his shoulders in a shrug. "We thought maybe meningitis, so we tested twice and the fluid was clear, no problem. Then I figured 'brain tumor,' and checked for that and . . . negative."

"You must have some theory." I reeled from the names of the things this was not.

He recited a string of Latin—diseases or conditions I didn't recognize, but which in their mystery sounded terrible. I didn't trust him to tell me exactly what they meant, so I asked him to write them down. He raised his eyebrows, but retrieved a notebook and did as I requested. I accepted the piece of paper he handed me and tucked it into my breast pocket.

I reached to touch Adam's hair. It was damp.

"We've been bathing him to lower the fever," the doctor said, anticipating my question. "It was near 105° when he arrived, but it came down to 102°."

Adam's cheeks were sunken, revealing the fine bone structure of his face. His skin shone, and the Band-Aid that held the IV needle to his vein reached almost completely around his forearm. I followed the line of his eyebrows with the tip of my finger, traced the intricate curve of his ears.

"Hi," I whispered.

"He can't hear you."

I put my hand above his lip. I had read once that smell is the oldest, the most basic of the senses, and now I thought that scent might, at some level, communicate my presence and make Adam feel less alone.

"Fill out the admitting papers, then go home and get some rest," the doctor said. "There's nothing you can do here. We'll give you a ring if he wakes up."

My hearing snagged on the word *if*.

"No, I'll stay. I'll use the pay phone in the lobby."

I intended to call my mother. After some initial anxiety about my decision to adopt, she and her sisters had welcomed Adam into the family with no hesitation. We had visited with them in Kentucky at Christmas, and their exuberance at becoming grandmother and great-aunts was instantaneous and overwhelming. They had cuddled Adam on their laps for hours, telling him his favorite stories, bouncing him on their knees. No one complained or showed disappointment when he ignored his carefully chosen gifts and played instead with empty boxes. No one called attention to the frequency with which he confused one of them with the other. If anything, they were even more at ease with his idiosyncrasies than I.

I dialed my mother's number, then hung up before the connection was complete. What did I have to tell? I had no surer sense of Adam's condition than when I had found him on the floor six hours ago. I couldn't promise that he would be all right, I couldn't give a name to his ailment.

I remembered the slip of paper in my pocket, and the woman at the reception desk directed me to a small medical library in the hospital basement. Research was a skill I was trained to value, and, with a cool academic objectivity I did not feel, I began to track down the names the doctor had written. It was as though by removing myself from the immediacy of Adam's situation, I would demystify and neutralize the danger. I discovered, however, that the doctor was simply guessing a diagnosis, and that the range of his conjectures was wide. According to the list, Adam might be suffering from anything from Rocky Mountain fever to a rare disorder that required the draining and recirculating of every pint of blood in his body. The only common denominator of the various unlikely diseases seemed to be the ambiguity of their symptoms; they all involved a comatose state, an unexplained fever, and rapid weight loss. Beyond that, their prognosis and treatments varied tremendously. The doctor, it was clear, had no idea what was wrong.

I telephoned Peter Blasco, a friend from college who was now finishing a residency in developmental pediatrics at Johns Hopkins.

"If I were you," Peter said after I had described the day's events, including the menu of diseases the local doctor had proposed, "I would get him to a major medical center as soon as possible. In your case that would be either Dartmouth, in Hanover, or the University of Vermont in Burlington. Which one is closer to you?"

I had never visited either town. "Hanover, I guess," I said. "It's about seventy miles south."

"As soon as he's stable, hire an ambulance and have Adam taken down there. I'll ask around to see who you should consult, and by the time you arrive, the information will be waiting."

It sounded like the reasonable thing to do. When I returned to ICU, Adam's condition was unchanged. I announced my intention to seek a second opinion, and to my dismay, the doctor took it as a grave insult.

"You'll do what you want, but it's your responsibility if you move that child."

"But you don't know what the problem is. You don't have a treatment."

"It's out of my hands now," he said and stalked from the room.

I was at a loss, with no idea of the right or wrong thing to do. If I didn't act, Adam's life was obviously in jeopardy, but if I did, I might endanger him further. I looked at the nurse on duty, but she wouldn't make eye contact.

"Do you know of an ambulance service?" I asked her.

She waited to answer, debating with herself, and then provided a name. They responded on the third ring and promised to be at the ER entrance in fifteen minutes.

"Don't worry," the dispatcher told me. "We get these runs all the time."

I signed the papers for Adam's release, and waited. The length of our stay in Hanover was unpredictable, and since there was no public transportation for me to return to Franconia, I went to find my car. It had been reparked in the lot, the keys left on the seat. My breath frosted the windshield, and as I warmed the engine, an arc of clear glass gradually spread before me. The afternoon was bright, vivid. To the right of the hospital was a small park with a picnic table which, in summer, must have been shaded by the swirling green limbs of two weeping willows. Now, however, the cluster of branches was a striking mustard color, illuminated against the blue sky. I drove past, and idled near the entrance to the emergency room until the red and white ambulance, its amber lights flashing, backed into the reserved space. I held the door as they rushed Adam from the hospital, an attendant walking beside the stretcher, holding aloft a clear plastic IV bag.

"Forget about speed limits," he said as he secured the rear hatch of the vehicle. "Just hang on our tail and we'll be there in record time."

I nodded, glad to take orders, glad to be under the direction of someone who knew how to defy the rules. Then, for the longest hour and a half of my life, I followed the siren down Route 10. Past every closed maple syrup stand and weather-vaned barn, along the curves parallel to the frozen Connecticut River, through every small town with its row of white brick houses, I repeated a single word: No.

We take the power of medicine for granted, because, after all, the magic absolutely *doesn't* work for each of us only once. I assumed that when Adam's affliction was given a name, it could be treated; then recovery would commence. It was inconceivable to me that the definitions of my life could change so abruptly and be so out of my control. The details of Adam's continuing story were vague in my imagination—what profession he would someday follow, how many offspring he might have, which passions and interests would direct him—but I had never questioned the duration, the progress, the happily-ever-after aspect of his life. Now my faith in order, in logic, in the payoff of determined effort, was shaken.

In the pediatrics visitors' lounge of Mary Hitchcock Memorial Hospital, I saw in the faces of the other waiting parents the same mix of confusion, rage, and anxiety that I myself was feeling. We watched each other, those strangers and I, like the finalists in a bad news lottery, each willing the other to win. Statistically, some of us would escape this night with our child and our lives intact, but not all. Every now and then, a doctor in pale green clothing would emerge to sit next to an anxious couple. They would converse in low, private whispers, while everyone else flipped the pages of their magazines, pretending disinterest to give them the illusion of privacy. In fact, we missed no detail. We watched the expressions of eyes, the intensity of questions, the touching, in comfort or celebration, of the listening parents. Their reactions sent conflicting signals: happiness brought encouragement but condemned our own chances; grief confirmed our worst fears, but was mixed with guilty relief.

It was almost 6 P.M., and I realized I had not eaten anything since yesterday's lunch in Montreal. I was unwashed, unshaven, my hair not even brushed. I had made no calls and spoken to no one but doctors and nurses. It was as if a day had been snatched from the sequence of my life. With the change in my pocket I got coffee from a machine and, while it cooled, I telephoned Peter in Maryland.

"I talked to one of the docs there who's examined Adam," he said, then paused.

"Someone's already seen him?"

"They gave him another spinal and the fluid is still clear. His vitals are strong, but there hasn't been any improvement. They're good people and they're keeping a close watch, doing everything they can."

"What do they think it is?"

"It's a puzzler. Maybe encephalitis, maybe a weird kind of epilepsy. Does he have any history?"

"No. I mean, I don't know of any."

"There's a Bob Storrs on staff who's going to drop by tonight. He's good and he'll be straight with you, but don't expect any ironclad answers. They'll schedule a bunch of tests and maye then have some idea of what caused this."

"Pete, off the record, what do you think?"

"One thing you learn in med school, Michael, is how really little we know. This could be anything from an allergic reaction to . . . anything. The problem is, his past is a blank. There might be some congenital problem he inherited, some trauma during his mother's pregnancy . . ."

"He was premature."

"That's as likely to be a symptom as a cause. The point is, tomorrow call the social service agency that placed him and see what they can tell you, but in the meantime, go to a motel tonight and get some sleep. You're not going to do Adam any good if you keel over."

Half an hour later Dr. Storrs, a tall, sixtyish Vermonter, approached my waiting room couch with a slight limp. He looked tired but compassionate. He sat beside me, rested his elbows on his knees, and spoke to the floor. His voice was so soft that I couldn't hear, so I leaned forward, aware of the sidelong gazes of everyone around me.

"I beg your pardon?" I said.

"No change, no change. He's a fighter, and we're getting him some nourishment along with Dilantin for the seizures. I think he'll rest tonight and maybe wake up tomorrow."

"What caused this?"

He shook his head. "You have a place to stay for the night? Get a room at the Chieftain down the road. We'll call if there's anything. No point in wearing down your resistance. You look like hell."

"But he'll be all right?"

Dr. Storrs raised his head and turned to me. His intelligent eyes were a gray-blue. "It's been a rough day all around. I think he's going to make it, but we'll have a better grasp when the test results come back at nine tomorrow morning."

He shifted the weight of his upper body forward and used the momentum to rise to his feet. He wore large, rubber-soled brown shoes and his fingernails were clipped to perfectly squared ends. He reached and briefly squeezed my shoulder, and then he was gone.

For the second time that day I was searching a hospital parking lot, but now it was dark and an almost imperceptible spray of freezing rain misted the air. When I located my car, I used a cupped match to thaw the lock, and then spent five minutes scraping a peephole in the frost collected on the windshield. I had no trouble locating the Chieftain motel, made unmistakable by the brightly lit green caricature of an Indian's head on its sign. The only room available had no telephone, so before I slept I stood outside in the public phone booth to call my mother. I rested my forehead on the cold glass as I spoke, as I told her what I didn't know and gave her all the reassurances that I myself wanted to hear. I had to shout to be heard above the sounds of horns and sliding cars from the road, and finally I cradled the receiver between my shoulder and my ear so that I could put my hands in my pants pockets for warmth. With my head cramped in that angle, I had no choice but to stare through the blurred, icy panes of the booth into the angry neon eyes of the motel's namesake.

I sat beside Adam's bed for another day before he opened his eyes. He had been removed from Intensive Care, but except for an occasional tremor that affected only his right side, he remained immobile, a small, quiet presence in the center of the white hospital bed. Plastic tubes connected and moored him to this world, and I watched as the level of glucose that fed his IV declined, drop by drop. I ate the food from Adam's tray, delivered without reference to his state of consciousness, and found quiz programs on the television set suspended from the wall. I barely ackowledged the consolation of well-intentioned visitors—staff chaplains and rabbis. When I could stand the brooding claustrophobia of the room no longer, I paged through the indices of heavy books in the adjacent medical school library, searching for any constellation of symptoms which matched my son's.

Adam's tests had revealed unusual electrical activity in the left temporal lobe of his brain, but more than that, the close scrutiny of a team of physicians had yielded a raft of auxiliary troublesome observations: his cranial circumference was abnormally low (in the fifth percentile), his joints were poorly articulated, he had a tendency toward curvature of the spine. When I answered questions about the rate of his development—his slowness to talk, to run, to grasp the fundamentals of toilet training; his indiscriminate friendliness to all strangers; his habit of rocking his torso back and forth—I did not miss the expressions of guarded concern on the doctors' faces.

"He simply had a rotten start," I explained to interns and residents on rounds, summarizing Adam's journey from neglectful biological parents, through state hospitals and foster homes, to me. "He's making excellent catch-up progress now."

They were obviously unconvinced. My words did not balance the fact of Adam unconscious on the bed.

"What do you know of the parents' habits?" Dr. Storrs asked late the second evening. "Did the mother get proper nutrition during pregnancy? Did she smoke? Use drugs? Drink?"

Denis Daigle's initial description echoed in my memory. "Adam was undernourished when he was removed from parental custody. He had failed to thrive," I quoted. "And yes, his mother drank, but I don't know what or how much."

He wrote the information on the chart.

"How could her behavior years ago be related to this attack?" I asked.

"We're grasping for straws here. There's new animal research that suggests that certain teratogens can adversely affect the developing fetus. I'll try to find out more about it. Quite frankly, your boy's condition stumps me. What he's presenting should add up to *something*, but I don't know what."

Gently he grasped Adam's wrist with his thumb and forefinger and counted a pulse. "He's got the heart rate of a long-distance runner. Maybe that's a sport he'll take up."

I took my encouragement where I could find it, and, back at the Chieftain an hour later, I lay awake on top of the bedspread, screening on the closed lids of my eyes scenes of Adam clearing white wooden hurdles, Adam tossing a javelin, Adam pushing out his thin harrier's chest to break the ribbon and win the race.

*

I bolted awake at a knock at my door, and after a split-second of disorientation I was completely alert.

"Yes," I called, noting that the light filtering through the Venetian blinds was the dun shade of early morning.

"You had a phone call from the hospital," a voice said. "They said for you to get yourself over there."

My heart froze, and all about me the items of furniture in the room rose in precise clarity, as if each had been outlined with a sharp black pencil. With the illusion of slow motion I concentrated on details I had not noticed before: the print of blowing autumn leaves above the bureau, the fact that one of the four screws on the chain lock was missing, the dark carpet stain just inside the room's entrance, where too many snowy shoes had been wiped.

"Your kid's awake and asking for you. Tell them to wait until after eight to call."

Now time raced. I splashed water on my face and didn't bother to lace my shoes. Halfway out of the parking lot I realized I had forgotten my coat, but instead of going back, I turned up the heater. The sky to the east had turned a coppery gold, and the piles of snow that lined the street were dusted with a fresh fall. The few cars out and about at this hour trailed clouds of smoke from their exhausts; the town traffic lights were not yet been tuned to their daytime rhythm, and at intersections they simply blinked yellow. I drove through as if they were all green.

I took the stairs two at a time and was running by the time I reached the door to Adam's room. Voices came from within, and I pushed inside. Dr. Storrs sat on the bed, blocking my view with the expanse of his white coat.

"Follow my finger with your eyes," he said to my son. "That's right: up, right, left, down. Now look at this spot on my forehead. Hold still. That's good. Good. Are you hungry? How about some breakfast?"

There was silence, and automatically I poised to inject my usual explanation. "He doesn't understand you. He doesn't have the vocabulary yet." Then I remembered the situation, where I was, and I closed my eyes to say thank you.

"Orange juice."

Thank you. Dr. Storrs stood up and Adam saw me.

"Orange juice, Daddy."

CHAPTER THREE

We were, as Dr. Storrs reminded me several times over the next week, "not out of the woods yet." Adam was clearly on the mend—his appetite was restored and he was gaining back the weight he had lost, his seizures were less frequent and seemed controllable through Dilantin—but there was still no indication of what had caused the attack. He was content to stay in the hospital and soon became popular with the floor nurses and orderlies. He greeted all visitors to the room as if each were the person in the world he most wanted to see, and his exuberance gave him a reputation that spread into the larger community of Hanover.

One afternoon while I was reading Adam a story—"The Little Engine That Could"—two young Indian men knocked on the door and entered the room. They explained that they were freshmen students at Dartmouth, which had recently repledged itself to a goal of recruiting and graduating talented American Indians, and that they had heard through the small-town grapevine that we were here. The Native American world is relatively small, and it's a rare event when you cannot find, within five minutes of conversation, some mutual acquaintance. Howard Bad Hand (a Rosebud Sioux), Duane Bird Bear (a Mandan-Hidastsa from the Fort Berthold Reservation in North Dakota), and I soon identified a few friends in common. While Howard and Duane amused Adam, they told me that they were part of a group of fifteen Native American students from around the country, and that the college was in the process of discussing the creation of an Indian Studies Program. Would I consider applying to teach in it?

I enjoyed talking with Howard and Duane. They had the familiar, sly sense of humor common among the Native people I had known in Alaska and among members of my own family, the kind of humor that relies on puns and double entendres, on self-deprecation and under-statement. I was culturally relaxed with them in a way I had almost forgotten. The students at Franconia were perfectly nice, but their frame of reference was often different from mine. By and large they came from wealthy backgrounds, though they attempted to hide this fact beneath layers of army surplus and thrift store clothing. They were earnest in their politics, sophisticated in their drugs, fatigued by the follies of The Establishment. They forecast their lives by the dates of their birth, by the turn of stars, by interpreting the lines in their hands or the whorls of their ears, and strove to be, above all else, mellow. They knew no funny jokes.

Duane, on the other hand, launched quickly into money-making schemes that were guaranteed to assure the financial solvency of the Native American Program.

"We could design an Indian Monopoly game," he suggested. "Instead of Chance you could land on B.I.A. [Bureau of Indian Affairs]: 'Your tribe has just won its case at the Court of Claims. Go back three spaces!' "

"Or," Howard interrupted, "we could write the pilot for an Indian science fiction sit-com: 'Indians in Space.' Silver lamé breechclouts and antennae instead of feathers. I love it."

I thought how good it would be for Adam to grow up around other Indians, how good it would be for me too, and said if the Native American Studies Program got off the drawing board I was interested. Duane and Howard promised to keep me posted.

Back in Sugar Hill with Adam, I was hesitant to inform Denis of all that had happened; the words of that clerk at the Littleton Hospital had lodged in my mind, and I dreaded any complication that might delay or even abort the finalization of the adoption process. A part of me felt guilty, as though Adam's sickness had been caused through my neglect or inattention. I blamed his weight loss on my not stopping for his dinner on the way home from Montreal; and, if I had but arisen earlier that next morning, I might somehow, through alert and quick action, have broken the ensuing chain of events. Perhaps Adam had collapsed because I had demanded too rapid a development in his abilities. Maybe Denis would think that, because I had to maintain a full-time job, I was not equipped to be the sole parent of a child with a possibly chronic medical problem.

The Franconia College administration was understanding, and my students were more than glad to forgo or reschedule the classes I had missed. Morning and evening doses of Dilantin seemed to control Adam's seizures, and he returned to his day care center. The patterns of our lives, for the next several weeks, returned to their normal routines, except that I was different. I took less for granted, paid closer heed to any variation in Adam's behavior lest it signal a relapse, and saw my son in a new light: for the first time he seemed not only precious, a miracle, but also precariously fragile. I feared for his safety on the playground, for his exposure to childhood diseases, for his next breath. I watched for aftereffects to his prolonged coma—languid behavior, memory loss, incoordination—and saw them all. Two or three times before I went to sleep I stood silently in his doorway and listened in the dark to the music of his breathing. I was waiting for something to happen, for us to move from the limbo of uncertainty into the stream of our future.

I had to wait for only three weeks.

Severe winter weather in interior New England is a fact of life, remarkable only when it fails to appear regularly or in large quantity. Shoveling out the car while the engine warmed was part of my usual morning regimen; Adam would amuse himself in his playpen until the driveway was clear, the windshield was scraped, and the defroster in operation. For me the exercise was as energizing as a cup of black coffee. The cold air was so sharp, the contours of the surrounding land so gentled by overnight snow, the morning silence so electric blue, that I rarely minded the inconvenience. The town plowers worked before dawn and the road down our hill was usually passable, so I got to the point of ignoring weather bulletins and tuning out the sound of sleet beating against the screens.

It came as a surprise, therefore, when one icy dawn in late February, dressed in my parka and goosedown mittens, I pushed against the outer door and found it blocked. The sun was not up, so I switched on the exterior light and was confronted by the gusting swirls of a blizzard in high gear. Drifts as high as three feet were piled against the house and, short of climbing out a window or removing the hinges from the locked door that separated our basement apartment from the rest of the empty house, there was no exit. The local radio station reported a "snow emergency" and announced the closings of everything from the Congregational church's Lincoln's Birthday baked-bean supper to the operation of Franconia College.

"We're trapped!" I whispered to Adam, who caught the spirit of the game immediately and made his eyes big in mock horror.

I removed his coat and boots, put a record on the stereo—Joan Baez singing "The Night They Drove Old Dixie Down." As always, the refrigerator was stocked to its limit. When there is heat, electricity, running water, and the makings of beef stew in the house, there are few pleasures to compete with that of being snowbound. The restrictions of nature enhance a sense of coziness, of the luxuriously slow passage of hours. I foresaw a whole day of what my library of child care books called "quality time" filled with father-son experiences that would mysteriously impress themselves upon Adam's psyche and which he would forever recollect in essence rather than in specifics, like the scent of a blanket just out of the dryer or the first taste of milk after a long thirst. I decided to cater and orchestrate our isolation carefully, to create an adventure, a healing, an interlude out of the ordinary.

With madcap abandon we looked at one picture book after another, not bothering to replace them on the shelf but instead creating a messy clutter on the rug. We made a village out of inverted cooking pots, plates and bowls, and convoys of trucks barreled through its streets. We had an early lunch of popcorn and peanut butter sandwiches and, if we liked the song on a record, we played it over and over as many times as we wanted. Adam clomped from one room to another in my unlaced boots, and we used our fingernails to etch designs in the frost on the windowpanes. By noon it was still storming and we had worn ourselves out, so we snuggled together beneath the blankets of my bed and soon, soothed by the muffled sound of strong wind, fell asleep.

Hours later, with the brief northern light already fading, I opened my eyes. It took me a moment to focus, to separate the continuity of some dream from the actual movement in violent progress against the side of my body, but suddenly, shocked into clarity, I was awake. Adam was on his back, his head angled to the left, his neck stretched to its fullest length. A slight froth of gummy saliva showed around his lips, and his eyes, half open, were blank. His skin was hot and dry to the touch, and his arm and leg jerked rhythmically as if synchronous with the slow beat of his runner's heart.

I had been told that seizures were not as bad as they appeared, that the correct response was to hold Adam close, to turn him on his side and ensure that his tongue not block his windpipe, to speak in a comforting pitch. To wait it out.

"Wake up now, Adam," I said, and cradled him to my chest. "It's Daddy. It's all right. Relax. Relax." His limbs shook like the wings of a great bird desperate for escape. Their strength, their blind purpose, frightened me, but I repeated, again and again, my message, and gradually, reluctant as a fish struggling on dry land, he relaxed into a deep stillness from which I could not rouse him.

I ran to the bathroom and returned with a washcloth soaked in cool water. His fever was so high that nothing took priority over breaking it, so I smoothed back his hair and stroked his face, leaving, everywhere I touched, beads of moisture to evaporate. I took encouragement from the frown that briefly compressed his features, and spoke again.

"Hey, Adam. Time for dinner. Come on, open your eyes."

He understood me. I could see him summon some shadow of consciousness and then, too weak, surrender.

"Sleep, then," I said. "You'll feel better when you're rested. It's fine, you sleep."

Without looking away from him, I reached for the phone, dialed "O," told the operator to connect me with the emergency room of the local hospital. I counted seven rings until I heard the voice of the doctor on call. It was the same man who had treated Adam before, and I told him who I was.

"Adam has had another seizure, a grand mal." I kept my voice calm, uninflected. If Adam was listening I didn't want to alarm him further by my tone.

He didn't answer immediately, then said, "Why are you calling me? I thought the only physicians who were good enough for you were in Hanover."

I experienced a flash of pure and fully realized outrage. This man, only a few years my senior, was instantly transformed in my perception from a well-educated professional, a potential friend even, into a criminal whose piqued ego took precedence over the well-being of my child. I was at no loss for words of accusation, of threat, but I stored them for later, for a time when I had nothing to lose.

"He was in the hospital for a week," I said as if I had not heard him. "He's on Dilantin and this is the first problem he's experienced since we got back. I should have called you earlier—I'm sorry—but I was behind at. . . . Listen, what should I do now? His fever has come down some and he's resting quietly, but I can't completely wake him."

"Let him sleep it off. It's probably nothing, but if you want another opinion you can always call Hanover."

I realized that I was hearing a conversation this man had rehearsed in his head and that by prolonging the phone call I was only adding to his satisfaction. I hung up, sat in the darkening room. My jaws were clenched in anger and I stared without seeing at the far wall. The bed began to shake as Adam descended into another seizure. It began with a twitch in his thigh, then a flailing of his hand which spread up his arm. His back arched as I pulled him to my lap and located the washcloth, still warm from his last bout. I held him so closely that our bodies exchanged their motions: as his finally became quiet, mine continued to rock from side to side, side to side.

That night, between Adam's second and third seizures, I did call Dr. Storrs, who listened without interruption as I described every detail.

"He may have some kind of flu," he said, "and the fever is causing the seizures. You're doing the right thing by keeping it down. Give him some baby aspirin—a small dose because of his weight—and keep him cool without risking a chill. If you were here, I'd say come over, but the weather is terrible. It would take you hours, assuming the road is passable, which it probably isn't."

I told him about the local doctor, but he was reluctant to comment directly.

"Most likely it wouldn't do Adam any good to be in a hospital, anyway. As long as the episodes don't last more than a few minutes and you're there to deal with the rise and fall of his body temperature, he's probably safer inside than he would be in a car going anywhere. Bring him down tomorrow for a blood level, and we'll see about increasing the medication."

I took consolation in those words as, through the night and without ever fully waking, Adam seized nine more times. There were moments when it looked as though he were grappling with an invisible opponent, larger, heavier, more experienced. He battled to avoid being pinned, to keep from having both shoulders subdued at once, to throw the bully from his body, and I was there as coach, as manager, and cheering audience. We didn't win, but we didn't lose. By morning, when we were exhausted, sore and punch-drunk, the match was called and Adam woke. I gave him some milk, a piece of toast, and bathed him in our metal washtub. All around the kitchen was the evidence of our perfect snow day—scattered books, over-turned pots, the dregs of unpopped kernels in an orange plastic bowl. That night, when we returned from the hospital in Hanover with a new bottle of pills, I finally cleaned it up.

Over the next few months, various specialists proposed a number of hypotheses to account for Adam's seizures. An electroencephalo-gram (EEG) test indicated a tiny lesion in the left temporal lobe of his brain, from which erratic bursts of electrical activity were discharged. These impulses in turn stimulated the movement of his right arm and leg and blocked normal functions of consciousness and motor control. The problem was inoperable under present technology, and might have been caused either by a congenital birth defect or by trauma. The favorite theory to emerge, supported by no evidence except the lesion's existence, was that at some unspecified and undocumented pre-adoption time Adam might have suffered a case of encephalitis, or inflammation of the brain. Popularly believed to be transmitted through horse ticks, this disease would account for the EEG readings as well as for the apparently chronic nature of his seizures. Adam was not epileptic, I was assured, though for all intents and purposes he could be treated as though he were.

The first long-term drug prescribed was Phenobarbital, a com-pound that tends to accelerate brain and motor activity in adults but to tamp it in young children. It had the advantage of being cheap, relatively free from side effects, and usually effective. In Adam's case, however, it acted only as a strong soporific; when he was not unconscious in a heavy sleep, he was lethargic, unresponsive to anything around him. Dilantin was substituted, but, while it allowed Adam to remain awake, the drug was not without problems. The strength of his dosage stimulated hair growth on his head, arms, and legs and, over time, his gums thickened and bled.

More subtle, but at least as troubling, was the realization that Adam's embrace of the world was muted by drugs whose effects were substantially unknown. He had only just begun to emerge as a distinctive personality, and I had so little with which to compare his present reactions, learning ability, or acuity. He seemed to me alternately sluggish and hyperactive, wired and unplugged. Child development books were useless in his case; most of those studies took no note of a child with Adam's history—premature, abused, abandoned, institutionalized, stereotyped, and now ill, all in his first three years. He fell beyond their range of normal precedence and prediction, a wild card for whom anything was possible but nothing was promised. There were no standardized graphs against which to measure his rate of speech acquisition, his level of knowledge, his fine-motor skills. He was a person from whom nothing could be reasonably expected, for whom every modest success was a triumph, every normalcy a miracle.

Adam and I, as son and father, were in a land without codified laws. No one could answer even the most basic question: will he get well? If his convulsions did stem from unrecorded encephalitis, then it was possible, *possible*, that they would eventually cease in the process of natural maturation. As he grew, the lesion could heal or else develop such thick scar tissue that he would no longer be dependent on medication. This might take place during puberty, but maybe earlier, maybe later. Maybe never. Yet if his problems arose from some other cause—some trait inherited from a curtained and legally sealed biological lineage, then they might become progressively more serious, even life-threatening. We would, I was repeatedly told, have to wait and see.

Meanwhile, day in, day out, morning, noon, and night, there was the medicine. It became my explanation, my excuse, for Adam's every disability. He could not, for instance, learn to count to five, the years of his age. For weeks he blocked on the number three.

"One, two, four, five," he would intone, despite my every effort.

"One, two, THREE," I would insist. "Three, Three, THREE."

"One, two, four," he would answer.

It had to be the medicine.

His identification of crayon shades was so inconsistent that for a time I thought he might be color-blind.

"This one is *red*, and this one is *blue*, and this one is *yellow*," I instructed as he watched. "*Red, blue, yellow.*"

But he never got them right, never for years. Again, the medicine was to blame.

Toilet training seemed completely beyond his reach, yet when I anticipated his need and put him on the toilet, he knew what to do and tried to oblige. But if I forgot, he forgot and was apparently impervious to the discomfort of a soiled diaper.

Other children in his day care center, including those much younger than he, had mastered in their speech the use of pronouns. They had no confusion in identifying themselves as "I" or "me" and the rest of humanity as "you," but Adam was stuck in the third person, referring even to himself by his given name. "Adam's bottle." "Adam sleepy." "Adam eat up." With me, with anyone, his constant question was "Do you love Adam?" and no matter how many times he was told a person's name, he would retain no memory. Except for me: "Daddy" he never forgot.

It *had* to be the medication.

The perimeters of my life had radically altered. I was offered the Dartmouth College job and accepted for the following year. Not long before Adam fell sick, I began a relationship with an artist named Eileen, who was also on the faculty at Franconia and who lived in a neighboring town. She had reciprocated my feelings, and within a short time we had become involved to the point where we had flashes of a future together. She and Adam liked each other from the start, and for hours at a time she and I had discussed our attitudes toward marriage—we were hypothetically for it, parenting, and the changes such moves would make in "a person's" life. Eileen's work had just begun to garner national acclaim, and she enjoyed the mobility and excitement of being single every bit as much as I relished my newfound domesticity. We were both happy with our independence, and that was part of the attraction. Still, our feelings for each other were powerful; in our rambling talks we were ready to reconsider almost anything.

When Adam's health improved and I returned to work, Eileen and I continued to see each other, and for a while our relationship appeared stronger than ever. On some days she invited Adam to visit for the afternoon, giving me a break and permitting the two of them the chance to know each other one-on-one. He was relaxed in her company, and her growing affection for him was obvious. Throughout

the spring we planned events—picnics, excursions in the White
Mountains, an Easter egg hunt—as a threesome, and when I
contemplated teaching at Dartmouth, I happily entertained visions of
a long commute, of finding a place to live midway between our
respective places of work.

Whenever the subject of Adam's ill health arose, as it inevitably
did three times each day when he took his medication, Eileen was
available to help in any way, always optimistic that his condition
would naturally improve. She was, during that critical period in
which I was forced to accept my son's physical disability, an unwavering friend, the source of good counsel and genuine concern. And
I drew the wrong conclusions.

As the end of the school year drew near, I talked to real estate
agents, found listings, and timed the mileage from various locations in
the direction of Hanover. The events of the past winter and spring
had eroded my confidence, made me cling to every illusion of
security. I wanted to fix definitions, establish rules that would act as
fences against surprise. I was suddenly afraid to be alone, the sole
arbiter of Adam's life, and so manufactured a one-sided picture of my
relationship with Eileen. I changed for her into the worst kind of
friend—one who tries to get his way by flaunting need—the very
opposite of the capable, no-ties bon vivant I had originally presented
myself as being. I badgered and pressured Eileen for commitments
until I forced her to defend the outposts of her own choices and drove
her away.

On the last day of the semester, I received a letter in my mailbox.
Eileen wrote that with reluctance and with some regret she had
decided that she was not ready for an escalated relationship with me,
or to take responsibility for Adam. She valued spontaneity, needed
mobility for her work. With a boyfriend involved in his own career,
this was not impossible, but with a child, especially a sick child, it was
out of the question. She refused to be an irresponsible mother and
therefore, for the time being, she could not *be* a mother. It would be
better for all if we made a clean break, and so, by the time I read
these words, she would be off to California for the summer. Her
feelings for us were entirely genuine, she said, but I needed more
than she could give. She was sure that someday, when the dust had
settled, we would be good friends.

As it turned out, from the vantage of seventeen years, she was right, and we are. Her determination was made with the courage and maturity of self-knowledge, but I credited none of this at the time. That day, I read the letter twice, standing in my doorway. There was no forwarding address, no telephone number. I was bereft, confirmed in my worst dreads, angry and frightened, forced to face the consequences of decisions I had freely made. Nobody had twisted my arm or promised that adoption as a single man would be easy. This was not a complete-on-these-two-pages inspirational story in *Reader's Digest*, and no deus ex machina was waiting under the floorboards to solve my problems for me. Within weeks I had to find a house, negotiate a move, locate child care, start a high-pressure job, and try to establish a new academic subdiscipline, Native American studies— a subject in which I had no formal degree. I had not finished my Ph.D. thesis, and I was faced with the prospect of caring for a chronically ill little boy.

Adam was sleeping in his bed, and I sat at the kitchen table. The outside door was ajar, and occasionally a flying insect would buzz into the room. A milk carton was on the counter, the television played, and I was late in returning a call to a real estate broker. My schedule for the rest of the day was listed on a piece of lined paper that rested near my left hand: correct essays, write letters, go to grocery (orange juice, bread, baloney, apples, eggs, paprika), laundromat, Eileen. She would be flying from Boston, and maybe I could rush there and convince her to stay, but I'd have to hurry. I considered waking Adam, changing his diaper, feeding him his lunch and medicine, driving with him in the car—Dustin Hoffman at the end of *The Graduate*. But somehow the prospect was too self-serving, too exhausting, too complicated, too unlikely to succeed. I had made my choices a long time ago; Eileen had a right to hers. So I remained seated while the shadows in the yard elongated their shapes, blurred. When Adam woke, we went to the grocery, came home and ate an omelet. I left the dirty laundry for the next day.

Our first house in the Upper Valley, as the stretch of New Hampshire and Vermont on either side of the town of Hanover is called, was a cabin on Lake Mascoma. Located in the town of Enfield, twenty minutes by car from Dartmouth, it had been listed as a "bungalow" in the classified section of the newspaper. At $175 a month, it seemed perfect. The interior was completely paneled in real, maple-stained wood, and the furnishings were spare but pleasant: twin beds in each of two small bedrooms, a narrow hall of a kitchen, a living room with a kerosene stove and a fireplace. The lake was a hundred feet down an incline that ended in a strip of sandy beach. The only neighbors were a family with two daughters and an elderly couple. Each occupied a wooden frame house that was a slightly larger, slightly more elaborate version of ours. All three were painted pale yellow and had green shingle roofs. Tall old pines framed the property, set back from a town road, and at night there were no yard lights to compete with the sky.

Adam and I each slept in rooms that opened onto the parlor/dining area. As the weather grew cooler that first year, our day would begin with the dangerous operation of lighting the stove. This involved crushing a few sheets of toilet paper, igniting the wad with a match, and then dropping it into a kerosene tank next to the fireplace just after the start-knob had been turned. When the timing had been precise and successful, a small explosion would sound and heat would begin to radiate. If my coordination was off, the least consequence was that I would have to try the procedure again. I hated to contemplate the worst possibility.

My new academic job was a challenge. Nobody at Dartmouth knew what Native American studies was supposed to be, but the unpersuaded suspected that it somehow involved basket-weaving and mysticism, a sop to radical minority students. The entire complement of the program's initial faculty allotment was .5 "full-time-equivalents," which meant that I was chair of half of myself, the rest of me parceled off to anthropology. To counter the community's politely unspoken doubts, I determined to make my courses unusually rigorous, and soon discouraged those who enrolled for no reason other than that it seemed the liberal thing to do. The students who remained were unsentimental about "the plight of the redman" and very smart.

I enrolled Adam at a day care center in Norwich, Vermont, directly across the Connecticut River from Hanover. Housed in an A-frame building with a huge, stuffed Snoopy perched in the window of the loft, it seemed an ideal spot. The staff was enthusiastic at the prospect of an Indian child—"so educational for our boys and girls"—and agreed to administer Adam's noontime medicine. They were undaunted by what they termed Adam's "developmental lag" and were the first in a long progression of people who were convinced that, thanks to their wide and pertinent experience, they could make a difference where others, such as I, had failed.

I hoped they were right. I rooted for their methods and wished them luck in teaching my son the number three, the colors, the letters of the alphabet. I seconded their assurances that within weeks Adam would be out of diapers and into training pants, the result of his acquiescence to subtle peer pressure. The move was going to be a new beginning for both of us, and I could hardly wait to log Adam's progress, to see steady growth, to witness the birth of motivation toward independence on his part. I waited for him to ask to tie his own shoes, to state a preference for one record over another, to make friends with children his age, to gain weight, and engage me with questions.

Every morning and late afternoon, as I drove him to and from his school, I talked a steady stream, pointing out interesting sights, asking about his activities, recounting tales of my adventures at work. At its midpoint our route traversed a railroad track, and this was the only thing on Adam's mind. He had noticed it shortly after we moved to the area and identified it with "The Little Engine That Could."

"Choo choo train!" he sang the first time we rumbled over it, and I, delighted at this recognition, chimed in.

"Choo choo!"

That night, on the way home, he watched for the crossing and when it came in sight, he said, "Choo choo." He did the same the next morning and the next evening, and the next and the next. For the two years he attended his day care, he never once failed to chime it, but he rarely said anything else. I would be talking to him about all the positive features of dry pants—the trips we could take without diaper bags, the luxury of rash-free skin, the approval and celebration of children and adults alike—and in the middle of it he'd say "choo choo" and cut me off. I could be close to the punch line of a story—"Who's been sleeping in my bed and is *still in it*?"

"Choo choo."

At such times I might reply with an attitude that was annoyed and frustrated, or, alternately, cajoling and happy.

"Choo choo," my five-year-old son would obstinately rejoin.

If I took a different road, a roundabout way, Adam was too

preoccupied with looking for accustomed signposts to listen to me. And if I followed the familiar path, no entreaty, no substitute topic or activity, nothing would turn his mind from its obsession. I thought it might indicate an affinity for railroads, that he might have some precocious interest, and I bought toy trains of every description—wood, electric, plastic. I found children's books about trains and read them at bedtime. I took Adam late at night to the train station in White River Junction so that we could watch the Montrealer roar past, its lighted windows a yellow ribbon in the darkness. If I couldn't beat the appeal of those damn tracks, perhaps I could, as in judo, use their strength with Adam as a trajectory, as a means of propulsion toward a wider appreciation of the world.

And through it all, Adam never complained, was always obliging, always repeated what I finally told him to say, smiled when I asked him to. But he was stalled on those tracks as surely as a car out of gas. He couldn't budge.

It was a small thing, a silly thing to have been upset about. Now that I don't drive that way anymore and that Adam thinks about some other things, those trips can even be fashioned into a funny story of parental overreaction. But at the time, after the first month, there was nothing humorous about it to me. Adam always crossed those tracks in the same way, as if he had never done so before. His monotonous response was like a kick in the stomach, a red flag or flashing light in my eyes. It was as if he were hanging from the rung of a ladder by his hands and refused to go forward, preferring to dangle in one spot until he dropped. He had grasped a single connection in the universe that resonated to him, and it was enough, it was sufficient, it obscured from his view everything behind it. He lacked the quality so celebrated in our species: the desire to see over the top of the next hill.

In the years to come those tracks would be replaced by other temporary monomanias—Garfield cartoons or cows or a single tape, played over and over on his Walkman—but there was never more than a single, solitary thing on Adam's mind at any one time. Ideas did not compete for his attention; he was loyal, sticking with a fascination until he wore it out. How he selected his passions I don't know, except that they had little to do with the array I tried to spread before him. There were times I thought him obdurate in his refusal to internalize ideas that would be good for him, stubborn. How great it would be, I often imagined, to climb inside his brain for an hour and arrange things, organize the files, discard the junk mail, and open a few windows. To be able to say, directly and without obstruction, *this* is important, Adam, *this* matters, *this* is worth knowing. For years I assumed I was fighting the effects of his medication, battering the barriers of his late start, scaling self-protective walls erected against the neglect he experienced as an infant. It was not until the following summer, when Adam was still five years old, that I began to have an inkling that my real adversary was the lingering ghost of Adam's biological mother, already dead in 1973 of acute alcohol poisoning.

CHAPTER FOUR

The previous spring Beatrice Medicine, a highly respected Standing Rock Lakota anthropologist, had joined me at Dartmouth as a visiting faculty member in Native American studies. Our previous professional association soon developed to the extent that she sometimes introduced me to people as her second child. A woman of wit, sophistication, and great compassion, she had taken a strong interest in Adam, and often we would share a meal with her and Ted, her sixteen-year-old son, at their small college-owned house in Hanover. They, together with many of the Native Americans and with Nina Sazer, who had founded Adam's day care center and had become a close and trusted friend, were our local quasi-family.

The undergraduate and medical students—Duane and Howard, Eva Smith (Shinnecock), Butch Guerue (Rosebud Sioux), Cleora Hubbard (Navajo), Harry and Gerri Buckanaga (Santee and Pine Ridge Sioux, respectively), Bruce Oakes (Mohawk), Karen Louise Erdrich (Turtle Mountain Chippewa), Travis Kinsley (Hopi), Lydia Begay (Navajo), Mike Hanitchak (Choctaw), Cathy Wilson (Nez Perce), Charlie Kaiaraiak (Inuit), Deborah Prairie Chief (Cheyenne), Charley Beech (Cherokee), Grace Newell (Paiute), Pedro Rado (Tlingit), and others—were hundreds or thousands of miles from home and not all that much younger than I. They for the most part treated me as a peer and Adam as a kid brother. Patient and accepting, they sometimes commented that he reminded them of a nephew or cousin back home. At the time, I assumed that they referred simply to his appearance.

After its first nine frantic months, the Native American studies department had become academically respectable. In July, Bea invited Adam and me to join her on a visit to her mother's house in Wakpala, South Dakota, on the Standing Rock reservation, and I was happy to accept. From a pattern composed of pieces of newspaper cut in the shape of arms, front, and back, Nina had sewn us father-and-son traditional powwow shirts. The material was dark navy crepe with tiny white polka dots, and each shirt was highlighted with thin strips of white satin ribbon across the chest and banding the cuffs. There was to be a large celebration in Wakpala during our stay, and Adam would be given a Lakota name. In anticipation, I had let both our hair grow for months: my mixed-blood brown was shoulder-length and wavy, but Adam's 4/4ths quantum was black, its rate of growth stimulated by the Dilantin, long enough to wrap in two slim braids.

I have a photograph taken just before we set out from New Hampshire; Adam's skin is clear, his eyes large and dark with straight, fine lashes. He sits on the wooden fence behind our cabin and looks over his shoulder at the camera. His hair shines where the sunlight filters through the trees, and he smiles. Dressed in blue and white striped pants and a red shirt, gifts from one of my aunts, he is far too thin; his arms are all bone, all elbow and wrist joint. He looks young and small for his age, and the expression in his eyes is confused, as if he is awaiting further instruction.

We were scheduled to meet Bea at the Institute for Indian Studies at the University of South Dakota in Vermillion in two days. I set out from New Hampshire before dawn and took the less-trafficked northern route through Canada. Adam was a good traveler, quiet in his seat, alert for the rumble of a truck or for the bump of railroad tracks. He didn't demand to know when we would arrive, didn't prefer one radio station over another, didn't ask where we were headed or why. When I stopped for gas, I lay him on the backseat and changed his diaper, and late in the afternoon at a convenience store on the upper peninsula of Michigan, I purchased bread, baloney, and cheese for sandwiches. At the cash register I had a sense of how boring the past eleven hours in the car must have been to Adam and, to reward his uncomplaining patience, presented him with a pack of Juicy Fruit—his first ever.

"Don't swallow the gum," I urged repeatedly. "When you're finished, put the old piece in the ashtray, or wrap it in paper and throw it in the trash. Only one stick in your mouth at a time."

Adam indicated that he understood. He chewed with cautious gusto, opening his jaws wide enough after each chomp to disengage the gum, then clamping down again. His whole being was concentrated on the ricochet of his teeth, the top row off the bottom.

He tried, but of course didn't succeed. After the initial gulp, his mouth was completely empty. It was clear I would have to supervise every piece Adam used, and the prospect of hours' worth of nagging discouraged me. I mentally crossed gum off the list of things Adam might have: another chip, insignificant in itself but part of a growing pile flaked away from the structure of Adam's future. I recalled the joke about the man who couldn't walk and chew gum at the same time. Now that my son was turning out to be such a person, there was nothing funny about it.

"Tell you what," I said. "Why don't you ride in the backseat and have the whole pack, one stick after the other. As soon as the flavor is gone, throw the wad away, swallow, then have the next one." I figured it was easier to get the problem over within five minutes, then forget it.

Adam was delighted at the largesse. From the rearview mirror, I saw him unwrap four consecutive sticks. His mouth worked vigorously, an expression of excitement on his face. This was the most interesting thing that had happened on our trip, as far as he was concerned. When the last piece was used up, I passed him a Handi/Wipe for his chin and shirtfront, and suggested he nap for the next couple of hours. I wanted to drive late so that we would reach Vermillion by dinner the next day, and that meant getting as close as possible to Duluth the first night. The road was uncrowded, the countryside lush and sparsely populated.

I tuned in a C & W station from Marquette and gave myself over to anticipation: in two days I'd be back on a reservation, eating corn soup and fry bread, listening to a northern plains drum. And for the first time I'd be there with Adam. I planned to teach him to fancy-dance when he got older, maybe even get some Lakota practice tapes and learn Sioux together so that he could speak his tribal language. There was a release that came from driving west; through the trees, the sky ahead opened like the end of a funnel, endlessly wide and high, a ceiling stretching without support above the horizon.

It was almost nine by the time I pulled into a large motel with a vacancy sign. Adam was awake by then, and we got out of the car and walked through the evening coolness to the lighted office. The manager, smiling at the sound of the entry bell, looked from me to Adam and back to me again.

"You have a room with two beds, please?" I asked. "My son and I have been on the road since four this morning."

The man glanced back at Adam, then answered. "Sorry, Chief. We're full up."

"But the sign said 'vacancy,' " I protested, then it hit me: *chief*. I bit the inside of my lip for calmness. "Well, is there another motel around here?"

"I couldn't say."

"There are laws against what you're doing, you know."

"Against being one hundred percent occupied?" He smiled.

I took Adam's hand and pushed back through the door, letting it slam. We stood on the step for a moment while I thought what to do next. Out of context, most strangers didn't place me as Indian, but with Adam, for Adam, it was going to be a different story. We were in a part of the country with many reservations, and that's where unapologetic discrimination was usually the worst. It was too late to call information for the number of the Michigan Human Rights Commission and report the bigoted manager—I waited until the next day at a pay phone to do that—and Adam was exhausted.

"Come on," I said. We got back in the car and drove fifteen miles before we saw another motel.

"Wait here. I'll just be a minute." This time, naturally, there was no trouble. The owner was hospitality personified, glad to see me, worried about the little boy all alone in the car, promising a quiet room where we wouldn't be disturbed. Maybe she would have been the same if Adam had been at my side. Maybe, but I didn't want to test it.

The room was paneled with reddish wood and lit by lamps with dark green shades. The beds were too soft and covered by brown velour spreads. But it was a place to rest, and the minute the door was closed I flopped backward on the mattress and stretched full length. Adam went to the TV and stood waiting for me to turn it on, but instead I held out my arms.

"Give Daddy a hug," I said. "You've been a good boy today."

Adam raced, then dove onto my chest, his body hard and light.

He loved physical affection more than anything. I closed my eyes, reached behind him and undid the band that confined his long hair in a pony tail, and began to absently comb it out with my fingers.

I immediately hit a snag. Then another. Another. Adam's hair was matted and sticky, clumped in pieces against his scalp. I propped up on one elbow for a closer examination, but I realized what it was before I saw it. Gum.

I took Adam into the bathroom to look at the damage under better light. Gnarled strands were wrapped tightly around and embedded in dried, twisted lumps. When I tried to pry them loose, bit by bit, the fine strands broke off in my fingers. There was no hope for a brush, and no doubt that the best solution lay in a close-cropped cut.

But I had tended Adam's long hair for months in preparation for his naming ceremony. I wanted him to have braids in the traditional way, didn't want to explain a nearly shaved head to a community of strangers. There had to be a method of washing the gum free. I located my address book and telephoned people around the country, desperate for suggestions. Finally, on intuition I tried my great-aunt Rena, well into her seventies and living alone in a small town in eastern Washington State off the Couer-d'Alene reservation. I said a quick hello and then summarized the dilemma.

"Peanut butter," she announced without hesitation.

"Peanut butter?"

"Not chunky. Smooth. Rub it in, squeeze it through, rinse it out. Works every time."

"You're sure?" I asked.

"Not chunky."

But, of course, when I took Adam in the car and found a late-night grocery store, the only type in stock was chunky. I bought the economy size and raced back to the motel.

"This is going to be a kind of game," I told Adam, as I stripped off his shirt and pants. "I'm going to put peanut butter in your hair. It'll be fun."

"You first," he said.

I could have argued, but figured what the hell. I scooped a two-fingered helping and smeared it on top of my head. "Now you."

The peanut butter gathered into oozing balls and sagging bulges. Against his tanned skin, Adam looked as though he were wearing a hat made of wet clay. I was as gentle as I could be, but my hands still must have pulled. After a minute of massage he started to cry, then wail.

"Shhhh," I said. "We're in a motel. You have to keep it down."

But his volume increased, and he scared himself with his own yells.

"Here, cry into this." I offered him a bunched towel and demonstrated how he could muffle it over his mouth and scream at will. I had visions of Michigan State troopers breaking down the door, sizing up the situation, and arresting me for kidnapping and torturing with peanut butter a half-naked child.

When the jar was scraped clean, I stood Adam in the shower, always his least favorite activity. Finally, a half bottle of Johnson's Baby Shampoo later, Adam was asleep on his feet, his hair sluiced down his back in an unclotted, sleek mane.

In Vermillion, and then on Standing Rock, people felt compelled to compliment it.

"Your boy's hair has such a shine," they would comment. "Such thick body."

I'd nod, accept their praise, make Adam say thank you. Then at night I would continue the slow process of removing tiny chunks of peanut, trapped by the comb's teeth. And if anyone noticed, over those next several days, how clouds of flies forsook all others to hover around Adam's head and mine, they were too polite to mention it.

We rendezvoused with Bea as planned and kept going. The drive across the length of South Dakota was a wonder. First, we stopped for an hour to visit friends on the Sisseton Reservation, near the Minnesota border, and then, around three in the afternoon, turned onto a state highway that led bullet west to Mobridge. The light held a long time, as for the next four hours we crossed plains as level and green as a billiard table. After dusk, it seemed as though we were traveling at the same speed as the sunset. The orb of the sun held steady just above the horizon, casting brilliant reds and golds into the low cumulus clouds. To the stranger, the land was devoid of markers, each mile the duplicate of what had come before and what was to follow. Yet that very lack of variety brought a sense of endless space, of expanse without limit or boundary. Our car could have been moving through air, so smooth was the ride, so unveering the course.

The light played over Bea's face as she entertained us with histories of her people's travels, her own past homecomings, and I thought about the nature of being a stranger.

Reservations are the residue of North America that, over the past five hundred years of contact with Europeans, Indians never gave up. They are, according to Justice John Marshall's Supreme Court rulings in the early nineteenth century, "domestic dependent nations," subsumed by America but not part of any state. They have complicated rights to internal self-government, to individual judicial systems, to impose their own taxes and make their own laws. They are, in a true legal sense, quasi-sovereign, each composed of populations who, since 1924, hold dual U.S. and tribal citizenship. Their political identity predated that of any other country on the continent; their right to exist and to continue to exist derives from an international recognition of "Aboriginal Claim," the long-term use and occupancy of a territory, theirs by fact rather than because of any written deed certifying ownership. More than three hundred reservations—so-called "Indian Country"—exist today, and, counted together with Alaska Native villages and regional corporations, they comprise just under one hundred million acres, ranging in size from parcels with the dimensions of a generous house lot to the Navajo Nation, roughly as big as West Virginia.

But reservations are more than property for the Indian people who live there. They are the past and the future, the tangible evidence that tribes were once as independent as any peoples in the history of the world, and the hope, if the treaties that recognized them are kept, for a return of self-sufficiency. They are networks of families, of extended interweavings of blood and generations, of resentments and forgivenesses, of shared space and time. They are places of historical and contemporary deprivation, of incarceration and religious restriction, of confusing, frustrating social inequities, and of too little cash. But they are also havens, home, where familiar words, be they spoken in the native language or in modern idiomatic English shorthand, are understood, where each ripple in the land has the significance of an old story, where you go when you need to.

No two reservations are alike any more than any two tribes are the same, but there are commonalities: government housing, missionaries, powwows, internal political feuds, disproportionate representation within the populations of the very old and the very young, ironic twists of humor, raging debates about alcohol, the Bureau of Indian Affairs, broken cars, quiet. People know each other, know who's who and who's related to whom. That counts for plenty and extends an umbrella of tolerance, acceptance, and noncriticism rarely offered in mainstream communities. If you belong, you belong. If you're a stranger, you feel it like a constant prickle of electricity.

If you march down a big-city street, nobody seems unfamiliar because everyone is. It's odd to encounter someone you know—it's remarkable; but to be an outsider in an agency town or on a rutted back road between reservation hamlets is to be *the* outsider, *the* maverick in a place where historically the visitor almost never meant good news.

A kind of protocol develops when you visit a number of reservations where you don't expect to know anyone. If you appear as unambiguously "Indian," it's easier—depending on how you're dressed; the question then becomes who are you with, why are you here? If you're a "could-be," a mixed blood, more validation is called for: conversations early on entail the ubiquitous litanies of "do you know's," establishing yourself as a person with the credentials of association, with an identity, with hypothetical references who would presumably be willing to attest that you are okay. It doesn't help to be pushy, to self-advertise with too much turquoise or beadwork, to talk too much. You're the petitioner, you're the one on trial, and there's no rushing the process. Local people are practiced in making their evaluations; they've had to be.

There's something deeply satisfying about being on your own reservation, something more than nationalism, more than security. It's a feeling of survival, of being a link in an improbable continuity. It's a responsibility fulfilled, an important promise kept, a preference for what seems less than what the outside world offers but in fact is more than imagined. Those fond of make-believe noble savages are devoted to the notion that there is a mystical quality at the root of the relationship between Indians and the land, but they misunderstand. Land is the opposite of magic: it's real, solid, firm. Land is legacy, it enables and supports life, it's both a source and a destination. Land is rocks, hidden roots, dirt, and buried bones, very personal and simultaneously communal. And if it's not yours by right of blood and memory, you always enter for the first time as a trespasser.

And so, as we approached Standing Rock, I was apprehensive as well as anxious. I didn't enjoy the role of stranger. I dreaded the introductions, the worry at a suspicious reception, the unease and loneliness of not being instantly identifiable. Even in the company of Bea, there were subtle tests Adam and I must pass. And to fail was to lose more than a moment's composure: it was to be judged lacking by the people whose estimation was most desired, most necessary. It was through the eyes of these unmet people that I would discover if in living in New Hampshire, if in teaching at an Ivy League school, I had changed. Their response was the litmus, for they, unclouded by self-interest, would know better than I.

I didn't talk about any of this to Bea; instead, as the sky around us darkened, we discussed statistics: the shocking facts of Indian health and welfare in South Dakota, the high infant mortality rate, the 80-percent unemployment in many tribal communities, the disproportionate numbers of Sioux in state prisons, the expected adult lifespan more than ten years shorter for an Indian man or woman residing on a reservation than for a white American. All were and still are dire circumstances without easy solutions, all are ills whose cause might be attributed—in an easy, knee-jerk finger-pointing—to "the government," the lack of money, the unkept promises, the endless bureaucracy of civil service. These were our standard public explanations, no less ultimately true because they were politically acceptable, but insufficient answers between two friends who had heard and said it all before. All the excuses were legitimate, more than enough reason for the overwhelming troubles of contemporary Native Americans. Nobody could blame a people for being beaten down by such circumstances clearly beyond their control. Side by side on that westward road, with Adam asleep in the back, Bea and I searched beneath the surfaces for more complicated causes.

Platitudes did not bring relief. If the government suddenly changed, if there were enough money, if the mechanics of social service processing moved faster, if the treaties were adhered to at last, would all the problems resolve themselves? Did contemporary American Indian adults bear *no* responsibility for the current crisis conditions? Was our behavior in no way contributory to the status quo? Were we powerless to effect changes or improvements on our own?

We shied from unwelcome conclusions, each of us citing grass-roots individuals who worked tirelessly and with enormous conviction in rectifying their tribal communities—educators, elected officials, social workers, doctors and nurses, religious leaders, activists, family organizers. These men and women operated with optimism, apparently immune to discouragement, using humor and wit to cope with the horrendous realities and disappointments that they faced many times a day. They were heroes and heroines, courageous and strong, sticking it out, often without recognition or compensation, because of principles and determination and the core belief that, if they could not eliminate suffering, they could at least wrestle it to a draw.

What we hated to acknowledge was the high burn-out rate these strategically placed workers experienced. How, after the initial burst of optimistic enthusiasm, after the "I can make a difference" rush of adrenaline, after coming to terms with the repetitious days and years of dealing with chronic minor annoyances, after constantly sacrificing grand-scale goals for the satisfaction of small victories, many eventually conceded, retreated, closed their eyes. Some became cynical, some found grim jokes in the horror stories they found themselves recounting, some joined the opposition, stopped being teetotalers or recovering alcoholics, and drank. There was an element of the inexorable about the process if you watched it from the outside, a limit of human endurance that, finally reached, collapsed. The determination for a normal, dependency-free life ebbed away with the persistent bandaging of small wounds.

The seven reservations in South Dakota—Pine Ridge, Cheyenne River, Standing Rock, Rosebud, Crow Creek, Lower Brule, Yankton, Sisseton—were full of people at various points in this cycle. These territories, cast like jagged-edged glass to the north, west, south, and east of us as our road bisected the wheat fields of South Dakota, were the surviving holdings of the Great Sioux Reservation, created by U.S. Senate treaty in 1868 and promised to remain forever intact. On a map it appears that the hub of each fragment is the small town where the government offices, the hospital, and the tribal police headquarters are located. These are the communities with paved roads, with snack bars and a mile-high TV antenna. Here are found the BIA high schools, the rows of prefab houses, color coordinated in their siding, all facing the same direction. Here telephones are not rarities, here helicopters land when they ferry the terminally ill to teaching hospitals in Minneapolis or Denver. Here is the grandest church, occasional plumbing. Here, if anywhere, is the treatment center for alcoholics, the refuge for battered women, the jail. Here grass is sometimes watered, making irregular, erratic patches of green to contrast with the yellow wild scrub that covers the whole country throughout the dry months. Here is the store, overpriced and stocked with high-starch foods, cake mixes, and setups by the case.

There is a sameness to these towns that goes beyond common architecture, government-issue paint. They seem somehow temporary, set on the landscape by a child with too few blocks, too little imagination. Now and then one encounters an effort, oftentimes never actually occupied or even completed, to construct a tribal office complex or community center with an "Indian" flair—cement walls with impractically geometric corners, gods-eye windows, chimneys fashioned to resemble teepee poles. These experiments are touching in that they were somebody's hope, some optimistic planner's dream that content might follow form, that in the right setting the old values, kindnesses, attitudes might reemerge. Much attention is devoted to the matter of compass orientation in these projects; picture windows attempt to open toward the vistas of mythological origin or to symbolically face the rising sun. But for all their grandness of conception, these monuments for the most part stand empty, forsaken in favor of cinderblock squares, or trailers tagged with bragging signs—THE UNITED STATES GOVERNMENT, OFFICE OF TRIBAL MANAGEMENT—and strung together with improvised, uninsulated enclosed walkways. Floodlights are big in these communities. They illuminate deserted streets and the entrances to buildings that are thought to need protection. Powered from generators or feeding off electrical lines, they create four-hundred-watt circles in the night, huge white beads that burn until dawn and sometimes throughout the day.

I thought of these beacons switching on as we approached our destination. The sunset had finally blurred into the smudge color of embers, and the signs along the highway said that it was fifty, forty, twenty miles to Mobridge, closest big town to Standing Rock, where we had rooms reserved in a Best Western. I reached behind me to check that Adam had not rolled from the seat and encountered his hair, still sleek from the peanut butter. Bea was sitting straight, as if urging the car faster. It had been almost a year since she was last home.

Though it was nearly ten o'clock, we drove past the motel and turned north onto a rough-surfaced two-lane road. There were stars now and a low moon. Bea pointed out landmarks as we crossed onto her reservation and headed toward the small settlement where her mother lived. This was no agency headquarters, just a cluster of houses built during the Great Depression, by the people whose families still inhabited them. The only signs of occupancy were distant lighted windows, usually no more than one per house, spaced miles apart. There was a blown smell of rain from the north where, we had heard on the radio, thunderstorms prevailed. This southern part of Standing Rock is a place so quiet that air itself has a low static sound, interrupted this night only by the roll of our car's wheels. We were a moving island, a thing of motion in a still, resting landscape, and it affected us. Our talk faded, the pupils of our eyes expanded, we breathed deeply into our chests, savoring the scents of hay and purple alfalfa.

At an indistinct juncture we turned right onto a rutted track of flattened grass and climbed a knoll to where Bea's mother, Annie Medicine, lived alone. The two-room house was low and square, smelled of bleached laundry and tea. Mrs. Medicine waited in the doorway and wore a low-hanging blue cotton dress, buttoned down the front, and slippers. She was a large woman with long, strong arms and heavy legs. Behind the thick lenses of her glasses her eyes were quick, thorough, counting. Her fine white hair was caught in a thick knot behind her head, and the skin of her high-cheeked face was clear, barely lined. She greeted Bea in Lakota, nodded at me and indicated a made-up cot, sometimes used by Bea's brother Marne when he visited, where I could lay Adam.

The room was clean, its walls hung with pictures of Catholic saints, crucifixes, and other religious objects. Every available flat surface—the bureau, the window sills, the top of the refrigerator—was a base for the framed photographs of smiling relatives. A thawed Sara Lee cake was set in the middle of the table next to a stack of plates and a bunch of forks. A kettle steamed on the wood stove.

Assembled in one corner were the items to be distributed in tomorrow's giveaway: blue metal plates, coffee pots, acrylic blankets, fringed shawls. There was an open envelope stuffed with five-dollar bills, a tablecloth still in its plastic wrapper, and coils of new yellow rope.

Conversation erupted in bursts, interspersed with comfortable silence. We behaved as if food were our real excuse for being there, and the clatter of plates passed, sugar and cream stirred into tea, were the music. We reported on road conditions, weather, and asked about plans for the annual powwow, to be held the next day. The topics were neutral, impersonal, information was diffidently offered, and yet somehow in the exchange of news a transition was made; I was less a stranger. It was not so much that I said the right things but that I did not say the wrong ones. I had not asked inappropriate questions, not seemed too eager. Adam awoke and stumbled to my side, rubbing his eyes, lured by cake. Mrs. Medicine approved of the length of his hair, found a comb and began to smooth its snarls and tangles. He stood obligingly between her knees as she sat on the edge of her chair and held his neck stiff. With the practice of many years she drew a center part and fashioned loose braids, secured with rubber bands from the pocket of her dress. As a final touch she licked her fingertips with a sweep of her tongue, worked the shorter strands above Adam's forehead into the design, then wordlessly offered her cooled cup for him to sample. She smiled at me when he did, and revealed that not only did she have a Lakota name to give to Adam but that she would bestow one on me as well.

Adam did not wake when I carried him to our room or when I removed his clothes, so I let him sleep in his undershirt, diaper, and rubber pants. The window in the bathroom was open and the night was cool and smelled of sweetgrass. We shared a double bed and I lay for a long time the way you do after hours of driving. I had so concentrated on staying awake behind the wheel that now, whenever I started to drift off, I jolted awake in the panic of an impending crash. I saw headlights on my lids when I closed my eyes and still felt the motion of the car, like an echo. I tuned into Johnny Carson and turned down the sound until it was barely audible; tonight he was the Great Karnak, mind reader extraordinaire, and dressed in a shiny turban and robe. Finally, lulled by the pattern of Adam's breath, I slept.

Even in my dream I am driving. Bea, Adam, and I follow a winding gravel track through the low Missouri River hills whose outline I have seen by moonlight against the sky, but now it is day. Suddenly and out of nowhere a trio of huge birds appears in front of the windshield, trapped by velocity against the glass. They beat their wings wildly, frantic to escape, but they are pinned tight. In the odd way of dreams I am at one with them, empathic, and I try to identify the sensation they feel. Then I have it: when I was a child I sometimes went to an amusement park. In Hilarity Hall, the fun house, there was a huge wooden bowl with steep sides sunk into the floor. When it was at rest the riders lay on their backs in the bottom, displaying their arms and legs at strange angles—elbows and knees bent as if running, for instance, or toes and fingers pointed as in a dive.

With the flip of a switch the bowl began to spin, slowly at first and then with increasing acceleration. As the speed built, each child would inch up the side, gripped by centrifugal force, eventually unable to move anything but the eyes. I remember my mouth was pulled wide as it seemed sure that I would inevitably be lifted past the rim and flung fast against a far wall, but there was nothing I could do, no anchor. There always came a moment of surrender, a relaxation of muscle in preparation for that flight, and it was that rush, that acceptance and embrace of any danger, that I touched in the minds of those dream birds as they blanketed the windshield with their splayed brown feathers. My vision was gone, and I took my hands from the wheel, turned in the seat to reach for Adam, as we flew toward impact.

I was holding him when I woke. His eyes were quick and alert and he agreeably returned my embrace. His back was bony, his elbows sharp. "I stayed dry," he whispered like an endearment, and I complimented him though I could tell it wasn't true. He not only had a hard time anticipating the need to relieve himself, he found it difficult to judge when he was or wasn't wet.

We were to meet Bea at nine in the coffee shop, and hurried to dress. I wrapped Adam's braids in streamers of red cloth, but left my own hair loose. I carefully slipped on a vest that had been passed down in my family; on a field of sky blue were patterned squarish floral designs in red and yellow cut-glass beads, captioned on one side with the word *wars* and on the other with the year *1906*, whose significance was now a mystery. Adam looked beautiful, his thin, sensitive face illuminated by the excitement of dressing in unfamiliar clothes. I gave him his morning anticonvulsants, fed him scrambled eggs, and by the time Bea arrived we were ready to go.

As we drove to the powwow grounds, we passed in daylight what had been mere dark shapes the night before. In the growing heat, steam seemed to rise from the ground and then collect at eye level, shimmering any perspective longer than a few feet. The sky was an empty arch, so dominant that it turned all that could be seen into a floating, suspended platform. The houses that, hours ago, had been only lighted squares of glass were a mixture, ranging from the sturdy brick or frame of leaseholders to fragile-looking shanties, each fortified behind a barrier of wrecked cars and twisted metal. We returned the waves of people sitting on their front steps or hanging washing on lines, and I told Bea about my dream.

She shook her head and opened her eyes wide, suggested that it must have been inspired by something I ate. We were late, and she was worried that her mother and sisters would have finished all the work of setting up the tables to hold the gifts and food. Her sisters, Marguerite and Lila, had been cooking for days in preparation for the feast: great quantities of corn and meat stew, fry bread, *waishapi*, a jellylike sweet made from June berries.

Indeed, a number of cars were already parked in a mowed field adjacent to the powwow grounds, and smoke rose from the fires and butane stoves set up in the serving area. The arena itself was a dusty oval, bounded on three sides by benches and tables arranged before a crescent of tall posts. An American flag hung limp from a metal post, and a large drum, surrounded by folding chairs, had been centered in the circle. Signs forbidding alcoholic beverages were nailed at each entrance, and off to one side a group of campers were clustered, the temporary home and changing area of the visiting dance competitors. These men and women were a dazzle of colored feathers, jingling bells, embroidered fancy shawls, and horsehair ruffs. They bent to adjust their leggings or tie their moccasins, they peered into mirrors suspended from open trailer doors to apply dramatic slashes of black or red paint to their cheeks, brows, and chins, and they made practice sweeps and dips to the beat of songs heard only in memory or anticipation.

Next to their confidence, their brilliance, I was shy and embarrassed. Who were we to be honored by the receipt of Lakota names, to be feasted and introduced in a language we couldn't even understand? It was a question I felt all too sure that everyone who had seen us must be asking, and I had no good answer. I held Adam's hand so that he wouldn't run or play on the ground, and he didn't protest. We sat together on lawn chairs beside Mrs. Medicine while Bea went to assist her relatives.

Annie Medicine was in charge without having to move or speak. She watched in turn each center of activity until she was satisfied, then her eyes moved on. On our drive back to Mobridge the previous night, Bea had reported that her mother approved of me, but I couldn't imagine why. To my mind I had been mute, unrelaxed, and had revealed nothing about myself. What was there to like?

"You weren't a fool," Bea had said, as if that told the story, so I tried not to be a fool again. I didn't ask Mrs. Medicine questions, though I had many. As the person and the father of a person she was about to name, what was expected of us? Were we to make a speech of thanks? Were there lots of names to be awarded today? All I knew was that the names conferred were owned by the giver, inherited from deceased relatives, reserved to be given to people who would carry some intangible trait forward. It was up to Mrs. Medicine to sift through her accumulation and decide "who" Adam and I were and would be, and yet she had so little to go on. A boy with long hair who liked cake. A man who had not yet been a fool.

I held Adam on my lap and waved mosquitos away from his face. So often I had been the reason for his presence at an event at Dartmouth, and yet here I felt as though I were his guest. It was he whom elderly women stopped to admire, he who was given the first taste of soup, he who blended, when I finally let him go, into a group of playing children who could have passed for his cousins. It was he who fit in.

The day stretched into late afternoon as we watched dance after dance. The drum was powerful, the male singers latticing together their falsetto voices against the pounding rhythms that first imitated and then instructed the heart. The crowd followed their favorite performers and cheered when a particularly deft move was executed, or hooted when someone failed to accurately judge the precise instant when all music, and therefore all motion, should cease. As Bea, Mrs. Medicine, her other children—Lila, Marne, Earl, Marguerite—Adam, and I sat in a row, men in cowboy hats and women, their faces framed by scarves, came forward to pay their respects, to smile and tip their hats and lightly touch, rather than shake, hands. All introductions were made in Lakota, so I had no idea how I was presented, who I was supposed to be, no identity except as Adam's father, as Bea's friend.

At four o'clock Annie Medicine pushed herself from her chair, hitched her shawl around her shoulders, and joined the master of ceremonies at the drum. Bea moved to take the vacant seat beside me in order to provide bursts of whispered translation, and the noise of the assembled crowd dimmed as people settled themselves on benches or spread blankets and faced the center of the circle. This was the main event. In a voice strong and sure, Mrs. Medicine addressed the group. Her body remained stationary, slightly hunched, but her tone and command were riveting. To me she sounded slightly argumentative, challenging, the words as clipped as bark scraped from a branch, but Bea's interpretations were benign, undramatic.

"She welcomes everyone on behalf of our family. . . . She says they do us honor by joining us on this day. . . . She is pleased to be surrounded by her children once again, especially her newest grandson. . . ."

Mrs. Medicine gestured with her hand for Adam to join her, and without hesitation he ran to her side. She stroked his wrapped braids, raised his chin with her finger, all the while continuing her speech.

"She has chosen a name for him," Bea translated. "A proud name of an important and brave man from the north—somewhere in Saskatchewan it would be now. This man was a person who endured many hardships and yet lived to a kind old age."

"*Can 'Ra*," Mrs. Medicine spoke, her hand on Adam's shoulder. "*Can 'Ra*."

"It's a good name, an important name," Bea said. "It means 'Wood Mountain.' He's a person I've heard them talk about. A man of gentleness, just right for Adam."

Earl, Bea's eldest brother, stood and brought an object wrapped in a Pendleton blanket to his mother, then returned to his seat. Carefully Mrs. Medicine unveiled a ceremonial pipe, its bowl carved of red clay, its shank made of polished wood and decorated with strips of beadwork and rawhide, and placed it in Adam's hands. The crowd shouted its approval, but Annie Medicine wasn't finished and continued to speak.

"Now it's your turn," Bea said. "Go stand next to them."

I walked across the dusty clearing, my eyes on the ground, my mouth parched. I imagined hostile stares, indignant looks, and felt presumptuous, embarrassed, isolated. No vest or polka-dot shirt, no long-grown hair or academic knowledge gave me rights here. I was a dry pond, a hollow bowl, a person who could be anyone because I was no one.

I was shocked back into reality by the impact of Adam's arms around my thighs. "Look, Daddy," he said. "Look what she gave me." He held the pipe for me to examine, but beyond it I saw his face, lit, delighted. Wood Mountain.

Mrs. Medicine grasped my wrist and held it while she continued her speech. The skin of her fingers was cool, powdery, and her voice had become slightly hoarse from so much exertion, and still she persisted, the sentences rising and falling like the cries of the singers, like the drum, for emphasis. I sought Bea's eyes, where she sat across the empty space, as if I could read in them some telepathic meaning. At first she looked calm, satisfied, supportive, but then, when Mrs. Medicine pronounced her final words—*"Wambli Rapau. Wambli Rapau"*—Bea's face froze, amazed, and she leaned forward in her chair.

There was no time to wonder, for once again Earl stood, approached, and gave his mother a wrapped bundle. From it she took a huge headdress of ancient eagle feathers, each tipped with a wisp of white horsehair and wrapped at the base with red thread. It was the kind of artifact I had seen only behind glass in a museum. It was the ultimate badge, the epitome, and Mrs. Medicine fit it on my head.

The drum began an honor song, and Annie Medicine led me in the dance, a halting two-step counterclockwise round and round the singers. Behind us Bea followed, holding Adam's hand, and behind her came Earl, Marguerite, Lila, Marne. Others joined the line, a few at first and then, it seemed, almost all the fancy dancers, all the spectators. For three minutes the world was in unified motion, as one with music, with the end of a long day, with the pleasure of gift giving and receiving. Mrs. Medicine moved gracefully, her body weightless, her glasses reflecting the sunlight, her breathing a steady counterpoint. The sudden cluster of people created an impression of swirling color, the turn of bright blankets, the billow of jersey shawls. Next to me appeared one of the most flamboyant dancers, a young man with white bone breastplates, blue- and red-plumed bustle, cowbells circling his shins, and a ruff on his head. Across his shoulders was an elaborate harness of more red and blue, and in its center was a small circular mirror. As he whirled and dipped, moved side to side, I caught glimpses of my reflection, my face surrounded by eagle feathers. It was such an improbable sight it made me want to laugh, to exult in the absolute unexpectedness of events as they unfolded, endlessly linked, one to one.

When the singing stopped the Medicines, Adam, and I moved to the table laden with assembled gifts, and the announcer began to call the names of people in attendance. As each was summoned, Mrs. Medicine selected a present, passed it to the recipient with a slight bow. Everyone then progressed down our receiving line with nods and smiles and well wishes.

Bea walked over to stand next to me, and shook her head. "If they could see you now at Dartmouth," she said. "You know, this makes you my son in the Indian way."

"Why did you look so shocked when your mother was speaking?" I finally had the opportunity to ask. "What did she say?"

"She always surprises me, that's all. How could she have known your dream? And then she chooses *Wambli Rapau*. She names you 'Eagle Wing.' "

CHAPTER FIVE

During those middle years of the 1970s I continually struggled to understand my little boy as he grew older. My recognition that Adam had a problem more serious than a "slow start" came in bits and pieces over the course of many years. In retrospect, the signs were all there, but at the time I stored in a file of nagging worry the poor hearing, the convulsions, the hundreds of repetitions of even the most basic instructions, the abbreviated attention span, the many minor, dismissable incidents, mistakes, and shortfalls. Finally, the accumulation became so numerous, so insistent, that anxiety spilled into my every thought. Yet even then, my capacity for rationalization proved almost limitless.

Up until Adam was almost seven, while he was a first and only child, there was no basis for comparison. I strove to accept uncritically his unique developmental schedule as appropriate. He was the product of so many special circumstances, so many adverse factors, that I publicly persisted in my defensive optimism long after a sense of dread had entered my nightly dreams.

As time passed I blamed racism: negative evaluators underrated Adam because of unconscious, unexpressed negative feelings about minorities. I discounted as "culture biased" the IQ tests that consistently scored my son in the upper sixties or low seventies. I periodically concluded that Adam's teachers must be incompetent, badly trained, or lazy when they failed to stimulate his performance in the classroom. I protested haughtily to principals, counselors, even, on one occasion, to the federal government.

Now, much later, I don't regret that one. Adam was enrolled in what I assumed to be an enlightened day care center, and I had thrown myself into the role of professional single parent. Still in my twenties, I was young enough to believe that all it took to juggle family and career was organization and good intent. I was aggressively confident, well versed in the literature and jargon of child rearing, and prepared to quote statistics to prove that nurturing was a *human*, and not exclusively female, potential.

I was ready for the doubtful look or the arched eyebrow, I was ready to exchange recipes and remedies while folding clothes in laundromats or waiting in line at Sears to have family portraits taken. I was not, however, expecting to vie with a population of high-achieving working parents—single or married—every bit as defensive as I about being employed outside the home.

The competition, I soon realized, would not be easy. The other moms and dads had read and taken notes on every how-to-be-perfect manual on the market. Their progeny arrived in the morning dressed in color-coordinated outfits with matching watches and down-filled winter gear. Each boy and girl sported hairstyles that had to have taken an hour of dextrous adult early-morning labor to create. These kids all had famous idiosyncratic habits—aversions to synthetic cloth or allergies to dust—that required special instructions.

Birthdays were the one occasion for each child to be center stage. And so lavish had the festivities apparently become the year before we arrived that the day care center had made a rule limiting the gala spread to foods explicitly made *by* the actual parents *in* their actual homes. This seemed reasonable enough, but as fall turned into winter and I witnessed, at the end of occasional days, the excessive remains of one extravaganza after another, I began to suspect that some people were cheating. How else to explain the ice-cream cupcakes, the individual hot-dog-and-baked-bean quiches, the fluted papaya cups filled with *crème fraiche*?

Adam and I still lived in the small wooden house by Mascoma Lake—the price was right for an instructor's salary. It was there that I retreated to think and plan as Adam's January birthday neared. Under no circumstances was I about to send him off with a concoction sneakily purchased at the bakery. I had something to prove.

I considered briefly the phyla of cream puffs and éclairs but rejected them as too risky. I was not an experienced cook, and my oven, while dutifully heating, was not up to wild extremes or precise temperature calibrations. I contemplated the possibilities of puddings but rejected them as too unorthodox, too bizarre. From every unconventional excursion, I came back to cake.

"What would be the best cake you could imagine?" I asked Adam one night as he played on the carpet with our Husky, Skahota. His reply was immediate and unsurprising, the declaration of his enduring passion.

"A choo choo train!" he announced, and went back to his game.

It was his birthday, so I didn't argue, didn't try to widen his horizon. This once I took his fierce attachment seriously and called Nina, who knew more about baking than I. Culling through her recipe collection, she uncovered directions for specialized pans made from cardboard wrapped in aluminum foil. Boxcars and caboose were a cinch, the coal car was a problem, and the locomotive was a challenge. But it was possible, it was Adam's enduring, maddening fantasy, and done right, it could be the most spectacular dessert ever to grace the two-foot-high day care table. I gave the project a week of my life.

Mounted on a piece of plywood, each of the six cars was at base an eight-by-four-inch-long rectangle of trimmed sponge cake, to which I attached paper wheels and connected toggles made of taffy. No food colors at the local grocery seemed bright or impressive enough, so I traveled one Saturday afternoon to a specialty outlet where, for two dollars each, I purchased small vials of blues and reds and yellows and greens so vivid, so ceramic in their luster, that a mere drop was sufficient to tint a bowl of white icing. But I was looking for more than a tint; I was after *bold,* so for good measure I mixed more and more edible dye into my palette until the hues that confronted me were dazzling. No caboose was ever so barn-red, no passenger car so grass-green, no plucky little locomotive, decorated with gumdrops, a hand mirror and a cheerful expression, so sky-blue. This was a little engine that *could,* and knew it. Black, for the coal car, was trickier, but I solved that dilemma with melted licorice that, when spread warm and allowed to harden, cemented the fragile sides into indestructible steel. I got behind in my lecture preparations, but finished the train at midnight the day before Adam's party. All around it I had constructed toy houses, cutout happy families (more than one shepherded by a lone adult male), grazing cartoon animals. Before going to bed, exhausted but smug, I asked Bea to come over and take photographs of Adam, Nina, and me standing before my creation. My son would have nothing to apologize for.

And it all came to pass just as I had imagined. When I carefully carried the plywood base from the car, and negotiated the door of the center, the train cake was greeted with exclamations of delight and disbelief by staff and children alike. Other parents, disrobing their sons and daughters from layers of mittens and boots and snowsuits, looked from the cake to me with expressions of betrayal and chagrin.

I had become the act to beat, the standard against which to measure. With a spin of the mixer I had achieved the status of Ideal Parent, the adult for whom no task was too great, no child's dream too onerous to grant. Yes, I was employed full time, but did I let that get in the way of my fatherly duties? The train cake told the story in capital letters.

The party, to which I returned to preside over later in the day, was memorable. In the flickering light of six candles (one to grow on), the children's eyes were sugar-glazed. The volume of their voices was loud with greed, and once the clapping ceased, they made fast work of all my labors. Within twenty minutes my ordered platter had become a surrealistic swatch of colors, with only the indestructible coal car, chipped at but undismantled, remaining as solitary witness.

Adam, who had eaten almost none of the cake in his excitement, was everyone's best friend, the hero of the day, and when we got into our blue VW station wagon to go home, he leaned across the seat with a smile so wide and happy it startled me.

"Thank you, Daddy," he said.

I looked at him, this little boy who really was, after all, what this was for and about. In his dark eyes there was one message only, one idea: his wish had come true. And I looked back in turn with a single realization of my own: in him, my wish had come true, too.

"Happy Birthday," I said.

The story should have ended there, with the cake eaten and Adam content and me reacquainted with the real meaning of things, but there was one final chapter. About ten o'clock that night, I was at the kitchen table trying hard to organize the next day's class notes when the phone rang. It was the director of the day care center, and her voice was frantic.

"What did you put in that thing?" she demanded.

"Why, nothing," I answered, worried that I had somehow violated some interdiction about natural ingredients. "Just flour and sugar and a few pieces of candy. What's wrong?"

"The parents have been calling me all night," she said. "They're hysterical. They're ready to take their children to the emergency room at the hospital."

"Why?" Now I was scared.

"It's when they put the kids to bed," she said. "When they took them to the potty. They noticed before they flushed! The water in the toilet bowl was green! Or bright blue! Electric yellow! *Orange!*"

I closed my eyes and saw again the jaunty cars, lined up and ready to roll. The train cake had made more of an impression than I had planned.

Days later, when every expensive hue had passed safely but remarkably through the digestive system of each child, the day care center's governing council inaugurated an amendment to the party rule: henceforth, all birthday fixings must be normal. The like of the train cake would never be seen again.

In the months that followed I kept a low profile, whisking Adam in and out with a minimum of fuss. I nodded agreeably to every announcement, hardly paying attention in my effort to avoid the frowns of other parents. Adam volunteered little information about his daily routines, and most of my energies seemed to go into his belated toilet training and into unsuccessful instruction in the art of tying shoelaces. Besides, I thought, in a few months he would go to kindergarten, and his progress would accelerate.

There was no public preschool in the town where we lived, so I filled out an enrollment card for the well-regarded program in Norwich, Vermont. As a nonresident, I would have to pay extra tuition, but I wanted Adam to have every advantage.

To my amazement, his application was rejected. I stormed into the elementary school principal's office and demanded an explanation. The man pulled from his desk a Manila file with Adam's name on it, glanced at the pages, then closed it on his desk.

"I'm afraid we don't have the facility to deal with learning problems," he said. "It's a matter of budget, you see, and I wish . . ."

"Learning problems!" I interrupted. "What learning problems? Who said he has learning problems?"

The man looked surprised, opened the file again and studied it. "Didn't they send you a copy of this?" he asked, holding out a typed sheet. "Some Dartmouth undergrad psychology students had a class project in which they observed kids at the day care center. I assumed they got permission."

I scanned the incriminating lines. Adam had been noticed sitting on the floor, rocking back and forth. Adam was more than five years old and not potty trained. Adam had turned off a record player in the middle of a song, oblivious to the fact that other children were listening to the music through earphones.

I had an instant and plausible explanation for everything. Of course he rocked—that was the way he had consoled himself as an infant when there was no one to cradle him. He had a late start in toilet training, surely not his fault. And naturally he turned off the record player if he couldn't hear the music; he didn't know about earphones. He was just trying to be helpful.

The principal listened patiently, but he wouldn't change his decision. They couldn't take the responsibility. They were not equipped.

By the time I got home, I was furious. I called the day care center office and railed against the impropriety of letting some nineteen-year-old student draw conclusions that would go into my son's school record. Why wasn't I consulted, I demanded to know?

The director was apologetic. I should have received a copy of the report, she said, and probably should have been asked to sign a release, it was an oversight on the center's part, but the observation project itself was highly professional. It was part of an ongoing federally funded grant to the Dartmouth Medical School intended to identify certain early signs in preschoolers that could predict later educational difficulties. The prognosis for Adam came as no surprise to the staff. He was a lovely little boy, and they were all crazy about him, but obviously he was "LD."

"LD?"

"Learning Disabled."

I demanded and got an immediate meeting between the director, the psychology professor who had assigned this project, and the Norwich primary school principal. Everyone was anxious to placate me and excuse themselves, but I would have none of it. When one of the psychologist's assistants attempted to engage in small talk before I had my say, I responded haughtily: "I believe in your discipline my mental state would be termed 'hostile.'"

Unbeknownst to them all, I had already fired off a long, detailed letter to the head of the National Science Foundation, the government agency that had authorized the medical school grant, charging improper procedures and unethical practices. I had already called a friend from my college days who had become a lawyer and asked whether I should bring suit to have the offending document removed from Adam's record. In my internal drama, I was a lion defending his cub against a pack of hyenas.

And I was correct to do everything I did, even if I was overly pompous about it. What the day care center and the project director and the school official had done in reference to Adam was sloppy and amateurish, poorly executed. I was sent a formal apology, the psychology professor was embarrassed, and Adam, the offending analysis eradicated from his record, gained the right to be considered for admission to the Norwich kindergarten if I would submit him to a series of diagnostic intelligence tests. With wrathful disdain, I rejected that last offer out of hand. I wouldn't even consider sending a child of mine to such a school, I said. I would put him instead into private home day care until he could enter the first grade in our town with a clean slate.

I was so busy being right, however, that I never allowed myself to tolerate the notion that a junior in college, a preschool teacher, a well-meaning administrator reading a set of simple observations, could recognize a danger that was invisible to me. I *willed* Adam to be fine, and he wasn't.

I approached the gnawing question of Adam's learning disabilities as though I were a trial lawyer and sought my own expert witnesses on his behalf. My friend Sally Deane, whom I'd met in Alaska, was getting a Ph.D. in psychology at Boston University, and I asked her to recommend someone good to thoroughly evaluate Adam's intelligence in order to determine if he did, in fact, have specific weaknesses and if so, how to strengthen them.

Sally provided the name of a woman operating out of a Boston teaching hospital, and with utter confidence I scheduled an appointment. I never doubted, at least I never acknowledged doubt, that Adam would be found in some way "gifted" and looked forward to hearing what off-the-scale talents he might possess. I believed, at that point in my life, in a kind of cosmic fairness, in the idea that for every disability there was an equal or greater ability. Adam was an innocent if ever there was one, and innocence could not be penalized. If he was slow at toilet training, that probably meant that buried in him was some surprising genius for art or music or poetry that was occupying his attentions. If he was methodical or repetitious in his verbal pronouncements—a clear no-no for a first grader—it surely indicated some good news that would surface later. Perhaps his orientation was toward higher mathematics or science, and he was simply bored with the humdrum of cutting and pasting colored paper.

I was sure I saw in Adam depths invisible to others, and that had to be those people's problem, not his, not mine. A real professional, a big-city Ph.D. with wide experience and a keen eye, would instantly perceive how special my son was, and in my vindication fantasy I returned triumphant to the Norwich day care center, to the selective kindergarten, to the Dartmouth professor who allowed Adam to be underestimated, and flaunted a glowing report. They would be chastised, self-accusing, horrified at their error. What's more, Adam's validation would be a true public service because it would spare other unusual children and their parents the trauma of this bitter exercise.

At dawn on the day of the appointment I garbed both Adam and myself with a serious eye for effect. We were dressed to impress: he in rather expensive matching maroon pants and jacket with a new white T-shirt, laundered tennis shoes, and Sesame Street socks. I made sure he carried a book to page through in the waiting room. His hair was neatly trimmed and scented with floral shampoo. His fingernails and toenails were clipped. His teeth were flossed and I had a toothbrush in my pocket for a last-minute touch-up, lest stale breath tip the balance of an otherwise favorable examination. He had new eyeglasses, the lenses polished to a glare, and a wristwatch, though even a rudimentary concept of telling time, I had to admit, seemed beyond him. He looked terrific—a handsome, attractive boy—and his face was lit at the prospect of taking the four-hour drive to Massachusetts. Who knew how many train tracks we would get to cross?

My ensemble was at least as carefully selected. The effect I sought was "professional colleague," and so I did myself up the way I imagined an urban psychologist might dress: conservative but with a few off-beat touches that indicated a mind no stranger to interesting quirkiness. A navy sport coat and tan slacks offset by one of my wide Paisley hippie neckties. I carried a zippered canvas case prominently imprinted "American Anthropological Association Annual Meeting—Toronto" in order to convey my erudition and willingness to banter in social science catch words. I think I even brought a copy of my résumé, just in case, as though I were interviewing for a job and not simply seeking an encouraging assessment of my six-year-old son's capacity to handle the first grade. In truth, I wanted to be a person so agreeable, so charming, that it would be emotionally difficult for a psychologist to disappoint me. Anything for a thumbs-up.

The waiting room was pediatric hi-tech, filled with bright Creative Playthings, puzzles, and connect-the-dot books. Clearly, this outfit was used to whiz kids—not a toy truck in sight. I took Adam to the bathroom, then settled in, self-consciously onstage, though our only external audience at this early hour was a self-absorbed receptionist. If Adam and I were costumed to produce a mild, vaguely upscale and pedantic impression, this woman was ready for Radio City Music Hall. Her teased and sprayed hairdo had the shape and consistency of broiler-frosted meringue piled high on a pie. Her arched, scarlet nails could only be described as talons. From the foot of one crossed leg dangled a shoe bearing a spiked heel at least four inches long. The frames of her eyeglasses were oddly fashioned, as though they were worn upside down, and were composed of a synthetic compound that gave off a pinkish, translucent glow. Her eyes themselves were set deep in welt-colored eye shadow, and her false lashes were so long they brushed her tinted lenses whenever she blinked, which was often. She wore a tight, short magenta dress whose superstructure, I suspected, originated at Frederick's of Hollywood, so exactly did her bosom resemble a perfect, horizontal "W."

Every pencil in the container on her all but empty desktop was a sharpened stake. Adam's name, the first on a short list centered on a single white sheet of paper next to the telephone, had been checked off upon our arrival. Her untouched cup, shaped like a goblet, decorated with a Happy Face logo, was half-filled with creamy coffee. The telephone had a receiver equipped with a shoulder prop, suggesting the possibility that there were moments in the day when both of this woman's hands were engaged—an event that I found hard to imagine. Certainly during the half hour that we waited, me stiff with anticipation, Adam increasingly restless, neither one of her hands had anything to do.

When at last Sally's friend appeared, she was warm and friendly, dressed casually in turtleneck and jeans, and focused her attentions immediately on Adam. She praised his wristwatch and socks (I scored points for myself!) and led us into a small consulting office. With efficiency she asked me a series of questions, always conscious of and sensitive to what Adam might overhear, about his background, school experience, and home situation. There was no judgment in her manner, and she listened patiently, reassuringly taking notes, as I over-explained, qualified, offered my own amateur diagnoses, to counter every worrisome sign. I found myself switching somehow to a textbook vocabulary, as if my ideas had more weight if they came from a senior researcher specializing in Adam, rather than from his advocate parent.

When the conversation was over, I left the room, and the psychologist administered a Wechsler Preschool and Primary Scale of Intelligence (WPPSI) IQ test, divided into two parts, verbal and performance. I can't say that I expected a miracle. I didn't know one was needed. I waited, instead, the way I had always waited for my own test results—with an attitude that could be summed up: surprise me. In grade school I had been fascinated with the analysis of my own Differential Aptitude Test scores, which indicated that I would be happiest either as a show business performer or as a YMCA social director. Forget the fact that I was tone-deaf and generally reclusive— the DAT said I had secret talent in reserve.

My son, however, was not destined to follow in my musical or medicine ball footsteps, nor was he likely to become, according to his WPPSI scores, a star in any other field. The psychologist's summation of Adam's performance was less than encouraging. His overall IQ fell into the "borderline" category, and his skills ranged from approximately a year below his age level in some visual tasks to considerably greater disparities from the norm in "areas requiring attention to auditory input." This translated to mean that Adam had trouble concentrating, particularly when dealing with abstractions. Furthermore, he was found to be more active than expected for his age level, impulsive in his approach to tasks, and highly distractible ("both auditorily and visually").

I listened, stunned with disappointment and worry, as she outlined a recommended educational program for "children like Adam." *If* he were to be in a regular school, he would require lots of external structure and would have to avoid "overstimulation." A teacher might want to provide him with a "study booth" set apart from his classmates to ensure a distraction-free environment. The main body of the psychologist's eventual written report concluded with the sentence: "In the same sense, monitoring of TV programs and movies would be even more important to a child like Adam, as he is highly stimulable and unable to inhibit the excitement once the wheels are set in motion."

It had never before occurred to me that Adam could be lumped into a definable category, that he was "like" anyone else in meaningful, predictable ways.

"But what else?" I asked her, straining for countervailing evidence, for some sign that linked Adam to a happy future, for an indication that his was but a temporary condition, a holdover from his famous slow start.

"There is one thing," she said and cleared her throat. "I wonder if Adam has been around enough . . . women."

"Women? Well, you know I'm not married, but we have lots of women friends, lots of women he's close to in the extended family—aunts, grandmothers, cousins. Did he say something negative about women?"

"Not to me." She seemed embarrassed, evasive. "But Estelle—the clinic receptionist whom you met this morning?—she privately told me that she was sure Adam was staring at her breasts before our conference. I thought I should mention it. Perhaps you should explain to him the differences between boys and girls. Maybe anatomically correct dolls would be useful."

It took me an instant to place whom she was talking about, and then with an enormous sense of relief I remembered. If the psychologist could be this off-base about one thing—Estelle had done everything short of neon lighting to draw attention to her chest, and one didn't need an advanced degree in body language to realize that Adam had simply exhibited the invited response—I could discount the infallibility of the rest of her report. I grabbed onto my amused indignation, made it my shield, convinced myself that yet another person had jumped to conclusions about Adam for extraneous reasons—his race, his single-parent adoption, his medical history—and had failed to recognize his true potential. The real problem, I persuaded myself, was not with Adam but with other people's perception of him. That part I could work on, the rest would come naturally. In the meantime I determined not to worry, to forget the blinking alarms, not to notice the growing consistency of outside opinion that something serious was wrong.

❊

In those years of Adam's early childhood, I trusted no diagnosis that wasn't encouraging, no road that didn't lead to a normal adult life for him. I rejected as impossible the judgments of the "experts" I had so far encountered, so the only choice was to become an expert myself. Equipped with enough data, I could overwhelm the nay-sayers and broker my son into success. If Adam's impairments were more than random bad luck, more than transitional stages, one obvious, personally nonthreatening source for their understanding was in the history of his biological parents. As I grudgingly began to concede that he might have *some* handicaps, some of them potentially beyond the ability of my love, of my energy, to affect or cure, I turned once again to the familiar reassurance of intensive study. I was trained to believe that the answers to almost everything resided in the library, ready for discovery if one looked in the right card catalogue and with enough persistence. Research meant authority, and author-ity, I once believed, spelled power.

I turned for enlightenment to the subjects I knew something about, relying upon my years of formal education, especially upon anthropology, the academic discipline which I daily "professed" in the classroom. What better motivation to grapple with the vagaries of "ethnohistory"—the understanding of a population's cultural behavior over time—than the championing of one's beloved child? Adam sprang from genetic roots that were, from what little I knew then, at least approachable. To investigate them was basically to pursue what I already did for a living. He was after all, though a snowflake like no other, the mysterious offspring of a particular man and woman—specific information about whom was barred to me—still the child of a tribe, still incontrovertibly an American Indian. My interests on the one hand might be focused on Adam, but his unique history was, in a sense, a microcosm of a much larger picture. I had never expected my son to teach me about Indians, but now I thought that perhaps a vigorous examination of certain aspects of recent American Indian experience could lead me to a new, helpful awareness of him.

In the best dispassionate social science manner, I determined to be objective. I would endeavor to consciously put aside my personal observations, my own intuitions and memories; they might be self-serving. I wanted the facts, the broad view, and the first line of offense was to systematically confront history.

CHAPTER SIX

Denis Daigle, my social worker, had been free to tell me very little about Adam's biological parents, beyond the fact that they were both Sioux from South Dakota. Confidentiality suited me fine, for it worked both ways. My major anxiety in the trial period before the adoption decree became final had been that someone would call or knock on my door, wanting Adam back. If that happened, I planned, in the best "Uncle Tom's Cabin" mode, to flee with him to Canada, to change my name, to disappear. The less I knew about Adam's natural family, the less they knew about me. Unfortunately, as I was to reluctantly discover, the less I knew about them, the less I knew about Adam.

But in the beginning, I didn't think I needed much information; in my naïveté and conceit I was convinced that Adam's life had in a real sense commenced once we were together. Whatever burdening psychological baggage he carried from his first three years could be culled the same way I divided the items that arrived with him in his strapped-together suitcase: the things that were useful, the things to which Adam seemed positively attached, we would keep; everything else would be replaced and improved upon. And there had been little to retain.

Before I came for him, Adam had been the most recent resident in an overcrowded state-approved home. His caretakers had several natural and adopted children of their own, as well as a steady flow of temporary placements whose board money provided a source of income. The man and woman struck me as well meaning but harried, disturbingly transparent in preferring their own children to those just

passing through. Their youngest son, Tommy, was closest in age to
Adam, and even Adam, confused and nonverbal as he was, picked up
on the hierarchy. For a year after he came to me he would correct my
telling of "The Three Bears," substituting "Tommy Bear" for "baby
bear." He brought from that foster home only two items that seemed
unambiguously his own: a single, scuffed, black cowboy boot,
children-size 4; and a small blue-and-white piece of quilting, fashioned with strings as a bib, so frayed and clearly homemade that,
though no one said so, I believed it must have originated with his
natural mother. These two treasures, which we still keep as heir-
looms, were all of Adam's past I thought we needed.

However, when in Pierre, I had overheard two state social
workers on the other side of an office partition discussing Adam's
background. The information was harsh, delivered in knowing shorthand, the repetition of a story so similar to others they daily
encountered that it had become familiar, old hat. The mother, one of
them confided, was dead at thirty-three; the father was in jail for
assault of some kind, who knew what? One of Adam's siblings had
been adopted by a Christian couple, the other was probably too old
ever to break out of foster care. Oh, and the maternal grandmother.
Somebody had seen her on a toot at one of the local taverns.

What they said was so disturbing that once I absorbed it, I politely
pushed it to the back of my mental file. The story of family
disintegration was too sad, too much the duplicate of others I had
witnessed or heard about in Alaska and Montana, in urban Indian
neighborhoods. It was the standard evidence I used in my lectures
when blaming "the system," yet this time it was my son who was its
primary victim. I found myself more angry than ever at the history
and social conditions that had led Adam's immediate family to such a
dead end, but at the same time, despite all my political rhetoric, I
could not exonerate parents who, out of weakness and self-
indulgence, had let their own children suffer. Whatever their excuse,
they were still agents of an oppression that left Adam alone in the
world, and for all my desire and will to extend to them the benefit of
the doubt, a part of my heart hardened.

Where was this partying grandmother when Adam's wrists and
ankles were scarred from ropes that tied him to his crib? Where was
she when he, as a baby, went hungry and developed chronic
pneumonia? Where was she when he was marooned unnoticed and

untoilet trained in the chaos of his foster home? I never openly admitted it, even to myself, but there was a side of me that let Adam's past life go with relief rather than regret.

But, of course, it wasn't that simple. A person's genetic history is a long chain, and the latest link begins with conception, not birth. Adam carried aspects of his ancestors in every chromosome, in every bead of his DNA string, in every gene. They were his raw material, literally the stuff he was made of. The parents who raised him, biological or adopted, could tease out the inherent strengths or unleash the weaknesses, but they couldn't change the outer limits of potential. These were ideas I didn't think about, ideas I didn't consciously credit, during those early days with Adam. I was a nurture man, all the way. Nature was the territory of eugenics or of elitists who espoused predestination for reasons of self-justification.

Graham Nash sang the anthem that became the credo of my generation: "We Can Change the World," and though I might not have been able to effect a U.S. withdrawal from Vietnam or make peace in Biafra, I had no doubt that I could give Adam back the life of independent choice, of unbounded possibility, that he was, as a fresh-minted human being, entitled to live. But this idealistic sentiment, for all its appeal, could not get Adam past the brick wall of the WPPSI IQ test. I determined one thing: if Adam could not disregard certain liabilities that came as part of his personal legacy, I could at least get a better grasp on what these land mines were and learn how to make the best of them.

I believed in the idea of external cause. If there was a problem, it must necessarily have a source, a reason, an explanation. If Adam's cognitive ability was permanently limited, as every evaluator seemed to agree, I wanted a culprit to accuse, a disease to blame, a named pathology. I had the kind of anger that could be ameliorated only through understanding, that could be accepted only after every stone had been upturned and every lead followed to its conclusion. The implied shrug I received in answer to my question "Why?" did not suffice. I wanted answers. Surely Adam's problem was not unique, an isolated instance of bad luck. Yet the litany of his definable symptoms—low birth weight, small cranial circumference, hyperactivity, repetitive mistakes, an early failure to thrive, attention deficit, seizures—did not in and of itself, according to the doctors and other professionals I consulted, point to any pat diagnosis.

I needed to find out who Adam was in order to discover who he could be, yet I was faced with little evidence, with precious few clues, and with court-sealed medical records that would take me fifteen years to crack open. I knew Adam's tribe. I knew he came from a shattered nuclear family. And I knew his mother drank and that she was dead before she passed thirty-five. A few years after Adam's adoption, his father was killed as well, a fact I learned through an inheritance report that arrived in the mail. This man, only slightly older than I, had been beaten to death by strangers in an alley in a Sunbelt city. Since his early teens he had been frequently arrested and incarcerated, mostly on charges that started with drunk and disorderly and ended in robbery or assault. He had listed his occupation as "artist" and had changed his name at least once. He had no property to bequeath except a fifty-dollar share in some reservation land leases.

I tackled one point at a time.

The Sioux, or Lakota ("the people," in their own language), lived before contact with Europeans in sedentary agricultural villages in the area west of the Great Lakes. They made fired clay pottery, hunted small game, enjoyed a social system in which men and women shared power and authority in all sectors of their societies. The Lakota got along with some of their neighbors, feuded with others, practiced a complicated religion, made music with flutes and rattles and drums, and prized oratory and story-telling above all other arts. They traded with culturally dissimilar peoples from many parts of North America and believed that the creative force, or *Wakan*, had formed their ancestors in what are today called the Black Hills (*paha sapa*), those strange, evocative, dark protrusions in the otherwise glacier-flattened landscape of western South Dakota.

When Spanish horses finally reached their lands via a trade route that extended from Mexico through the Pueblos to the Great Plains, the Lakota for the most part elected to forsake their stable communities for the excitement and challenge of constant movement. The horse for them was an agent of revolution, as the wheel or the automobile has been for other peoples in other times. It set them free on the long, mostly uninhabited corridor of open land between the eastern prairies and the Rocky Mountains. This was a country stocked with buffalo, the ultimate one-stop-shop animal whose harvest could feed, clothe, and shelter a society that didn't demand too much in the way of material possessions; the tribe, to the horror of latter-day Western anthropologists who don't think such things should logically happen, "abandoned the pot" and embraced a life-style at once more risky and more thrilling than horticulture.

The plateau west of the Missouri River, while starkly beautiful, a sage-scented expanse of yellow grass cut with deep gullies, was a precarious abode, a land of poisonous snakes and scrub weed, of wolves and coyotes, where eagles and hawks dominate and prey at will upon earthbound creatures. The climate is measured by extremes of cold and heat, drought and flood. The high plain has no ocean coast; rather, its boundary of reference and mythological inspiration has always been the changing sky, the source of light by day, of star-pointed direction by night. The hues of dawn and dusk are the palette in an otherwise monochrome universe. In a territory circumscribed by the luxury of far vistas, the birds of the air are most at home.

Scouring winds rise unpredictably, in dry summers lifting dust into cyclone devils or igniting the live match of lightning wherever it touches down, in winter whipping snow to such gray frenzy that to stray a foot beyond one's door without a secure tether is to lose all bearings. In traditional times, for human beings to survive at all in such an environment was a measure of ingenuity and invention. It required fast reactions, a constant fluidity, an unshackled, parrying response to whatever surprise nature might spring. Life was chance, and death was immobility.

For a few glorious generations, the Lakota shared all the earth that mattered to them with other Indians—Cheyenne, Arapaho, Crow, Pawnee, and Assiniboine—groups whose basic attitudes and values the Lakota could appreciate, even when intertribal relations were not friendly. As might be expected from a people who opted for bareback itinerancy rather than for plowed fields, the Lakota prized independence and individuality; even the issue of whether or not to go to war, even the gender role an adult might play, were matters of personal responsibility.

The Lakota had a live and let live attitude toward the first trickle of Europeans and Americans who penetrated their territory in search of trading partners in the late eighteenth and early nineteenth centuries. When gold was "discovered" in the Black Hills, wagon loads of unruly white entrepreneurs, prospectors, and bandits invaded and tore at the sacred earth, slaughtered buffalo by the thousands, and left the carcasses to rot in the sun. It was widely known that other tribes had tried to live in peace with these newcomers and had still been massacred or deported, so the Lakota mounted a fierce, now legendary resistance. With the defeat at the Little Big Horn of General George Custer, a man who had been murdering unarmed Indians for a decade, the Lakota and their allies shocked the nation at the very moment of its Centennial. Their victory, which by any contemporary standard must be understood as temporary self-defense, earned them a stereotype for being "warlike" and became the excuse for the federal government to partition their aboriginal territory, supposedly protected forever by Senate treaty.

To a nomadic people, the imposition of tight restrictions on movement was in and of itself devastating. Confined by martial law to restricted reservations poorly suited to farming, devoid of buffalo, and administered by an overabundance of corrupt government appointees, the Great Sioux Nation, as it was once called, was politically and spiritually crushed. In light of their history and cultural values, the Lakota who survived the ensuing waves of disease and military attacks, like Wounded Knee, to which they were vulnerable, were especially susceptible to feelings of despondency, embittered dependence, and demoralization.

An unfortunate collision of circumstances—bad example, misleading precedent, high anxiety-producing developments—surrounded the introduction of alcohol to the Lakota by French, British, and American trappers sometime between 1790 and 1830.[1] In the heyday of their independence, most of the tribe's males and some females had traditionally conducted a vision quest, or *hanbleceya* (a "crying for vision"), around the time of the onset of puberty. One by one, they were expected to forsake the safe haven of their families, often for the first time in their lives, and, alone and unequipped with provisions, to brave the unknown of open country. Ideally, they remained isolated until, in an induced altered state of consciousness brought on by fear, fasting, thirst, stress, and faith that something extraordinary would happen to them, they experienced a flash of insight. This introspection revealed a highly personal mandate for adulthood, an identity, and was an event of unparalleled importance in charting the course of their lives. If, in later years, a reconfirmation was desired, or if circumstances changed, a second *hanbleceya* might be sought via a sun dance or other ritual.

The significance within their culture of the act of vision seeking predicted to some degree the Lakota's eventual acceptance of alcohol—initially named in Lakota *minnewaken* (the "magic water")[2]—which seemed to offer a more efficient and less painful route to altered consciousness. Used to seeking and then trusting the validity of a dreamlike state, some Lakota males found the early effects of inebriation appealing. Moreover, they lived in a time that cried out for explicating visions: certainly at no previous period in tribal history had there been a greater need for enabling and enlightening insights in order to understand the direction their world was taking.

The literature of frontier transactions is filled with data about the introduction of "spirits" to unsuspecting Indian tribes. European trappers and traders, usually the first members of their societies to reach the interior of the continent, did not exhibit the drinking patterns condoned in London, Paris, or Madrid. The loud, raucous behavior for which they were infamous would not have been tolerated in their home countries. But when Indians met such men, they had no way of knowing this, and were inclined to be broad-minded. European traders, after all, were the conduits for manufactured goods—nails, knives, tools, mirrors, cloth—that Indians wanted to acquire.

A protocol surrounding the trading event developed, which included speeches of welcome and good intentions by tribal leaders, a distribution of food and especially liquor by the traders, an exchange of items, and a final celebration. Many early reports indicate that Indians were initially repulsed by the taste of the concoctions made from fermented corn and other ingredients that the traders insisted they accept. This may have been intensified by a physiological response—prevalent in many East Asian and American Indian populations, in which the skin reacts to alcohol with an unpleasant flushing effect—and by the loss of dignity, of control, that drinking engendered. Certainly the brew's taste was as new to North America as the social rules governing its use—rules whose only available guide was the group of rowdy foreigners who produced and distributed the often bootleg hootch.

Tribe after tribe learned not only *to* drink, but *how* to drink from

Europeans whose bad manners, determination to get drunk, and lack of restraint were notorious, and eventually this "trapper style" of liquor consumption became incorporated into some Indian communities. To the more sedate missionaries, homesteaders, and merchants who arrived later, who had never met a white mountain man but who carried as part of their own cultural baggage a bevy of negative rumors, stereotypes, and fears about "savage redskins," the fact that Indians used alcohol at all and the manner in which they seemed to react to it confirmed every horrified suspicion. An accident of circumstance thus over time hardened into self-fulfilling prophesy. Drinking in sprees, drinking everything in sight when it was available (with intermittent periods of abstinence), drinking until drunkenness turned into unconsciousness—all part and parcel of the European-introduced trading ritual—became the hallmark of popular American folk belief about the way Indians "naturally" responded to alcohol.

For proper European administrators and for latter-day United States bureaucrats, this supposed phenomenon was as good an excuse as any to impose restrictions and prohibitions (beginning with the Indian Trade and Intercourse Act of 1834) on people who were culturally different and, more to the point, in the way. And these strictures themselves produced a mini-industry. For unscrupulous profiteers, running liquor to Indian territory became the eighteenth- and nineteenth-century equivalents of modern cocaine or crack rings. For Indians whose practical options were increasingly limited, whose lands were confiscated, whose languages, religions, hairstyles, and preferred foods were banned by laws enforced by nervous, well-armed soldiers, drinking in "unacceptable" ways became one of the few possible modes of protest and ethnic self-expression. It was a means of refusing utter colonization, of affirming group identity, of not complying with oppressive, resented, intolerant, and intolerable statutes. It was also a means of oblivion, a quest for the illusion of power,[3] an escape from a reality of frustration and failure[4] in which the whole familiar world seemed to have ended. The life ways, the spiritual beliefs, the oral literature, the social conventions that had been honed over thousands of years were suddenly illegal, inefficacious, and inaccessible.

But rather than resolving the contradictions of existence, as a *hanbleceya* did for a receptive adolescent, the drug of alcohol magnified the confusion; rather than integrating the individual into a productive life within his or her society, the excessive use of liquor shattered the delicate web of shared custom, duty, and perspective that imposed meaning on even the ordinary chaos of life.

In recent years, many concerned people—social scientists, tribal leaders, health administrators—have struggled to understand and explain the phenomena of alcohol use among American Indians. In the several Indian communities in which I had lived—indeed among some of my own relatives—drinking was such a fact of life that not only had I never seriously questioned it, I had been at times an enthusiastic participant.

When people exchanged mock-cautionary tales of the strange and dangerous events that took place during a bout of drinking, I always had a few experiences of my own to contribute. There was the time my date at a party fell down a flight of steps halfway through the evening, then got up and danced until dawn, neither of us realizing until the next day that she had broken her arm. There was the winter night that, on a dare, I left a sweat bath to roll naked in the snow like, someone claimed, the Finns did. I fell into a drift, became drowsy, and would have frozen to death if a cousin hadn't thought to look for me. Almost everyone had such self-deprecating stories, funny because against all odds the teller had somehow survived. Relating these departures from normal good sense and propriety had a leveling effect as well: no matter who or what you might otherwise be, you were still a helpless idiot like everyone else when it came to booze.

In the long run, I was fortunate in two respects. First, I always eventually wound up flushed and physically sick after the consumption of more than two or three drinks, though this fact alone might not have been enough to discourage me. It was simply too easy when the bottle was passed in a social context to disregard the resolutions I had made the previous dawn while sitting, miserable, alone, and exhausted, on the bathroom floor. Second and more important, my immediate family practiced sobriety and moderation; despite my occasional youthful excesses, their example gave me strength.

I "understood" drinking, therefore, but in an altogether unreflective, unanalytical way. I knew how to act in a drinking situation, understood the fun it could be. I recognized the dangers, but I had no distance. To get an unskewed grasp on the drinking environment in which Adam's biological parents had lived required that I supplement my own experience with the theories of others. There certainly was no lack of material. With little effort I amassed dozens of opinions, articles, books, reports, and statistics pertaining to the whys and wherefores of alcohol use among Indians. Some of them were easily dismissed, like the idea of the bush aviator who ferried me one morning from Fairbanks to a remote Alaskan Native village where I had been invited to conduct a two-day workshop for teachers. This pilot, whose nickname was Punky, warranted close scrutiny. He and I were alone in a single-engine plane, flying above a thousand miles of uninhabited wilderness, and as he chatted he polished off a nearly full bottle of Wild Turkey.

"You want to know why they get shit-faced so fast?" Punky asked me, then took a long swig. We both knew to which "they" he referred.

I wondered if there was any way I could figure out how to operate the maze of dials and switches on the control panel if he suddenly passed out. Was there an instruction manual in the glove compartment? Was there a glove compartment? Would some calm air traffic controller "talk" me down like in the movies if I managed to grasp how the radio worked?

"It's their *genes*," Punky continued without waiting for my response.

"Their *jeans*?" I said, misunderstanding him.

He nodded knowingly. "Indian genes are bigger than white genes. So when they fill up with hootch it takes longer for it to get absorbed."

I was about to protest, to tell Punky he was a pea-brained lunatic, but when he saw an eagle flying below us, shouted "Bombs Away," and jettisoned his empty bottle, I kept my mouth shut. Genes it was, you betcha.

But the chilling facts were harder to dismiss. In the estimation of *The Final Report of the American Indian Policy Review Commission*,[5] alcohol abuse was "the most severe and widespread health problem among Indians today." Nationally, around half of the adult American Indian population was chemically dependent to some degree. In practical terms this meant that almost every Native American was plagued, directly or indirectly, by alcohol. A 1975 study revealed that over 50 percent of the Indians surveyed had immediate-family problems due to drinking. Alcohol-related deaths occurred at six and one-half times the national rate, and 71 percent of Indian arrests reported in 1960[6] were alcohol-related. The death rates from accidents and gastritis were three times greater than for the general population, and in 1973 the Indian Health Service reported that terminal cirrhosis occurred among 27.3 individuals per 100,000 as opposed to 6.1 individuals per 100,000 in all races.[7]

In 1976, 4.7 percent of Indian deaths were homicide or violent as opposed to 0.5 percent for the country as a whole. In South Dakota, where Adam was born, one-third of the prison population was Indian, though the state is 95 percent white.[8] The suicide rate nationally was currently two and a half times greater than that of the general population, and even higher among the young; Indians had a shorter lifespan than any other population group in the United States. Indeed, compared to the misery produced by the chronic, boozy cycles of despair and violence, waste and dependency and poverty prevalent in so many rural and urban Indian communities, the "dry" past seemed like a world of unpolluted emotions and clear thought, of familial and social relationships free from ethanol, the active chemical ingredient in ordinary alcohol. A golden age. A paradise.

An army of sociologists, anthropologists, psychologists, and nutritionists promoted hypotheses that endeavored to address why and to what extent some Indians drank, but how was I to puzzle out the relative credibility of the scholarship? Some explanations were obvious: alcohol-induced indifference was probably for some a means of coping with cycles of poverty, divorce, job loss, guilt, or even death of a family member—all too common events on a reservation or in an urban ghetto. But surely these were more symptoms than causes. The truth of the matter was that alcohol threatened the million and a half contemporary Indian people as virulently as, five hundred years ago, a plethora of Old World diseases had decimated Western Hemisphere populations, eliminating by infection, in some cases, nineteen out of twenty people in a given community within a brief period of time.

I turned for answers to the work of one person whom I instinctively trusted. Writing about the Standing Rock reservation, the place where Adam and I had received our Lakota names, in her doctoral dissertation, "An Ethnography of Drinking and Sobriety Among the Lakota Sioux,"* my friend Bea Medicine had examined a

---

* My argument and documentation in the following pages often parallels and is derived from that of Dr. Medicine's thesis. Acknowledgment is gratefully made.

modern American Indian community—her own—in crisis. Hers were the observations of a sympathetic, but meticulously trained insider. Her study, extending from 1969 through 1983, focused on the place where she was born and raised, an 848,000-acre federal reservation spanning the borders of North and South Dakota. Many of her interviews were conducted in her native Lakota language; as a result, the responses she elicited seemed likely to me to hold a depth and candor only rarely found in orthodox anthropology. As an enrolled member of the tribe, she had the advantage of inspiring the implicit trust of those with whom she spoke. Furthermore, she wrote about a place which, though not the reservation where Adam's parents had lived, was probably very similar to it.

The approximately 8,000 Indian residents of Standing Rock had, at the time of Bea's study, an unemployment rate of 60 percent and an average educational attainment level of 9.0 years. Much of the land was leased to non-Indians for livestock grazing purposes, and the federal government was the predominant employer. Bea's work on alcohol dependence there built on several previous investigations, notably a 1962 monograph by J. O. Whittaker and a 1972 study by Luis Kemnitzer.

Whittaker's findings were alarming: of those 15–17 years of age, 50 percent of males and 40 percent of the females reported drinking; of those 20–29, 99 percent of males and 72 percent of females drank; of those 30–39, 93 percent of males and 85 percent of women drank.[9] Bea reported parallel, and in some cases, higher and increasing, percentages within these population groups.[10] Furthermore, Whittaker adds:

> 44 percent indicated usually drinking until drunk; 68 percent had been arrested for drunkenness, 35 percent two or more times, 42 percent had experienced blackouts, 25 percent of the latter with increasing frequency; 14 percent had either been hospitalized or had sought medical advice for a body ailment due to drinking; and 9 percent had had delirium tremens. Sprees or binges, ranging in frequency from less than four a year to once a week, and in duration from 2 to 7 days or more, were reported by more than half of those who drink.[11]

In his sample as a whole, 31 percent abstained, 45 percent drank occasionally, and 24 percent drank regularly (that is, more than three times per week). Factoring out male informants, 18 percent of the women in 1962 did not drink at all.[12] Data from Standing Rock and the Pine Ridge (also Sioux) reservation in South Dakota suggested that the greater the economic security, the greater the alcohol consumption,[13] especially on paydays, the times when lease checks reached landowners, or when cash from land sales was received. In other words, abstinence seemed in part to depend upon lack of funds rather than on internal decision.[14]

A variety of sources reported that alcoholic consumption among the Lakota was traditionally, for the most part, a public, rather than a private, affair. Gordon MacGregor, in his *Warriors Without Weapons* (1945), listed the four cardinal virtues of traditional Lakota society as generosity, bravery, fortitude, and moral integrity; Bea maintained that of these, generosity was the most crucial; when applied to drinking behavior, this meant that alcohol, whenever available, was distributed "to any and all, of either sex and any age, who may be present when a drinking session begins. To refuse a drink is tantamount to a slap in the face,"[15] because it deprived the host of his or her *right* to be generous.

The Standing Rock observations also supported those that Kemnitzer made in regard to a segment of Pine Ridge society:

Small children are present at drinking parties, and infants are taken to bars and there suckled, or beer and wine is mixed in their bottles. Children under twelve play around the drinkers in bars, and by the age of fifteen are in drinking groups of their own, but do not participate in public bar drinking until they are older. Adolescents are also sniffing gasoline and glue as well as drinking alcoholic beverages. The drinking behavior is also expressed in the play of younger children.

Two young boys are playing with toy cars. They pretend to load the cars with people, drive the cars to White Clay for wine, get drunk, and wreck the cars on the way home. Little girls playing with dolls make up a situation where the "parents" get drunk and fight.

Thus, values and behavior reinforcing traditional drinking patterns are transmitted by example and instruction to children of all ages, and drunken behavior becomes "normal" behavior for a significant segment of the population.[16]

Alcohol consumption, it was clear, was more than a neutral artifact, a thumbed nose at an oppressive culture. When its use was habitual, it became physically addictive, a drug that a person couldn't easily do without. Moreover, through a process not yet fully understood, the offspring of alcoholics (especially, it appears, of alcoholic fathers) seemed to show, in study after study, a greater tendency toward similar chemical dependence in their own adult lives, whether they grew up in an environment in which heavy drinking took place, or whether, removed early from the influence of their biological parents, they were adopted and raised by teetotalers. This was not to suggest that all children of alcoholics were predestined to become problem drinkers themselves, but only that men and women in this category have a statistically greater probability of drinking to the point of abuse, if they start at all.

This vague, but undeniable sense of legacy was the curse of many families, many communities, many cultures around the world— American Indian groups among them. The explanation was a conundrum, a chicken-and-egg, "Catch 22" cycle in which there was no clarity: does a social toleration for excessive drinking create a multi-generational pattern of inebriation, or does some biochemically altered or random genetic predisposition underlie an acceptance of destructive behavior? Where did the emphasis lie, in choice or in compulsion? Was the best solution in preventive education— implying volition—or in outright government-mandated prohibition? Whatever the theoretical response, it was evident from the utter failure of federal restrictions against Indian drinking, lifted by Congress as recently as 1953, that the latter path not only didn't work, it made matters infinitely worse. Indeed, a law making it illegal for an Indian to possess a whiskey bottle with a broken seal absolutely encouraged "blitz" drinking, if only to eliminate the evidence.

I constantly tried to relate these theories to an understanding of my son's lineage. While Adam's father might be accounted for by the fact that drinking had been epidemic among Lakota men for some time, as late as 1969 Eileen Maynard was able to write, "The woman who does not drink is respected and the woman who drinks is criticized. Especially open to censure are women who neglect their children because of drinking or who hang around bars unescorted."[17] And Bea noted that traditionally "some women believe that excessive drinking can cause miscarriages or stillbirths. The majority of women do not drink during pregnancy. For some, this may be a time when they give up drinking entirely. A few young women in their twenties, who were carrying illegitimate children, often drank excessively but did not state a reason for this."[18]

Was this what happened to Adam's mother? Was she such an exception? How did she avoid her society's sanctions and drink herself to death? If there was something new under the sun, I learned, it was in the growing percentage of reservation women who were heavy drinkers in the age group of eighteen to forty-five—the years of fertility, pregnancy, and motherhood. Some pointed to the rise of the equal rights movement, to politics that encouraged women not to bow to any pressures, peer or otherwise, that seemed to discriminate between the genders.

More convincing to me, however, was the subtle argument that increasing rates of female drinking derived from a greater overall rate of alcoholism within society. If a predisposition toward ethanol dependency was inherited, then the number of people affected by alcoholism had the potential to expand geometrically from one generation to the next. And if, as seemed obvious, men and women were less likely to use contraception or other forms of birth control when drunk than when sober, then sex in the context of alcohol would produce a disproportionate number of unplanned pregnancies. It was not surprising, therefore, that a substantial swell in a group's drinking behavior often resulted in a population explosion, with an accompanying decline in the average mean age. Such conditions propagated themselves, in every sense of the word.

Whittaker recorded in his 1962 study that while 55 percent of his female respondents drank, only 20 percent of their mothers did so,[19] and Bea reported that "the increase of drinking among Lakota women appeared to be accelerating"[20] at the time of her fieldwork; furthermore, she saw no evidence of an abatement in this behavior after the birth of children. In fact, "from 1960 onward, drinking by females during the child-bearing age became more frequent,"[21] probably because for women who grew to adulthood after the ban on alcohol consumption was lifted, "drinking was almost a puberty rite."[22] Moreover, many parents associated a surge in drinking on the part of younger women with the rise in teenage pregnancies.[23]

> Generally, a female learns drinking behavior in the family setting. In most cases her father and mother are drinkers, and her initiation into drinking is not a problem to them. Many families actively encourage young daughters to accompany them on drinking bouts. Others carefully guard their daughters from peer group interaction. . . .

Families who encourage daughters, or do not discourage them, to participate in drinking, are fatalistic. The girl will drink no matter what they do. The daughter who drinks may become a form of insurance as a source for alcoholic beverages. She can recruit White ranchers, farmers, and even police officials to support the drinking habit she acquires. Her extended kin, if composed of heavy drinkers, share in this symbiotic relationship. Indian women who fit this description very often form liaisons with bar owners, bartenders, and business men to guarantee a source of liquor. This relationship may become a source of livelihood. [24]

Whittaker's 1980 follow-up study on Standing Rock supported the idea that an overall increase in the level of drinking had taken place, [25] and Lakota culture was particularly ill-suited temperamentally for combating this trend. Several researchers have pointed out that what opposition there was to drinking behavior tended to be passive, [26] a theory reinforced by a study of Canadian Cree, [27] which indicated that excessive drinking did not produce the kind of guilt or violation of self-image that it might have done among an analogous group of non-Indians. Whittaker found that 38 percent of his Standing Rock respondents did not even disapprove of a man beating his wife when he was drunk. [28]

In Bea's experience, "drinking and deviance (incarceration for drunkenness and aggression, suicide, and homicide) were tolerated on reservations." [29] "Individuals who drink," she wrote, "are not chastised by the in-group, nor are they punished or made to feel guilty. This characteristic of Lakota life does not serve as a strong social control mechanism." [30] In fact, she concluded, "the single and most salient feature counterproductive to achieving and maintaining sobriety is the sustained pressure to drink, which begins at an early age for men. This is also beginning to be true of Lakota females." [31] In her thesis Bea explained that "the individual who strives to a changed life style can be certain of alienation from the social group," [32] and almost inevitably experiences feelings of great loneliness brought about by a sudden lack of friends. [33] "Statements such as 'You think you're too good to drink with us,' or 'I didn't know you're such a *wasichu* (White person),' or 'So you're not a Lakota any more,' are examples of pressures to drink which can be unnerving to non-drinkers." [34] In fact, "the first response to the sober person is one of disbelief by family and community members." [35]

The situation, as I tried to make intellectual sense of it, seemed rife with internal contradiction: the cherished cultural norm of personal prerogative seemed to work only one way. An individual who was drinking or drunk could not be criticized because it was his *right* to do what he wanted—except if he wanted *not* to drink. Then the group as a whole was free to make fun of or banish him. What was this "you think you're too good to drink" business, anyway?

I was reminded of a vintage joke. Two men, one white, one Indian, have been on a pier fishing for crabs all morning and have filled their shallow pails almost to the top. They leave their spot to take a lunch break, and when they come back all the crabs have escaped from the white guy's bucket, but the Indian's is just as full as it was an hour before. "I don't get it," the white man says in exasperation. "It's simple," his friend replies. "These are Indian crabs. As soon as one starts to climb out the others drag it back."

According to virtually all the material I could find, a willingness to drink excessively on occasion stands as almost a requirement for membership in certain Indian groups—almost a definition of ethnic identification. As Gretchen Lang put it in her study of urban Chippewa in Minneapolis, "giving up alcohol means giving up a pattern of life that is much more complicated than simply abstaining from the beverage."[36]

Bea maintained that economics is partially responsible for this attitude, arguing that "the flexibility and pooling of kin (*tiospaye*) for labor and income has allowed the Lakota to exist in a marginal situation. Mutual but unspecified reciprocities have allowed the Lakota to cope with chronic and on-going socio-economic deprivation."[37]

Affecting this pattern was complicated because in large part, as Bea observed, "Drinking is not seen as a problem for most Lakota Sioux."[38] There were indications, however, that this might be changing.[39] Some of the men Bea talked to had stopped drinking after they "thought about the trouble the Sioux were in," from which she gathers that "there is an awareness on the part of the people that many of the dissonances of Lakota life—family deterioration; loss of Lakota values; spouse and child neglect; accident rates largely due to drunken driving and petty crimes, especially stealing to obtain money to drink, are all related to abuse of alcohol."[40]

Perceptions vary, however. Few people mentioned the obvious health factor as one of the reasons they practiced sobriety. Alcoholics Anonymous, and the drug Antibuse, effective for many non-

Indians who are chemically dependent, have not in general proven successful in Native American communities.[41] On the other hand, according to Bea, "being 'reformed'—as some Lakota say—has been a part of the maturation process that some men have followed," though it has not been "a predictable event."[42] Women who had been drinkers but stopped in their forties—either because they had by then become grandparents ("their children are grown, now"[43]) and wanted to set a good example, or simply because they were "tired of drinking and carousing"[44]—are called *winyan tanka* (women, big), which has connotations of "maturity," in Lakota.[45]

All the scholarly evidence suggested that alcohol, over the past 150 years, had become so absorbed into the social systems of many American Indian groups that it could not be easily excised. For generations, certain types of drinking had often functioned as public demonstrations and reinforcements of solidarity, identity, and good times. Liquor had become part of an accepted context, and to refuse a drink could be interpreted as a denial of essential community values. All the same, there was no disputing that alcohol abuse was at the heart of many of the debilitating problems from which Indian people suffered—directly causing some (accidental deaths, cirrhosis of the liver) and aiding and abetting others (poverty, family disintegration, child abuse). It had wiped out my son's natural family.

Bea exhorted that "courage and a certain self-isolation seem in order for the maintenance of sobriety,"[46]—the former, a quality regarded among the Lakota as a primary virtue, the latter, utterly disparaged. When Whittaker queried his informants as to how they thought an alcoholic might stop drinking, 73 percent answered that it simply took willpower, 21 percent said the person would need assistance, and 6 percent thought religion was the answer.[47] Bea interpreted "willpower" to mean a traditional concept, *chin ka cha*, "self-actualization or exercise of personal autonomy in a decision-making process."[48] Another route to a change in attitude, she speculated, might be the practice of *ah wa bleza ki*, to examine one's self, to cogitate, to become introspective.[49] Perhaps the important concept of *wacunza* ("to cause harm," especially to a family member) could be a powerful inhibition, when understood in connection with alcohol use.

The underlying premise here is that unless one is able to cogitate upon one's actions, and place some perspective upon these acts, one is unable to deal with problems that are based on interpersonal relationships. . . . The process places the remedial behavior upon the self-awareness and reasonable character of the person who is causing the dissonance. This is the ultimate focus upon individual autonomy (*chin ka cha*). . . . There is no force outside the individual, such as *wakan* ("sacred, omnipotent power") or slight feelings of guilt, via the Christian ethic, that places the locus of control upon the individual. This then may offer an explanation as to why many Sioux relate an achievement of sobriety to "will power." The greater emphasis on individualism, or, at least, individual decision-making . . . is [related] to these concepts of personhood.[50]

"A person is allowed an unstructured freedom of choice," she maintained. If a man or woman behaved in a particular manner, it was assumed that "he/she prefers to be that way," and "no force outside the individual is able to intervene."[51]

Some tribal alcohol counselors and workers reported that participation in an organized Western religion which imposes strong sanctions against liquor use (e.g., Mormonism or fundamentalist Christianity) assisted some clients who wanted to break a pattern of chemical abuse; others argued that recourse and appeal to systems of traditional belief might be a partial solution. Thomas Mails pointed out, in his study of the renewed sun dancing at Pine Ridge and Rosebud reservations, that drinking "is, in the view of every medicine man and leader, a curse of incredible proportions."[52] Joseph Jorgenson understood the primary objectives of the current sun dances to be remolding of the individual participant and a general critique of the social system.[53] As always with the Lakota, however, there was a strong emphasis on individual responsibility. A person seeking help from whatever source did not expect and was unlikely to respond to specific instructions or orders. Instead, in Bea's words, "he or she is simply asked to *ah bleza* one's actions and implement change."[54]

As with all hard challenges, true motivation must come from within.

CHAPTER SEVEN

Adam's story is the center of this book, but its cast of characters is large. In 1974, when Adam was six, Denis helped me adopt another boy, a little over twenty-four months old, also from a South Dakota Sioux background. I gave my second son the name of my former, recently deceased fishing partner in Alaska, Sava, a man of great patience and skill, of good humor and even temper.

Sava Stephan was a believer in bizarre theories, the more improbable the better. He was sure, for instance, that Cook Inlet salmon could tell when the seas were so rough that no sane human being would venture forth on them in a small wooden dory, and so, Sava argued, the worse the weather the more fish there were trying to make a run for it past the village. This belief, in part, accounted for the fact that he took me on as partner. I was not much good at tying nets or steering a boat, but in my eagerness to learn the trade I was the only man or woman in town willing to risk my life to prove his point.

The highlight of our shared experience came the second August I was in Tyonek. The morning was gray and cold, the wind whipping waves into battering rams. All along the coast of Cook Inlet experienced gill-net fishermen took one look at the threatening skies, threw some coal on the fire, and broke out the playing cards. Not Sava Stephan. "Oh boy," he said in Tanaina. "They'll really be running today."

Driving rain blurred the lenses of my glasses as we pushed the boat off the sandbar. Over several layers of sweaters, long underwear, and jeans, we wore hip boots, slickers, and low-brimmed rubber hats, but I still felt wet and cold. The nets we dragged into the prow were already water-logged and heavy, and the salt rubbed into old cuts on my hands as we hoisted them, yard by yard. There was a protocol to setting nets: Sava steered alongside an anchored, floating barrel; when we got close enough I grabbed the loop of rope and secured it with a simple knot to a matching rope on one end of the net. Then, as the net played out, we approached another barrel, positioned just the right distance away, and the procedure was repeated. This was not easy for me even when the inlet was glassy and calm, for it required fast hands and perfect coordination, neither of which were my strong points.

That day it was murder. We were about a quarter mile offshore, and the gale was so strong I could barely hear Sava's voice from where he sat at the other end of the boat. My command of Tanaina idiom got shaky under stress, and I found myself mentally translating each of his commands into English before following them—thus throwing off my timing. I managed to grab and tether one end of the net to the first barrel we passed because we hit the bottom of a wave at exactly the right moment. Then I dumped length after length of webbing over the side while Sava aimed at the red buoy that marked the other terminus. This time we were high while the barrel was low, so I reached with one hand far over the bow to snag the loop while gripping the rope at the end of the net with the other. For an instant I had them both, the link between, then I heard Sava shout some instruction.

"We're too far away," I painstakingly translated his words. *"Let it go and we'll come back."*

I did as I was told, but made one mistake: I released the net and held onto the barrel. In what seemed like slow motion—I remember I had in my mind a cartoon picture of what was going on even as it was happening—I was pulled over the side and under the freezing water. My boots began to fill, one of the two danger signs of drowning in Alaska (the other being hyperthermia, even in summer), and I realized I was good for only one strong kick to the surface. I scissored my legs, broke into the air, opened my eyes, and saw Sava leaning over the boat looking for me. Our hands met, and with enormous strength he hauled me in.

They say that after a brush with death the world looks different and that was true for me, but by the time I caught my breath, I realized that it was because I had lost my glasses. I had clear vision ap-

proximately to the end of my arms; everything beyond that was a myopic blur. Whatever help I had been to our team effort was now lost.

"Maybe it's too rough," Sava concluded with some regret. I knew
in his imagination legions of crafty fish were at that very moment
rushing beneath the dory, eluding even him.

"May*be*," I allowed. And then the motor sputtered and cut off.

"It's just wet," Sava decided. "Have you got anything small and
waterproof to wrap around the spark plug?"

I searched the pocket of my slicker and found a clear plastic sack
with a few caramels in it.

"Perfect!" Sava discarded the candy and wrapped the bag around
the plug. It worked too—the thing started right up—and then the
plastic caught fire. Sava quickly dumped a bucket of water on the
engine to put out the flames before the gas tank exploded, but that
left us permanently adrift without power. The wind was rising, and
the boat was tossed in every direction.

"I guess we'll wait it out," Sava called above the noise. "Throw the
anchor overboard."

I could barely see, so I crawled forward on all fours and found the
heavy piece of iron by touch. "To the right or the left?" I yelled, as
the prow rose and dropped beneath me.

"To the right, to the right," he answered. I was proud that I
understood him so well and heaved the anchor in the correct
direction. The only problem, it wasn't attached to a rope. We heard
a splash in the distance, squinted at each other through the rain, and
had nothing to say. Then Sava did the only thing possible: he threw
back his head and laughed. "This is a good story," he said when he
finally caught his breath. "This is a really good story. Don't worry. It's
too good not to get told."

And he was right. The boat eventually caught a huge wave and,
like a surfboard, we were carried back to shore, past the rocky parts,
right up the bed of a small river, and eventually we beached without
much permanent damage to the hull. When the storm finally sub-
sided and the tide went out, we even found the anchor, even
retrieved the empty, tangled net, even found my glasses, one lens
protruding from the mud and reflecting the late afternoon sunlight
like a beacon. "They got away *this* time," Sava said, his theory
undented by our experience.

Several years after I left the village, Sava Stephan, then only thirty-five years old, had a heart attack and died while successfully slam-returning a volleyball in the Tyonek school gym. I gave my boy his name in hopes that he also would grow into a man whose ultimate resource was laughter.

Adam was delighted to have a brother, and Sava was a terrific toddler. Whereas Adam was long and lean, Sava was compact, sturdy. From the first he had a generous smile and a thirst for independence. I had recently purchased, with five hundred dollars down and two thirty-year mortgages, an eighteenth-century farmhouse—a "handyman's paradise," the real estate agent had said—about a thirty-minute drive from Hanover. With Nina's help I wallpapered side-by-side upstairs bedrooms for the boys; Adam's was a jungle of black-and-tan zebras and lions and giraffes, and Sava's was a bright scattering of red birds, green fish, and yellow deer. Each room had a window overlooking Skahota's square doghouse, placed in the shade of a sugar maple tree in the yard.

Over the years we have lived in the house there have been continual improvements—the green paint got scraped from the original wide-pine floors, plumbing and insulation were upgraded, one after another the rooms were filled with books and second-hand furniture—but from the very beginning it felt like home. The water supply came by gravity feed from an underground well located up a hill half a mile away; there was a level meadow ideal for a big vegetable garden, and our eleven acres were rich with apple trees, raspberry, blackberry, and gooseberry bushes, and even boasted a small, shallow pond. The property was located some distance from a main road, and even with the cacophony of frogs and crickets in the summer, it was quiet and serene. Few cars passed by, and Adam and Sava could play undisturbed for hours on end while I sat on the granite slab before the front door, reading and taking notes for my lectures.

I was amazed at how quickly Sava acquired language and mastered new tasks. He was toilet trained within two months, practiced repeatedly until he learned to tie his own shoestrings, and did his best to be helpful. Despite the five-year difference in their ages, the two boys functioned at the same level in many areas, a fact that, at the time, I determinedly regarded as a convenience and a blessing. In that first year we were all together, when I went in to teach at Dartmouth, Sava stayed at a local day care home where Adam went after school. I dropped them off at 8:30 and picked them up at 4:00.

I had little time for an independent social life—my waking hours were divided between family and work and a few good friends—and I had no complaints. I rarely hired baby-sitters, both because I couldn't afford it and because in general I only went out after dark if Sava and Adam were invited, too. They got used to putting on their pajamas and falling asleep in unfamiliar beds after dinner on weekend nights while I helped with the dishes and talked late with other faculty members. At the end of the evening I would start the car engine, turn on the heater, then rouse the boys, one at a time, and carry them, wrapped in blankets, to the backseat. I'd play the radio softly as we drove the quiet roads home, and when we pulled into our driveway, we always waited for the song to end before we went inside.

I emerged from my first investigations of Adam's learning problems with a sheaf of data that fulfilled the demands of my preconceptions; I had identified scholarly explanations for his situation that exonerated not only me as a parent, but Indians in general. Some Indians drank because some Indians drank. Maybe we had a particular biological susceptibility to alcohol, maybe the drinking patterns were just cultural by-products. We were hapless innocents, duped by a foreign scourge. I could eloquently explain the whole process to a classroom of Dartmouth sophomores and have them beating their breasts in unison within fifteen minutes. There were a thousand logical, external reasons why Adam's situation was inevitable and nobody's fault.

But those reasons didn't do me a damn bit of good the day I almost lost him.

I sat that morning in the spare bedroom I used as an office, writing the text for my first book, while Sava and Adam played in the bathtub. I had hit a snag in my attempt to describe in nonspecialized language the convolutions of federal Indian policy and was trying to concentrate, but at some level I was monitoring the patterns of splashes and shrieks that came from the next room. Suddenly, there was a lull, then I heard Sava say, "Out, Adam, out now." He sounded too calm and genuinely worried.

I ran to find out what was going on. Sava was sitting in the water looking as though he might cry. "Adam won't play," he said. Then I saw Adam, the right side of his body jerking, his head completely submerged. I pulled him out, lay him on the rug next to the tub; he didn't seem to be breathing. I arched back his head, pinched his nose, covered his mouth with my own, and blew into his lungs. Between each breath I tried to reassure Sava with words I didn't myself believe: "It's all right, honey," I said, counting all the while. "Everything's okay." I had never given artificial respiration before and couldn't be sure I was doing it the right way, and I was torn by indecision: should I continue my efforts or rush to the phone and dial for emergency assistance? It was clear I should do both, and for the first time ever I was deeply horrified at my arrogance in trying to be a single parent. If there were two adults, Adam would have a better chance.

In the end I couldn't leave him, and after what seemed like a very long time I felt him stir in a way different from his seizure. He coughed, retched, vomited water. Sava began to cry, and I reached out a hand to comfort him. "No this is *good*," I said. "This is very good." Adam was operating on his own, drawing angry, wonderful, ragged breaths. I rested his head on my lap, lifted Sava from the tub, and wrapped him in a towel.

"Sing to Adam," I suggested, and without hesitation Sava began his standby: "I've Been Working on the Railroad." I leaned back against the cold porcelain of the tub. Yellow looseleaf sheets of research notes, now blurred and spotted with water, remained where I had dropped them. Adam's chest was so thin, stretched so translucent, that I could follow the patterns of blue and red lines beneath his skin and watch the pulse and push of his heart. His lips, flecked with drying froth, were gray from shock or chill. His eyes were closed, his black lashes thick against the pale brown of his cheeks. I held each of his hands in one of my own; where they budded through my clasp, his fingertips were still puckered from the bathwater. I strove to divert my anger. Who did he look like, I wondered? The shadow of whose face did I see before me?

The composite picture of Adam's mother that I had occasionally tried to build in my imagination was hazy, indistinct, shaded more by what I knew of her life than by the cast of her facial features. My research said this woman had violated Lakota traditions by her use of liquor during pregnancy, but then again, the articles maintained, she had been pressured by her peers to do so. If only she had become a teetotaling Mormon, listened to the oblique advice of appropriately nondirective counselors, better examined her own conscience.

But that she had done none of those things was not her responsibility, I had read again and again; she was not liable because she was subject to societal forces that had predestined her behavior long before she was born. Her own mother, the famous bar-hopping grandmother on a toot, was but another cog in a long network. Not her fault either. In fact, everyone with a face or a name was herself a victim. My son's grievous physical and learning problems, whether they derived directly from the hostile environment of his mother's drinking, from her alcohol-related neglect and abandonment of him, or from some other source, were *really* the legacy of some anonymous French trapper, the result of some innocent ancestor's belief in transcendent visions, the product of some taunting fool who was emotionally threatened if Adam's mother said no to a shot of whiskey when her son needed her care.

Much as I admired the industry and insights of the scholars I had consulted, I had closed their books impatient and still dissatisfied. I understood and agreed with everything they said, but when I remembered Adam, stumped at counting any number above ten or thwarted by a jigsaw puzzle intended for three-year-olds, all the theoretical explanations seemed too pat, distant, more sophisticated versions of a noncommittal shrug. All the oppressive history in the world did not balance the injustice of Adam's personal tragedy as he reclined helpless in my arms. Human beings were more than programmed robots, slaves to their socioeconomic circumstances. Ultimately, for a reason beyond anything I had thus far been able to comprehend, the several people directly responsible for the start of Adam's life had cared too little about what happened to him.

Abstract explanations were of little practical use to me. Their often patronizing oversimplifications were worse in their bland and fatalistic acceptances than the know-nothing excuse of "bad luck" with which I had begun. The fascinating cross-cultural theories about "Indian drinking" and social mayhem were ghostly cerebral creations with no substance to them. Adam's ongoing inability at age seven to tie his shoes, to know the conceptual difference between lunch and breakfast and dinner, to maintain focused attention for the length of a Donald Duck cartoon, to take a bubble bath without a life-threatening event—those were realities. On some gut level I didn't give a hoot about the anthropologically explained or politically correct *right* of individual choice, about a self-serving cultural apology that each person was beyond reproach even for destructive behavior that extended to babies. I wasn't buying any complicated justification that presumed to condone the bad hand Adam had been dealt.

The next fall, I enrolled Adam in the Cornish Elementary School, located about a mile and a half from our house. The yellow bus collected him at 7:10 A.M. at the foot of the road. He carried his noon meal—a sandwich, a banana, a cookie, two Dilantin tablets, and one Tegretol pill—in a tin Raggedy Andy lunchbox and was always anxious to get going. I don't think he missed more than a few days because of ordinary illness in his initial eight years of public education; he seemed impervious to colds and flu and the range of childhood diseases, as if his chronic physical problems, some of them—such as curvature of the spine or an overabundance of permanent teeth or hearing impairments—waiting for a more advanced age to surface, were enough.

Adam's first-grade teacher was Alice Hendrick, a woman of many years' experience, of utter patience and optimism and understated skill. She had taught six-year-olds for so long that even when speaking to adults, she clearly enunciated each word and gave frequent, supportive, rather unnerving compliments. "What nice shiny shoes you're wearing," she once said when I attended a PTA meeting. "And you arrived right on time!"

The population of Cornish was a curious northern New England hodgepodge, part old Yankee farmer, part recent hippie commune, part Dartmouth College commuter, reflected in the names of Adam's classmates, which ranged from Old Testament prophets to innovations like Sunshine and Cardamon. The entire school was composed of only slightly more than one hundred students, and within a month every teacher knew each one of their names.

Mrs. Hendrick took a special interest in Adam. Dismissing as ridiculous my offer of extra payment, she encouraged me to drop him off at her house on Saturday mornings during the school year and several days a week during vacations. She shared my faith in his potential and brought to bear all the skills she had acquired over a long career. At the time, his progress struck me as maddeningly slow, but now I look back and realize that Mrs. Hendrick accomplished in one year something that by rights should have taken much longer: she taught Adam to read. It wasn't easy, but gradually he was able to recite the words, to chime the sounds off a page and into the air. He recognized the relationship of phonics and print, formed his lips, and expelled breath. Writing followed, once he had the general idea. His printing was slow and laborious, the letters remained for years at nonuniform size, many of them inverted or reversed, but it was legible. Adam had a new vehicle for communication, for ingesting and producing information. I believed it was the major breakthrough I had been expecting, that I had assured one and all was just around the corner.

From 1974 through 1979, Adam regularly saw a pediatric neurologist at Kennedy Memorial Hospital in Boston. Dr. Edward Hart was thorough, measured in his assessment, and highly professional. With the series of memos, recorded after each of Adam's visits, I can follow a wobbly pattern of growth, of blood tests and increased medication, of body weight gained slowly—fifteen pounds over five years, to a grand total of sixty-six pounds at age eleven. It is a record that speaks of hope and setback, of seizures and good manners. Adam seemed always to be better than he had a right to be, but never as good, on a subsequent visit, as the previous encouraging signs might have predicted. It is a record that clinically describes Adam with great precision and with sympathy, but which makes no promises, notes no soaring strides.

Those visits tamped my optimism, but Adam's reading fed it. I suppressed the fact that he had very little comprehension, that he retained almost nothing of a story he might speak. I did not listen as he read without reference to punctuation, without pauses at periods. He slid from the punch line of a book to "The End" to its copyright information without noticing the discontinuity. I ordered him a set of special computer-printed volumes in which the protagonist was always "Adam" and the cast of characters included Sava, Skahota, and me, but the rest of us paid more attention to these wonders than he did. Reading was important, was a true step, for Adam, but if it was his bus ticket to adulthood, it was no express.

I arranged for my Dartmouth teaching and advising schedule to take place in the morning hours, so that by 3:30, when Adam got home, I had already collected Sava from his day care and we were there, waiting. In many ways it was an idyllic period, and I used to joke that we were living on the cover of a 1955 *Saturday Evening Post*.

We had our share of accidents too—one time I cut my finger badly when Sava and I were home alone together. Blood was everywhere, and yet before wrapping my wound in a towel and driving to the hospital, I ran upstairs to change my clothes. I wanted to make a good impression on the emergency room staff. By the time I arrived, reassuring Sava all the way, I required a transfusion.

Professionally, as well, it was a time of some turmoil. To be retained, much less promoted, at Dartmouth required a constant production of publications. I taught an overload of courses and simultaneously lobbied to increase the faculty of Native American studies and the number of Indian students admitted to the school. One problem was particular to Dartmouth. Before there was a Native American Program the school had "The Indian" as its unofficial mascot. Fraternity boys would dress up in paint and feathers at the halftime shows of football games, and the crowd would respond by shrieking "wah hoo wah." No harm was probably intended, but to the Indian students who arrived in Hanover it was an offensive display, a tacky caricature with minstrel show overtones. When this reaction was presented to the trustees, they, with some embarrassment, abandoned the symbol, but some alumni and a few students were recalcitrant. *They* were the Indians, they argued. If Native Americans didn't like it, they should remember they were "guests" at Dartmouth and could be asked to go home. It was an ultimately boring, silly controversy, but it did hang on. Year after year the NAS students and I would have to explain why it was just as inappropriate for the Caucasian sons and daughters of Dartmouth to play stereotyped Indians (wild, savage, noble-hearted and stoic) as it would be if they took it into their heads to be rhythmic Blacks or wealthy Jews. The symbol became symbolic to all concerned, the issue on which the constituencies of a changing institution slugged out their differences. It was an annual nuisance that wore out me and every other Indian in town, but there was no way we could give up.

There was much uncertainty on all fronts, professional and personal, and so I *had* to have had anxieties, doubts, money worries. Our well completely dried up on at least two occasions—once from January until March—and I was forced to lug drinking water to the house in old milk cartons and melt snow for the rest. My mother's house in Kentucky was struck and almost demolished by a tornado. And yet, somehow, everything must have seemed to me to be under such control that in the spring of 1976 I telephoned Denis to initiate a petition for a third adoption.

"Impossible," he said. "It'll never happen."

"More impossible than you think," I answered. "This time my request is specific: I want a daughter, and she must be very young so that there is a reasonable gap in age between her and Sava."

Denis laughed, but he did agree to see me. I confess, I was not entirely honest with him at all times. I never, for instance, revealed the scope of Adam's problems, never mentioned the growing proliferation of opinion that his educational possibilities were severely limited. Instead I emphasized Adam's progress, all the new things he could do, all the wise pronouncements he had made, all the interests I was sure he was on the verge of having. There was no doubt that Adam was a happy little boy, affectionate, emotionally secure, still thin but otherwise healthy-looking. His adjustment to Sava's arrival was a model of sibling harmony, and his eclectic memory—he could recall the exact position of every piece of furniture in the Catholic Charities office during a previous visit, though sometimes he could not remember the names of his classmates—served well to make a positive, immediate impression.

In addition, to allay Denis's fears that I was taking on solo too large a burden, I made subtle hints that waiting in the wings there was a woman, almost a fiancée as I described her, who would someday marry me and be the mother of my children. This mystery female was a paragon—an Indian lawyer-activist who yearned for parenthood, had a huge and loving extended family, and was, by way of a bonus, tall and beautiful and possessed of a sterling disposition. It got so that Denis would ask after her when he and I spoke about the progress of the adoption application, and I would always report on her latest triumph or provide a telling anecdote to demonstrate her developing devotion to Adam, Sava, and me.

There were moments, I suppose, when I came to believe in her myself, though the fact was that between teaching, chairing and promoting the Native American Studies Program, and looking after my two little boys, I had almost no time or energy for a wide network of social engagements. Instead, I depended on family visits, on interaction with some Indian students, on neighbors, especially on a few good friends. My life was so full of the children and career I wanted and never expected I'd get, that to ask for more seldom occurred to me. I had the uncomplaining single-parent examples of my mother and grandmothers for role models, and within its own context my everyday routine seemed the quintessence of normalcy.

It must have seemed that way as well to the staff of the South Dakota Social Services Agency, because one June morning Denis called in some amazement.

"What would you say," he asked, "to a ten-month-old baby girl?"

"I would say 'when,' " I answered.

"What would you say to next week?"

"Monday."

Somehow all the schedules got adjusted. I found a substitute for my classes, and Nina—who lived nearby with her son, a marvelous little boy named Joshua whom she had adopted from El Salvador and who was from the first day she saw him in love with every experience life had to offer—would take care of Adam and Sava while I was away. I flew for the third time to Pierre and, that very afternoon, met my daughter Madeline. She was, as promised, perfection: wispy black hair, bright dark eyes, enormous cheeks that made her face look square as a Mayan god. She had been in a foster home since birth and, except for a nasty case of diaper rash, she was in excellent health. When I first saw her, she was dressed in pink organdy and sat, placid and serene, in the middle of a playpen. She had a natural reserve; she appeared to ask for nothing, but when a bottle or a cracker was placed in her hands, she was delighted. A few months later, Madeline's first two-syllable word was "goody," and she used it for every occasion.

"Time to get up, Madeline."

"Goody!"

"Lunch, Madeline."

"Goody!"

"Find your pajamas, Madeline."

"Goody!"

And she meant it too. In no time at all, Adam and Sava took their sister's presence for granted, Skahota endured yet another new set of exploring hands, and Sava's day care home made room for one more on three mornings a week. With Madeline's arrival the warp and woof of our family life seemed richer, more complicated, in gathering rhythm. In addition, my career was going well—a book and several more articles were published, my teaching evaluations were positive, an outside team of experts recommended that Native American Studies be made a permanent academic program at Dartmouth, and after six years on the faculty I was promoted from assistant to associate professor with tenure.

When I think back on that time, this is the scene that is conjured: at the sound of Adam's tread on the road Skahota barks eagerly, I take a sheet of steaming cookies out of the oven, and Sava pushes a chair to the table for Madeline. We always had cats living in our barn, usually named according to a prevailing theme—the most friendly were Sierra Madre, Sierra Leone, Sierra Blanca, and Sierra Nevada—and in this vision they stretch and prepare to join the party.

It is impossible that our lives were really so well ordered, so under control. On my old calendars I see the notation of many doctor visits, medical appointments in Boston. I constantly read books about learning theory and tried innovative experimental programs, searching for an approach that would be effective for Adam. My first inclination, a sort of 1960s flower child theory, was to be nonintrusive and natural, to let Adam find his own appropriate level, to allow him to be "free." I was inspired by a cartoon I had hung on the refrigerator. It showed a classroom in which all the students faced forward in perfect rows of desks—except for one American Indian student who sat on the floor and looked the other way. The exasperated (insensitive) teacher berated, "Why can't you be like other people?" Well, I was not going to be *that* guy! Beneath the caption I had written: "Don't worry if Adam: 1) wets his pants; 2) disrupts a group; 3) does sloppy activities; 4) refuses to do activities; 5) does nervous hand movements, etc.; 6) is grumpy; 7) hits; 8) takes a long time." I doubt if my good intentions lasted very long.

On the "positive reenforcement" front, I mimeographed a check-list of Adam's daily home and school activities, each of which, when executed, gained him a "star." A minimal accumulation of stars at the end of the day produced a "certificate," and a designated number of certificates could be spent, like money, for toys, fast food, or anything else he desired. The sheets, titled "Adam's Day," included such categories as "Sat Still at Breakfast," "Stayed Dry in the Morning," "Was Cheerful at ____," and "Got Undressed by Self."

The concept of saving, however, was lost on Adam, and still is. He is a living embodiment of the Roman poet Horace's adage "*Carpe diem*" ("Seize the day"). Tomorrow, as a concept, is no competition for *now,* and after a month or so of mixed results the lists were put aside. Denial of privilege was no more effective. There was nothing Adam wanted enough that the threat of its loss would alter his spontaneous behavior. If I said, "Adam, if you don't stay dry, you'll have to wear a diaper to school," he would, without embarrassment, wear a diaper. If I threatened to banish him to his room unless he sat still during an activity, he would accept the consequence without complaint—and *I* would feel like a rotten bully. Not that there weren't bursts of progress, whole weeks of operation on a new plateau in some area or another.

With total concentration, occasional hysteria, and insistent instruction, I could coerce, encourage, or manipulate Adam into modifying unacceptable behavior. But the moment I stopped pushing, ceased to monitor, he reverted to old habits. Nothing seemed "automatic" with him. There was no branching curiosity, no internal motivation to be more grown up, no quick building on previous experience, no secure gain. Regardless of how much energy I, or his teachers, expended, Adam, for the first hundred or so repetitions, always eventually wound up back at Go. His maturation was a pitched battle between our exhortation and his indifference, yet outwardly he remained serene, forgiving of adult frustration, content with and impervious to whatever new method we might employ.

Sweet disposition was Adam's talent, and it was so striking that it often obscured his lack of progress. In recent years I've wondered how I could have closed my eyes for so long to the fact that Adam had enduring disabilities—three years after his adoption I wrote a psychologist that I was "convinced that there is nothing permanently wrong with Adam. I'm sure you hear that from every parent with whom you work, but I think I've been open in making a judgment. . . . While it is obvious that he is developmentally young for his chronological age in certain areas, his improvements have been dramatic, erratic, and far more rapid than I would have predicted." I concluded my five single-spaced pages by noting: "I guess if I could wish one thing for him it would be for him to be more vulnerable—for disapproval and approval to matter more than they do—for him to get his kicks out of other people more. He has this insulation, and a good thing he did, of course, in his past, but it's time for it to come down a bit, and I need to know how to help him to trust. He is a sweet, loving, affectionate, and gentle boy—as nice a person as I've ever met."

A succession of teachers reacted the same way, as evidenced by the observations they sent home at the end of every school year. "Adam is a delightful boy and a real pleasure to have in my class," commented his third-grade teacher. "Adam is a very loving child. I enjoy working with him," said his fourth-grade instructor. "He's doing *so well* this year! It's hard to believe it's the same youngster," wrote the school principal at the beginning of the fifth grade. All these good men and women were determinedly optimistic. They praised Adam's "progress" in things like map making and social studies, his fondness for reading books, his great interest in art, the leaps he was making in friendships and self-control. They proclaimed his mastery of basic arithmetic ("He understands the process of addition and subtraction and has computed problems with the use of counters and the number line. . . . He has demonstrated good ability and understanding with regard to our unit on geometry"), vocabulary, telling time.

I saved these encomia in a scrapbook as an antidote to discouragement. They testified to what I wanted to believe, and I quoted them to psychologists and doctors and new homeroom teachers as proofs. It is only now, in retrospect, that I see them for what they were—collective delusion, wishful thinking. At no time in his life could Adam, by any stretch of the imagination, read a map or comprehend the principles of geometry. In eight years at the Cornish School he never once received so much as a telephone call or an invitation from a "friend." He never stayed in his seat for more than a few minutes unless he was supervised.

When Adam was young, people fell in love with him and with the idea of him. He was a living movie-of-the-week hero, an underdog who deserved a happy ending. On top of that, he had good manners, an appealing face, me to broker and block for him. He was the only full-blood Indian most people at his school had ever met. His learning problems at first appeared so marginal, so near to a solution. With just the smallest nudge they would pass over the line into the normal range. Every good teacher, every counselor, every summer camp director Adam encountered in grade school and high school viewed him as a winnable challenge and approached his education with initial gusto and determination. He teetered in his ability so close to the edge of "okay" that it seemed impossible that, with the proper impetus, he would not succeed. I understood this conviction perfectly and succumbed to it for fifteen years. I sometimes had the fantasy that if I could penetrate the fog that surrounded Adam's awareness and quickly explain what was what, he would be fine. He was just slightly out of focus.

The fact was, improvement was hard to come by and even harder to sustain once it had appeared. Reviewing those end-of-the-year teacher reports, it is now clear that in grade after grade Adam was working at the same level on exactly the same tasks. Every year he started fresh, showed promise up to a point, then couldn't take the next step. His learning curve resembled more than anything else one of those carnival strong-man games in which a platform is struck with a weighted mallet and a ball rises up a pole toward a bell. In my son's case, sometimes the bell rang, but then the ball always fell back to earth. He was the little engine that couldn't make it over the mountain, and, in frustration and disappointment, without ever actually saying so, all but a dedicated few eventually stopped thinking that his trip was worth their effort.

But what a few those were. It may sound odd to say it, but Adam has been in his life incredibly fortunate in some areas, and special education teachers are one of them. Olivia Alexion arrived at the Cornish Elementary School when Adam was in the second grade and led him through the maze of the next seven years with unflagging affection and devotion. She was very young, barely out of college, but possessed a patience and long view that perfectly equipped her for the job. Ms. Alexion was a realist who acted as though she had a short memory—that is, she had the ability to forget setbacks and to maintain steady optimism even when, year after year, she was required to repeat identical lessons for Adam. She and I formed a kind of conspiracy, an allegiance that sometimes demanded daily communication so that his victories at home or at school could be consolidated, built upon. We were the day and night shifts of the same factory, and Adam was on our assembly line, inching forward at a slow pace, but forward all the same. She wrote hundreds of notes about his activities, recorded each incremental step, celebrated each tentative advance, railed against each slippage. She believed as fiercely as I that Adam had unrealized resources. She was the antithesis of detached.

What was in it for her, I privately wondered now and then. Was it ego? Was it the will not to be defeated? She worked long hours for little pay and spent many evenings researching in the library to develop new techniques. At first I hesitated to sing her praises too loudly to other parents with children in special education—I didn't want to give away how much attention she was devoting to Adam— but it turned out that we all felt the same way about her. She concentrated on each of her students as if he or she were the only child in the world, and because of her each of them surpassed what had been regarded as maximum potential.

When Adam was halfway through the fourth grade, Ms. Alexion decided to schedule a WISC-R IQ test for him on a Saturday morning in January. She believed he had previously tested "low," and that in an ideal examination environment his scores would show significant improvement. She and I would sit in the room while Adam was questioned and this, she was sure, would alleviate his feelings of anxiety as well as mute his tendency to become easily distracted in any new situation.

The results, however, fell into the same range: a verbal IQ of 63–77; a performance IQ of 63–81; and a full-scale IQ of 64–76. As always, there was a wide scatter pattern. Adam scored best on picture completion and object assembly and lowest on block design, coding, and similarities. In other words, tasks that had to do with abstract reasoning were the most difficult for him.

This wasn't what I wanted to hear, so I all but dismissed the results in a long, rationalizing letter to Ms. Alexion. I noted that the WISC was "in significant part culture biased" in favor of "mainstream America"—as if Adam, the son of a Dartmouth professor, living in Cornish, New Hampshire, came from some exotic society. While allowing that, at age ten, such "terms as 'alike/different,' 'older/ younger' " were confusing to Adam, I brought all my anthropological mumbo jumbo into play in denying the accuracy of his scores: "The sequential arrangement of pictures to form a story that 'makes sense' depends for its validity on a shared understanding of proper organization. The idea of 'ordering' a story, rather than trying to make sense out of the existing order presented, reflects a Western sense of 'controlling' the world rather than the idea of dealing with the world 'as is.' " I was really cooking.

"The test stresses some types of performance over others," I protested. "The oft-repeated direction 'work as quickly as possible' has little meaning for a child raised to emphasize process rather than strict efficiency." Was that how I raised Adam? And yet, how persuasive I sounded to myself. I could explain anything where Adam was concerned. In my defense of him, his liabilities were nothing more than pointers to the fact that, as an Indian, he conceived the world in different, preferable, terms. To read the sheaf of my letters during those years one would gather I believed that Adam was lucky not to be able to tell time, to tell a nickel from a quarter from a penny, or to consistently discriminate between large and small. The world, American culture, individual assessors had the problems—Adam was just as he should be.

I must have been a formidable force for Adam's teachers to deal with as I tried to intellectually or culturally coerce them into sharing my views. I talked more than I listened, demanded reports of "progress," and vigorously protested any opinions that seemed to limit Adam's chances. To judge him lacking in innate ability, I darkly hinted, implied poor teaching, racism, or a defeatist attitude. My justification for pressure was rooted in my wish that Adam be all right, but it stemmed also from pride, from my arrogance, my terror.

I look back now at Adam's Cornish report cards, at all those *Satisfactory*'s and *C*'s in math and science and history that I had insisted appear, all those passing marks, when in truth he didn't grasp for more than a minute any of the material. To what extent was Adam's steady progress from one grade to another due to my bluster? How far did Ms. Alexion lead him by the hand? To what degree did his teachers, for liberal or self-image reasons of their own, need to believe that he should be granted the benefit of the doubt? Yet the further on paper Adam got ahead, the further he fell behind.

CHAPTER EIGHT

On the second Saturday of May 1979 I dressed Adam, Sava, and Madeline in their dance outfits and drove to the open field at Storrs Pond in Hanover for the annual Dartmouth powwow. I had attended every year since the first such celebration in 1973, and it was an event of song, dance, good food, and get-togethers with old friends to which we greatly looked forward. The previous autumn, on a visit to the Choctaw Reservation in Philadelphia, Mississippi, I had placed an order for new blue shirts for the boys and a bright red dress for Madeline. They arrived just in time and fit perfectly. Each was highlighted by the distinctive zigzag ticking that marked them as Choctaw, and the kids looked gorgeous. Madeline, at age four, had hair long enough for real braids, and our friend Eva Smith had sent her a shawl and the boys new feather bustles and shoulder harnesses—Adam's in pink and white, Sava's in yellow and black.

Not to be outdone, I donned an overabundance of my own finery: a dark blue satin shirt decorated with roses—a treasure I had found on sale at Macy's; a heavy, blue turquoise ring; soft deerskin moccasins from the Micmac reserve in Nova Scotia; and my proudest possession—the full-beaded floral vest I had worn for our naming ceremony. I wore a choker made of porcupine quills around my neck and topped myself off with a tan cowboy hat. I was *ready*.

This particular powwow was special because it was to include the first reunion of graduates who had been part of the Native American Program, and I anticipated seeing many former students now going to school or working at various jobs around the country. Butch Guerue had become a tribal judge on his home reservation of Rosebud.

Duane Bird Bear worked for the Environmental Protection Agency, and Eva was finishing medical school at Georgetown. No one had any idea how many of the old gang would show up, but it promised to be an interesting and emotional evening, starting with a reception in the Hanover Inn after the outdoor activities ended at six.

All three of my children danced that day. I stood watching and experienced such a pang of pleasure that it was hard to talk. None of the kids were champs by a long shot, but they were fearless, even Madeline, who gamely trudged and shuffled into the midst of the adult competition, dragging her new yellow shawl, dodging women contestants three times her size. Adam was a whirling blur, thrilled for once to be free to move in any erratic way he chose, and Sava, very serious, tried his best to imitate the maneuvers of the expert male fancy dancers. It was a glorious afternoon—warm and sunny— the spring after a long winter. There were booths selling fry bread and honey, corn soup, various crafts. The Program had survived at Dartmouth for the magical seven years. It had passed its internal and external evaluations and had attained a quasi-permanent official status. There was much to celebrate.

Later, in the cool and dimly lit lower meeting room of the Hanover Inn, while Adam, Sava, and Madeline slept in the corner on a stack of Pendleton blankets, I sipped a glass of punch and gossiped in an alcove with Butch and Cathy Wilson, then in law school at Arizona State. Familiar faces were everywhere, and we interspersed our conversation with waves across the room. There was a sense of shared relief, of that particular kind of first-time nostalgia that hits people in their twenties and early thirties when at last they understand what that vaunted emotion is all about. We congratulated each other on getting older because we were all still young enough to regard aging as an improvement, not yet as a decline. We were playing, to a certain extent, at mutual adulthood. The difference in age between me and my former students seemed to have collapsed, to have become less significant. We were more or less of a single generation now, me at one end and the youngest of them at the other, veterans of the same campaign.

A tall woman entered the room through the far door, and for a moment I couldn't place her. She was slim, graceful, had long brown hair, and was dressed in a plain rose calico jumper.

"Who's *that*?" I asked Cathy.

"Karen Erdrich. She's changed. I heard she goes by her middle name now. Louise. I wonder if she's still writing."

"Yes," I said. "I spoke to her on the phone about six months ago. She's the editor of the Boston Indian Council newspaper."

As Louise crossed the room toward where we were standing, various memories came back to me. We had arrived at Dartmouth in 1972, she as one of fifteen Native American freshmen in the first class in the school's history that matriculated women, and me as a first-year instructor, hired to establish the Native American Studies Program. We had attended a welcome picnic at a park along the Connecticut River, and she and I had found ourselves standing off to the side while some of the more energetic Indian students played volleyball. Her hair was arranged, early-seventies style, in a tight permanent that ringed her face, and she wore a miniskirt and red cowboy boots. After talking for a few minutes with Adam and me, she had imprudently offered to take Skahota for a romp. He was not used to a leash and seemed to regard it as a kind of sled harness. While she tried to look dignified and in control, he repeatedly towed her from one end of the park to the other.

Louise had mostly kept to herself as an undergraduate, but she had made a strong impression. She was an artist and had once offered to illustrate a short children's story I had written. Her drawings were bold, quirky, better than my text. At another time, when she was a student in a Native American Studies class, she had proposed that, instead of a term paper, she would produce a fictional account of the first meeting between the Delaware Indians and the Swedes, based on an actual historical incident that she had come across in her reading. It seemed that the governor of New Sweden (later Delaware), a self-aggrandizing bureaucrat, had commissioned local Indians to make an entire suit for him out of wampum, the shells used for money. He figured this would render him an impressive figure, worthy of great awe and respect. The price he offered was right, so he got his suit, but by the time it was completed, he had gained so much weight that his body had to be greased with butter before it would fit—and then it lasted intact only through his first deep breath. It was a great story, and Louise told it with a humor that somehow communicated both the poignancy and absurdity of contact between cultures.

Though I knew Louise less well than I did some of the students during her years at Dartmouth, we had been friends and shared in common the experience of being from mixed-blood backgrounds. We kept in touch by Christmas card notes and occasional phone calls after Louise graduated, returned to North Dakota, and was appointed a traveling poetry teacher as part of a state humanities program. Her assignment was to move from one small town to the next and conduct a two- or three-day poetry workshop in the local public school. Occasionally, she would call me from the road, from a tiny clapboard hotel on the plains, just to share a funny incident, like the time she stopped in a place that had two water towers, at either end of the main street. In a burst of creativity, each had been labeled with a word: one was "Hot" and the other "Cold."

In the three years after college, Louise had worked on a Nebraska Public Television film about Indians; she had attended the infamous trial of American Indian Movement defendants in Fargo; she had worked at a truck weigh station along an interstate. More recently, she had received a master's degree at the Writing Workshop of Johns Hopkins University and was now living in Boston. I hadn't actually seen her since 1975, and, except for a couple of undergraduate poems published in Dartmouth literary magazines and the children's story she had composed for my class, I had read nothing of her work.

Louise finally drifted to where Butch, Cathy, and I were standing. She wore no makeup, no jewelry except for dangling abalone earrings. She was the most beautiful woman I had ever seen.

"How's your boyfriend?" I asked, instantly regretting the first question that popped into my head. I had an idea she was still seeing the handsome sculptor she had dated as an undergraduate.

She shrugged. "It's a kind of rough time."

I tried my best to look sympathetic. I have no idea what else we said to each other during that first in-person catch-up conversation, but somewhere along the line I learned that Grace Newell, head of the Native American Program, had invited Louise to Dartmouth in two weeks to read her poetry, and that there was a chance that a year from January she might be in Hanover as a writer-in-residence.

Fourteen days later a baby-sitter watched my children while I sat in the first row of folding chairs at Collis, the campus building where "alternative" activities were scheduled, waiting for Louise's reading to begin. I was something of a philistine as far as modern poetry went—most of it, like a lot of classical music and jazz, forever seemed to be over my head. I hadn't mentioned this to Louise, of course. She was nervous about public performance, and I wanted to be a supportive old friend. I also wanted to make a good impression.

The lights dimmed, and Louise stepped behind the podium and opened a Manila folder. She was wearing a white blouse, a black skirt, brown boots, and the same earrings. She tapped the microphone with her finger to make sure it was on, then she took a deep breath and began.

I had never heard anything remotely like it. She started with a set of narrative poems about life in a small midwestern town. Characters, at once absolutely original and yet also familiar, came to life, fought, loved, died, were born. Vivid stories, tight and condensed as black holes in space, rolled forth one after the other. The emotions were archetypical, universal, baleful and tragic as Greek myths, yet they were set in the most ordinary of contexts and were all the more powerful for it. Next, while the audience was still stunned—nobody even thought to break the spell by clapping—Louise read a section of what she described as a novel-in-progress: the tale of a Chippewa woman who bested a group of men at a card game in a butcher shop and their fury over the loss. It was alternately hilarious and terribly sad, a building swirl of impressions that clung to the imagination with incredible power.

The lights went up, applause finally rang out, but I sat still, as dazed as if I had been hit over the head with a stick. Some English professors had arranged to take Louise into the dining area next door after her reading, and I followed. While they were going through the cafeteria line with their trays of herb teas and organic desserts, I touched Louise's elbow. "Do you want to visit in the lounge?" I whispered, as if she had nothing else to do.

She nodded and whispered back. "Okay."

Like spies about to make an information drop, we sneaked out, leaving the English professors to crane their necks and try to puzzle what had happened to Louise. She and I found a quiet corner with two chairs and a table and sat without saying very much. I had no proper vocabulary to describe my reaction to her writing or reading, and, after her stage fright, she was drained with relief. Finally, I drove her back to the house where she was staying. I turned off the ignition, and we sat for a moment in the dark car. I barely knew this woman, and yet it occurred to me to ask if she wanted to get married. To me. Crazy. Not like me at all. Instead, I just shook her hand when she got out of the car. Lightning romance, I firmly believed, only happened in the movies or in bad paperbacks, and besides, the kids and I were all set to go to New Zealand for nine months in about a week's time—I had been awarded a research fellowship. There was no chance in the world that anything but friendship could develop between Louise and me, yet I did ask for her address and gave her mine in the Southern Hemisphere.

Much, much later my mother-in-law confided to me that her daughter had called her late that very night, had gotten her out of bed.

"You won't believe this," Louise had said. "But I met the man I'm going to marry."

The children and I rented a car, drove to JFK airport, flew to Los Angeles, changed planes, and flew to Avarua in the Cook Islands, where we broke our trip for a few days in a palm-thatched guest house on a perfect, empty beach. At mealtimes we ate breadfruit, papayas, and fish caught by the man who lived next door. It was paradise-as-advertised, with brilliant starry nights under the Southern Cross, friendly local people, and sunrises that could break your heart. In the afternoons while the children napped under palm fronds, I organized my notes and made plans for my proposed study, a comparison of the Treaty of Waitangi, the solemn pact between Maoris and the British, with analogous U.S.-American Indian agreements.

The months immediately preceding our departure had been hectic. I was finishing my part of an extensive bibliography for the American Library Association, eventually published as *A Guide to Research on North American Indians,* and also had to prepare our house for sublet. I applied to go to New Zealand because, among other things, it had a reputation for being progressive in special education. I thought the experience of living there might be good for Adam, as well as for Sava and Madeline. We had arranged by mail to rent a house on the grounds of a Baptist seminary in a quiet residential neighborhood, and the University of Auckland had offered me an office and library privileges in the Department of Maori Studies.

Adam, Sava, and Madeline enrolled at the Victoria Avenue School, presided over by Miss Bishop, a meticulous and rather reserved headmistress. There was a great deal for the kids to get used to—short pants uniforms for boys, a new set of idioms and accents, a bevy of misconceptions about American Indians—but the transition was relatively easy. The children's school was less than a mile's walk away, and I could arrange my schedule at the university to be home before them every afternoon.

Madeline and Sava, in particular, made friends easily, as they had in New Hampshire, but for Adam, Victoria Avenue was simply another version of Cornish. The teachers reported identical problems—he wouldn't stay in his seat, he had a very limited attention span, he had no mastery of "the basics" of mathematics or a grasp of general knowledge. And they praised him for the same familiar qualities—a sweet disposition, politeness, a great wellspring of energy. He was put back a grade, spent time in the resource room, but made only fitful progress. Several times he lost his way walking home, even though the school and the seminary were on the same street, and his response to any new experience was one of increasing wariness or indifference. He was agreeable to the trips we took, but he had little reaction to places or people we encountered. I made the rounds of the usual specialists—neurologists, psychologists, learning theorists—but they produced no new insights.

On the broadest of conceptual levels, Adam had no idea where he was and had no particular interest in finding out. A situation was comfortable for him when it became rote, troubling and ignorable when it wasn't. More than most of us, he carried his world inside his head and imposed it when possible wherever he was. His enthusiasms were all in the area of expressed affection—he could be counted on for an embrace, an exuberant response to being tickled or swung in the air, but there was no engaging him in conversation. The extent to which he paid no heed to the details of his environment was truly staggering; he had never absorbed much of the minutiae of information that for most people form the basis for common sense. After seven years of formal education, most of that with intensive professional tutoring, he was unable to make change for a dollar, avoid a mud puddle if it lay in his path, or discriminate between a clean and a dirty dish.

The months in New Zealand passed quickly and, for me, productively. Maoris had, if anything, a less protected legal status under their Waitangi compact than American Indians enjoyed under federal treaties, and yet there persisted throughout much of the country a firm belief that relations between indigenous Polynesians and the descendents of English immigrants (called *pakehas,* or "white turnips" in the Maori vernacular) were by far the best on the planet, a shining example of inter-ethnic harmony for all to follow. We were invited to a number of *marais,* the traditional meetinghouses of Maori clans, and I exchanged stories late into the night, trading tribal mythologies and survival strategies, jokes, and recipes. I delivered a series of lectures at the universities in Auckland and Wellington and collected boxes of notes, photocopies, and clippings. During the children's school vacation we used rail passes to travel with a friend from Dartmouth throughout the South Island, from the glaciers to the sea coasts to the ski regions. Finally in December, at the peak of the subequatorial summer, we flew to Australia for a week and then home to the United States.

I was glad to be back. One thing I had missed in New Zealand was the easy garrulousness of most Americans—the casual habit of strangers speaking to each other at a coach stop or in the checkout line of a supermarket. And so, since there was not much of my grant money remaining by the time we landed in Los Angeles, I rationalized that it would be fun to take the bus across country. I wanted to be in touch with "the people," to feel the pulse of my native land, I told myself, and besides, it was dirt cheap. Forget the fact that we had nineteen pieces of luggage to worry about. Forget the fact that Adam was not all that easy to manage and that Sava and Madeline were at the time eight and five years old, respectively. Forget the fact that in the Northern Hemisphere, December was not the warm season. Nina, who now lived in L.A. with her son Joshua and daughter Natalia, drove us to the Greyhound station and commented that my whole idea was a weird combination of Jack Kerouac and Erma Bombeck.

That trip was an education. I began to suspect something in those initial dark hours as we crossed the desert toward Arizona, a suspicion which was repeatedly confirmed on the many subsequent days and nights as we headed northeast—namely, that a bus company official searched each terminal for the strangest individual and awarded him or her a free passage to anywhere. Perhaps this was done by way of providing a floor show for the other, normally sedate passengers, I don't know. But it invariably worked out that Mr. or Ms. Nutzo presided in close proximity to the traveling Dorrises. I tried to position Sava and Adam on the seats directly in front of Madeline and me so that I could keep an eye on them, make certain Adam didn't have a seizure, be certain they were covered with their coats at night.

The first evening out we, and the rest of the bus, were treated to a long commentary about the pros and cons of sadomasochism, delivered by a woman enthroned diagonally across from us. In her opinion, the balance definitely tipped in favor of a few whips and chains. On another occasion there was the man with an illegal cat under his shirt. He had to be physically ejected in Springfield, Missouri, and then stood outside the bus demanding that we, his fellow passengers, be the judges. As the sun rose on the leg from Indianapolis to Louisville, I watched, fascinated, as a slinky transvestite picked up an—I presumed—unwitting Hoosier. They eventually, but not soon enough, asked the driver to let the two of them off at a deserted spot along the highway before we crossed the Ohio River, and for miles I tried to picture the startled look inevitably bound to light the Hoosier's face. From Pittsburgh to Port Authority terminal in Manhattan all the travelers except for us seemed to be armed with huge boom boxes, which they blasted at top volume on competing stations.

Other than the unavoidable stiffness in my back, I loved every minute of the ride. The kids and I ate chili for breakfast out of thick white bowls at wind-battered stations in western New Mexico, played nonstop spot the license plate games across Oklahoma. A disagreeable word did not pass between the four of us for three thousand miles. We visited friends and family all along the way, sometimes only briefly between connections and sometimes overnight. By the afternoon we arrived in New York, a two-day pause before our last change of buses, I was ready for the trip to be over, and abruptly it was: the newspaper headlines were full of John Lennon's murder, and on a cold, raw night I left the kids with my Aunt Ginny and joined hundreds of others in a silent vigil outside the Dakota, the apartment house where he had lived.

On an afternoon shortly before Christmas we boarded a green-and-white Vermont Transit bus and headed north through a countryside covered in snow. It was familiar territory, the completion of the loop of our journey. All nineteen bags—filled with everything from Cook Island seashells to copies of Maori-related statutes—were accounted for. We were healthy, renewed, anxious to see Skahota, our house, our neighbors. And for me, something more: Louise was scheduled to arrive the next day to begin her appointment as writer-in-residence.

She and I had corresponded weekly during the past seven months, often enclosing souvenirs with our letters. Initially, she sent me leaves from the MacDowell Artist's Colony, where she was reworking her manuscripts, and I reciprocated with South Seas postcards of unusual plants and birds. But an unexpected thing had happened: away for the first time in years from the pressures and demands of my Dartmouth job, I had begun to write poetry and short stories. I had been published now and then in college magazines while I was an undergraduate at Georgetown, but my work had never caused much notice, and once I embarked on the process of graduate school, anthropological research in Alaska, and full-time teaching, I never seemed to find the time or the inspiration that creative writing demanded.

Now, suddenly, it was all I wanted to do. I'm sure I was in part inspired by Louise's example—she was the first person I knew well who was a "real" writer. In any event, I began to send her pages of my compositions along with my letters, and she in turn sent me poems and stories of her own. The nature of our friendship—its possible ramifications—went nervously unacknowledged, only vaguely hinted at, in this exchange, so it was a relief for us to have something upon which to focus, and we fell into the habit of writing long commentaries on each other's drafts. From the outset each of us was frank and honest—we praised what we liked and questioned what we didn't. And every excruciating criticism Louise made, I had to admit, was right on the money.

I brought Adam, Sava, and Madeline with me when I went to the Lebanon Airport to meet Louise's flight from Fargo, via Boston. I wanted her to begin to know the kids, and they her. She remembered Adam from her undergraduate days, of course, and had met Sava and Madeline at the powwow almost a year before. I had talked to and written her about each of them, about Adam's health and school difficulties especially, but if she was going to get to know me better, it could only happen within the context of the children. They and I were a package, a unit bound together by years of interdependence and affection.

I was late, or the plane was early. When I stopped the car in front of the glass wall of the terminal, I saw Louise immediately. She was alone standing by a yellow metal trunk, facing away from me, and wore a long black coat. I hesitated for a moment, watching her, before opening the door. It was the night of her poetry reading all over again. We had never been out on a date, never said a non-oblique word of affection to each other. I knew her better through her fiction than through any real time spent together. And once again all I could think of was to propose marriage. I took a deep breath. I didn't want her to decide I was crazy, didn't want to scare her off. That night, while Adam, Sava, and Madeline slept on the bed in the Hanover apartment she had rented, Louise and I talked about our manuscripts until four in the morning, then I took the kids and went home. The next night she came out to our house for dinner and stayed—us still talking editorial fine points—until 3:00 A.M. It went on like that for what seemed to both of us like quite a while. By the time the question of matrimony finally came up, it was only a matter of when.

Louise's family background was Turtle Mountain Chippewa on her mother's side and German-American on her father's, and she was the eldest of seven brothers and sisters, the youngest of whom was only a couple of years older than Adam. She was used to dealing with children, and so approached the issue of her impending motherhood with equanimity and enthusiasm. There were so many adjustments to be made in both of our lives—the abandonment of the self-image of being single, among the most imposing—that neither she nor I had concentrated much worry on the particulars. We loved each other, she loved the children, they loved her. The working-it-out part would naturally follow.

I did wonder, after so many years of having me completely to themselves, if the kids would be hesitant about accepting another adult permanently into their lives. I introduced the subject one night after the children and I had finished a dinner capped by blackberry pie. Adam was thirteen, Sava was nine, and Madeline was six.

"We've got something to talk about," I said, dozens of TV sit-com precedents whirring in my brain. I had watched this scene played many times: the opening episodes of "The Brady Bunch" or "Eight Is Enough"; the many false alarms on "The Courtship of Eddie's Father." There was a pause while I waited for their attention, and in the quiet I realized a new dimension to the situation. The announcement I was about to make was the end of a long chapter in my life. A single parent was *who I was;* over the past decade, it had become my identity in a very basic sense, a source of power and self-definition, a proclamation to the world on the subject of the male capacity for nurturing, an against-the-odds achievement that was the accomplishment on which I relied when everything else went wrong. The decision to become an adoptive father was the part of my past about which I had never harbored a regret or a second thought. Without that secure status I would, in a sense, have to start over in the construction of my private vision of self. There was no denying it—the feeling that welled up in me at that moment, within the general context of excitement and anticipation for the future, was the sharp grief of departure. I would never again be the only important person in my children's lives. This moment was a border that, once crossed, would be forever closed.

"In October," I said, "Louise and I and you are all going to get married. She'll live here and wants to become your mother."

"What will she eat?" asked Madeline, not skipping a beat and regarding protectively the one piece of pie left in the pan.

I looked at my daughter. Was this question an obfuscation for a deep-seated terror of rejection? Did she fear that she would be replaced? I studied Madeline's face. Her eyebrows were drawn tight in concentration. Her mouth looked slightly belligerent. Her chin was raised. Her only dread, I realized, had to do with a particular slice of pie.

"The meals will be bigger when Louise is here," I reassured her. "She'll eat the same things that we do."

Madeline smiled, a great burden lifted.

"I knew it," Sava announced smugly. "I told you they were, Madeline." He was proud to be right, unfazed by any changes this move might signal.

I turned to Adam, waited for him to speak. Of the three, he was from the beginning the most spontaneously affectionate with Louise, but he was also the child most bonded to me. Now he took his cue from his brother and sister and without a word began to clap his hands, cupping his palms for amplification. The sounds boomed through the air, little explosions like the pop of fireworks. Irresistible . . . and one by one, the rest of us joined in.

We got married in the fall of 1981—the five of us—between two weeping willows in the freshly mowed backyard. Present were a few friends, Louise's sister Heidi, and a justice of the peace. We had asked for a simple ceremony, and that's what we got—it took all of five minutes, including the part we wrote ourselves, the part in which we promised to be good to the kids and they promised to be nice to us. It was a sunny day in a year when the colored leaves had lasted a long time on the trees. Louise's mother had made her dress and sent it from North Dakota, and I had ordered a bridal bouquet made from anemones and roses. Our house overflowed with flowers, the thoughtful donation of a practical neighbor who had brought them from a funeral home so they wouldn't go to waste.

Adam was the first of the children to call Louise "Mom," and once he began, sometime that first winter, he injected the word into every sentence he spoke. His transition back to school, however, was bumpier. We had returned to New Hampshire from the South Pacific in December, just as the Southern Hemisphere was entering its summer vacation. In New England, however, the school year was in full swing, and as a result, the children had only a short break between virtually twelve straight months of classes. Adam's grade level was ambiguous, but it was agreed that he would spend one additional full year in Cornish before beginning high school. Everyone—Ms. Alexion, the principal, and I—felt that this extra time would give him security and an extra cushion.

For the first two years of marriage, we were a family in the midst of merging the several lines of our individual lives. Louise determinedly attended conferences with Sava's and Madeline's teachers and joined me at various of their grade-school pageants and productions. There were innumerable sports events that demanded our presence, but the night I remember best was the ancient Roman extravaganza in which moms and dads were served spaghetti and grape juice by their toga-clad offspring. We sat with other parents at long cafeteria tables in the town hall and applauded as verses were recited in halting Latin. The *pièce de résistance* of the evening was a dramatic skit entitled "Persephone's Dilemma," in which the goddess of spring waffled endlessly about whether to stay in the underworld with her husband or join her mother "upstairs."

After half a decade of rejection slips from magazines and literary journals, Louise's short stories had finally begun to be published. In order that she could write full time, I accepted an additional job as director of Dartmouth's liberal studies graduate program, which operated primarily during the summer terms. I further supplemented our income with occasional consulting and lecturing trips that took me to Indian communities as far away as Alaska, California, and New Mexico for brief, intense visits.

All the while we had in our minds a whole set of clichés having to do with turning corners, crossing lines, tying up loose ends, becoming a single unit. In December of 1982, in the judge's chambers of our local county seat, Louise legally adopted my children. I listened as Adam's, then Sava's, then Madeline's name was read, heard them say yes, and watched as each child in turn was embraced by Louise. As she and they signed their names to papers that formalized the pact we had already begun to live, my eyes followed the line of ornate woodwork that bordered every wall of the room. The surface gleamed with wax, and the corner joints were fitted together so seamlessly that the carved pattern appeared unbroken, as if it had been crafted from an enormous tree. On our way home we stopped at a restaurant for clam chowder and toasted each other, one and all, with steaming, raised spoons.

Louise was anxious for her parents, brothers, and sisters to know Adam, Sava, and Madeline, so, though three months pregnant, in July she took the children to North Dakota for a two-week visit. She drove our old and dilapidated Chevrolet Malibu and made the acquaintance of many a mechanic along the route through Ontario, Michigan, and Minnesota. Then, when she returned in August, our well ran dry. We could not afford to have another one dug, so for seven weeks, while waiting for a replenishing rain, we ported the ubiquitous milk cans from the plentiful water supply of the Dartmouth gym. We ate lots of TV dinners and fruit because that meant we didn't have plates to wash.

When in the spring of 1983 Adam "graduated" from the Cornish Elementary School, he still could not add, subtract, count money, or consistently identify the town, state, country, or planet of his residence. Ms. Alexion had taken a leave of absence due to failing health, and everyone agreed that Adam was too old to repeat yet another primary-school grade. Delay would accomplish nothing. His next step, therefore, was Stevens High School in Claremont, New Hampshire, a thirty-minute ride away.

One June afternoon, Louise and I, with Mrs. Storrs—the new special education teacher and, coincidentally, the daughter-in-law of Adam's first Hanover doctor—met with the Stevens staff to explain what we knew of Adam's learning problems and came face to face with a group of people absolutely confident in their ability to succeed.

"I have never failed in twenty years," a woman who taught social studies proclaimed. "I have this unbendable rule: one staircase goes up, the other goes down. I stand at the top and direct traffic."

Louise and I glanced at each other, unsure if this statement was intended as fact, as metaphor, or as a reference to the Sandy Dennis movie, but did not dare ask in the face of so much experience and self-assurance. We obligingly filled out Adam's course cards: two hours in the resource room, basic math, civics (managed by the woman with the unblemished record), PE, English. We bought Adam a new wardrobe, peppered the remaining summer months with optimistic projections, and crossed our fingers in the hope that all he needed for success was a new environment, more responsibility, a fresh start with higher expectations.

Things, however, did not go smoothly, beginning with the school bus at the end of the day. On some afternoons Adam missed it altogether; on others he boarded the wrong one and rode to the end of the line in a direction opposite to ours. Every four o'clock was a question mark, a distraction: would Adam show up at home? Would the phone ring? Would *we* have to get on the phone to track him down? Then there was the issue of homework. Midway through the fall, Adam had a test on the mechanics of government. His teacher transmitted a stern note instructing us to coach him on four chapters in particular. He *had* to pass, she said. The first section dealt with, among other things, the Senate Rules Committee.

Poor Adam. Louise and I operated like a tag team throughout that weekend, each of us drilling facts at Adam in tandem until we couldn't stand it any longer. We might as well have been speaking Tagalog—nothing penetrated. The totality of Adam's incomprehension frightened us, I think. We became obsessive, as if the only thing in the world worth knowing was the procedure by which a bill got to the floor of the House. Civics took on, for us, the aura of Truth, and we were in a contest. If Adam could learn this, which as a freshman he was expected to do, then he had hope of an independent future. We were fighting for his life and lost every ounce of perspective we possessed. We yelled, we shouted, we begged, we threatened, we wheedled, we cried, we applauded each chance correct response. The Weekend of the Rules Committee was in a sense our last stand for normalcy, and in making it we became crazed, unfair, the worst kind of parents. By Monday Adam and we were shell-shocked, mentally gaunt, dispirited, and exhausted. On his test Adam didn't get a single answer right. The teacher forwarded the paper in a sealed envelope with another note, this one with a logo of a frowning face: "I *asked* you to help him on this."

But she got hers. After January I wrote a long letter to the principal expressing our concern that Adam seemed unhappy and was making little progress. The next day the telephone rang.

"I received your letter," the principal announced. "It was *typed*." This last was said in a tone of accusation. "I have scheduled a team conference with all the teachers and the district superintendent for next Tuesday."

I never did figure out why typing was so much more alarming than handwriting, but my letter put the school system on red alert, and the meeting was fully attended. The faces that confronted us as we walked into the room were defensive, less than friendly, and for the next hour we listened to a recital of Adam's failures, shortcomings, recalcitrance. He was uncooperative, willful, stubborn, and careless. He continually forgot the combination for his locker, he touched other students "inappropriately," he was perpetually late to class, he ate his lunch before arriving at school, he would not stay in his seat, he did not ask questions about the math facts he didn't know. When, at our suggestion, they had found Adam a training job at a day care center, he fought with four-year-olds over who got to play with the blocks. Yet he had the *ability*, each teacher stressed—he simply didn't choose to use it. It wasn't so much that Adam *did* anything so bad, but that he was passive toward learning, incurious, maddening in his intellectual immobility. Administrators, counselors, instructors, and staff vied with each other to parade their fruitless efforts, to lodge their complaints, to appeal to our sympathy.

"Every day I stand on the second-floor landing between periods," the civics teacher's voice rang out. "And every day *he* breaks the pattern, disrupts the flow. I see this *disturbance*, and it's *him*, going down the up, up the down. It throws everyone off. No matter how often I instruct him he gets it wrong." The woman's voice shook. She was unhinged.

"What do you suggest?" we asked. Confronted with such unbottled anguish we felt subdued, almost apologetic. We had experienced the frustrations these people were describing but were unnerved in hearing them expressed by a group who only months before had been positively smug.

"Send him to a psychologist," they seemed to say in unison. "Once, twice, three times a week. Here's one we recommend. Young, full of ideas, a Ph.D. We've spoken to her already. She'll find out why he's so resistant."

Adam had an initial session with this woman, and then Louise and I went to see her, told her for two hours our version of Adam's history while she made notes. She was sure she could help our son, she said at last. She had heard many stories like his before. His IQ tested in the dull-normal range, and so there was a sufficient mental capacity— he *could* pass his courses. Moreover, he had liked her, connected with her, in their conversation. They had achieved rapport. He probably had a low self-image, perhaps stemming from being an adopted child. Her shirttail theory, preliminary she emphasized, was that all he needed was encouragement, trust, acceptance. There was no missing the direction of the verbal finger she pointed, but we were beyond the stage of flinching. If we were Adam's problem: great. We could change, be whatever it took. The psychologist scheduled Adam for extensive private sessions every Monday, Wednesday, and Friday afternoons. Louise and I would be summoned when she had something concrete to report. And one other thing: she did not take Blue Cross.

We went home, encouraged once again because someone in authority had affirmed that Adam's problems were correctable. Furthermore, we were glad that Adam had a new outlet for expressing his emotions. He would need it. A few months ago we had learned that Ms. Alexion, at age thirty, had been diagnosed with terminal cancer. Despite the pain of her many operations, she continued to maintain contact with Adam, closely followed his program, offered advice until, to the grief and sorrow of all who knew her, she died. It was a sad time for everyone, but especially for Adam. Ms. Alexion had been his teacher, his prod, his applause, his measure, for eight years, and she more than anyone was responsible for the growth he had demonstrated in the classroom.

Months passed, and the only communication we received from the psychologist came in the form of bills. We saw no improvements in school performance, but what did we know? Adam's breakthrough might come at any moment, and we didn't want to throw things off track by being precipitous or pushy. Finally, in May, as the spring semester was about to close, and when our son had achieved passing grades only in his resource room courses, we made a second appointment ourselves.

"I'm glad you came in," the psychologist began. "I'm afraid there's nothing I can do for Adam, but I think he's enjoyed our talks." We waited, expecting something more, but the silence in the room lengthened.

"That's it?" I demanded. "But surely you have some advice. What about sex education, for instance? How should we approach the topic of sexuality with Adam? He's just reaching puberty."

"That *is* an issue," she agreed.

"Should he stay at Stevens High School? Have you seen progress?"

She shook her head, closed her eyes in contemplation. "It's hard to figure. He *should* be capable of better work, but . . ."

"Is it us, then?" Louise asked. "Are we doing something wrong?"

"Adam is very fond of you," the woman said. He's almost *too* well-adjusted, *too* secure. He assumes you'll always take care of him. Perhaps that's why he doesn't strike out more on his own."

"Are you suggesting that we shake his faith?"

"Oh, no. He's basically a sweet boy." She stood up, signaling that she had nothing further to add.

"Will you send us a written report and evaluation?" I asked. "After all these weeks, you must have some pragmatic suggestions."

"Of course," she smiled. She seemed anxious for us to leave, so we did. With the exception of a one-page summary of our conversation and a report of Adam's test results—his IQ remained steady at 65—we never heard from her again.

Halfway into Adam's first trip through the ninth grade, Louise's volume of poetry, *Jacklight,* came out to good reviews in 1984, and a week later our daughter Persia was born. In the same month a New

York publisher accepted Louise's first novel, *Love Medicine*. My *Guide to Research* received a citation as an outstanding academic book of the year. Our family life was full, exciting, unpredictable, in full flower. Persia was a happy, rewarding baby, content to sleep in a Snugli against either of her parents' chests while they wrote. Adam, Sava, and Madeline were affectionate elder siblings, gentle and attentive.

During the summer after Adam's frustrating year at Stevens, Louise and I tried unsuccessfully to find him a job, if only to occupy his time. He spent two weeks at a YMCA camp, but otherwise had nothing to do, no real interests other than his proclaimed "hobby" of stacking wood. He had a desultory attitude toward the various chores we assigned him, until by accident we hit on a job that engaged him completely: uprooting the burdock plants that proliferated on our property despite our unceasing efforts to stem their inexorable tide across the fields.

We impressed upon Adam how important was his contribution. Without his help, we said, our property would be overcome with the prickly weeds, and Adam assumed the mantle of responsibility with uncharacteristic zeal. Once he focused on a task, we had previously observed, he tackled it in bursts of such monomania that he often forgot to eat and would expend himself until he nearly fainted with exhaustion. Moderation was a middle road he didn't understand, and it was as hard to get him to stop work, as it initially had been to get him going. That summer, fighting burdocks became his crusade. Sometimes late at night he would creep from the house to find seedlings, and there were mornings he began his patrol before dawn. But burdocks were a worthy opponent. No matter how many wheelbarrow-loads of tan stalks Adam dumped into the trash pile, there were always more hearty plants to dig.

Late in August Louise and I met with the principal of the Cornish School—the district still "responsible" for Adam—and he suggested we transfer our son to the Vocational Education Program at Hartford High, White River Junction, Vermont. There he would be part of a small group of students, all of whom had handicaps of one kind or another. We met with the director, Ken Kramberg, a low-key young man who surprised us by actually listening to what we had to say. The first question he asked was whether it mattered to us if Adam eventually was awarded a high school diploma. Would we be satisfied if, at the end of four or five years, he received a certificate of attendance and could hold a full-time job?

"After looking at his scores and talking to Adam, I think he has a real shot at a mostly independent adulthood," Ken said. "But I wouldn't want to bet on his ever passing geometry." Ken's was the voice of reason, and we gave our full approval to the program he proposed.

Hartford High's philosophy was practical, at the other end of the spectrum from the Rules Committee approach. In addition to some academic classes, Adam would have an extensive daily course in "survival skills": how to shop for groceries, do the laundry, cook simple meals, fill out an application, take the bus, choose which clothes to wear, and clip his nails without being told. After a year or so he would be placed in part-time employment, monitored on-site by the school staff. Adam would rotate through a variety of possible occupations for which he might eventually qualify: inventory clerk, grounds maintenance, assembly line operation, food preparation. A match would be sought between his interests and his abilities, and when that was found, the training would become intensive, specialized. The goal, by the time he was twenty-one, was a regular paycheck, an apartment, a start to a satisfying life.

It was a long commute from Cornish to Hartford—Adam had to leave the house by six-fifteen and didn't get home until after five, but we saw an almost immediate improvement in his attitude. For one thing, the abandonment of the quest for a diploma meant that he had no more homework, and that alone relieved a great deal of tension and frustration in our household. Released from the grind and despair of the previous year, Louise and I suddenly had our evenings and weekends returned to us—to spend with the other children and with each other. We felt energetic, enthusiastic. The nagging sense of constant failure—ours as well as our older son's—was replaced with moderate expectations, optimism, a sense that we were at last on the right track. By the time our third daughter, Pallas, was born in April of 1985, our day-to-day family life seemed temporarily to have attained a modicum of balance and direction, and we took advantage.

CHAPTER NINE

In 1982, while in the Twin Cities to deliver a lecture at the University of Minnesota, I had paid a courtesy call to Stan Shepard, a program officer at the Bush Foundation. The Native American Studies Program at Dartmouth was forever on the lookout for new sources of funding, and Bush had a reputation for having an interest in American Indian higher education. Our conversation produced no grants to my program—the foundation for the most part confined its philanthropic activities to the states of the upper Midwest—but it did result in an invitation that was to have a profound and enduring impact on my understanding of Adam's condition.

Stan proposed that I join him on several of his upcoming trips to South Dakota reservations. As a matter of policy, Bush staff members, accompanied by one or two outside consultants, normally did a site interview with each organization that had a pending application for financial support. While I was by no means an expert on tribal matters in South Dakota, I did have academic credentials and some experience in the general area of Indian affairs.

I was glad for the opportunity to visit the West, to take a break from the routine of teaching. I missed being among adult Indians, missed the staccato cadence of speech, the gentle in-jokes, enjoyed the long drives through almost empty country. When you've lived for a while as a part of one tribal community in North America, any reservation can have the feel of home to it. Louise did her writing at our farmhouse, seated at a high stool before a desk made from a spare door. The children were all in school, and so when the Bush invitation came, for the first time in ten years I felt completely free to accept, with no anxiety or guilt, an interesting job that kept me away overnight.

The Holiday Inn in Rapid City might as well be ten thousand miles from the village of Pine Ridge on the huge Sioux reservation of the same name, but on good days it takes only two hours to drive between the two. The road, that early spring morning as Stan and I set out, was the warmest spot on the land, a wet, black Magic-Marker line upon which the snow had melted faster than it had on the scruffy range that stretched on either side. The route south winds through a corner of the Badlands, turns to skate the edges of jagged arroyos and undercuts sheer bluffs as barren during seasons of cold or drought as any desert.

And yet everywhere there was the rush of life. Prairie dogs stretched upright like sentries to watch the approach of our rented car, then dove for cover so late that only a glance in the rearview mirror confirmed their escape. The silhouettes of deer surfaced now and then on the peripheral rises, fragile dark cutouts outlined by sky. Overhead, eagles and red-tailed hawks made tangents to the circle of approaching, dissolving horizon which on the high plains, or at sea, so perfectly describes the curve of the earth. In the leased fields cattle grazed with their noses pressed to the ground, their satin lips pulled back into smiles that allowed their teeth to scrape for frozen grass. Stan and I had been told to watch for antelope, for elk, but saw instead only the cartoon-flat impressions of rattlers, a stationary parade of snakes. Hung over from the long winter, lulled by the sun, they had dozed on this north-south highway and were crushed beneath the wheels of speeding pickups, dawn delivery trucks, low-slung vintage Pontiacs, peeling from one out-of-the-way dot on a large map to another.

The only stations we could receive without static were country and western or National Public Radio, a curious rivalry of heart and mind that somehow complemented each other in the steady, uninterrupted turn of miles. There was time for both. We crossed the reservation boundary, an invisible divide just shy of the Long Branch Saloon in Scenic, the single enterprise along the way. It was a combination bar and emporium that retained, like a memory that couldn't be reconciled, one sign forbidding Indians to enter and another offering beadwork for sale within. Behind the building stretched a tangle of smashed cars, their bright paint turning monochrome in the constant assault of weather.

Our destination was a rehabilitation and treatment center for teenagers with "chemical dependencies," the only such facility, according to its application for Bush assistance, on any reservation in North or South Dakota, Nebraska, Wyoming, or Montana. Project Phoenix had maximum occupancy of under twenty beds, a capacity far too small for the demand. Its population arrived as referrals from tribal courts, boys and girls at the end of their rope at fourteen or fifteen, children addicted not only to alcohol or conventional drugs, but to those very popular reservation highs, favored only in communities so poor that nothing else is available: "huffing" (the inhalation of fumes from a gas tank); glue; clear nail polish; dimestore perfume; Sterno, rubbing alcohol. These were the hard-case kids, the ones with no place else to go, and there was an ever-expanding waiting list. In the budget cuts to Indian health care, already begun under the new Reagan administration and soon to double, triple, Project Phoenix was the last stop. It was go there, or sleep in abandoned cars. It was there or tribal jail, a single-cell lock-up that housed adults and juveniles together, regardless of the nature of the offense. It was there or nowhere.

As we drove the county roads toward Kyle, Stan and I reviewed the nightmare statistics and wondered, could the crisis be this bad? Was this the language of hyperbole, of a sharp-cookie administrator who knew how to push the right buttons of a St. Paul foundation? We believed that we had no illusions about the extreme deprivations on Pine Ridge, Cheyenne River, Rosebud, and yet . . . the conditions described in the narrative sounded like something out of *The Inferno*. This was America, this was the Reagan eighties, the me-decade. Pine Ridge had, in the eyes of the Supreme Court of the United States, the status of a nation, a government-to-government relationship with Washington.

We took the turnoff onto a potholed road that led to the jail, a small, squat modern building with a brick and glass facade. Next door, as if underlining the words we had just spoken, contradicting the doubts we had expressed, was a ragtag cluster of battered mobile homes, a prefabricated house, a few parked pickups. Over the entrance, a knocked-together wooden platform with a mat for wiping muddy boots, was a sign, PROJECT PHOENIX. The director, a smiling

Sioux man of about forty, stepped out to greet us. He wore glasses, had a breast pocket full of pens clipped onto a plastic lining to protect his shirt from ink stains. The staff had been worried about us, he said. They had expected us earlier. They had fixed a dinner in our honor, and we'd better eat soon or it would be spoiled.

Stan apologized—we had miscalculated the time it would take—and we followed the man through the door into what he called the common room, the place alternately used for group counseling and television, for in-take and recreation. The room was empty of people. Its walls were lined with cheap couches, with plastic lounge chairs. Coffee tables were laden with clean ashtrays and neatly stacked magazines. The linoleum floor was spotless: we had indeed been expected. On the panel-board walls were posters—many of them featuring Indian-looking characters—warning against addictions of every type.

There was a noise behind us, and I moved to make room for three young boys, "clients" the director called them, to enter. Ignoring our presence, they turned on the TV, dropped onto chairs and couches, and stared straight ahead.

I stared too. They could have been Adam's twin brothers. They resembled him in every facial feature, in every gesture, in body type. They came from a living situation as different as possible from an eighteenth-century farmhouse in rural New Hampshire; they were bare survivors of family crisis, of violence, of abuse—otherwise they wouldn't be at Project Phoenix—and Adam, after the dislocations of his first three years, had been protected, defined as "special," monitored in his every phase of development. Yet there was something so uncannily familiar to me about these boys, about their facial expressions and posture, their choice of television program, their screening out of all but a few elements in the environment that surrounded them. The correspondences seemed too great for mere coincidence; they were not superficial either. The fact that these boys and Adam shared the same ethnic group was far less central to their similarities than was the unmistakable set of fine tunings that transformed disparate individuals into the same general category. Some common denominator was obvious—clear as it would have been if in a gathering of people only a few had blue skin, were seven feet tall, spoke a language no one else understood.

The director saw my confusion and shot a question mark in my direction.

"I have a son," I told him and reached into my wallet for a photograph.

He examined the picture, nodded, and handed it back. "FAS too, huh?" he asked.

The bureaucratic world of Indian affairs is full of triplicate acronyms—BIA, HEW, JOM—but this was a new one on me.

"FAS?"

"Fetal Alcohol Syndrome," he said. "Most of the kids we get are FAS or FAE—Fetal Alcohol Effect. They come from alcoholic families, mothers who drank. Your wife too?"

"He's adopted," I answered. "And, yes, his mother did drink. But he's been with me since he was very small."

"Doesn't matter. There aren't many FAS who live with their birth mothers after a certain point, or if there are, we don't see them. Whatever the booze does, it happens before the kid is born." He reached for Adam's photograph, which I still held.

"You see the eyes?" he pointed out. "The small head? See how thin he is? He's what, thirteen or fourteen? If you didn't know better, you'd think he was a lot younger."

I saw what the man meant. He was right on every count. I looked back at the boys sprawled on the couch. In their fixated concentration on the program, their mouths gaped in a too-familiar way.

"Do these boys, the ones who come to Project Phoenix, have learning problems?" I asked. "Do they have trouble with things like money?"

The director laughed, not unpleasantly but not with real humor either. "Are you kidding?" he said. "Money. Time. You name it. And the worst thing is, they don't learn from experience. We train them, run them through counseling, set them up with voc-ed, whatever, and in a couple weeks or a couple, three, days the court's petitioning them to come back here. Same story. They stole. They huffed. They didn't report in to their parole officer. They were fooling around with some girl who didn't like it."

"What finally works for them?" I asked, ready to go home and try whatever he suggested.

"What works for them?" he repeated. "What works? Not a goddamn thing."

A woman came out of the kitchen, smiled, and called us to the meal she and others had fixed. Three tables had been pushed together, and on them was laid out a full traditional Thanksgiving dinner: turkey, stuffing, mashed potatoes, cranberry sauce, molded jello salad, sliced bread, and margarine in a bright yellow tub. It was offered with an unassuming largesse and hospitality that bespoke traditional Indian people, a generosity toward guests both ingrained and natural, a celebration of values the more striking because it occurred in this place of overpowering need. Every dish had been prepared with care and tasted delicious, but I had to force myself to eat. I kept glancing through the door at the boys watching television— because of space limitations they would eat their helpings of this meal later with the other clients. And I kept seeing Adam. I didn't know any more about FAS than what the director had volunteered, but I held onto those three letters like clues. When I went back to Dartmouth, I would flesh them out.

Over the course of the next three years I made many Bush Foundation visits to Dakota reservations—to Pine Ridge, Rosebud, Standing Rock, Turtle Mountain, Devil's Lake, Crow Creek—and the contrast between the grim conditions I observed in the West and the manicured, academic detachment of Dartmouth became increasingly more difficult for me to reconcile. There is a luxury to intellectual neutrality, and also an arrogance. The same sought-after "objectivity" that led a campus ethics committee of which I was a member to formally abjure "immediate" issues stood as a convenient barrier to all confusing intrusions that might disrupt the flow of dispassionate thought. Scholarship by its very nature aspires to be above the ebb and flow of daily events, to take the long view. There is no enduring place for the frantic, the desperate, the hysterical.

The life of the mind is ideally serene, and so when I moved to the classroom from the poverty, the multiplying economic and health crises that defined the existence of northern plains Indians, I protected myself with glib rejoinders. It would do no good to rant at the undergraduates who sat in rows before me. They were by and large the sons and daughters of the privileged, blooming with good health, dressed in the newest fashions. The problems with which they came to me as advisor were for the most part wonderfully solvable. Any sense of reality outside their experience had to be insinuated, couched in unthreatening language, if it was to be heard. Generalized guilt, of course, was easy to engender, but equally easy for students to forget in the stroll to their next lecture, their aerobics class, their enormous dining room. In their heart of hearts these well-intentioned young men and women were irrefutably sure that the miseries of the world were not their fault, and in any case their course schedules ensured that each instructor would barrage them with appeals for the relevance and centrality of his or her concern. They had learned to be wary, to withhold their fervor.

Even the Native American student organization took a measured approach to the demands of crises on distant reservations. The admissions office had perfected its techniques since the early 1970s, and the Indians who matriculated at Dartmouth were now often drawn from more affluent economic backgrounds and were less a contrast with their campus peers. The dropout rate was down, fraternity/sorority membership was up, and many had daily concerns far removed from the anger I felt upon the completion of each round-trip to Rapid City or Pierre. I lost my patience with them, and therefore my credibility, for a year, because of one meeting in which I too passionately exhorted the group to spend the bulk of its activities' budget on an issues-related conference or on a direct donation to a community child-neglect project instead of over-financing the annual May powwow.

It seemed that the more I delved into the ballooning emergency of fetal alcohol syndrome among Indian people, the more I became unmoored from the internal preoccupations of the Ivy League. For many in Hanover, New Hampshire, the burning question about Indians still, after more than a decade's debate, centered on the nickname formerly given to the athletic teams. Every year new generations of freshmen had to be "educated" to the idea that it was inappropriate to turn the image of an oppressed people into a caricature, a negative *or* positive stereotype, for half-time entertainment. As early as 1974 the Board of Trustees had officially concurred with this assessment and banned any official use of the logo. However, in protest against this supposed restriction of their right to be insensitive if they chose, some alumni and a few students proudly hawked Indian-head paraphernalia: door mats, emblazoned clothing, bumper stickers. They took opinion polls, passed out petitions on street corners, even decorated themselves with jagged stripes of greasepaint to assert their position.

Such willful ignorance was hard for some, Indian and non-Indian, to digest, but, juxtaposed with Pine Ridge, for me it became numbing. I returned from one early-October excursion on a red-eye flight and came directly to campus to prepare for my class. I had spoken to no one since leaving a facility near the village of Porcupine devoted to treating little boys who had been sexually abused by drunken adults. The place was run by a Roman Catholic brother, soon to be transferred by his order for a bureaucratic reason incomprehensible to all concerned, and though the need was great and growing, the shelter would likely soon be closed for lack of funds.

As I rummaged through my lecture notes, trying to construct a two-hour explanation of the political underpinnings of the Iroquois Confederacy, there was a knock at my office door. I opened it to three elderly men, the expressions on their scrubbed faces bright and eager. Still in the mode of reservation protocol, I automatically deferred what I was doing to their advanced age, invited them inside, and offered my hand; but they held their ground.

"Are you Professor Dorris?" the middle one of them asked.

"Yes," I smiled.

"Well," he glanced at his two companions and then, in concert, the trio pulled open their coats to reveal Indian symbol T-shirts and loudly chanted, "Wah Hoo Wah"—the former Dartmouth Indians' football cheer.

We faced each other, not two feet apart, and yet in different universes. The old grads were pleased with themselves: they had risen early, dressed with intent to insult, and bearded their tormentor in his den. Mission accomplished. What did I have to say to *this*, their eyes demanded.

I took a step back and closed the door. I had received in the mail an application from the Rockefeller Foundation for a year-long independent study fellowship, and that day I filled it out, requesting support for full-time research on fetal alcohol syndrome and its impact on some of the reservation communities I had visited. I called Louise for her consent, then formally petitioned the dean for a leave of absence.

The following winter I was promoted to full professor, *Love Medicine* was the dark-horse winner of the National Book Critics Circle Award for Fiction, a draft of Louise's second novel, *The Beet Queen*, was completed, and my Rockefeller grant was approved. I was earning an extra paycheck by teaching an advanced aerobics class for fifty participants three times a week at the gym in Hanover, and I had begun my own novel, *A Yellow Raft in Blue Water*.

Louise and I had become involved more and more with each other's writing, from the conception of fictional characters to the final copyediting of a manuscript—though each of us faced the blank page or word processor screen alone. By the time any submission left our house, however, we had achieved—after many a heated literary argument—consensus on every word. As a result, both of us felt responsible for and protective of whatever book, article, poem, review, or story was published, regardless of who got the cover byline. We knew every paragraph by heart, so frequently had it been rewritten and revised.

One April evening after supper, Louise and I unfolded a map of the Midwest and circled the possibilities where we might settle for the twelve months of my fellowship beginning in August. We wanted a location reasonably near to her family and to the reservations I needed to visit, a place with an academic library, with access to an airport, with a good day care center for Persia and Pallas, and, the bottom line, with a quality school system that would benefit Sava and Madeline and where Adam could continue the type of instruction he had begun at Hartford—all of which pointed to a college town. We made circles around Missoula in Montana, Winnipeg in Manitoba, St. Paul, Bemidji, and Northfield in Minnesota, Fargo and Grand Forks in North Dakota, and Rapid City in South Dakota, then contacted friends and associates in those places to see if they could help us find a large, furnished dwelling to lease.

Stan Shepard ultimately provided the best lead: Bill Woerhlin, a history professor at Carleton College in Northfield, an hour south of the Twin Cities, who had worked with the Bush Foundation on several occasions. Bill's wife, Molly, answered the phone when we called, and in a matter of days she had put us in touch with a realty agent who mailed photographs of our ideal house—a huge Victorian a block from campus with six bedrooms and a rent we could afford—and which was available on the exact date we wanted to move in. I talked to the director of special education in the Northfield school system, and she assured me that Adam's current program could be mirrored. Carleton College generously offered us library privileges. We had never spent much time in southern Minnesota, but sight unseen we signed a year's lease, made a down payment on a Dodge Caravan—which would transport all seven of us—and as soon as the Dartmouth summer term was over, we packed our things and headed west.

Less than a month later I was on my way back to Pine Ridge, informed by three years of sporadic textual research on the disability I had first learned about at Project Phoenix. I had reexamined and closely analyzed the record of Adam's medical and psychological examinations, and had reviewed as objectively as possible my memories of his life experience. I had spoken by telephone to some of the most illustrious scientists breaking new ground in the field of teratogens and genetics, and had attended dozens of lectures on the subject of birth disorders. Now I knew at last what questions to ask, and the time had come for me to listen firsthand to the voices of men and women directly involved with the victims and perpetrators of fetal alcohol syndrome.

In 1968, the year Adam was born, four French scientists published a modest research paper (*Les enfants de parents alcooliques. Anomalies observées*) noting certain recurrent birth defects disproportionately represented among 127 children of alcoholic parents. It was not until 1973, when Adam was five years old and had received his Lakota name, that another team of experts, this one at the University of Washington in Seattle, carried that initial observation a step further. This group, headed by Dr. David W. Smith of the Department of Pediatrics, observed retarded intrauterine growth in ten out of twelve newborn infants of mothers with chronic alcoholism; they ultimately described an apparently consistent pattern of physiological deformities in these children, and gave it a name: fetal alcohol syndrome (FAS). Not instantly recognized as a major breakthrough by most of the academic community, only three scientific or clinical papers on the subject appeared worldwide that year. But it was an idea whose time had come. West German research reports in 1975 and 1976 were followed by Swedish studies in 1975 and 1977, and by 1979, more than 200 FAS-related articles had been published. In 1985, the year Adam was hired at his first part-time job—filling salt and pepper shakers—the annual rate of FAS-related professional documentation had increased to almost 2,000 articles.

The notion that maternal drinking was bad for a baby's health was, of course, not new. The Old Testament of the Hebrew Bible contains a very specific proscription in Judges:13—

> And there was a certain man of Zorah of the tribe of the Nanites, whose name was Mano'ah; and his wife was barren and had no children. And the angel of the Lord appeared to the woman and said to her, "Behold, you are barren and have no children; but you shall conceive and bear a son. Therefore beware, and drink no wine or strong drink, and eat nothing unclean, for lo, you shall conceive and bear a son. No razor shall come upon his head, for the boy shall be a Nazirite to God from birth; and he shall begin to deliver Israel from the hand of the Philistines." Then the woman came and told her husband, "A man of God came to me, and his countenance was like the countenance of the angel of God, very terrible; I did not ask him whence he was, and he did not tell me his name; but he said to me, 'Behold, you shall conceive and bear a son; so then drink no wine or strong drink, and eat nothing unclean, for the boy shall be a Nazirite to God from birth to the day of his death.' "(2–7)*

As early as 322 B.C., Aristotle, in his *Problemata,* noted that "foolish, drunken, or hare-brained women for the most part bring forth children like unto themselves, difficult and listless." Plato suggested that alcohol should be barred "to any man or woman who was intending to create children. . . . Children should not be made in bodies saturated with drunkenness." Plutarch (120 A.D.) observed that "one drunkard begats another," and the Babylonian *Talmud* (200–500 A.D., Kehuboth 32b) warned pregnant women: "One who drinks intoxicating liquor will have ungainly children." In ancient Carthage there existed a ban against consuming liquor on the wedding night for fear that a defective child might be conceived.

During the so-called "gin epidemic" in England from 1720–1750, when cheap drink was for the first time widely available, the British

---

* Dr. Ernest L. Abel, in his fine and comprehensive book *Fetal Alcohol Syndrome and Fetal Alcohol Effects* (New York: Plenum Press, 1984, 1987), argues (pp. 2–25) that the subsequent proscriptions against drinking, often cited as evidence that ancient societies recognized the danger of maternal drinking, can be misleading. He makes the valid point that the underlying reasons for these laws and maxims must be understood within the context of the historical period and culture in which they existed. However, the fact remains that though the explanations for these rules may have had other than modern scientific roots, their impact was clearly therapeutic. Before Hebrews grasped the biological concept of trichinosis, they forbade the eating of pork for religious reasons. The end result was the same: it suppressed the incidence of food poisoning. Similarly, no matter why some societies discouraged pregnant or potentially pregnant women from imbibing alcohol, it turned out to be a wise thing for them to do.

Royal College of Physicians warned in a report to Parliament that parental drinking was a "cause of weak, feeble, and distempered children." A century later, another scientific committee advised the House of Commons that the children born to alcoholic mothers had a "starved, shrivelled, and imperfect look." It was even worse than that, according to William Sullivan, a physician for a Liverpool prison. In 1899 he published findings to the effect that alcoholic women had a stillbirth and infant death rate of 56 percent, more than double that of their nondrinking female relatives.[1]

The 1973 Seattle researchers presented their findings in the British journal *Lancet*, identifying a number of newborn traits which they associated with maternal drinking. These included prenatal and postnatal growth deficiency; a particular pattern of facial malformations, including small head circumference, flattened midface, sunken nasal bridge, and a smoothed and elongated philtrum (the groove between the nose and upper lip); central nervous system dysfunction; and varying degrees of organ system malformation.[2] In other words, some infants produced by women who consistently used large amounts of alcohol during their pregnancies were smaller, developed more slowly, and looked different from the babies of mothers who used no alcohol; they also more or less shared certain other health problems which clinically set them apart from the newborn population as a whole.

On the surface, this was a startling, radical, even infuriating assertion to some physicians who, in good conscience, had been long in the habit of actually prescribing a calming glass of wine or beer, or an occasional celebratory drink, to their pregnant clients. There were even instances in which premature labor was forestalled by means of an intravenous injection of an alcohol-based solution.

As recently as 1974, a standard reference and medical school textbook, *Pharmacological Basis of Therapeutics* by Louis Goodman and Alfred Gilman, maintained that "alcohol gains free access to fetal circulation, *but it does not seem to harm the fetus.*"[3] Though this misinformation was corrected in the 1980 and subsequent editions of the volume, it was the voice of instruction for many students who are presently now practicing doctors and supported the established habits of many of their patients and colleagues. Social drinking, after all, is considered part of American culture, a basic right, like smoking or hand-gun ownership; a notorious period of national lawbreaking occurred in response to the legal prohibition of liquor sales in the 1920s, and in many states the production of wine or spirits is a major industry and employer. "*Our* mothers drank," protested many indignant dissenters to early FAS warnings, "and look at us."

Such a reaction prompts a number of possible responses, the most benign being that women in their mothers' generation probably didn't, as a class, consume as much as many women do in the 1980s. Statistically, in contemporary North America nine out of ten women of child-bearing age are said to drink occasionally. Reliable figures suggest that seven out of ten of these women drink regularly, on the average of one drink per day. Five to ten percent of the women in this same age group qualify as confirmed alcoholics—and the overall total of women within the population who consume ethanol in any form is dramatically on the upswing. In recent years, the ratio of new female drinkers to male has increased by two to one. Among college students, for instance, the estimated number of male drinkers rose about 3 percent between 1953 and 1974; during the same period, the equivalent figure for females was 12 percent. This disturbing trend (matched by a similar surge in female smoking) may be due to any of several causes, but it undeniably parallels other broad, more positive social changes for women within the same time period. Thanks to concerted political effort, women have made statistical gains vis-à-vis men in such areas as salary parity and education, and have achieved greater leadership roles in business and government. However, the process of discarding oppressive and stereotypical roles has not been universally beneficial: liberated of external sanctions discouraging their participation in what were previously guarded as exclusive "masculine" domains, women are now "free" to do, and increasingly are doing, just as much harm to their bodies by use of drugs and chemicals as their male counterparts. But there is a key, biologically based difference. Drunk expectant fathers may, at least as far as it is currently known, hurt only themselves and those unfortunate enough to get in their way; drunk expectant mothers can grievously and irreparably cause harm to their unborn infants.

For the past two decades, it has become irrefutably evident that alcohol is a teratogen (a word deriving from the Greek roots "*terrato-*" and "*-genés*," literally, "to make monsters"), the scientific expression for a chemical agent that in certain dosages can cause birth defects. Alarming articles in respected, usually staid, professional publications such as the *American Journal of Obstetric Gynecology* have attested to the fact that alcohol passes the placental barrier freely in certain animals, such as rhesus monkeys. Acute intoxication of the embryo has been recorded for both lambs and human beings. The human fetus has a reduced capacity to eliminate alcohol, and therefore concentrations tend to be higher *in utero* than in the rest of the mother's system by the end of her intoxication and are likely to endure there for longer periods. The baby in the womb becomes more drunk than its mother with every drink of liquor, wine, or beer she takes. By the time she feels tipsy and thus socially or physically compelled to refuse a refill, the child she carries could, in effect, have already passed out. And, as Dr. Cortez F. Enloe, editor of *Nutrition Today*, put it in 1980, "for the fetus, the hangover may last a lifetime."[4]

The physiological process by which the damage takes place is not precisely understood, but in general it is fairly uncomplicated. When a person ingests more alcohol than his or her liver can process, the excess is released into the bloodstream to circulate until it can be detoxified. Once the placenta of a pregnant woman is formed, any raw ethanol present in her body envelops the fetus, where it is distributed in the liver, pancreas, kidney, thymus, heart, and brain, concentrating in the gray matter of the developing child. It may interfere with zinc metabolism, with hormonal balance, or with the ability of the placenta to carry oxygen, thus creating anoxia and subsequent brain damage, especially during the first and third trimesters. Alcohol is a dehydrating agent, so it absorbs water. This is the reason it stings abraded tissue, and this may well be the reason that the brain of a newborn whose mother drank appears desiccated, smaller than it should be—water has been sucked out of the developing cells, killing them outright or rendering them functionless. (The ability of the fetus to eliminate alcohol is only about 50 percent of the adult capacity, meaning that the same amount is present twice as long.) The amniotic fluid itself becomes a kind of alcohol reservoir, and as Dr. Enloe observes, "the mental computer that is constantly bathed in ethyl alcohol soon adapts to that milieu. Short circuits develop and no amount of education in later life can realign them."[5]

Despite the clear logic of these arguments, the scientific community was characteristically cautious in creating or applying a new label to describe this and related conditions. A "syndrome" is little more than the name given for a collection of symptoms that seem to regularly coexist but for which there is rarely a single diagnostic feature and no specific biochemical, chromosomal, or pathological test. For a condition of "full" FAS to be identified, a number of highly specific criteria had to be simultaneously present in a candidate, including: (1) significant growth retardation both before and after birth; (2) measurable mental deficit; (3) altered facial characteristics; (4) other physical abnormalities; and (5) documentation of maternal alcoholism. Many of these points, of course, are hard or next to impossible to calculate. What constitutes "normal" size or growth within the human species? How can genetically inherited features such as nose shape and eyelid formation be compared between members of one race and those of another? What constitutes a working definition for "alcoholism"? Other characteristics were hard to pin on alcohol as their single cause.

Many factors such as nicotine, environmental pollution, malnutrition, certain ingredients in over-the-counter medications ingested during pregnancy, or even inherited genetic traits might account for some of the specific side effects (arterial and ventricular septal defects in the heart, aberrant palmar creases, joint abnormalities, convulsions, hydrocephaly, abnormal EEG activity, small teeth with faulty enamel, curvature of the spine, hearing problems, cleft lip, cleft palate, club foot, increased risk of perinatal death, epilepsy) most often associated with FAS. Moreover, various practices known to be dangerous to fetal health, especially smoking, poor diet, and drug ingestion, are often found coterminus with extreme drinking patterns—one study showed that 65 percent of heavy drinking was associated with smoking in excess of one pack of cigarettes a day—and thus undoubtedly exacerbate or complicate the ravages of alcohol poisoning. Can alcohol consumption be isolated and factored out as the causal core of the collective problem?

The answer is unambiguous: a pregnant white rat that doesn't smoke tobacco or marijuana, take pills, or drink caffeinated coffee but that eats a balanced diet will still deliver a predictably deformed offspring if, in a controlled experiment, it takes in enough ethyl alcohol. Auxiliary bad habits undeniably make a condition worse; drinking causes it.

In regard to human beings, a growing handful of researchers argued that it was more than coincidence when the full range of FAS symptoms consistently appeared in the babies of alcoholic mothers. They devised ex post facto diagnostic tests in which photograph albums of children from various ethnic groups—some of them suspected of having fetal alcohol syndrome, some of them assumed to be healthy—were sent without any designation to other scientists and physicians, who were asked to identify by looks alone which individuals were likely to be impaired. The respondents, with only their own past clinical experience upon which to base their guesses, were highly accurate in selecting the photos of the children at risk for FAS. The compilation of these surveys yielded a composite "FAS face," recognizable to anyone—doctor, counselor, teacher, social worker, parent—used to dealing with the victims of maternal drinking.

It was certainly familiar to me when I first saw it in 1979; it could have been the picture of Adam.

Clinically, alcohol is an insult to the fetus that can be manifested in a wide range of symptoms.

But probably mental deficiency, in varying degrees, is the most debilitating aspect of FAS in those children who survive. The mean IQ for such individuals falls, according to various studies, between 65 and 80, from, in the terminology of psychological testing, "mildly retarded" through "borderline" to "dull normal," although individuals with IQs as low as 15 or as high as 105 have been positively diagnosed. FAS children at all ages and stages of growth lag behind their peers in everything from rate of language acquisition to development of academic skills in arithmetic. Often these learning problems are not apparent until considerably after birth, and they seem to appear quite independently of environment.

Whether children are raised in the chaotic households of their unreformed alcoholic biological mothers or nurtured in stable, sober, loving natural or adoptive homes, the disabilities surface with uniformity. Overriding the nature/nurture debate about whether genetic inheritance or environment has the predominant influence on the construction of human personality, the permanent limitations caused by alcohol seem to be fixed *in utero* and modified only slightly and perhaps temporarily by anything that happens after birth.

Problems with brain cells and organization, like the formation of vital organs, joints, and absolute body size, cannot be repaired. A baby enters the world with all the raw equipment he or she is ever

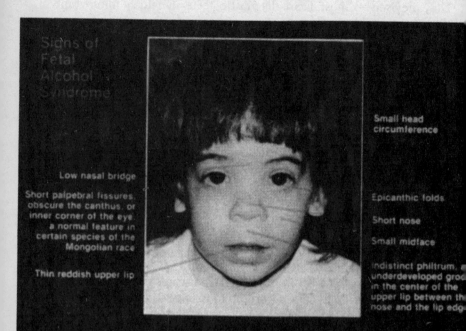

Signs of
Fetal
Alcohol
Syndrome

Small head
circumference

Low nasal bridge

Short palpebral fissures,
obscure the canthus, or
inner corner of the eye,
a normal feature in
certain species of the
Mongolian race

Thin reddish upper lip

Epicanthic folds

Short nose

Small midface

Indistinct philtrum,
underdeveloped groo
in the center of the
upper lip between th
nose and the lip edg

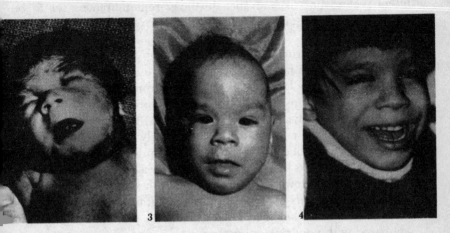

Child with Fetal Alcohol Syndrome photographed at day one, eight months, and four and one half years. This child was diagnosed at birth and has spent all his life in one foster home where the quality of care has been excellent. Despite good school programming, his IQ has remained stable at 40 to 45.

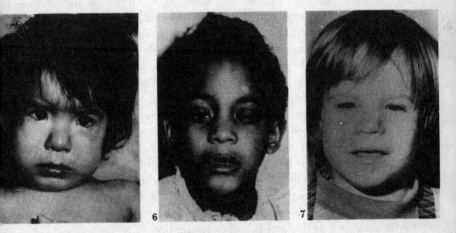

Patients with Fetal Alcohol Syndrome from three racial groups. Photographed at one year, three years and nine months, and two years and six months, respectively.

going to get. What's lacking at delivery may not be obvious for ten or fifteen years, but like advance birthday remembrances set to be opened only at certain ages, the beautiful boxes may turn out to be empty or half full.

If all this were true only of children having "full" FAS, it would be bad enough, but in fact that population represents only the smallest visible tip of a very large iceberg. The syndrome can be detected at birth only in the most severe cases, usually occurring exclusively in the offspring of truly alcoholic women, that is, those who throughout the duration of their pregnancy have regularly consumed more than 100 grams of ethanol each day. That works out to approximately eight beers or slightly less than a pint of whiskey or a bit more than a bottle of wine per day. However, one recent British study[6] has shown that as little as 100 grams per week in the first trimester doubles the risk that the baby will be in less than the tenth percentile for weight compared with nondrinking mothers.

FAS is an equal opportunity affliction. Its victims have been born to women from age fifteen up, of all nationalities and income groups, who ingested every type of liquor, including to some who neither smoked cigarettes nor took any drugs but alcohol during their pregnancies. Rarely will a first baby show signs of full FAS— statistically the average age at birth for the mothers of FAS diagnoses is thirty years, by which time many have borne two to five previous children. As a group, such women rarely seek out prenatal care and often have severe health problems of their own, including, but not confined to, a high incidence of pancreatic and kidney disorders, cirrhosis of the liver, iron deficiency anemia, venereal disease, and general malnutrition. Significantly, many expectant mothers in this category actually lose weight during the course of their pregnancies, since much of their caloric consumption comes from alcohol and is nurturing neither to themselves nor to the child they carry. Underweight women who drink necessarily have higher blood alcohol levels than their heavier counterparts, and protein deficiency might well be due to a lower rate of metabolism and elimination. The cycle of maternal cause and effect is self-perpetuating.

Furthermore, in these women central nervous system (CNS) illnesses, including delerium tremens, are not uncommon. The mothers of those first FAS babies identified in the Seattle study, for instance, were severely at risk themselves, with only about half of the original group surviving more than two years after giving birth. Many factors are important in determining how a particular adult will react to a given dose of alcohol: age, previous pregnancies, duration of drinking history, nutrition, timing (that is, at what stage of pregnancy she consumed specific amounts of ethanol), individual metabolism, or an inherited genetic predisposition related to maternal or paternal drinking behavior. The reaction of each woman to alcohol is unique; the same absolute amount may produce a host of separate outcomes, and different amounts may produce almost identical outcomes, depending on the particular case.

For a woman who imbibes alcoholic beverages more moderately (say, a cocktail or a couple of glasses of white wine several nights a week) or more sporadically (teetotaling, due to morning sickness, for the first trimester; only an occasional beer in the second; then a one-time binge in the third—a critical stage of fetal brain development—in which she consumes five or six drinks in a span of a few hours), the destruction inflicted on the newborn child may be scarcely noticeable to the naked eye, but its effect may still be devastating. Dr. Ronald Forbes, writing in the respected London journal *Public Health* (1984), argues on the basis of several studies that drinking "either before pregnancy or prior to recognition of pregnancy is linked to a variety of neonatal problems, even with an average of only two drinks a day, regardless of whether the drinking is daily or irregular. One ounce of absolute alcohol* daily before pregnancy is associated with an average of 91 grams [1–2 ounces] decrease in birth weight.[7]

Fetal Alcohol Effect (FAE), the name given any preparturition alcohol-induced developmental impairment that entails less than the full complement of FAS symptoms, is harder to diagnose, more subtle, but in many respects just as debilitating as the full syndrome—and it is far more widespread within the general population. As Dr. Frank L. Iber points out in a seminal article:[8] "The most exciting recent data reveals new (and disturbing) information about the learning ability of rats and mice born of mothers who have been on diets containing only relatively low levels of alcohol. Anatomically, such infant animals appear in every way to be normal. However, when tested at various stages in later life, it becomes obvious that

* The average drink in a restaurant is rarely less than an ounce and a half, and in clubs it's about two ounces.

their learning ability is impaired. . . . It ranges from slight to marked impairment in the ability to learn as demonstrated in such standard tests as shock avoidance maze running, and complex tasks of adaptation experiments that are well characterized in rats." In 1983, Professor V. Cernick announced to a pediatric conference in Canada that only 34 percent of the FAS babies he studied showed the physical deformities considered typical of the syndrome.

At birth, according to Dr. Ann Streissguth and Robin A. LaDue,[9] infants with FAS may be tremulous, irritable, overreactive to sounds, and have feeding difficulties. They typically fail to thrive and show a weak sucking ability. Alcohol effect might surface in a single heart or joint malformation, or it might cause cerebral palsy. In maturing children, the legacy of maternal drinking may become evident in tests that indicate marginal mental retardation or in perception disturbances, short memory span, distractibility, interrupted or unusual sleep patterns, and emotional instability. Later in life, these children may be hyperactive, inattentive, impulsive, fearless, indiscriminate in their reaction to friends and strangers; they may also demonstrate poor motor function or thinking disorders.

In relatively mild cases, FAE might be suggested by a repeated failure to master the multiplication tables, to grasp how to gauge time, or to conform to patterns of social functioning that depend on an internal appreciation of long-term consequences or "morality." It might be indicated by persistent head and body rocking, clumsiness, difficulty with peers, or life management problems. Dr. Forbes reports that FAE children may "show poor judgement and may repeat behaviours that have had bad outcomes in the past. . . . Some of these children have been observed using large vocabularies without really understanding the content of what they are saying. As a result, they may initially sound more capable than they are."[10]

In other words, they don't learn from their mistakes, and they don't know what they're talking about.

Certainly it is true that, considered alone, any one or even two of these deportments might be nothing more than a passing phase of a normal child's development. Certainly, it is true that when grouped in clusters of three or four, these symptoms might be accounted for by any number of causes *other than* or *in addition to* maternal drinking. But when they occur in tandem, when the physical and behavioral anomalies more or less coalesce into a repeated, cumulative set of fixed actions or signs, the alarm bell sounds. The very opposite of deduction by default, a diagnosis of fetal alcohol syndrome or fetal alcohol effect is a reluctant conclusion pressed out by the overpowering weight of connected evidence.

CHAPTER TEN

Early on a September morning in 1985, I left the Rapid City airport in a rented tan Citation. It was chilly, drizzling, foggy. The recent rains had made the sagebrush grow tall along the side of the road. Here and there were glistening catches of light where water had collected in potholes. There was an unfinished ambience to the landscape—like a construction site without the construction. Crops of sunflowers were rolled in huge bales to dry in the wind. Two flocks of wild turkeys, each an even dozen, wandered by the side of a gully, and a small herd of antelope, tails white and erect, watched from a swell. I followed the procession of telephone poles that linked the Pine Ridge Reservation to the outside world and tuned in KILI-FM, All-Indian radio, to hear traditional honor songs, intermixed with Elvis Presley tunes, for a twenty-year-old boy, yesterday's suicide.

There was no marker to indicate the reservation boundary, but the road changed from the smooth surface maintained within the Badlands National Monument. The ground on either side was a neutral color like snow, like sand. I had an eleven o'clock appointment with Jeaneen Grey Eagle, director of Project Recovery, the drug and alcohol rehabilitation effort officially sanctioned by the tribal council. I located the office in the Pine Ridge village, on the government buildings' street angling north from the four-way stop at the center of town.

Jeaneen was young, attractive, harried, angry. The eyes behind her glasses were intelligent, measuring, deciding whether or not she would have patience with my questions. Her long black hair was pulled back from her forehead with a beaded clip. She wore a Navajo turquoise necklace, and was dressed in sandals and an electric blue karate suit.

She had grown up on the reservation, and after a time away for higher education, she returned to marry Robert Grey Eagle, a University of New Mexico–trained lawyer, now the head judge of the tribal court. As a couple they practiced a curious amalgam of the traditional and the modern: they took sweat baths for spiritual renewal, and Robert had participated in the sun dance, but on another occasion, while attending a South Dakota State convention, Jeaneen found herself snowed in for several days at the Rapid City Holiday Inn with the rock group Quiet Riot and had thoroughly enjoyed the experience.

Jeaneen was praised by everyone to whom I had spoken about fetal alcohol syndrome. "She's the person who knows the realities," I had heard often from sociologists, psychologists, public health service doctors. "She's on the front lines, the person in the thick of the problem. She's smart, she's tough-minded, and she tells the truth." Now I could see what the people I had contacted had meant. Jeaneen was a woman at the center of a crisis. I turned on my tape recorder, tossed out an opening question, and she took over the conversation for three hours.

In Jeaneen's description, fetal alcohol syndrome lost all vestige of academic jargon, all cool distance. It was lethal, on the increase, the more dangerous because it was both commonplace and preventable. Jeaneen's was not an analysis composed of fine distinctions, of cautious calibration, but rather a pastiche of broad strokes, the kind of identification made at the scene of an accident when a quick take is the only hope of saving lives. She was a different kind of expert than I had previously met in FAS readings and lectures; on the subject of maternal drinking she was a zealot, battle-fatigued, impatient with ambiguity; she was not without compassion for chemically dependent women, but she reserved her sympathy for their victims.

I listened to her with the relief that arises from lifted isolation, with the attitude Cassandra might have had if just one other seer had concurred when she foretold the destruction of Troy. Jeaneen's perspective on FAS was no more gentle, no less dire, than my own—on the contrary, in that it was more informed, hers was much worse, confirming and reflecting my most hyperbolic fears—but in her I quickly sensed a strong ally who wore no blinders. Jeaneen must have felt a hint of the same thing. The interview gradually evolved into a conversation, and the conversation into the first foundation of a comradeship.

"People think that I'm Chicken Little saying the sky is falling," she said. "They don't seem to understand the far-reaching consequences of this. They are conditioned to live day to day. I don't know if that comes from having a hard time financially or what the reasons are. I wish there was some way to try to talk to people about long-term effects that this is going to have. How we're breeding a society of people who are not capable of living even in *this* world, let alone the other world, leaving the reservation."

"I don't think you're Chicken Little," I said. "FAS is the most destructive thing to hit Indians since the European diseases five hundred years ago."

Jeaneen agreed and regretted that she lacked the funds to implement a more constructive program.

"I would open up a women's center," she said energetically. "Take in some pregnant women and provide treatment for them. And also have a special care center for FAS children. I think we need a clinic just for those children alone, where experts would work with them at a medical level and at an emotional level as well as at an educational level. FAS children do not have the capability of living within this society. The ones I have seen are so hyperactive—we have them bouncing off the walls down here, tearing the walls apart. Those children end up abused an awful lot. My husband, being a judge, has to issue so many temporary custody orders. Last week there was a ten-month-old baby that came before him, and I wanted to take that baby so badly. I had to force myself not to do it."

While we talked, Jeaneen's eight-month-old son, Jesse, slept in a small crib behind her desk. She often looked at him, smoothed his hair, as if to remind herself of the real issues.

"The problem is in epidemic proportions. You go down the block, and out of ten children you see five, six of them with FAS or FAE. I keep banging my head and thinking, 'How can they do this? How can they do this?' There's an attitude of 'Oh, that's not going to happen to me.' You see these women who are drunk every single day, and—you ask the doctors and nurses up at the hospital—there have been babies born whose skin, the whole baby, smells like wine. It's like they're pickled and the amniotic fluid is saturated with alcohol. But a lot of times when a baby is born, the [FAE] is not diagnosable from the child's facial features, and difficulties like epilepsy don't show until much later. You know how that goes."

I knew how that went.

". . . Of course, the babies that are born are usually smaller . . ."

According to the health records I had recently received from the South Dakota Department of Child Welfare after years of petitioning, and had since reread so often that I knew them by heart, Adam had weighed three pounds, twelve ounces at his premature birth. "He is not developing at normal rate," his health profile had stated in 1969. "Medical care necessary, feet not normal. Development has been below average, in that at the age of seventeen months he did not walk. He would pull himself up by the furniture and could stand with the aid of a chair. He crept and made cooing noises, but he did not talk, nor did he have any words in his vocabulary. He experienced convulsions—one was in the course of recovery from a severe dehydration with 'enteritis' [inflammation of the intestine] at about six months, and the other occurred approximately two months prior. Pneumonia during the first year of life. Frequent ear infections. *The cause of his physical and mental retardation*" that anonymous Public Health physician had written in the dark ages before anyone in America had ever heard of fetal alcohol syndrome, when the medical textbooks still confidently stated that ethanol had no intrauterine effect, "*is that the cause is undeterminable* [italics mine]."

I brought my attention back to Jeaneen, who continued, unaware of the impact her words had upon me the parent as opposed to me the dutiful researcher.

". . . the growth slows down and the physical stuff starts, but these women don't realize it even then. Why can't they see what's happening? Why don't they care? People say, 'How many FAS kids are born up here?' and I say, 'I don't know because Indian Health can't diagnose it unless it's real obvious.' We had a client come in with a baby in nineteen seventy-seven, and the baby had convulsions, it had DTs [*delerium tremens*] after it was born. I couldn't believe a baby having DTs—it was real hard for me to comprehend. We all have a magic barrier that prevents bad things from going through. But that baby still has convulsions and is real hyperactive. She can't talk.

"The *New York Times* called us a colony—our average income is like three thousand dollars. Our infant mortality rate is almost triple that of the state of South Dakota, for whites, okay. So here we are, and people have children to increase their welfare checks. That's basic economics. I don't think President Reagan's ever heard of that branch of economics, but I know people who've gotten pregnant to get a bigger check without stopping to think, 'Okay, this child is going to cost x amount of hundreds of dollars to feed, clothe, and shelter, and welfare is probably not going to cover that amount.' Okay? But in dollars and cents it means a raise. We get a four-percent cost-of-living increase. Well, they go for nine months, have another child, and do the same thing. And then use up all the money in the first week of the month. We have a terribly high birth rate here, and we have a high infant mortality, and we have a high incidence of children born with physical defects. And that's probably it: people are reproducing to get an increase in food stamps and welfare benefits."

I was momentarily taken aback by Jeaneen's candor. She spoke without internal editing, as if too weary of the problem to seek euphemism. I glanced at the tape recorder, its wheels sealing up our thoughts like the filling in jellyroll, and her eyes followed mine. I moved my finger toward the stop button, raised my eyebrows in question. Was this off-the-record? She shook her head. From somewhere a trust had grown between us, and now it was my turn to risk an unpopular opinion.

I wondered aloud whether some of the mothers Jeaneen talked about might not be merely products of economic deprivation and historical exploitation, but might themselves be victims of fetal alcohol effect. They would therefore find it hard, if not impossible, to cope with money and preplanning. Adam had received ten dollars from his grandmother for his seventeenth birthday, and I let him take the cash to school.

"Where's the money?" I asked him when he got home. He had purchased a doughnut: he gave somebody ten dollars, took a doughnut, and asked for no change. End of transaction. It had occurred to me that many adults and young people with undiagnosed FAS or FAE were perhaps in jail for small crimes like shoplifting—offenses that seemed to them like a good idea at the time because they couldn't project the consequences if they were apprehended. And they *would* tend to be caught, over and over. They were not clever thieves.

Jeaneen immediately understood my point. "We had an arrest record within one given year equivalent to like sixty-five percent of this reservation's population," she said. "And that statistic means a lot of repeaters, not that sixty-five percent of the people here committed crimes."

Jeaneen looked out the window, took a phone call, indicating that I need not leave the office. I busied myself with the papers in the file I had brought along—newspaper clippings, demographic studies of reservation versus urban Indian drinking patterns. The theoretical goal of anthropology is an "etic," or outsider's, perspective, combined with an "emic" (group member's) insight, and it's a juggler's balance rarely attained. The participant/observer I learned about in graduate field-work classes walks the top of a dam between a stranger's constraint and an insider's abandon, and a misstep in either direction is dangerous. My training resisted the intimacy of shared experience offered by Jeaneen's honesty, and when she was finished, I cleared my throat and moved on to the next subhead on my prepared list of questions.

Was there a particular chronological age when a mother was more at risk for having an FAS child?

"It depends on her *drinking age*," Jeaneen answered. "I've seen FAS/FAE children born to really young women, but these were girls who started drinking early. I guess another factor is nutrition. If a woman doesn't eat what she needs while she's pregnant, she com-pounds the effects of alcohol."

I asked Jeaneen whether, having lived on this reservation all her life, she thought that local women were now drinking more or less than previously.

"I was a data coordinator back in the seventies," she answered. "At that time the average age for the women in the alcohol program was like forty-nine, and we had roughly sixty-five to eighty-five percent males. We've got more women clients now—probably sixty to sixty-five per-cent. Their average age is about twenty-five, right smack in the middle of childbearing years, and they're drinking heavily.

"What kind of stuff?" I asked. In Alaska I had known people who made home brew from potatoes, yeast, and sugar, then aged it in a plastic garbage can for a week. The most potent shots came from the bottom.

"A lot of beer, a lot of wine. Not so much the hard liquors because there isn't immediate access to them. We're a 'dry' reservation, but we have our bootleggers, and then two miles over the line here we have five or six little beer joints that do a record business, like they're second to Omaha in alcohol sales for the state of Nebraska. Millions of dollars cross that line. And so many die annually on the road to that place it's got the name 'Killer Highway.' Seven people killed at one time, three people killed at another. They just recently had a poster contest for a sign, and this guy drew a skull, real graphic—it scared the heck out of me. It said, SLOW DOWN, DEATH AHEAD. And the skull has a war bonnet on."

"What's the beer of choice?"

"I believe Budweiser is. Anheuser-Busch, I think, should be more than happy to commit funds to an FAS project."

This sounded to me like a practical idea, and I asked if she had approached the management of the company in St. Louis.

"Somebody did back in the seventies," Jeaneen recalled. "They tried to get backing for some prevention materials, but nothing ever came of it. The wine here is called muscatel. It's in a green bottle, which is why you see all the green glass around on the ground. It's real cheap. It costs like seventy-five cents a bottle, and the bootleggers sell it for like two and a quarter. The scary thing is, the people now are starting to drink Lysol. They call it Montana gin. I asked a doctor a few months ago if he had any research on what Lysol would do because we have women who are pregnant, street people, who are drinking Lysol. I need to know what it is going to do to the children."

I mentioned a recent fad that a former student of mine who lived on Rosebud had told me about: kids would puncture an aerosol can of Lysol, spread the fluid on bread, and call it a Lysol sandwich. It didn't take many bites to fry their brains.

Jeaneen shook her head. "I know of a man who was perfectly sane, had perfect eyesight, could see a bug crawling across the street coming toward his house, and now he's almost blind, his mind is practically gone. It's almost like he has Alzheimer's disease, just real pathetic. He drinks Lysol."

But why, I asked? Why poison when the wine was so cheap?

"To get high. Plus, it can be stolen from the store, and it stretches a lot further than muscatel."

I had no idea what the kick of Lysol might be like.

"They say it's between a gas high and an alcohol high," Jeaneen reported. "You get a ringing in your ears and you feel drunk, you feel like you huffed gas."

Years ago, when I lived on a reservation in eastern Montana, I had known people who sipped perfume they bought in tiny beveled bottles at Woolworth's. Was that still a beverage of choice?

"Yes, every now and then."

But the modern age had arrived in Indian Country. "We have a lot of young people here who are using cocaine, marijuana, acid." Jeaneen ticked off the list on her fingers. "They wanted me to teach a high school class on teenage pregnancy. I had my first baby at seventeen, so that's one subject I'm qualified to talk about. So what I did was use a game. I gave each student a hard-boiled egg, and they had to take care of it like it was a baby for exactly a week's period. They had to document when they had their eggs in their possession, when they neglected them."

I had heard of this technique before, but Jeaneen had given it an extra twist, adapting it to the specific conditions of Pine Ridge. Each girl had drawn a slip of paper to give her a temporary, fictional identity. She could be thirty-one years old and a housewife, or a person who started her day with a bottle of beer, or an alcoholic. Then the students drew again and some of them were pregnant with a second child. Some of them kept drinking or swallowed an aspirin or took acid. Some of them had FAS or FAE babies, and Jeaneen would have them write down how they felt about their guilt.

"I think I ruined a whole generation," she laughed. "These girls no longer wanted to get pregnant!"

What happened to a child with FAS or FAE on this reservation, I wanted to know. What would have happened to Adam?

"Up at Oglala Community School there's a cooperative for children with learning disabilities. When the kids get into high school, though, they don't have that safety net underneath them, and very often they drop out. You go to any mentally handicapped program on the reservation, and you look—most of the kids are FAS children."

Jeaneen had mentioned a subject close to home for me. Adam's eventual life after high school was a territory I could barely imagine. Would he live away from home? Have a girlfriend, a wife? His future was an island I could just make out, but it was a mirage separated from the present by deep water. How was the transit accomplished?

"What happens to them when they drop out?" I asked.

"They usually marry or have children. Then they divorce, and the woman gets on ADC [Aid for Dependent Children] and stays there and continues to have children, and we're back into the cycle. You get a second generation. You know how often FAS people need glasses, braces, wheelchairs, crutches; but here they're like a whole segment of society that's forgotten about or shoved under the table. We don't have a way to document how many there really are—that's the biggest problem."

Jeaneen herself was reluctant to give a rough estimate. She was aware of the relatively low incidence of FAS reported in some published studies—five or six impaired children out of every thousand born in particular communities, but I could tell she didn't give these figures much credence. Neither did I—though I understood where they came from. Firm diagnosis was made only in ironclad instances where every known symptom was manifest. Scientists recorded the bare minimum number of cases, a practice ultimately as unrealistic in terms of generating an accurate count as would be the assignment of an FAS label to *every* infant who gave evidence of only one or two symptoms. The truth necessarily lay somewhere in between.

Jeaneen protested that she had no proof, no absolute documentation to support her subjective impression of the percentage of fetal alcohol victims on this reservation, but I pressed her for an intuitive response. She was, by virtue of the length of time she had worked in her job, in a better position than almost anyone to hazard a guess. She might lack a backup statistical sample, but she had the virtue of being known and trusted in her community; a social scientist who passed through the reservation for only a few days and attempted to survey a population at once reticent to share its secrets and taught by experience to be hostile toward nosey non-Indians might emerge with some very suspect data. What's more, Jeaneen impressed me as having good instincts and a bias against gratuitous exaggeration. She had nothing to gain from me by inflating or deflating her figures. Again I put the question: of those Sioux children born on Pine Ridge, how many did she *think* might be impaired by prenatal drinking?

"I would say right now we probably have about twenty-five percent of our children here on this reservation, and that's conservative. It's probably higher, but twenty-five percent would be a solid base."

One-fourth of the population! I thought out loud, combining that incredible figure with the patterns of FAS behavior my written sources associated with adult activity. If it was true, as logic would suggest, that FAS kids grew up to have more kids, to have them earlier, to drink during their pregnancies because they were harder to counsel, then that meant that more and more impaired infants would be born in a given community.

What percentage of pregnant women did Jeaneen guess currently drank at a level that might be dangerous?

She stared at me, almost defiant, as if to see whether I would believe what she was about to say or whether I would join the ranks of those who called her Chicken Little. She bit her lower lip, decided.

"About fifty percent," she said in a flat voice. "Fifty percent are drinking on a weekly basis, on weekends. That's probably conservative again. When I went to prenatal clinic, I used to look at my peers, and then I was thinking it was like eighty percent who were still drinking while they were pregnant, though they had all heard of the FAS stuff."

We exchanged a look. Even if she was off the mark, even if she overstated the case by as much as half—and I didn't think she did—the figures were horrendous.

"What can be done?" I finally asked.

"Our real problem is finding a way to reach the entire community, those people who are more prone to abuse alcohol. We have to get the laws *here* enacted. It doesn't matter what anybody else says outside, we need to get some of those women in jail. That's what it takes—really severe and harsh methods, but to ruin a small child's life, then that's . . ."

Adam was once that small child. If his mother had been locked up, prevented from even one night of drinking, how much more awareness, how many more possibilities might he now have? If she had come after him with a baseball bat after he was born, if she had smashed his skull and caused brain damage, wouldn't she have been constrained from doing it again and again? Was it her prerogative, moral or legal, to deprive him of the means to live a full life? I had no doubt that there were compelling reasons for her weaknesses, for her mistakes, but reason didn't equal right.

Was it likely that such laws would be passed? What civil liberty overrode the torment of a child?

"We've talked about what the best approach would be," Jeaneen said. "It would have to come from grass-roots people, and what it would take is education first."

"And the law," I insisted. "What would the law entail?" I thought of the judgment of Solomon: to appease two rival parents the king proposed to sacrifice the disputed baby. Should a parental entitlement, in the case of FAS, be abridged by the state to save the child?

"If a woman is pregnant, and if she is going to drink alcohol, then, in very simple language, she should be jailed. We cannot . . ." Jeaneen chose her words carefully, regretfully, relating both sides of the argument. "There is no treatment center here that will take a pregnant woman. There's no place to send them. How do you monitor besides checking on them on a daily basis? The women say that it's their choice to drink or not. But if they want to have children, they're going to have to take care of them—and they don't wind up doing that. Most children end up with foster families, very often are abused on top of being FAS or FAE."

She unconsciously made a fist with her hand, then spoke her mind.

"They just need to put in jail those women who drink when they're pregnant. That's probably what it's going to take, because if a woman's hard core, then she's going to drink."

Adam's mother had been hard core. In the report I received, her cause of death was listed simply as "ingestion of denatured alcohol"— *antifreeze*. Incarceration might have led to treatment. It might have saved her life.

Was there even room in the jails?

"Each solution that comes up is a problem within itself," Jeaneen sighed. "Jail is no place for them, but it's the best alternative for someone who would otherwise drink while she was pregnant. I know of one case in particular in which they have jailed a pregnant woman; they kept her in for like a week, and then her family came and started to get angry about it. She was told that—*the family* was told that—they had to keep her sober, and they were told what could happen to the child if she kept drinking. They were told that if they did not keep her sober, she would be jailed again. And it worked. The family did start keeping her home and watching her so that she didn't drink. Once they were told that she was being kept in jail not for her sake, but for the child's sake, then it was understood."

"Do you ever yourself get really angry when you see a pregnant woman who's drinking?" This was an instinctive, unpremeditated question, intrusive and personal, none of my business. I was ready to call it back, when Jeaneen nodded.

"I know of one case in particular of a woman who has five FAS girls," she said. "One after the other, each of them in foster care, and every time I see her pregnant, I wonder why she can continue to have children. I've even asked—it's probably morally wrong for me as a person to question God's will—why is she continuing to have children when she doesn't want them and they are FAS? There should be some way to make her stop. She's not taking care of them. I've talked to my husband about it, and I think he feels sorry for me because I've gone so far in my thinking about forced sterilization for some of these people. I don't think that's out of the question—I think in the future that's going to be a reality. But I'm not going to be the one to sit and say, 'You can't have any more.' It would take a council of people from various agencies to determine who can and who can't, and that almost sounds like *1984*."

Her words were shocking, antithetical to every self-evident liberal belief I cherished, yet through my automatic silent denial I felt some current of unexpected assent. It was because we were talking about *babies*—babies who were going to be carried to term. Jeaneen and almost everyone I had spoken to had stated categorically that abortion was a choice almost never made by reservation residents, either because of religious beliefs pertaining to the sanctity of life or because medical facilities were too expensive or inaccessible.

I thought of my son and of all the things he'd never experience or even realize he was missing. What would happen to him when Louise and I died? By all evidence, he had been deprived of the miracle of transcendent imagination, a complex grace that was the quintessence of being human.

Grief can drive you places you never expected to go.

After a pause, Jeaneen continued, echoing my confusing thoughts. "You go back to the moral question, that a person does not have the right to ruin somebody else's life from the beginning. A child is innocent and has not asked to be born, nor is it asking to be abused—and I *do* look at it as child abuse. If a woman is willing to abuse her child before it even has been given a start on this earth, then she probably isn't deserving of another child, but who's going to make the determination?"

"I know," I said. "Even talk about the prohibition of alcohol raises the ethical issue of who can make a choice of what's good or bad for somebody else."

"This one lady comes down here—I can't even force myself to look at her any longer. And it's not in my daily agenda to hate. I try to assess rather than hate, because hate seems to use a lot more energy. *But I hate her.* I hate her for what she's done to her children. And I feel for those children. They'll never be . . . they'll never be *humans,* I guess, as we know humans, because they've never been given that chance. They can never love because they're not going to know the concept. One little girl was so severely affected that she'll never be accepted into society. In fact she'll be stared at, she'll be gawked at. What would we do to somebody who was doing this to our children? We would probably hang them at the street corner. But because alcohol is so accepted, we've become passive to the subject of FAS children."

In her anger, Jeaneen's voice rose, awakening Jesse, who began to cry. Jeaneen lifted him from the crib, let him dip his hand into her cup and stir the cooled coffee at the bottom with his fingers. It splashed on her karate suit, but she paid no attention. "He's eight months old and kind of realizes—like he spent all this time and probably just figured out you're a stranger," she explained. "Plus he's getting teeth. He was born on Jesse James's birthday. Somebody got confused one time and called him Billy Jack."

What would Billy Jack do about FAS, I wonder? It's not a dilemma that gloomy-faced movie stereotype of the macho Indian could solve with a blunt chop to an opponent's neck or even with a hokey snake ceremony. Who would Billy perceive as the enemy? The answer was not long in coming: the bootleggers, of course. They would be sleazy, white, operating out of a messy, smoke-filled shack, and Billy would smash through the door with a few well-placed kicks. He would be furious, vengeful, ready to fight against guns, knives, fists wrapped in chains.

But what if, when the splinters settled, he found inside only a group of pregnant teenagers, gentle voiced, some beautiful, smiling, buzzed on muscatel? What if he were confronted by a thirty-year-old nursing mother, a half-gone can of Bud in her free hand?

We took a break for lunch—Jeaneen went to pick up a bucket of broasted chicken and fries ordered from the village all-purpose grocery store. I stood and stretched. Through the open window came the sounds of a small town at midday: the calls of children at recess, the occasional dull drone of overflying planes on their high passage from one coast to another, the slam of car doors as people parked in front of the government buildings. Far down the road the country stretched flat and empty. The sky hung so low, seemed to dip below the edge of the horizon, to curve under the distant perimeter, that I had the impression I was looking out from on the top of a mesa, from on top of the world. The wind was blowing, and there was caramel color to the fields, mixed with the green from the previous night's rain. It was not so bright a day that the clouds, highlighted in violet, made obvious shadows on the land, but rather they cast subtle shades. The white hills to the north were so smooth and close-cropped that they appeared to be padded in felt, the beacons of other islands across the moving tides of grass. It was a landscape that defined the word *open*, the opposite of the enclosed, blurred myopia that was Adam's legacy. He came from a country that encouraged the farthest sight, but he forever stood in a well shaped by a bottle.

Two figures approached, walking on the bank of the highway. Even from this distance it was clear that they staggered, were propped against each other for support. They were women dressed in dark clothing, scarves about their heads. The younger of them wore quilted lavender snow boots, and the older woman, unlaced men's shoes and thin white anklets, little girl socks. Her bare shins and the hem of her dress were caked with dried mud, and I watched while she stepped without notice through a large puddle. They got nearer, and I could hear snatches of their conversation as they argued loudly in a language I didn't understand.

The one in shoes berated the woman in boots, then alternately pleaded and cooed in the singsong voice of a lullaby. The one in boots shook her head. She absolutely refused whatever was being asked. The old lady began to cry, to shrill high-pitched words ragged with fury. She batted away the other's arms, stopped where she stood, and sank to her knees, keening, until her younger companion helped her up, calmed her, said something so funny that both women laughed and had to grip each other for balance. Cars raced by them without slowing down, and finally they passed within a few feet of my window. Their features were similar. They had the look of a mother and daughter.

I checked my watch when we finished eating. It was nearly three o'clock, and I had a long drive to Rapid City. I proposed that we spend another half hour in conversation today and that I return in a month or so to continue the interview.

"Okay." Jeaneen rocked Jesse in her arms, rolling her desk chair rhythmically back and forth to lull him into sleep.

I turned on my machine, adjusted the sound level, and Jeaneen picked up where she had left off.

"I talked with my husband while I was waiting for the order at the store," she said. "I've given him a lot of FAS education on how to identify people as I've done the research, and he's finding that he's dealing with a lot of FAS adults in the courts. You can tell from the physical characteristics that they're FAS—from the hands, the lines in the hands, different things give them away. And he says these are the people who cannot deal with the bigger realm of things. What we were talking about. He said they almost deal moment to moment. They don't stop to think they can't spend their paychecks now because what are they going to eat next week. So then they go into people's homes and they steal. He gets so frustrated. He used to believe that everybody could think like he thinks, that they could project a week from now, a year from now. But now he says he's got to back off. If he sees somebody with the obvious characteristics of FAS, he tries to take things a little slower with them because they do not understand the way he understands. Their comprehension is much different. I say, 'You see a lot of this?' and he says, 'Yes, more than I ever expected was out there. People in their forties and fifties.' "

The light was fading as I gathered up the papers Jeaneen had given me, packed away my recorder, and said good-bye. I broke the speed limit going north through the Badlands, past Scenic, past the sites of abandoned forts. At first I replayed the tape, listened to Jeaneen's soft voice, modulated so as not to disturb her baby's slumber. I made mental notes to myself of the points to follow up, the statistics to compare, the theories to bounce off other experts. I concentrated on details in order not to think of wider implications and tried to regard today's conversation as a productive collection of material, nothing more. But it didn't work. I was driving through the western remains of the Great Sioux Nation, through Adam's birthright, and before the sun disappeared altogether, I allowed the stillness of helpless reflection to descend. In every direction I went, I trailed those two women, weaving the road into Pine Ridge, my oldest son—all of us—in their erratic wake.

CHAPTER ELEVEN

By October, we were well established in our routine in Northfield. Persia and Pallas were enrolled at a day care center at the Oddfellows Senior Citizens Home located across from a Malt-O-Meal plant, and every morning when I dropped them off, the air was heavy with the smell of cooking grain. Sava and Madeline were busy discovering the perks of town life—the convenience of being able to walk to a store or a video arcade, of having people to visit on foot. Louise and I had made good friends of our next-door neighbors, discovered favorite paths through the Carleton College Arboretum, and established a pattern of an hour-long nightly walk out past the town's boundary and down a lane bordered by unmarred prairie. Northfield was on the southern approach pattern to the Minneapolis–St. Paul airport, and we timed our excursions by the count of jets, twinkling red and white among the autumn constellations.

Under the supervision of the middle school, Adam began a part-time job at the local Pizza Hut. His duties were to police the parking lot for rubbish, to refill as needed the salt and pepper shakers on each checkered table, and to make sure that a supply of paper napkins was always plentiful. It was in many respects the ideal employment: he received a silver sateen windbreaker with his name inscribed on it and was entitled to eat a free pizza for lunch every day. Of course, there were complications. Some of the teenage staff members soon caught on that Adam was an easy mark, agreeable to anything they suggested, including repeating to the boss obscene words he didn't understand. Moreover, he required frequent, if not constant, supervision on the job, or else his attention would wander and he would stray from his tasks. As had always been the case in the classroom, he performed best in a one-on-one setting—not the standard context of a fast-food restaurant.

When we had moved into our house, Adam had chosen a bedroom located high under the eaves on the third floor, and most days he preferred to go there after school, remain until dinner, then go to sleep early. In that sanctuary he created a distinct environment: windows that were opened were left wide, regardless of the outside temperature, until we closed them. His radio was left playing until late in the night. When the thin music drifted down to our room on the second floor, Louise or I would wake and climb the stairs to shut it off. Adam kept a collection of Garfield cartoons neatly snipped from the Minneapolis Sunday newspaper, and every night, when we shook him awake, told him to go to the bathroom and put on his pajamas, we would find these cutout sheets spread beneath the burning desk light. No amount of cajoling could induce Adam to socialize in what was, in fact, an extraordinarily hospitable community; unless we organized an activity specifically for him, our son kept to himself.

In late October I, along with Bea and others, was appointed a United States representative to the Inter-American Indian Congress convened in Santa Fe. The three-day meeting brought together delegates from throughout the hemisphere with the stated goal of sharing among North and South American native peoples some common concerns, programs, and strategies, but the atmosphere was distinctly political. Certain nations with notoriously repressive policies toward their indigenous populations sent ambassadors who were, to say the least, less than critical of their governments, and even within the U.S. contingent there ran an ongoing feud between supporters and detractors of the current presidential administration. Any slight impact my brief talk on the concept of tribal sovereignty might have had was far overshadowed by flamboyant behind-the-scenes machinations and intrigues that constantly raged in the hallways and conference rooms throughout the modern convention center. One of my fellow delegation members, an otherwise sensible man whom I had known for many years, became obsessed with the conviction that our hotel room was bugged and spent an hour peeping behind the southwestern motif paintings and under the sunburst bedspreads. It did no good to point out to him that neither of us had anything remotely secret to say to each other.

On the way back from the meetings, I stopped in Albuquerque for an interview with Dr. Philip May, a University of New Mexico sociologist who for four years had headed the sole government-funded FAS prevention project dealing with Indians. I had read Phil May's published papers, his detailed reports comparing alcohol consumption among various Indian tribes and communities, and he came highly recommended by Jeaneen Grey Eagle, who had participated in one of his training sessions.

Phil picked me up at the bus depot and drove me to his home, a squarish, neo-Pueblo–design house in a quiet neighborhood. He was a tall, blond-bearded man, serious and intent, within days of the end of funding for his second two-year project—a fact that both galled and frustrated him. His wife and teenage daughter were out shopping for a prom dress, and while he and I got acquainted, Phil gathered and laid a stack of desert cedar branches in his barbecue pit, preparation for a cookout. The day was so mild that we stayed outdoors, a pitcher of lemonade between us.

His involvement with FAS research, Phil summarized, stemmed from the late 1970s when, as part of the International Year of the Child, the Indian Health Service (IHS) allocated $120,000 to assess the impact of alcohol on children in tribal communities.

"Three or four people who were asked to come in and plan that project happened to believe that FAS was a topic of great interest. They'd seen a tremendous increase," Phil recalled. "The most influential person was a physician who went to Tuba City [on the Navajo Reservation] in nineteen fifty-six, right out of med school, and stayed. She retired in seventy-nine. During that period of time FAS had been discovered, and over the years, particularly in the last five years, she had seen more and more women delivering while they were intoxicated. She herself had delivered some FAS kids. I offered my services half time, so I became director."

The initial goal of the study, as Phil described it, was to generate factual data pertaining to the scope of the problem. Its success depended upon both the willingness of people in various of the IHS service areas to propose likely cases and the ability of a university diagnostician to correctly identify fetal alcohol-related problems, distinguishing FAS or FAE symptoms from those generated by a host of other causes.

"The referral system brought us a lot of funny-looking kids who were developmentally slow," Phil said. While we spoke he held a ballpoint pen in his hand and flicked the point in and out of its case. It was the mark of a professional researcher, the instrument of his trade at the ready for a stray piece of information.

A specific treatment and rehabilitation plan was drawn up for each child, and by the time the funding ended in 1982, most of the potential FAS victims in seven of the twenty-two areas had been evaluated.

"Local communities really liked the topic of FAS," Phil said, stressing the unusual degree of cooperation the project had received. "They were so frustrated with many adult behaviors with alcohol that they realistically and fatalistically didn't think they could resolve. And here was FAS, a totally preventable problem that affects innocent people. Plus, it is very much on the rise. If we nipped it now, we could get back to where we were fifteen years ago when it didn't seem to be as big."

We went inside to the cool of Phil's study. My recorder was still running as we settled ourselves in comfortable chairs. His desk was piled with overstuffed file folders containing reprints of scientific articles, copies of federal specifications, a jumble of yellow pages covered with handwritten notes. The tangled bureaucracy of Indian Affairs is methodically slow and daunting, as refined in its pigeonholed regulations as any claustrophobic labor union. Its penetration required the mastery of a language composed almost exclusively of capital letters, dashes, and numbers—incomprehensible to anyone outside the system, but so central to communication within it that a layperson who ventured into a closed-door meeting might think he was listening to computer shorthand. The mechanics and effective manipulators of this officious monster were usually careerists, civil servants who after years of paper pushing grew contemptuous of the naïveté of those who lacked a GS rating. The overburdened, over-regulated system resisted the inconvenience of new ideas, the designation of unsolvable predicaments.

I listened as Phil described the gauntlet he and his colleagues had run in effort to continue their project. Their renewal proposal was battered and chipped away at every stage by backbiting, jealousies, cliquishness, cynicism, and apathy. It did not surprise me. The conditions he threatened to expose were expensive to address, vastly complex, and unpleasant to acknowledge. They involved that gray area most irritating to those who get their instructions from printed rules: ethical ambiguity. And Phil May—Ph.D., Anglo, outspoken, thorough but temporary, and lacking a federal ranking—was a natural adversary. Despite the success of the pilot study, despite the lobbying efforts of the National Indian Health Board, the National Tribal Chairman's Association, and the National Congress of American Indians, continued support took months to materialize.

"Finally they got Congressman Yates [of Illinois] and several other people concerned," Phil said, "and that put three hundred thousand dollars in the IHS budget that was to be spent for FAS [for each of the next three years], ostensibly to follow up the stuff that we started. And that became a political football."

In Washington they didn't play touch. I had heard a rumor on Pine Ridge that Indian Health was about to lose a million dollars of its budget to AIDS research. I thought of Jeaneen Grey Eagle, struggling to coordinate a prevention program in an area as large as a small state on a $1500 annual grant.

I mentioned to Phil that everything I read, everyone I talked to, seemed to concur with the doctor from Tuba City who felt that the incidence of FAS was increasing.

"The availability of alcohol has increased tremendously over the past decade," he pointed out. "But it's not just a function of availability. There are a lot of other things, particularly the way that cultures adapted and the kind of norms that are instituted about it. . . . One factor is the traditional women's roles. Drinking is *much* more acceptable among Plains women; it's a *little* bit less acceptable among Navajo women; it's the *least* acceptable among Pueblo."

Yet there were further layers of complication.

"The rigidity of Pueblo drinking norms for women is so inflexible," Phil explained, "that after the period of adolescent experimentation, a woman is faced with a decided choice: to quit—and the vast majority do quit. But those who decide that they are going to continue drinking essentially cut themselves off from mainstream Pueblo society and wind up in a highly alcoholic peer group away from traditional culture. The ostracism effect takes over, and they become producers of multiple FAS kids. They might have two, three, and four. We had two Pueblo mothers who produced five FAS or FAE kids before they themselves died. So ostracism in that sense backfired on the Pueblo."

Phil bombarded me with statistics: by his admittedly conservative count, one of every fifty-five babies born in some Plains tribes was impaired by either FAS or FAE, a figure much higher than he estimated among the Pueblo or the Navajo groups that had been surveyed. Even that figure was misleading, however. The multiple births of FAS babies to a single mother made incidence appear more widespread in the population than was actually the case. It was a matter of concentration, not distribution.

"There are a limited number of people you have to influence to solve the problem," Phil stated with conviction. "We felt that was really encouraging, and we gave lectures to over eleven thousand community Indian people. As we sit here, Wednesday's our last day of operation, and we have educated eighteen hundred trainers in the United States, the vast majority of them Indian, who are to carry on prevention activities in their communities. Now what percentage of them will, I don't know. They have the knowledge, and now they can decide what they do with it."

The issue of strategies reminded me of some of the extreme measures Jeaneen had mentioned as possibilities on Pine Ridge, and I asked Phil if there had been any discussion in the places he had surveyed of incarcerating, as a stopgap measure, drinking pregnant women who had already borne an FAS baby.

"That's happened on one reservation," he allowed, but preferred not to identify which one. "Other tribes have considered it. The Navajo have tried to get heavy maternal drinking actually classified as prenatal child abuse by bringing it under their Child-Abuse Act. Most tribal child-abuse laws have the legal advantage, the judicial advantage of bypassing certain civil rights. Indian governments can do whatever they want."

He was correct there. A number of U.S. Supreme Court decisions, the most telling being *Santa Clara Pueblo v. Martinez* (1978), had established that the Bill of Rights did not necessarily apply within the sovereign boundaries of federally recognized reservations. By provision of treaty, Indian nations generally had the right to devise unique codes of conduct applicable to their resident members. Those laws took precedence over the tenets of American justice, even when they appeared to those who did not subscribe to the tribe's value system to be discriminatory and anti-Constitutional.

I would soon hear and read more about the concept of "fetal rights," as several major cases came to the docket in California and New York, in response to a recognition of the damage a woman could do to her unborn child if she took cocaine or refused to follow a prescribed diet. There was no clear evidence that such legal measures were effective—some in fact argued that they were counterproductive in that they discouraged abusive women from seeking any prenatal care whatsoever, lest they be prosecuted—but they all arose from the same impulse: rather than wait for irreversible and probable harm to be caused, aggressively prevent it from happening. This strategy entailed, in the eyes of those who endorsed it, a choice between the lesser of two injustices. The restricted woman suffered, if that was indeed the correct term, for less than a year in order that the human being she *chose* to bear—this was a crucial point—would not be incapacitated and a burden on society for a lifetime.

One aspect of Phil's research that troubled me was the disparity between the FAS/FAE incidences his data yielded and the higher estimates I had heard from others. Jeaneen had been confident that 25 percent of the children born on Pine Ridge suffered some degree of impairment from maternal drinking. Granted, she was not a clinician, but her figures did not vary all that widely from those of Eva Smith, now a renowned doctor at the hospital on the White River Apache Reservation in Arizona and principal investigator of the community's FAS Prevention Education Project. Eva had come to Dartmouth as a transfer student in 1972 and had remained a close friend of Louise's and mine. After college she received her medical degree from Georgetown, and two years later she was named by the American Medical Association as the outstanding family practice resident in the United States.

I had seen Eva last at a convention of the Research Society on Alcoholism in San Francisco and had put to her my ubiquitous question: how serious was the fetal alcohol problem? What percentage of the children born at White River might be classified as FAS or FAE?

"I'd say at least ten percent, and probably higher, for FAS," she had answered. "For FAE behavioral effects that will not manifest themselves until years after I leave the community—for those I'd go as high as twenty to thirty percent." I had never known Eva to exaggerate; she was widely respected as judicious, unflappable, professional. Shortly after our interview she moved to Washington, D.C., to coordinate Indian alcohol programs nationally. Why then were her percentages more than ten times greater than Phil's?

"We worked with kids from birth through fifteen years of age," Phil explained. "As a matter of fact, we actually worked with some kids up to twenty. And we found two adults in their twenties and thirties and included them in our surveys. But . . . with a lot of these kids, if there's any doubt, we essentially diagnose them as normal. We're very conservative about that. We could have elevated the statistics quite a bit if we put borderline cases into the surefire category."

Did he therefore mistrust Jeaneen and Eva's higher numbers?

"It would depend on what they're using for their numerator," Phil said. "A lot of these estimates say that half of the kids are affected by alcohol. The way we diagnosed FAE is that we had a thirty-, thirty-five–item checklist and certain features, a number of which had actual measurement—each kid would have a certain quantitative score in addition to a clinical judgment. Any kid we diagnosed as FAE had a very high score on that scale, in that their palpebral fissures [eyelid formations], or their head size, or their I.Q., or their length and weight per age—those kinds of things—were in the lowest fifth percentile. So we're not talking about kids who have been merely *affected* by alcohol. There are lots of kids we diagnosed as normal though we knew the mother drank, and pretty heavily. I don't think we diagnosed *any* kid as FAE who had an intelligence above 85. We gave them one whole standard deviation from the norm—we were that conservative."

Conservative was not the word. Even in the premier University of Washington study, the measure of all FAS research around the world, the range included subjects with I.Q.s greater than 100. Exacting standards such as those Phil employed had the advantage of removing any possibility that a person who did not have fetal alcohol impairment was included in the sample, but they also ensured that many people who were probably affected were not counted.

As Phil continued talking, moreover, I caught a hint that there might be another reason why the scope of his identified group was so relatively narrow: it was personally difficult for him to believe, to imagine, that the worst-case scenario could be true.

"One estimate has come out of Montana," he said incredulously. "A noted dysmorphologist [an expert who studies unusual bodily structure or form] says that one in four kids on reservations up there is affected by alcohol."

"Just like what Jeaneen figures for Pine Ridge," I injected.

Phil acknowledged this, but went on. "I have major trouble with that because I don't think those tribes have worse drinking problems than some of the Plains reservations in our study. And I'll be doggoned if every fourth kid, every tenth kid is affected." He shook his head vigorously, dismissing the possibility as unthinkable. "I can't see any culture or any group of people with a problem that bad. I just can't see how any group could survive like that."

It was unbelievable. But that didn't necessarily make it untrue. The verdict on survival was still out. Plus, I found myself impatient with the safety of shying away from a projection because the future could not be documented in advance. I was more inclined toward the theoretical stretch of Professor Ann Streissguth, a prolific researcher at the University of Washington, who identified "bad judgment" as one of the most subtle, most difficult, but most telling symptoms of FAS or FAE. According to her, this condition had less to do with intelligence than it did with the inability of a person to evaluate the consequences of his or her actions.

Her recurring observation of this phenomenon among her patients rang very true for me. Adam perpetually had a hard time with certain abstractions: Bigger than/smaller than. Planning ahead. Saving money. And, carrying this a step further, it logically struck me that someone like him, someone who happened to be a female, could not relate to a warning that "Nine months from now something bad is going to happen for the rest of your child's life if you drink today." It would be an impossible concept for a counselor or obstetrician to convey, and it would not successfully hinder drinking during a pregnancy. I kept coming back to the obvious deduction that fetal alcohol victims were behaviorally among the most likely people to reproduce fetal alcohol victims. For them, logical argumentation had the least sway.

"I think there is a real danger, no doubt about it." Phil followed my train of thought and provided an example of his own. "Those kids aren't really that aware of the consequences. When you go out to the Navajo Reservation and you look like me, when you walk into a room with a bunch of little Navajo kids there, they associate you with discipline and/or shots, neither one very pleasant. Most Navajo kids will stay to themselves, they'll actually cower from you. But FAS kids don't. A little Navajo kid out there with FAS will come up and just grab you by the leg and say, 'Hi, how're you doing?' Really just love you."

His words jogged my memory. "He's such a loving child," people said of Adam when he was little. He would approach total strangers in public places—airports, grocery stores, the lobbies of movie theaters —and wordlessly embrace them. He showed no more hesitancy than he had toward me at our first meeting when he had looked up from his trucks and said, "Hi, Daddy." Everyone, anyone, stood at equal distance from him. Persia, now much the same age as Adam had been in those days, invariably clung to my legs for a good five minutes in an unfamiliar setting, using the security of my presence to get her bearings, chart the lay of the land. But Adam, before he had retreated into himself in his early teens, had approached the world like a blind man walking in an endless summer meadow, as if there were no danger of false steps, no possibility of obstacle, no hidden pitfalls.

That fearless trust was one of the things I had most loved about him, most admired, most bragged upon. "He's never met a person who wasn't kind to him," I remember expounding, but that was ridiculous. Before the age of two he had been battered, starved, and neglected. He had every reason to be shy. Yet it took years of the persistent rebuff and harsh mockery of his schoolmates before Adam learned to await some signal of permission before automatically touching another human being.

I looked around Phil's study, at the books that overflowed the shelves and were stacked on the floor, at the printouts and professional journals, at the Rolodex bulging with phone numbers and addresses. This room was one of the crossroads where the lines of inquiry intersected: social science supplementing biochemistry, personal testimony combining empirical experience with theory. It was the place from which answers or at least directions should emerge, so I brought up my most frightening microchip of deductive reasoning: *If* education and counseling were the major thrust of the prevention effort; and *if* FAS and FAE victims were, relative to women of childbearing age as a whole, unmoved by logic; and *if* women who were FAS or FAE victims had more children, started having them earlier and continued having them longer; and *if* those women who could understand the advertising campaign cut back on their drinking during pregnancy and those women who couldn't comprehend the arguments did not, *then* would not the proportion of FAS victims necessarily grow within any given population? Wasn't the increase exponential? Wouldn't the figures double in ever-abbreviated spans?

Phil took a long route in responding to this concern. He had problems in drawing large conclusions about precisely who was bearing FAS or FAE children.

"We haven't seen too many of the mothers because so many are missing in action or dead," he said.

I returned to a topic I had raised on Pine Ridge—the question of the average age of a woman whose offspring might be most impaired by her drinking.

Phil confirmed Jeaneen's observation. "Full FAS is much more common to women over twenty-five. The body is so much better able to eliminate alcohol when it's young. And second, the standard Indian woman's drinking career is cumulative. They get drawn more and more into really excessive drinking groups—where the sole occupation, almost, is recreation and alcohol. It becomes their whole life, and it takes awhile for them in that kind of peer group to leech out trace minerals and to begin doing damage to their livers. You know," he added parenthetically, "women are much more susceptible to cirrhosis than men because of the fat content of their bodies and of the hormone balance.

"So Indian women who continue drinking in that kind of an all-or-nothing setting," he went on, "begin to do immediate damage to their bodies in the mid-twenties. We've diagnosed one hundred and thirty FAS kids, and of the eighty-five that we've followed closely on seven reservations, only seven were born to women under twenty-five." He paused, considering the implications of his data. "A woman has to abuse her body for quite a while. We've seen women who've been intoxicated virtually their entire pregnancy, but if they're young enough the kids don't come out *looking* or acting that damaged, at least at young ages. It may show up later on, the poor judgment."

I remembered reading of the connection between the point in her pregnancy that a woman drank alcohol and the impact it had on the developing fetus, and asked Phil how much was known about this correlation.

"It's just a matter of time." He rubbed his forearm, and his face took on the almost wistful expression of a scientist who knows that firm answers will eventually turn up. "Ten or fifteen years from now you'll be able to say, 'A dose at x weeks does this.' If the mother drinks heavily the first trimester, then all the structural kinds of things happen. Second trimester, the major thing at risk is size and intelligence, but particularly miscarriage. In the third trimester, it's mainly intelligence."

As ever, when I pondered or talked about this subject, the personal and the professional overlapped. I listened to Phil's catalogue and matched it to Adam's late mother. From the symptoms Adam exhibited, she must have drunk through all nine months, increasing toward her due date. Like all regret for events that might have unfolded differently, this profile made me want to travel back in time, to be at the side of this woman—unknown to me yet touching every part of my existence through Adam. I wanted to meet her during her pregnancy in order, if necessary, to slap the crucial drinks aside, to persuade her to save the quality of our mutual son's life. How many glasses of wine or home brew or beer would she have had to refuse? How much was too much?

"If a woman were only binging for a week," Phil said, "there's no way a kid would be diagnosed as *full* FAS unless it was a real critical week, like somewhere in the third week, the tenth week. Most of the women we see are either heavy bingers or alcoholics. It's not just the size of the dose—it's the dose, the timing of the dose, and the age of the woman."

Phil, and all the people who toiled in this field, constantly encountered women like Adam's mother. I asked how he advised they be approached? How did he talk an alcoholic with a learning disability into not having an occasional drink or not yielding to the impulse for a single night of partying during the course of her pregnancy?

"We try to hit that whole thing real hard," he said. "Probably the most effective slide that we ever show—and we use close to a hundred slides—is a picture of a severely damaged FAS kid's brain next to a normal kid's brain. We talk about timing and dose. We always point out that there are some kids—and there were some in Seattle—who looked and behaved fairly normally with the exception of being a little slower and a little bit behind in school, or a little smaller. But when those kids died, when those kids had autopsies, there were a few who had signs of heterotopia, some scrambling of the layers of the brain cells, and when the researcher went back and asked the mother about her drinking history, he found that she had been a moderate to moderately heavy drinker."

I had seen that classic photograph, seen others like it in which the brains of teetotaling lab mice were compared to those of mice that had been force-fed a diet of ethanol. And even to a person like me who had no real knowledge of how the brain functioned, how it *should* look, the contrast was startling. Alcohol shrunk the brain within its cranial case. A normal cerebrum looks squeezed into a too-small space, packed so tightly that it is creased and folded over itself. But a brain stunted by alcohol has parts that are smooth as a creek stone; it rests within an abundant, vaulted chamber, an insufficient organ to power a complex body. And yet, as Phil said, sometimes an FAE victim had no telltale outward physical abnormalities indicating that the brain had been prevented from attaining full development.

Again I asked: how much drinking did it take to do harm? Was there any guaranteed "safe" level of alcohol that a woman could ingest without posing some danger to her baby?

"We push *absolute abstention*," Phil answered emphatically, and slammed the flat of his hand on a stack of papers at his side. *"It's the only sure way.* We talk about knocking IQ points off. If you don't drink, you may be carrying around a genius. But with repeated doses of alcohol, *even a few*, you may be knocking one, two, ten, fifteen, twenty, thirty points off that kid's intelligence. If we have a lot of drinking mothers, we may someday have whole societies with lower average intelligence. I really believe that, but it's too big an inferential leap for some people to make."

We let the words sink in. This was the bottom line again: survival. I thought of Aldous Huxley's *Brave New World*—where social classes were determined before birth by manipulation of fetal intelligence. I thought of those who called Jeaneen "Chicken Little" and how they must be among the ones for whom this "inferential leap" was too broad. I thought of the generations of Indians, of ancestors, who had managed to survive into the twentieth century despite invasion and plague and government policies aimed at cultural genocide: would our story end with alcohol, a liquid so deceptively fragile that it could evaporate in ordinary air?

Total abstinence for the duration of a pregnancy was an idea that seemed overly extreme the first time I heard it, but after I learned that identical warnings had been issued by the Surgeon General of the United States, the Royal Society of Physicians in England, the American Medical Association, other organizations responsible for maintaining public welfare, and even Jane Brody in her popular nuts-and-bolts *New York Times* health column, it sounded less radical.

It sounded like common sense.

A car pulled into the driveway. Doors slammed and we heard women's voices. The family was back, and Phil's wife, Doreen, an attractive, smiling Pueblo woman, walked into the room carrying a large white shopping bag, her teenage daughter just behind her.

"Success!" Doreen exclaimed, then paused while we were introduced.

"Let's see it," Phil said, with an air of spousely resignation.

"Better get that extra job," Doreen joked while she removed the lid from a rectangular box. There was a swish of tissue paper, and then a formal gown of stiff, dark-blue taffeta was revealed—tasteful, sophisticated, a grown-up dress. Phil tried to suppress his smile, but he was pleased, proud of the pleasure that lit his daughter's eyes.

The interview was almost over, but before I departed for the airport, I wanted to return one last time to the symptom least likely to be identified for treatment: bad judgment. It was potentially such an ambiguous concept—actions that might be frowned upon in one society might be the evidence of distinct and approved values in another. But by ignoring all aspects of the category of judgment as a possible FAE common denominator, the aggregate number of those affected by maternal drinking could be vastly underestimated. Were there any practices that were automatically suspect, regardless of the culture in which they appeared?

"Certainly there are universals." Phil tipped back his chair, balancing on the rear legs as he thought of examples. "Self-destruction; behavior that's not protective, not health protective, not future protective."

I mentioned the example of "Lysol sandwiches" I had heard about on Pine Ridge and Rosebud.

"I thought they were draining it into water. Hairspray . . ." Phil said, familiar with the habit. "They even have beaded puncture tools, I understand. They take a piece of wood, of willow or something, drive a nail into it, cut it off and sharpen it, then bead it and wear it on a belt: 'Lysol user.'"

I related a story Eva had told me about a rash of medical problems on a reservation she knew that had to do with children abusing typing correction fluid stolen from their teachers' desks. They'd paint it on the tips of their fingers, inhale during class, and get high. But if they exercised too soon afterward—rode their bicycles home, for instance —their lungs would harden and they could die of asphyxiation.

"Risk taking in some cultures, especially on the plains, is so valued," Phil acceded. "There are people on Pine Ridge I just love. I just love them. But, going back to fifteen years ago when my wife and I lived there, so many seem to always find new ways to do themselves in. And I don't know why. It could be the residual effects of alcohol."

There are optical illusions that confuse the eye. You look at an illustration from one angle, and you see a goblet; then you take another perspective, and the picture inverts to the profiles of two people facing each other. That was how it was for me in absorbing information on fetal alcohol syndrome: social theory—the prized value of "risk taking" or another such standard euphemism—would blink on and then alternate with the reality of Adam's life, his closed-door future. Relativistic equanimity was no excuse. None. As an outraged father I would run roughshod through civil liberties, convoluted politics. I would reinstate prohibition, jail offenders, impose protective standards. But then the image would change again. I would assume once more my professorial role as nonjudgmental liberal defender of different strokes for different folks, hypothetically prepared to grant the individual excess in order to preserve the group's collective right to follow its own course.

How did I reconcile this grand position when the price seemed to be paid in the currency of hundreds or thousands of Adams? Was I an insider or an outsider on this issue? Did I have a vote? Did my subjectivity light dark corners where others didn't want to look, or was it a blatant violation of sound ethnographic procedure, skewing my research to the point where it became merely self-serving?

I posed the question of great internal debate throughout Indian Country: should liquor sales be legalized on reservations? Would that help at all?

"It depends," Phil answered thoughtfully. There's a place on one reservation—a package store called The Flame. You don't have any-thing going on inside but people are staggering all around The Flame and drinking under the trees. It's crazy. Yet a positive drinking en-vironment can eliminate some real problems—mortality and arrests. There are so many variables. The place we call by the pseudonym

"Plains Reservation Community" in the published research had a horrendous problem with FAS up through Seventy-seven or Seventy-eight. We screened a whole *bunch* of FAS and FAE kids. Then government per capita payments stopped. We saw one full-FAS kid born after Seventy-eight up through Eighty-two. *One.* There may have been some other FAE kids or some that were damaged to a mild degree, but the classic ones weren't being born there anymore. The payments were supposed to start up again last year, so I don't know what's going to happen. But here's a variable that might be unrelated and incidental, and it seems to affect the rate."

The obvious conclusion to draw from Phil's example was as appalling to me as had been Jeaneen's first introduction of the idea of forced incarceration for pregnant, drinking women. And yet I couldn't help remembering Bea's findings on Standing Rock: that some bingers and alcoholics continued to drink until the money ran out. Was the answer to FAS, therefore, to keep people poor?

"In that particular case, yes," Phil answered, then shook his head, denying the words he had just spoken. "At least make sure that their money is coming in some other way."

Forced sterilization, paternalistic government programs, men making decisions about women's bodies—the stuff of federal Indian policy for the past hundred years. These things were not solutions; they were the damned ingredients that caused the problems. It was my turn to recoil from the inferential leap.

"They can take the per capita stuff and just have a bunch of work programs, basically," Phil continued, returning full circle to the expectation with which our conversation had begun, to the optimistic hope that his years of hard work would reap positive results now that the funding had expired. "That's an interesting reservation. We flew all over training our little hearts out to create a local knowledge base that hopefully ten or fifteen years down the road will have spread the word on FAS so that at least everybody knows about it. Now whether that knowledge will result in a behavior that is positive, we don't know."

But Phil couldn't persuade himself, couldn't console himself with this vision. "I think we can only assume it's going to get worse, though," he conceded unhappily. "It's safe to assume that unless we are active now, it's going to get worse."

But why, then, was Phil's prevention education program being phased out by the Indian Health Service, just when it was operating at full steam? Did someone in Washington think FAS would go away by itself or that it was not a big problem, just a passing hobbyhorse for the International Year of the Child?

Phil looked depressed and explained the semantics. "They say the project is not 'defunded' but that the contract is ended. Four or five months from now they'll create some FAS advocates and take our materials and use them." There was no mistaking his bitterness. "By taking over FAS they're getting *the* jewel so far in prevention because it's a magic topic; we've impressed that on them, I think. They're taking it, and they're taking it over."

Phil opened a drawer in his desk, as if to find one more document, one more exhibit for his case, then closed it without even looking inside. "It was so neat to trip onto a subject like FAS," he said, almost wistfully. "Where the response was universally positive and universally productive, at least in the discussion phase. That kind of reception gave us lots and lots of press, and the guys in Washington just became increasingly jealous of it."

Universally positive? What about those hundreds of Indian audiences he had talked to, I wanted to know. How did they receive the bad news of FAS?

"A lot of people, when they start seeing the slides—I mean old people who are not into health literature—they sit there and kind of shake their heads, and they start talking about somebody they've known. 'That's so and so's niece,' or 'That's my granddaughter,' or 'So *that's* why Juanita does so and so.' And it really clicks with them."

I could empathize. Everything I learned about fetal alcohol syndrome had to it the ring of the personally familiar. Either the facts corroborated something about Adam I had already noticed, or they alerted me to the oddness of behaviors that I had previously taken for granted. There was a perverse elation to this growing awareness—a juxtaposed mixture of relief and sadness and anger that Louise and I shared whenever I returned to Minnesota and related a new installment in our investigation. I guess the word for it was "knowledge." And if knowledge, in this case, wasn't power, at least it was better than ignorance. It was heartening for us to discover that Adam was not alone, that his collection of disabilities had a name, an explanation, a circle of interested professional researchers. We had a sense of "Aha!" to the gathering body of information. As each curiously shaped piece was fitted into the puzzle, more definition took shape. We had a clearer idea of what we were looking at. But the simple accumulation of facts, of classifications, of parallel cases yielded ultimately false encouragements. They did not lead to cure or resolution but only to a deepening, hardening conclusion. We recognized others—parents, educators, scientists—who dealt, emotionally and practically, with the victims of maternal drinking. We waved to them, shared anecdotes and details, pooled our scraped-together facts and figures, but in the end the communication was more of condolence than of enlightenment.

The next long visit to South Dakota, this one via Pierre in mid-December, did not have an auspicious start: fifteen minutes out of the Sioux Falls airport, at ten thousand feet in blizzard conditions, the small commuter plane on which I was traveling shook once, violently, then lost altitude. The perky blonde flight attendant made her way to the front, grasping the backs of seats to stay upright, and disappeared into the cockpit. Out the window the ground continued to approach at an alarming rate, and a woman two rows up from me began to loudly quote the Twenty-third Psalm. The frozen landscape below was as far from green pastures as I could imagine, but I caught her drift—especially the "Yea, I go down" part.

A moment later the flight attendant emerged from the forward compartment. She was less composed, and I strained forward to read the name tagged between the brave silver wings on her breast. I wanted to know the identity of the person who was about to announce my doom. It was Cindy.

"There's nothing *majorly* wrong," Cindy chirped into the microphone, her cheerfulness-training firmly in place. "It's just that the windshield kind of blew in on Jim—the pilot? But Bob's going to run us back to Sioux Falls, real low, so fasten your safety belts and put out those cigarettes."

In the seat pocket under my tray there was a complimentary copy of *Redbook* magazine. I opened it to a short story and read with such intensity that to this day I can recall whole sentences. With every lurch, a recent memory dislodged in my brain and fell into my consciousness. Our life that year was full of juxtapositions—Louise and I were editing the galley proofs of *The Beet Queen*, progressing through the manuscript of *Yellow Raft*, and struggling with a mountain of technical articles about fetal alcohol syndrome. One weekend we were in Chicago for the Indian Achievement Awards banquet, the next we were ensconced in a luxurious Japanese hotel in Little Tokyo for Louise to accept the *Los Angeles Times* fiction prize, and less than a month later, prohibited by strep throat from our planned Thanksgiving visit to my in-laws in North Dakota, the whole family sat around a table in the only restaurant in Northfield serving dinner on the holiday.

The meal was composed of the traditional elements, but in unorthodox formats: *shredded* turkey, canned fruit cocktail that had been *heated* in a base of lemon pie filling, *cool* peas, cranberry sauce in the shape of its can. The dining room to which we had been assigned along with others who arrived with small children was part of a hermetically sealed Quonset hut. Window frames had been nailed to the walls, but instead of clear glass each pane consisted of a square of mirror. The effect was surrealistic—outside was inside was outside—made the more so by the loud Musak accompaniment of Liza Minnelli belting out a song bemoaning the "little-town blues." This remembered tableau was much in sync with my mental image of Co-pilot Bob, sleet stinging his square-jawed face as he steered our steep descent.

We landed safely, got our pictures in the newspaper and free rooms at Howard Johnson's, then took off again the next morning and arrived at our destination without incident. The Pierre airport had changed little since my trips to pick up each of our older children, but the roads of the state capital were icy. I was not worried. In anticipation of inclement weather I had special-reserved a four-wheel-drive monstrosity the rental agent insisted upon calling "the vehicle." The vehicle was large, red, and unwieldy, but it did suggest the invincible aura of a tank—or of a bunker—and it had a radio, which I turned on as soon as I was out of the lot.

"The fabulous Narjini brings the magic of the sultans to central South Dakota," an enthusiastic voice announced. "Three sets of twenty minutes each of belly dancing at the Silver Dollar in Fort Pierre."

The fine snow blew low across highway 83S in parallel threads, visible wind at war with the occasional truck sifting dirt from its rear trapdoor. Given any time to themselves, the drifts would completely obscure the road, turn it the same beige slush as the sky. The only contrast to the surrounding blandness was the line of huge metal grids, stark and predatory as Masters of the Universe toys, through which electrical power flowed. On the radio news there was an obituary for a local enlisted man killed in a Newfoundland air crash—for a boy who once had held the broad jump record at Hoover High School.

This time I was headed for the second largest Sioux reservation, almost the size of Pine Ridge and just as destitute. Rosebud is an ironic name, suggesting fragrant springtime, for this place that the U.S. Census Bureau identifies as encompassing one of the two poorest counties in the United States—the other is on Pine Ridge. This is a region of grueling poverty, where the unemployment figures regularly reach 80 percent and where the average lifespan for an Indian man is less than sixty years. I had an appointment with Brenda Demery, a public health nurse and another of Phil May's trainees, whose position and duties were roughly equivalent to Jeaneen's, though slightly broader in nature.

The village of Rosebud is nestled in as much of a valley as the northern plains can muster, a gentle indention where buildings are set at slightly different levels. It is an old town for South Dakota, and in dead winter its closed doors and smoking chimneys were as enigmatic as that other "rosebud," the cryptic password of *Citizen Kane*. Brenda's office was located behind the hospital in a squat brick building. Inside, the overhead lights were bright, the rooms decorated with the now-familiar framed posters admonishing against unsafe substances.

Brenda was a businesslike, compact Lakota woman. Her handshake was cautious, pro forma, giving nothing away. She mentioned she was from Fort Yates on the Standing Rock Reservation, the place where Adam and I got our Sioux names, and that she had worked on Turtle Mountain Reservation in North Dakota, where Louise's grandfather—he was once tribal chairman—and grandmother live. For the last several years, Brenda had resided on Rosebud, and recently she had adopted two children, each from an alcoholic family background. Both, she said, had experienced some physical and developmental problems, "but not FAS. They're not as severely affected as that."

"A couple of years ago Indian Health realized that FAS was becoming a major problem," she told me once we were seated and the tape recorder was activated. "We're seeing more and more of it.

The governor of South Dakota has appointed a task force, in effect for a little over a year now, but one of the problems is that we have no sure way of identifying FAS children. Within the state we have identified so far just thirty-three children, and thirty-one happen to be Indian. We all feel that there are definitely many more. Most of our physicians are elderly; they grew up in the communities where they practice, and it's very hard to live in a place where you make that identification, that this child is FAS. When you bring in an outside resource, they can take the *blame* for having identified that child. Also, in the Aberdeen IHS area we don't have permanent medical staff. In one year alone we had over two hundred and twenty doctors at the hospital. They're here for maybe two, three, four weeks at a time, and, of course, if there's a child born with FAS, they wouldn't want to make the diagnosis."

I must have looked puzzled by this statement, for she answered my question before I asked it.

"They wouldn't be around to see it through, or the parents might be upset—both of those. Unless a child is very severely affected, they just don't have the training to identify FAS. A lot of doctors who've been out of school for a while have heard the term but don't know much about it. You need a pediatric dysmorphologist, a doc who specializes in children's genetic problems, to make the diagnosis, and we don't have any in this state—though I heard one just moved into Sioux Falls and we'll try to latch onto him. Once the kids are identified there are resources."

Always on the lookout for something new to try for Adam, I asked what those might be.

"An FAS child can qualify for SSI, supplemental income. With a lot of the physical problems that these children demonstrate we can filter them into crippled children; a cardiologist comes every six months, a neurologist comes about once every three months."

I thought of the resources that have been available to Adam—Harvard-trained specialists, a university medical center—and what little impact they have made upon his life after years of concerted effort. In so many ways he remained little different from those boys at Project Phoenix. Would, in fact, his long-term prognosis have been radically different if he had been born and raised on Rosebud? If Louise and I had never entered the picture?

"In most cases with FAS, I would say about eighty to ninety

percent, the children are removed from the home because of the drinking that is involved."

Just like Adam was, but by then it was too late. After he was born, the damage had been done. I stopped myself. I had bobbed across the barrier that was supposed to divide me as parent from me as dispassionate interviewer, seeker of truth for its own sake. The more people I talked to—in this year of talk—the earlier in each new conversation this lapse seemed to take place. To get back on course, I relied on one of my now stock questions. Every fact had to be confirmed at least twice for me to believe it.

"Do the mothers of these children tend to be older?"

"You don't find many under the age of twenty-four. A lot depends on how long they've been drinking and what they're drinking all the time," Brenda said, echoing the conclusions of Jeaneen and Phil. Now this response could be filed under "true."

I moved on to the sticky issue of identifying fetal alcohol effect. Brenda took a deep breath, drummed her fingers on the desk for a moment, and looked around the room as if to find a better answer than the one that occurred to her. I had the sense that she, too, was retreating from the emotional charge this topic inevitably seemed to deliver.

"It's hard to define because there are other kinds of birth defects that can cause a child to have mental retardation and learning problems, not just alcohol consumption. You basically have to go on the history of the mother or the family. Awareness is beginning to improve a lot. FAS is something that people are interested in because it involves children. One of the hardest things here is to get women to understand that when they drink, the alcohol goes into the placenta, and the baby's actually drinking. You will hear comments like, 'I drink but my baby doesn't. There's no way my baby drinks just because I do.' "

It was a familiar dilemma, and I repeated examples I had heard from around the country. Everywhere I went, I found the same chain reaction: parents who abused alcohol produced children who abused alcohol produced children who abused alcohol. Where did it stop? Did the cycle persist because of cultural conditioning—nurture—or because of nature, because of residual fetal alcohol effect? If it were substantially the latter, as I had begun to suspect, it would be almost impossible to interrupt through ordinary means.

Brenda appeared to be dissatisfied, as if there was more to the story than either of us conveyed. She frowned.

"You have to remember that children here know or see only one way of life," she said. "This is the way that they've grown up. They *like* their parents. Hard as that may seem to some people to accept, this is their mom and this is their dad, and they love them. And just as hard as it may be for some people to accept, mothers and dads love their kids. You can't make the judgment that they don't care. Yes, it's difficult to work with these children. You make them understand that their parents were affected by a *disease*. That's a big thing on this reservation: alcohol is not accepted as a drug to which people become addicted—not just physically addicted but mentally and emotionally addicted. It's hard to get this across to even medical people who work here all the time.

"Eighty percent of the people who come in here are drunk," Brenda said, indicating the neighboring hospital with a sweep of her hand. "They come in because they're accident victims, they're intoxicated or something. You get burnt out. It's not easy to empathize, but you have to keep your objectivity."

Brenda's words—impassioned, on target, absolutely right— reflected that larger reality, where victims are victims of victims in an endless linkage that's been smithed by history, by racism, by economics, by bad luck. There are so many avenues for indignation and sympathy, so many people who are not themselves to blame. But finally I couldn't completely grant the blanket pardon that was implied. A person who lives in the world, no matter what his or her social or psychological context, seemed to me more accountable than a baby who had not yet been born. To some degree, a choice, no matter how buried its trigger, had been made by one party in this sorrowful transaction and not by the other. My ultimate allegiance was to that person Adam was not allowed to be, to the baby carried by every woman who wouldn't—or who couldn't—stay alcohol-free for nine crucial months.

But I didn't say any of this aloud. I was here to listen, not to engage in a debate that had no right position, no winning answer. I didn't even think Brenda and I had points of significant disagreement; on any given day, reacting to any particular incident or individual, the weight of outrage might shift from one ruined life to another. So I moved on to the next question I had written in advance in my notebook: what was being done on Rosebud to tackle this problem?

"You have to start with the young, and the younger they are the better," Brenda said. "At Headstart, when they're three or four years old. If they're older, in high school, it's harder because they've already got experiences behind them, already got their way of thinking.

"To be perfectly blunt . . ." she stopped, weighed her words carefully, then began again. "IHS makes the statement that FAS is definitely a problem, but as far as anybody really *doing* anything about it—doing any teaching or other types of education, it's pretty much nil. Phil May came out here a little over a year ago and set up training sessions on the reservation with anywhere from ten to thirty people. He sent us material and gave us flyers, slides, everything, so that we could go out in our communities. And then every time we led a session, we were to forward to Albuquerque the evaluations people gave to our presentation. As far as I know, Jeaneen and I are the only ones who have ever done that. People are aware it's a problem, people *say* it's a problem, but when it comes down to putting money in a program or in making a real effort to do something about it, it's pretty much an individual effort. We try to do the best that we can do, but when there's just one of you to cover a hundred and fifty miles, it's . . ." she paused, straightened the calendar on her desk, looked harassed. "And plus we're responsible for other things. There are twenty-four communities on the Rosebud alone."

Once again Brenda seemed to hear herself, then pulled back from anything that sounded too accusatory. This was no simple matter of disorganization or lack of goodwill.

"On all the reservations people will say that health is very important, their number one priority, but when you look at what the tribe is doing, all their resources and energy are going into economic development, water rights, land rights, because these are the immediate, foreseeable things that they need. We need food, we need resources, we need to have a paycheck. It's hard for these people who are worrying about where's my next meal coming from, or am I going to have enough fuel to get through this winter . . . it's hard for people to think down the line, twenty years from now, this is what's going to happen to my child. You can't see downrange, you can't see the far-reaching effects. Right now is what's in front of you. The need to survive."

Her words rang out in the afternoon quiet of her office, in the eye of the tornado.

"You have some people who *can* see down. You have teachers that are concerned, you have health professionals. But for the most part, these are people who have come in from the outside. They're not people who have lived here all their lives or have probably ever been on a reservation before. Their concept of things is different from those of us who have been here and lived here. There really is a difference between Indian and non-Indian culture. They can't get that understanding. Family is important, even if you come from a drinking family. Family is number one. And people think you're helping if you don't tell the cops that they're drinking. You don't want to get them in trouble. You kind of cover up and hide for them. Because they're family. That's what families do. And it's hard to get people to understand that what they are really doing is hurting. You need to get that drinking person into help even if it's against his or her wishes. It's hard to get the community to change. That's why we have a lot of abuse. Women abuse mostly, but there's male abuse. It's accepted. It's an accepted part of the community, and it's an accepted way of life. It's hard to change people's attitudes. You've got to go step by step."

Brenda—at once adoptive parent of a child who had been hurt by alcohol and trained professional, coping daily with the details of counseling, prevention, education—was without self-deceptions, but was caught, as were so many people who struggled directly or indirectly with this problem, as indeed to an extent was I, in the vortex of conflicting loyalties: cherished principles and beliefs versus unwelcome insights.

"All Indian people have been affected by alcohol to some extent," she added. "We've all had a relative who is considered alcoholic. And in some families you tend to go the same way, or you want nothing to do with it. It's hard to find a middle road."

CHAPTER TWELVE

During the winter and spring of 1986, I spoke to doctors, lawyers, parents, tribal leaders, teachers, social workers, psychologists, chemical dependency counselors, and police. From Project Cork, a Dartmouth computer-based information clearinghouse on matters related to alcoholism, I received several large shipments of scholarly articles, biochemical studies, and statistical surveys, and tried, with my limited knowledge of hard science, to highlight my way through with a yellow marker. I attended the annual conventions of experts in the field of addiction and chemical dependency, corresponded with Ann Streissguth, the psychologist at the University of Washington whom everyone regarded as the professional with the best and longest overview of FAS behavior. I filled several imitation wood-grain port-a-files with my notes.

It seemed, sometimes, as though I were throwing darts at a blank wall, and every spot I hit was a bull's-eye. There was no irrelevant information, yet no single source provided the breadth of a comprehensive picture. There were weeks, months, at a time in which I wasn't sure if I were pursuing answers to questions about Adam, alcohol, Indians, women, cultural disintegration, ethics, or economics. The book I had intended to write—a footnoted study of the national implications of fetal alcohol syndrome—was evolving more and more into the chronicle of a personal quest for understanding.

As I accumulated the painfully honest, unvarnished testimonies of others, I worried that it would be hypocrisy to disguise in print our own family situation, my own motivations and biases. Yet that was a kind of exposure I had not anticipated and did not desire. I had never been drawn to write an autobiographical memoir, never planned to step out from behind the shield of invisible authorship. Some novelists base their characters on real people. Their fiction is thinly veiled fact—but Louise and I are not among them. Our stories, our characters, are consciously invented creations, not stand-ins for ourselves. This book would necessarily be different.

I discussed the question with Louise and with Adam. Were they willing for our experience with FAS to be the central organizing principle in this book? I spent a long time explaining the matter to Adam and read my initial notes aloud to him to demonstrate the extent of our background that might be included. He had rarely shown much curiosity about his adoption or about his biological past, but I had never kept any facts from him. We had talked often about his physical and learning problems—detailed, mostly one-way conversations on the drives to doctors' offices or in meetings with school personnel. He was a veteran of professional counseling, and though I had no notion what he ultimately made of the information at his disposal, he was familiar with the terminology.

As an anthropologist I was sensitive to the matter of informed consent: I did not want Adam, because of any lack of understanding of what publication meant, to agree that this book reveal material he would rather keep under wraps. But how could I explain to him, who rarely read, that total strangers would thumb through a version of our lives—through our weaknesses as well as our strengths—and draw conclusions we might not like to hear?

My profession was a not very provocative mystery to Adam, something that had more to do with "where" than with "what," so his basic question about the enterprise I proposed was matter-of-fact: he didn't understand what would make me write a book. It didn't make sense to him for me to spend so much time doing something I had told him I didn't want to do in the first place.

"If I write the book this way," I told him, "maybe what happened to you won't happen to somebody else."

"Okay, sure," he said. It was no big deal to him. Privacy was not a priority.

"Look," I suggested. "If I'm going to tell about my life and your life, it would be fair for you to do the same thing. Write down everything you can remember, the good stuff and the bad stuff, and we'll put that in the book too. Then you can tell the story the way you saw it."

An expression of interest crossed Adam's face. The idea appealed to him.

"How would I do that?" he asked.

"Just start," I said. " 'The Adam Dorris Story by Adam Dorris.' Take your time, and include anything you want."

And he did. He looked at our photo albums for inspiration, sifted through his accumulated possessions, and every so often he would produce a few pages, especially after his grandmother and aunt gave him a used manual typewriter on which to compose. Louise read the text as it was written, I didn't. His and my perspectives had to be independent, not responses to each other. But I think Adam got a certain satisfaction from the fact that he and I were engaged in something of the same task. In our house his bedroom was immediately above my office, and sometimes as I sat before my computer I heard the thump of banged keys from above. "The Adam Dorris Story by Adam Dorris" became by far the most sustained project he had ever attempted—a work of which he was proud, a work he was anxious for people to read.

And when, as this book was nearing completion, Adam and I finally traded full manuscripts, I found our memories of events to be complementary. Adam's accomplishment was, for him, the equivalent of painting the ceiling of the Sistine Chapel. It was the best thing he had ever done, far exceeding what many would say he had the ability to do.

Once Adam had embraced the project, I lost my last excuse to back out. He had been accurate in his perception: I didn't want to do it, didn't want to relive painful memories on paper, didn't want to produce a book that would fit into no neat category and would necessarily fail—because of its subjectivity, if not for other reasons—to satisfy many experts. The issue of fetal alcohol syndrome touched upon ethical questions for which I had no clean answers. It involved theoretical and moral positions which at best were ambiguous and at worst were directly opposite to my own political preferences. Mired in contradictory evidence, I was every bit as conflicted and irritated as Jeaneen, every bit as distressed as Brenda, every bit as frustrated as Phil. Omniscience was a myth I discarded early on. There were no signposts to follow. When you decide to have a child, you are hostage to an uncertain future. The fine print of the contract is invisible—it appears, as if inscribed in lemon juice, only under the heat of the bright light of unfolding experience. Control is a delusion, and the only absolutes are retrospective.

Once we accepted that our family was intrinsically part of this book's narrative, reminders and analogies arose everywhere we looked: a child with the distinctive facial characteristics of FAS might approach me on the street. At a Northfield party, Louise jinxed the festive mood by prevailing upon a pregnant Carleton professor not to have wine with her meal, and all the way home we discussed whether it had been the right thing to do. Yes, we finally decided, but that kind of intrusion did not win us friends in the short run. I had a similar encounter in the restaurant of the Minneapolis airport. A woman, certainly well into her second trimester, sat at the table next to mine and ordered a martini.

"Excuse me," I said. "But it's really not safe to drink when you're pregnant. I'm working on a book, and . . ."

"Mind your own business," she snapped back, then turned to her friend and loudly complained about how typical it was for a man to think he knew more than she about her own body. When her drink arrived, she caught my eye and held up the glass in my direction. "Cheers," she said, and took her first sip.

There was a part of me that wanted to whip out my wallet, show her Adam's picture, tell her his story. There was a part of me that wanted to make a citizen's arrest or to plead for her baby's brain cells. There was a part of me that wanted to ask her if she intended to fill a formula bottle with gin and vermouth, to feed *that* to her child when it was born—since there would probably be less harm done at that stage than what she was doing today. But I kept silent, turned away in embarrassment, hoped that she was young enough, un-stressed enough, well nourished enough to minimize the dose of poison she was sending to her growing fetus with every self-satisfied swallow. It was no pleasure to be right.

We took Adam to St. Paul for an evaluation of his scoleosis. His spine had quickly and irreversibly developed a sharp curve to the left—a thoroughly predictable symptom of fetal alcohol damage, according to published scientific papers. His job at Pizza Hut was continually jeopardized by his performance, his apparent inability to function without direct supervision. He seemed to have reached an educational plateau beyond which any moves forward would be slow, erratic, of short duration before disappearing. As Adam got older, the contrasts accentuated between him and other young people his age or even younger, and as this happened, I saw him retreat into solitude, take fewer risks.

And yet he did not learn from his mistakes, inconvenient or maddening as they often were. He clung to established order with tenacity, refusing to adapt to fluctuations in his external environment. If he had successfully worn a T-shirt and no coat in the summer, then by golly, he'd slip from the house in identical clothing in January, even though the temperature was well below zero. When he learned a new skill, he would more often than not focus on some extraneous detail within the overall structure, and drop anchor. The whole constellation of actions, the essential mixed with the accidental, would become entrenched, and no single part could be selectively jettisoned. There were no gradations, no interchangeable parts to a pattern once he embraced it. Right clothes = T-shirt. Period.

On television it is chic to portray the learning disabled as invariably conscientious, anxious to please, desirous to make a good impression or to compete in the Special Olympics. People around them recognize their industry, their effort, their purity of spirit. Bill, the retarded character played by Mickey Rooney in two popular movies-of-the-week, and, more recently, Benny on "L.A. Law" are impossible not to admire. They balance their drawbacks with such respectable strengths that they are models of preconcupiscent, unspoiled humanity, children of nature whose inherent nobility Rousseau would recognize in a flash.

Adam was not like that. Though I knew him to be sweet, gentle-hearted, and generous, the face he showed to the world was sullen. He avoided work whenever possible, refused to pay attention to his appearance, was slow to motivate, and only occasionally told the truth. His attitude discouraged even those who began their association with him enthusiastically. Most people, even in the so-called caring professions, need some return on their labors, some reassuring sense of progress taking place, of gratitude or response, but Adam, for whatever reason, was rarely forthcoming with any of this. He took what was offered for free, he usually cooperated in any new venture when the spotlight was focused on him, but as soon as the pressure was off, he seemed to slough whatever skills he had been assiduously taught. He was not, by and large, rewarding, and in all but a few rare and special instances, we watched as various adults lost hope in his potential. With it went a measure of their commitment. Once Adam passed beyond the circumscribed limit of teachers' or social workers' technical responsibility—even if they had worked with him on a daily basis for months or years—they dropped out of our lives. Few bonds endured longer than the law required.

This was not due to a lack of basic compassion. If Adam's disability had been multiple sclerosis or blindness or dyslexia or simple epilepsy, if it had been deafness or a speech impediment, I think he would have been more appealing to the health workers periodically assigned to his case. Certainly he had a range of physical ailments—he took two different types of medication three times a day to control his seizures; he had hearing and sight and balance problems; his spine twisted; his teeth were too large and too numerous for his mouth; and his coordination was chronically precarious.

But his greatest problem, the day-in, day-out liability with which it was hardest for the world to cope, was his lack of a particular kind of imagination. He could not, cannot, project himself into the future: "If I do x, then y (good or bad) will follow." His estimation of consequences was so hazy that it translated into an approach to action so conservative that it appeared to be stubborn. He existed in the present tense, with occasional reference to past precedent. Every leap was off a cliff and into an unknown depth, perhaps too shallow, perhaps bottomless, and so he tended to dig in his heels.

And when he did venture forth, sometimes tentatively, sometimes with the brashness of having nothing to lose, he made wrong choices, saw only part of the picture, was either too literal or too casual in his interpretation of detail. If left to monitor his own medication, he might take all three of a day's doses at once in order to "get them over with" or might sequester them in a drawer "so that I won't run out." He might take a dollar bill out of my wallet, even when he had ten of his own, "because I wanted to save mine." The question "why" has never had much meaning for Adam; the kind of cause-effect relationship it implies does not compute for him.

In April, on a visit to Little Wound—a school of some 750 students, kindergarten through twelfth grade, in Kyle on the Pine Ridge reservation—I had a long interview with Mona Richards, a special education counselor, Elaine Beaudreau, a vice president at

Oglala Lakota Tribal College, and Sharon Cuny, an elementary grade teacher. Both Mona and Sharon had adopted children diagnosed with fetal alcohol impairments. From the first word our conversation was unguarded. Listening to their experiences as parents and as professional educators I had a recurring sense of *déjà vu*. We communicated in an insider's language, a vocabulary scoured, for once, of gloss or apology or subterfuge. Among ourselves we didn't need to temper our sentiments, didn't need to leaven our anxieties with protests of parental affection—which we accepted as a given—but had the liberty of telling each other the truth as we had come to know it. For two hours we opened the doors to our secret rooms, merged the parallel universes each of our families inhabited.

We met in a bright, empty classroom. The alphabet ran the base of the ceiling like a border, each letter illustrated by a picture. A bulletin board was crowded with students' drawings having to do with Mother's Day, only a couple of weeks away. Suns were yellow, skies were blue, and stick women grasped the hands of stick children as they stood together beside houses with smoking chimneys. Mona invited me to join them for lunch in the cafeteria, but I asked if, instead, it would be all right if we simply talked in this place where there were no distractions. All three women had brought sandwiches from home, so they had no objection. We sat in small desk-chairs arranged in a rough circle as if for a reading group, and as we spoke or listened, we bent our too-large torsos forward toward the center. At first, as we exchanged introductions and biographical information, our voices were muted, careful, modulated to a library volume, but within moments the air was crowded with our testimony.

"At least a third of the population of any school system on the reservation, a third of the student body, have some kind of emotional or learning problem that, once you get the family profile and see the drinking that goes on within it, could be attributed to FAS or FAE," Elaine estimated. She was a vivid, articulate Lakota, a longtime resident of Pine Ridge who received her college and graduate degrees at St. Scholastica and Wyoming. She radiated authority, self-assuredness. FAS was by no means a new topic for her, nor was this the first time she had expressed her frank opinions.

"The bulk of the population of those students goes into the FAE category, and what do you do with them?" she continued. "Do you spend a lot more of your time dealing with lack of attention span and not being able to behave and not being able to concentrate, versus academics? You can take that further: what are we doing as a society, meaning the reservation, for the next generation, if half of our population is going to be FAE adults?"

I asked to what extent it *was* an adult problem.

"We probably have two or three generations of FAE people," Elaine said. "We've probably got grandparents, probably have people who have died who have had that syndrome."

"Do the mothers tend to keep the FAS kids they bear?" This was a question I never failed to ask, for it touched on two key issues, one objective, the other subjective. What was the cost to society, especially to an already economically strapped place like Pine Ridge, of a woman who drinks during her pregnancy? And what about Adam? What was the likely sequence of events in his life that led him to join our family?

Sharon answered with an emphatic monologue. She was a pale, slim young woman with light brown hair, dressed in pale shades of yellow and blue. She did not give the impression of being the scrappy fighter that she was.

"I've had my little boy since he was five years old. [His mother] walked off from a family of twelve. Then after he was with me for six years, she wanted her kids back. She got four of them, and social services recommended she not have more than that because she couldn't handle them. She stopped drinking, she went back and told the judge that she wanted them back, and she got three more, so that made seven. And within a month she was back drinking.

"I got a call, an emergency call, and I was afraid he was dead, that was all I could think of. 'Is he alive? Is he okay?' I said when they called. They said, 'Yes, but we need to send him back to you. Do you want him?' It was a very volatile situation, and they had to get him out of the home. He had been staying with the principal of the school the last two nights. . . . He came back terribly withdrawn, almost like a baby. It's taken him a year to get back to where he was before he left. He's doing better, but I'm not ever going to let the courts get him again.

"He's the only one of those twelve kids who's full FAS; the rest of them are to some degree FAE. He's had everything from cerebral palsy to epilepsy, and he has all the other things: he was small, curvature of the spine, not stretching out, walks on his toes—the works. Poor little guy. But he was lucky enough to have the mentality to be able to function in the school system. He's fortunate there.

"What can I expect in the future? What can I expect of him? Will he be able to live without me? He's so dependent. There're so many things he can do, yet some of the basic things of life, he can't. It's just very difficult. Will he make it through eighteen? Can he ever learn to bathe, brush his teeth, and do the basic things he needs to?"

"Yes," I reassured her. "My son can. But I watched him tie his shoes the other day and thought, 'there's a year of my life.'"

"At least," Sharon laughed, then smiled at me. "More than that, I think."

"Motivation is a real obvious problem," Elaine suggested. "Counselors deal with it. So do teachers, whoever, any person working in social services. FAE people are full of apathy, they don't care, they don't seem to have this need for survival or the desire for it. They don't even have the idea or conception of doing anything beyond the needs of what they're used to. Like getting up and eating a bowl of cereal: 'I'm told I have to do this at such and such a time, and that's all I do.' And not even thinking beyond.

"I've even seen it with FAE adults, again the motivation. They will sit in my office and give me terminologies like 'I just don't care,' and 'I don't know why I did it, why I did that.' They don't really understand their own feelings of what's going on inside them. Then take that a step further: a lot of these people are parents already, and a lot of these parents are . . . teaching and giving examples for that same kind of behavior to their little children. So where's the crack? Where's the division? Is this a physical thing versus a learned behavior? It's complicated."

I listened to Elaine and thought that people unfamiliar with fetal alcohol impairments would not fully comprehend what she meant. They would think, "Well, sure, a lot of folks aren't as motivated as they should be. You can't attribute *that* to maternal drinking." They would think Elaine and Sharon and Jeaneen and I were conveniently associating with every dysfunctional behavior to alcohol, using it as the scapegoat and easy explanation for a range of problems found in every society throughout history. Who could prove such a nebulous correlation? And yet, despite coming as we did from different backgrounds, having widely variant experience, we found ourselves in utter agreement: Elaine was on to something important and true.

Mona, the special education teacher, was the adoptive mother of a child probably impaired by prenatal drinking. A warm, intelligent Lakota woman recently returned to Pine Ridge, she had received a B.A. in sociology from Black Hills State College and then continued to take advanced courses in counseling. "I was a late bloomer," she admitted, referring to the years of work before she returned to school to get her degree. "I remember in psych and socy classes they talked about 'failure to thrive.' I wondered why these kids never developed normally. I related to some of my own relatives who had really tiny children, and I knew they always drank a lot, and I'd wonder if their kids were 'failure to thrive' children and if it was related to drinking or proper nutrition or emotional neglect. It was hard to determine which part was really it. I guess that's why I got so carried away when I got to FAS."

There is a word for the condition of "failure to thrive": *marasmus*, derived from a Greek root. It means literally wasting away or progressive emaciation. It brought to my mind that first photograph I had seen of Adam, all knees and elbows and large dark eyes.

"They call us 'The FAS Ladies' here," Elaine joked, bringing me back to the present.

"We just keep pounding away." Mona's remarks, informed by the convergence of professional and personal observation, were devastating to hear. At each new level of candor we four seemed to pause for breath, to check each other out for continued approval before proceeding. In that fluorescent atmosphere of artificial daylight we willed ourselves to be vulnerable.

"[Students affected by FAS or FAE] don't try to do any more than what they're assigned," Mona commented. "Some of them have trouble even getting the basics. They have so hard a time learning how to read and write and doing the little things that they need to do in life. They have no motivation, very little desire." She raised, then lowered her shoulders. "There're so many kids that just need *comfort* in this classroom."

The word startled us, made us amused at our own needy intensity. "I guess they're not the only ones," I said, expressing the recognition that we all felt.

"My son has a difficult time," Mona continued, shifting to the personal. "He has a lack of reasoning abilities, and I think that you learn those somewhere along the line, that you have to think about things and reason. He has no patience, and if he can't get it like that"—she snapped her fingers—"he cannot sit down and think about it, reason it, and come out with a good decision."

In this almost conspiratorial atmosphere of shared insights and private fears, I dared to hypothesize further than anything I could substantiate with hard evidence.

"How does this translate when the kids get to be teenagers and beyond?" I asked, then proposed an answer to my own question. "I have a suspicion that a lot of kids who commit suicide cannot conceive of themselves dead and therefore give in to the spontaneous act. A lot of kids who commit theft or who ingest dangerous substances may not be able to help it, in a sense, because they don't reason, as you say, beyond a certain point."

Mona nodded. "There was a little boy in here a few days ago who was trying to huff chalk. They try almost anything." She returned to the example of her adopted son, Kevin.

"Like his foot got run over by a car because it didn't occur to him to look before crossing the street, and he stepped right in front of a car," she said. "It causes me nightmares thinking about what happens when he gets old and starts off taking drugs—what's he going to do? He can't reason anything out and say, 'Okay, this is wrong.' Somebody teases him and tells him to do something. He's just a total reactor. He doesn't ever make decisions on his own. If the teacher's in a good mood and really has a good time with him, then he'll have a great day, and he'll learn a lot. If somebody else does something, the kid next to him pokes him with a pencil, he'll go in the opposite tangent. His whole life is that way. Will he ever be able to drive a car? Will he ever be able to hold a job, ever be responsible for himself? He's going to be thirteen in May, and he's the size of my third-grade kids. He's in a fifth-grade classroom, and he should be a seventh grader. I got him at five, and he was still wearing diapers. He was the size of a baby. But he's come a long way, and I treat him like he's a normal child, even though I know he has a lot of difficulties. I have to get after him to do his exercises. He needs to do them because his tendons are like this, he can't touch his heel down."

To demonstrate she pressed the toe of her boot into the floor, then strained without success to flatten her heel. Her face was a reflection of the hours she had worked with her son. She wore a mask of pain, the look of a person who'd been called upon in an emergency to bind an ugly wound or to cradle a broken bone.

"He had to do these exercises for like twenty minutes a day." She laboriously pushed her heel lower and lower. "It's torture. He'll cry as he walks on his toe all the way across the room. Makes me feel like I'm killing him.

"Everybody in the house says, 'Gee, Mom, do you have to *do* that to him?' I say, 'Yes, I do.' But now I've tried to get it so that he does them, and he will not. I gave him a schedule; he's got a schedule written on his closet door so he won't be embarrassed in front of everybody else, and it says 'When I come home, I change my clothes. I do my schoolwork, I do my chores, I fix my bed and pick up my clothes'—all these things I have written down on a list, every one. 'When I get up I brush my teeth, I bathe, I wash my face, I comb my hair, I put on clean clothes.' He'll go for a week with the same clothes on. He doesn't care. It doesn't bother him in the least.

"And then eating—he'll sit at the table and wait for me to put food on his plate. He will not eat if I am talking to somebody or if somebody comes to the door. If I put one thing on his plate, he will eat that, and when he is done, he will get up and leave. That will be it. He won't eat anything else. Now I'm trying to convince him: 'You feed yourself from the table. You put it on the plate . . .' He'll go days without eating unless you give it to him. Then he gets sick. If you don't feed him right, he gets sick, everything from ear infection to flu. I worry that he gets his vitamins, I have to make sure he eats, make sure he bathes."

I listened with fascination, thinking of the many lists I had made and hung on the refrigerator for Adam, remembered changing his diapers at five, how I still have to hound him to take his anticonvulsant medicine, how when not reminded, he won't shower, eat, or change his clothes. Yes, it could be a mere coincidence: that this boy on Pine Ridge and my son in New Hampshire have almost identical behavioral profiles. Yes, it could be a coincidence that both of their mothers drank, that they have similar physical impairments, that the boy's adoptive mother, in her worried complaint, strikes precisely the same chords that Louise and I have struck on many other occasions. But in this room, on this day, we four people have cast off the caution of coincidence: we're after common denominators. Mona and I looked at each other, communicated without words.

"One thing, totally unscientific, that stems from coming to terms with my own son," she offered. "I impose on him a bunch of things that I *think* will enhance his life and that I *think* he wants, and then I feel bad because he can't have what I think he wants. In fact, when I'm being realistic, I know he's a very different person than I am. Because of FAE he doesn't want the same things. It's a chore for him to come when we all go out to dinner as a family, because it's 'Sit up straight, chew with your mouth shut, put your napkin on your lap, blah, blah, blah.' He would really rather not go. He'd rather stay home, he'd rather do a repetitive task. I'd hate it if I were him, but he doesn't hate it. And this has been something really, really slow for me to accept because we tend to project our personalities on our kids. That may be a clue to treatment. There may be a different life-style that non-FAE people don't understand that might fulfill an FAE person. But I don't know what that is."

None of us did. Each of us glanced at the others, waiting for ideas, suggestions, proposals, but the sense of Mona's words echoed in the room and defeated the easy answers.

"We try to change the tribal code," Elaine said after a long pause, breaking the spell.

This issue inevitably seemed to return to law, to external coercion in the absence of self-restraint, to a deprivation of liberty as a last resort. Again and again the people to whom I've talked, especially those on the front lines, face to face with the innocent victims of maternal drinking, came to the sorry conclusion that no arbitrary freedom was worth the cost in lives that FAS entailed. "Do unto others as you would have them do unto you" instructs the most elemental commandment of social intercourse. That is the rule, the "categorical imperative," as Immanuel Kant termed it, at the base of all cultures. It is the necessary condition for survival, but perhaps in its subtle permutations it is not part of our natural instinct; perhaps it must be learned, imposed. When that primal impulse does not flow of its own accord, laws have been written to mandate it.

"We've talked about the legal aspects," Mona rolled a yellow pencil between the thumb and index finger of her right hand. "These children are abused before they're ever born. I finally got some papers about intrauterine child abuse. And Jeaneen Grey Eagle's husband has been prosecuting women who are pregnant and who are always drinking, and so we wanted to go over the tribal code with him and see what section he's using."

"What's been the response to all this?" I asked. These women were so much more action-oriented than I, clear in their analysis and purpose.

"We're real pioneers," Elaine said. "We're fumbling through."

"There's an awful lot of resistance," Mona interrupted. "Probably because of the alcoholism. Only in the past five years have they started talking about alcoholism and having AA [Alcoholics Anonymous] meetings down here. But then some people say you get brainwashed by AA."

"Jeaneen told me that people are saturated with FAS information right now," I said. "One group won't come to a meeting because they claim they've heard it all before, and another group says, 'I drank during my pregnancy and my kids are fine . . .' "

"I myself get saturated with FAS." Elaine took a breath, adjusted one of the turquoise rings on her fingers. "But the answer is very simple: you don't drink. Abstinence will prevent FAS from ever happening to your children."

There is nothing quite like the awakening of spring on the plains. Winters are marginally colder in Arctic latitudes, the January ground is frozen a few solid inches thicker, lakes must be a bit deeper in order to maintain the necessary oxygen to keep fish alive beneath the ice. But the miracle of thaw in the Dakotas is the absolute contrast it awakens in thermometers. One March blizzard day the windchill factor is $-60°$ F, and the next afternoon a warming Chinook has blown away all memory of frost. Spring, even more than mercurial autumn, is the buffer zone between the unbelievably frigid and the extraordinarily hot. It's the wink of normalcy in a land where the July and August highs can top 120 degrees, the soggy, fertile renewal of fields once scraped smooth by mammoth glaciers only to become the bottom of a huge inland sea and then, silty with rich loam, to rival any region of the earth in their hospitality to seed. Spring is not as much an intermission between the great solstitial extremes of winter and summer as it is a clement oasis where human beings temporarily survive without the crutch of furnace or air conditioner.

It was late April, and I came back to South Dakota for an extended period, my itinerary traversing the state from Aberdeen, where I had appointments with a variety of administrators at the Bureau of Indian Affairs regional offices, to the small reservations of Fort Thompson and Crow Creek, to Rosebud, and, finally, where this phase of the journey began for me, to Kyle and with Jeaneen on Pine Ridge. In the past nine months I had become not only a collector of information but a carrier of messages from one embattled outpost against the growth of FAS to another, the bearer of strategies, gimmicks, and isolated success stories.

In my suitcase was a range of prevention and education materials that had been developed by various of the programs I had visited: bumper stickers, bookmarks, flyers, posters—some that intended to amuse, some that aimed to frighten—all warning against the dangers to a woman of drinking during her pregnancy. These were the hopeful productions of limited budgets, the equivalents to wartime exhortations dropped from airplanes in order to influence civilian populations. It was hard to picture the precise scenario in which they would be effective—few of the typical mothers who gave birth to full-FAS children were likely to be so intent on their reading that they wouldn't want to lose their page, but what the hell, it *could* happen. A person *could* get stuck in traffic behind another car and be forced to read and reread a message glued on a trunk.

I was driving due north at night with the windows rolled down. Cool, watery air, the residue of an afternoon storm, washed over my face. The road was so ruler-straight that a well-balanced car could steer itself, and in the blackness the only reminders that this was earth and not some uninhabited planet were the far-between porch lights of isolated farms. Two times I stopped: once to telephone Louise from a solitary booth and share with her my amazement at the weather, and the other time to simply stand in the wind, to listen to the silence, to exalt.

Aberdeen is a small city empowered by federal bureaucracy. It has the look of an officious county seat, its brick buildings too big and sturdy to be justified by the civic population alone. It has more than its share of motels and "family-style" eateries, the better to accommodate the stream of conventioneers and petitioners who are drawn by the regional headquarters of the BIA. Its tidy suburbs reflect the security of civil service incomes, guaranteed for life, for the duration of the mortgage. There is a stolidity to the appearance of many citizens on their lunch hours, a purposefulness to their gaits as they proceed from office to Country Kitchen or Perkins or Golden Skillet. Aberdeen has the feel of a town protected by impenetrable red tape looped in triplicate in a charmed circle that repels all unwelcome invasion.

Even the city's name evokes the burr of order, thrift, austerity—an ironic contrast to the constituencies that Aberdeen is mandated to serve. The perspective from Barren Butte on Standing Rock or from atop the bald hill at Wounded Knee—where at the end of the nineteenth century Big Foot and 145 of his men, women, and children were massacred by the Hotchkiss guns of the Seventh Cavalry—is of a different, more violent reality. Life for most people on the reservations within this Bureau of Indian Affairs designated "area" is harsh, chaotic, and brief. Beneath the thin fiction of official policy there swirls a whirlpool that no neat category or printed federal guideline can tame. "Aberdeen" is an innocuous and therefore misleading label for a desperate legacy of forced assimilation, violence, graft, and indifference. It is a caption so ordinary, so unexceptional, that it confers invisibility, deafens the roar, obscures the fatuity of stopgap management and short-term planning. In Scotland, Aberdeen is perched securely on a granite ledge above the crash of the North Sea. In land-locked Dakota, its aluminum-sided namesake abuts Pine Ridge.

I met with Sandy Karlsgaard, the special education coordinator for half of the federally funded schools in the region, including Marty, Whirlwind, and Wahpeton, where Louise's parents have taught for thirty years.

"In the law there is not the category Fetal Alcohol Syndrome," Sandy informed me. "There is a category called 'other health impaired' where medically defined conditions affect the ability to learn, okay? It seemed appropriate to us in the Area to include FAS/FAE with the stipulation that it was a condition identified by a doctor, not by a physician's assistant, social worker, nurse, but *truly* a medical diagnosis. We issued a memo saying that within the Area for any audit purposes we would accept FAS children as 'other health impaired' and eligible for not only special ed instruction but whatever related services, including physical and occupational therapy, speech, etcetera are available. That's how we're specifically addressing that. In addition, we know that because of the sociological aspects and the psychological ramifications, it is not always an easy diagnosis to obtain. Many of the symptoms of the manifestations in the classroom are also compatible with the mentally retarded, or sometimes where there's normal intelligence, there's some of this other manifestation . . . attention span, distractibility. And we strongly suggest that under FAE, some children are being served under the appropriate category but are not truly identified as FAE. It's kind of an unofficial sort of term."

Sandy was immaculately dressed in a blue suit with a gold pin on the lapel. Her hair was precisely coiffed, and her makeup and nails were exceptionally correct. She gave the impression of being a woman with the reins in her hand, watchful lest the team she was driving fly out of control. Her expression said she didn't much like "unofficial sorts of terms."

"Do you have any idea of the number of referrals your office receives in the category of fetal alcohol syndrome or effect?" I asked, attempting her idiom.

"Almost negligible. It has to do with reluctance."

I mentioned that a school social worker at Pine Ridge had told me a few months ago that she thought that between 40 and 50 percent of the kids in her school were affected to some degree by maternal drinking.

"Again, that has to do with personal opinion as opposed to 'special documentation,' " Sandy stated. "That official documentation is negligible, not the opinion. The *opinion* . . ." she stressed the word, making the distinction clear. "We know that in IHS research there's information about it being the number one cause of mental retardation and so forth. I have a variety of fact sheets that are public information, and I can give you some that might be helpful."

I wanted to get to the core of the disparity between the crisis conditions I had heard about and seen firsthand for the past year and the low official statistics coming into the central office. Did the problem arise from simple ignorance? Did the doctors not know how to make a diagnosis?

"FAS is relatively new, and at the same time there have been presentations at our annual in-service workshop for all special ed personnel in the Aberdeen Area. It is not as new with IHS as it is with the general public. And yet we're still very much in the process of educating people about it. Because of the fact that it is one hundred percent preventable, we have a sociological factor that makes some people reluctant to deal with it. There is a concerted effort to educate regarding alcoholic intake and pregnancy. In the state of South

Dakota it's broader than just in the Bureau. Under Governor Janklow there's a task force with the ultimate goal of educating students, children, starting at the high school level and then working backward into prevention efforts, starting with surveying the students to see if in fact they are aware. We've had an item in the legislature this year regarding whether there should be a notice posted where alcohol is dispensed. 'This could be hazardous to the unborn.' There are some revolutionary approaches."

Revolutionary? Was it so revolutionary to tell the truth?

Sandy went on to describe by their acronyms the dormitory programs at the Area boarding schools, counseling efforts I heard about from every other BIA administrator, all highly cooperative, with whom I talked over the next two days. Aberdeen seemed determined to address FAS as but one within a larger context of competing troubles. The Bureau, one official after another explained to me, was overextended, expected to solve a host of complicated problems, and lucky to keep its head above water. I met people who had frequently seen FAS and FAE children. They sympathized but were prevented from serving them directly until they were officially designated as FAS by licensed physicians. The testimony of the Jeaneens and Brendas and Monas and Elaines, even the statistics of Phil May, didn't count because there was no MD behind their names. Yet the Aberdeen Area Office was *the* sanctioned conduit between Washington and the Sioux reservations, the dotted line on the flow-chart of goods and services stemming from nineteenth-century treaties and Senate-mandated laws. The problem had to be "visible" to Aberdeen if it had any chance of moving up on the crisis agenda.

All along the way, as I drove the length of South Dakota, alternately nicknamed "The Sunshine State" or "The Coyote State," flocks of migrating white birds rose from the highway like clouds of swirling smoke. It was an eight-hour trip from the agricultural northeast to the southwest, the quadrant dominated by the Sioux-U.S.–disputed Black Hills and by Pine Ridge. I looked forward to seeing Jeaneen; of all the people I had met in the past year she seemed to me the most practical, the most straight-shooting in her approach to FAS.

We talked once again in the small Project Recovery office, this time joined by Charlotte Brave Heart, another counselor. Jeaneen's hair was curly from a fresh permanent, and her desk was laden with Manila folders, film canisters, FAS prevention bulletins. On the floor was a suitcase packed with the Avon cosmetic products she sold to supplement the family income. Cold cream was the popular item every spring. Even young skin gets raw when exposed to the "Alberta Clipper" that descends from Canada all through the winter.

Jeaneen wasted no time in plunging into the subject of our mutual concern, reeling off a long list of the latest atrocities, the most recent examples of the toll that maternal drinking was extracting. "Last weekend we had a lady in jail who is nine months pregnant. We said, 'Do you know that your baby is probably just as drunk as you are?' Then she was discharged from the hospital, and the frustration of hearing that was just something else. I asked them if I could go in and bring charges against her for abusing her child, and my husband Robert said no, from the legal perspective I really didn't have a standing. I was not *directly* hurt." Jeaneen shook her head, as if this was the craziest idea she had ever heard. "Right to life," she sarcastically repeated the catch phrase. "How can you enact the law when the Supreme Court doesn't recognize it? Legally, you can detain a woman for assault and battery. What is 'life'? The question needs to be asked. I would almost have to be the child itself to bring a complaint."

I trotted out my inevitable question: why is this happening, why now?

"I noticed," she said, "that one generation back alcohol really hit us. People who are now in their forties are the products of FAS and FAE, and look at them and at the way we live here. It's like we don't live for tomorrow—everything is instant. 'I want it now.' People don't think of the consequences of acting out and having bad behavior. They're really surprised when somebody dies of drinking because it's something that they don't consider harms your body. It's a real self-centered and a real 'today' type of thing. Nobody saves for tomorrow, we all know that. When the grant-in-aid checks come rolling in, people don't think about the end of the month. 'Now we can eat all this good food'—they buy t-bones and ribs. A whole generation of irresponsibility, and I think a lot of it is mothers drinking and neglecting their children. Drinking means passing out, right? Passing out before everybody else does."

I closed my eyes, recalled how utterly, how smugly, I had silently rejected Phil May when he proposed much the same thing: that available funds equaled an increase in FAS babies. Was his analysis easier to dismiss because he was not himself an Indian, because he did not come from and currently live on a reservation where a high proportion of drinking took place? Jeaneen, however, provided me no such facile escapes. Her observations might sound right-wing to me, might fly in the face of what I wished to believe, but they were forged by facts that had been confronted, not hypothesized. She was no happier to face them than I, but she was less flinching.

I still didn't necessarily agree with what she was saying—I still coughed up qualifications, rationales, and I still mentally insisted that there had to be other avenues of explanation and resolution—but I could not feel superior in my safe, politically correct fortress. In the pitched battle against fetal alcohol syndrome, the paths of right and wrong constantly converged, crossed over each other. There was little in the way of moral high ground in the trenches, and the body count justified the imposition of martial law. Repressive legislation brought serious dangers of abuse and misapplication, but to do nothing or to do too little was, for the casualties, worse than doing too much.

"If you had total power in the world . . ." I said. "If you could do anything—but keeping in mind issues of human rights and civil liberties . . ."

Jeaneen laughed. "You just *knew* I was just going to eliminate *them*. Okay, *not forgetting* the fact that there are civil liberties and human rights, I still think that somebody needs to—I don't even know who this somebody is . . . I don't like to use these abstracts, but at some point there have got to be mechanisms in place that are going to make women who are drinking stop having children if they're going to keep drinking. They have to make a choice. I have yet to meet the natural mother who kept her FAS child."

Rarely, either, had Eva, rarely had Phil. Those children, a few of the lucky ones among them at least, were now with Brenda, with Mona, with Sharon. With Louise and me.

"They are not taking responsibility for what they are producing," Jeaneen insisted. "Yes, there are human rights—there was an uproar about IHS sterilizing women, and I don't agree with IHS. I don't support eugenics. *Yet what we're talking about here is the survival of Indian people.*

"Not so long ago I did a presentation, and the council members were all looking at each other, looking for the symptoms, joking. I never realized it was this bad—I was really sorry that they had made light of it. What do you do? Do you require a license for somebody to have a child? I don't have a plan. I don't want to think that things will go that far, so I haven't really put ideas together. Who's going to sit in supreme judgment of people and say, 'You've got a problem and therefore *you* cannot have children'?—On the reservation, women are keepers of the family—I don't want to do that. But it almost looks like somebody has to."

"But if *you're* reluctant to think that far, who would?" I asked. "It's not something that anybody wants to think about, but over and over as I talk to different people around the country it seems like we're not *approaching* a crisis but are in the *middle* of one, one that is going to grow geometrically. When eventually the tribe as a whole has to vote for a crucial choice, a significant percentage of the population may be impaired in their ability to take a long view. What happens then?"

I was not shouting, but the volume of my voice was close to it. For a moment Jeaneen and I seemed to glare at each other, adversaries by default. I was the messenger she would like to shoot, and she was the only person I had met who might have a workable solution, and she didn't.

Charlotte interjected a mediating comment: "There's a thing called denial that's directly associated with alcoholism." Her words broke the tension. We had strayed across the boundary of restraint, of dispassionate description. I found myself doing more talking than asking questions, as if this were the last chance I would have to speak my mind.

"I guess I could use a dose of denial," I said, and both women smiled. They had each reached my current level of profound bafflement so often that it was familiar territory to them.

"I have the same questions that you have," Jeaneen said, "and I haven't found any answers. I've searched my soul. I've thought, 'What can you do to help these children cope?' I don't know, I don't have the answers. I can't stop it."

"The thing I keep returning to," I said, "is 'bad judgment.' Seventeen years as part of our family does not counteract for Adam that instant of not seeing the big picture. He takes something that doesn't belong to him, or he gets goaded into going to his boss and saying cuss words he doesn't understand. Try to explain to that man how bad judgment is not a matter of simple intelligence or an indicator of a rotten person, but just inability, absolute inability."

"How can a person live without judgment?" Jeaneen wondered. "It's something that nobody really focuses on until you run into it. Then you realize how valuable it is."

"It's not something that shows up easily on tests," I agreed. "We're banking on the fact that it won't occur to Adam to want to be independent for a while. Unless somebody says to him, 'Hey, you can go out and live on your own, forget all these rules . . .' And his version of living on his own! We were driving in the car once, and he was mad at Louise and me and said, 'Maybe I'll get myself my own apartment.' Our eyes lit up—we were mad at him, too. We said, 'Adam, what do you think it would take for a little apartment, to go to the grocery, to pay your bills, how much money would it cost each month?' He was seventeen years old, special education teachers had worked with him for twelve years on the idea of money. He said, 'Fifteen thousand dollars a month.' He can't make change for a dollar, and he had no concept of it. He'd spend it, too, if he had fifteen thousand dollars a month. If somebody said, 'Here's a doughnut, give me fifteen thousand dollars,' he'd do it."

There was no humor in our laughter, but it was a relief.

"A lot of people who are perceived as being social misfits may well have this as the base of their problem," I went on. "You know, I talked to the other kids at Adam's work and told them what cruel little bastards they were for playing tricks on him. Then I sat down with Adam and said, 'Don't let yourself be used by other people.' And he can understand it when I'm right there, but one of the reasons that we have always lived in a very controllable environment—in the country and now in a small town—is that he would be a sitting duck if he went to a school where there were drugs or drinking. He wouldn't last a day.

"And that would just compound all his other problems because then people would say that he was the way he was *because* he was drinking—the symptoms look the same. I think, here's one boy I've spent a good part of my life speculating about, like how he is going to survive and function without Louise and me supervising him. What do you do with a whole big population of kids like Adam in a community that already doesn't have the resources that it needs? No one has found an educational method that works. We sure haven't."

Jeaneen and Charlotte listened with the sympathy of understanding, so I didn't stop, I didn't take cover, I didn't disclaim. Our family situation was a small drop in a huge bucket, in and of itself statistically insignificant, yet it did involve a human life. If the single case ever ceased to matter, ever stopped being the source from which every other concern arose, the battle would be lost. In the months to come I was to hear alarming numbers—an estimated 70,000 fetal alcohol-impaired children born each year in the United States, unguessable legions more around the world—but these were, in the end, not faceless megaliths but collections of individual tragedies, each one a long and uniquely sad story.

Jeaneen and Charlotte knew how to deal in particulars. They let me talk as long as I needed, nodding kindly whenever I paused. They sat still as the light in the room faded, and whenever the telephone sounded, they let it ring. They listened with hearts that years of struggle, years of small and large defeats, had not toughened. They heard the voice behind my words, the cry of any father, any mother: not *my* baby. Not my *baby*.

CHAPTER THIRTEEN

In the 1971 Hollywood film *Escape from the Planet of the Apes*, Dr. Zira and her two companions, all highly evolved apes with advanced degrees, have time-traveled to the present from a future in which chimpanzees, gorillas, and orangutans rule brutish human beings. Their twentieth-century reception, however, is less than cordial. In the course of the movie these peace-loving ape-o-naughts are hounded into hiding and are eventually murdered. The lone survivor, the last hope for the continuation of all that was cerebral about the world of tomorrow, is Zira's new-born offspring, hidden unobtrusively in a traveling carnival. We are left with a final shot of his face, his eyes sparkling, as he tries to teach himself to speak—and because of the compassion, reasonableness, and enlightenment of his slaughtered parents, we anticipate his success.

At least I did so when I saw the movie in the year it was made. It was not until I watched it rerun on cable TV that I noticed one detail I had previously missed. Halfway through the action, Dr. Hassline, the presidential science advisor, offers a glass of "grape juice plus" to the very pregnant Dr. Zira, and in no time at all she becomes drunk. We are led to believe that she tipples more of this ancient world beverage at every opportunity, and her relish and lack of restraint are a source of mirth to one and all.

Dr. Zira was an older mother, under stress, off her usual diet. She had to be in her third trimester when she started her binges. The little fellow in the circus wagon didn't have a prayer.

*

The closest thing in 1989 to a presidential advisor on the subject of alcohol is the surgeon general, and Mr. Koop's advice is simple and direct: *abstinence at the time of conception, during pregnancy, and throughout nursing is the only guaranteed safe practice.* Congress, following the laws of some enlightened states, has finally passed a bill mandating that a series of warnings—one of them dealing with the dangers of drinking during pregnancy—be printed on all liquor bottle labels. In Seattle, Barry Epstein, an attorney from New Jersey representing a group of FAS victims, has brought suit against several liquor manufacturers. He alleges that the executives of these companies knew or had a responsibility to know that, used by women at the wrong time, their products could very probably cause birth defects, yet no serious efforts were made to warn the public. Epstein contends that the mothers of his clients were not aware of the risk they were taking when they imbibed certain brands of beer, whiskey, and wine, and as a result they did inadvertent damage to their offspring, all of whom were born with lifelong fetal alcohol impairments. Therefore, he believes that the liquor companies are liable for a share of those children's enormous medical costs.

Who has the responsibility for the knowledge of safe practice? Certainly, every woman and man who elects to bring a child into the world has a moral obligation to the life he or she has participated in creating. Whether that duty is or should be enforceable by civil law is a matter of debate, but there is no ambiguity that an infant carried to term depends upon the good sense and judicious behavior of his or her parents. The mother is most directly involved in a physical respect, although that in no way absolves the father from his obligations to his son or daughter.

But even the most well-intentioned parents can be led astray if the medical establishment fails to make available adequate public information. As I write these words, Louise and I are expecting a baby in a month, and to refresh our memories about breathing techniques we stopped by the Pregnancy Resource Center of the Dartmouth hospital to check out a few books. While Louise browsed, I pulled the thickest and most official-looking volume on the shelf—one of several copies of *Pregnancy, Birth & The Newborn Baby*, published by Delacourt Press and listing as its authorship no less an authority than The Boston Children's Medical Center. Automatically—because of my book, because of the preoccupation of our lives—I checked in the index under "alcohol" and turned to page 87. "There is no reason to restrict alcohol in moderation during pregnancy," I read. "Many women find the occasional drink a pleasant persuasion to relax. But that before-dinner cocktail, particularly if it is accompanied by a snack, can be the downfall of many who have trouble controlling their weight."

Incredulously, I turned to check the copyright—1972. The book was out-of-date, but what trusting parent would suspect that? A mother would be proud of herself, confident in her before-dinner cocktail, after receiving the go-ahead from a big green book from The Boston Children's Hospital, displayed and offered for free borrowing by a major medical center. And unwittingly she might to some unknowable degree poison her child.

It is obvious that a drunk driver in a suburban neighborhood is a hazard to the well-being of children, but what about the doctor who fails to become familiar with both the *facts* and the *probable facts* about a practice as potentially dangerous as maternal drinking? What of the health librarian who permits egregious misinformation to be distributed? Have we learned nothing from the lesson of Thalidomyde? Defective automobiles and kitchen appliances are recalled by their manufacturers when it is demonstrated that they pose a threat to safety. Why not recall authoritative books that contain lethal advice? Every informed store clerk or bartender or waiter who sells liquor to a pregnant woman without apprising her of the possible side effects is, in a way, the knowing deliverer of a letter bomb. Is it worth the risk of causing offense, of provoking a hostile reaction, to issue a caution?

Yes, it is.

In the summer of 1986, before our family returned from Minnesota to New Hampshire, I arranged for Adam to participate in a four-week Outward Bound program along the boundary waters that constitute the U.S.–Canadian border. Ann Streissguth had advised me that some of the FAE clients with whom she worked in Seattle had profited from such an excursion; they had become more self-reliant, had stretched themselves in response to the rigorous demands of life in the wild, and I thought it would be a good cap to Adam's experiences in Northfield. I wrote long and detailed letters to the Outward Bound staff, forwarded extra supplies of anticonvulsant medications, and bored Adam with earnest conversations about safety. He and I used his Pizza Hut savings to purchase some brightly colored, top-of-the-line gear, and in early June everything was in place for his departure. Except for a few weeks at a YMCA summer camp in New Hampshire, Adam had never spent time away from the family, but he seemed neither eager nor reluctant to be off.

Louise and I, on the other hand, were full of anxiety. Were we doing the right thing? Would Adam wander off alone into the woods? Would he have a seizure while acting as the catcher for a trust-drop, thus not catching his partner and allowing an unsuspecting teenager to fall off a cliff? Nothing spurred our worries as much as the contemplation of the famous Outward Bound "solo"—the crowning glory of the whole venture, in which each person was left alone overnight with minimum supplies and expected to survive through the wiles he or she had accumulated. Would Adam be terrified? Eaten by a bear? Never heard from again?

Certainly, these are the fears of every parent as a child strikes out independently for the first time, but in Adam's case there was an extra dimension. This was, after all, *our* idea, not his, and therefore if something went wrong, it was entirely our responsibility. Furthermore, could any amount of cautionary correspondence adequately prepare Outward Bound staff to anticipate what Adam wouldn't know? They would unavoidably assume too much—it takes a long time to realize what an impairment in abstract reasoning implies. Nevertheless, when the day the course was to begin arrived, I walked Adam to his ride, embraced him, and let him go. "Sink or swim" is one of those glib phrases that are tossed off lightly only when the real possibility of "sink" seems remote.

Over the next twenty-eight days, we called the Outward Bound headquarters in northern Minnesota several times. No, they invariably replied, they had heard no reports from Adam's course, which they interpreted to mean that all was well. Yes, they had forwarded our letters, and, yes, they would call immediately if there was even a hint of trouble. These conversations were reassuring, yet not a waking hour passed when I didn't imagine disaster; every ring of the telephone stiffened my spine. We bought an answering machine to monitor calls on the occasions we were out of the house, and when we returned to a blinking red light, I didn't relax until the tape had fully played out with routine messages.

Louise drove one car, loaded to capacity, back to New Hampshire, and with her went Sava, Madeline, Persia, Pallas, and our cat, Angel. Strapped to the roof of the Dodge Caravan was an enormous plush parrot Sava had won at a carnival booth during Northfield's Jesse James Days celebration. I watched my family turn the corner of Second Street and head east, and that garish bird seemed to salaam at me in solemn farewell.

I was to meet Adam in Duluth the following afternoon, and as I took the interstate north, my mind was almost blank. My imagination simply would not construe the hypothetical events of Adam's experience. A part of me hoped for a magical transformation—for a northern woodsman, plaid-shirted, robust, laconic—and part of me dreaded being informed by a concerned, horrified Outward Bound leader that Adam had disappeared, evaporated into the forest.

I parked at the airport, the assigned rendezvous, and walked through the sliding doors. The lobby was full of laughing, high-spirited teenagers, exchanging addresses, recalling highlights, a few boys and girls kissing each other passionately. I scanned from right to left, and then I saw him, sitting alone, dressed exactly as I had sent him off. In that split second before he noticed me, I studied my son: he did look bigger, shaggier, intact. His expression was neutral, a mask of non-involvement, but he had lived. He raised his eyes and they lit with recognition. We ran toward each other, arms wide, and then held each other close for what seemed a long, long time as if to make sure that this was truly happening. Adam was almost exactly my height. He felt so solid, so strong. It was a moment of coming together that made a fifteen-year loop with our first encounter in the playroom of the Social Services Department in Pierre, a moment without forethought, without questions, with no words except the names we gave each other.

At last we stood apart, nodded, smiled. I don't know which of us was the more relieved. He picked up his knapsack and walked with me to the car. There was no one to whom he wanted to say good-bye.

"Did you like it?" I asked. "Was it wonderful?"

"No," he said.

I waited for him to go on, to elaborate, gripe, fill me in, but there seemed to be nothing he wanted to add.

"Why not? Weren't there good parts about it?"

I opened the trunk, dumped in his equipment, unlocked the

passenger door. Adam shrugged and thought hard as he settled into his seat.

"Well, I did fall down a ledge," he offered, as if this were the best thing that had happened, and as if his announcement needed no further explanation.

I went right for the heart of my worries. "What about the solo? Tell me about that."

We strapped on our safety belts, and I steered out of the parking lot, down the long sloping hill that leads from the airport into Duluth and then to the road that follows the lake shore into Wisconsin.

"Solo?" Then he remembered. "Oh that. Yeah."

"Did you spend a night all alone? What was it like?" In the Outward Bound brochure this ordeal had been described in detail by various participants. Some had used the intense time to review and evaluate the meaning of existence. Some had experienced personal epiphany, had heard in the nervous cracks of twigs and the snorts of unseen animals the shape of their future lives. Some had constructed complicated lean-to's, had foraged nutritious meals of berries and roots, had rediscovered the making of fire.

"Oh. They dropped me off on this little island," Adam recalled. "It was about suppertime."

"And then what?" I prompted. What thoughts had occupied his solitary night?

"I don't know. I went to sleep. They had to shake me to wake me up the next day."

I never could decide if Outward Bound had made much impact on Adam. On the one hand, how could it not have? Twenty-eight days was twenty-eight days, and, if nothing else, it had to have demonstrated to him that he could cope without the constant presence of his parents. On the other hand, once back with me, Adam rarely seemed to think of his adventure and gave every impression of having forgotten most details before we stopped at a motel in Sault Ste. Marie the first night. The tremor of his initial real brush with independence seemed to pass through him imperceptibly, a 1.5 on the Richter scale of his equilibrium.

I had expected that, post-Voyageur of the boundary waters, Adam might resent and want to modify restrictions in his previous routine, but he settled back into familiar patterns without protest. Eventually, we received a letter from the young man who had led Adam's course, and we read it for clues that we might have missed. But again, there was little to go on. Adam had not charmed his fellow participants. He had slowed them down, needed too much attention, lagged behind unless goaded into action. The course leader was as mystified as I concerning whether Adam's self-image had expanded. Adam, he reported with some vexation, was a tough nut, but not a bad kid.

I couldn't have put it better myself.

As we passed through Ontario and Quebec, then made a long diagonal plunge across Vermont, Adam and I listened to Bruce Springsteen cassettes, exclaimed over the occasional bump of railroad tracks, and ate hamburgers. When we stopped for the night, I cut his toenails and fingernails, showed him how to shave his chin, flipped on the TV to "Hollywood Squares." We made good time and arrived back on our farm only half a day after Louise, the children, and the cat. Their trip had been uneventful, with one exception. While they were traversing the long Tappan Zee Bridge over the Hudson, a strong updraft had suddenly enveloped the Caravan. From inside the car Louise felt a tug, then heard a flapping sound that she soon identified as the end of a rope beating against a side window. One of the binding constraints that crisscrossed the roof had come undone, and as she watched helpless and fascinated, the giant parrot ascended over the guardrail, suspended for a red and purple instant in midair, and then plunged, yellow beak poised like a bird of prey, to the river far below.

Once at home, we resumed the regular pattern of our lives. Adam, now eighteen years old, reenrolled in the Hartford Vocational Program and took up where he had left off. He was temporarily placed in part-time jobs in the local veterans hospital and at a beer keg factory, continuing all the while with his "life skills" classes. Sava and Madeline returned to their old schools—of late neither one had been having an easy time with academic subjects, and each required special educational assistance. Persia and Pallas began a new day care program with a wonderfully industrious and conscientious woman who lived directly across the street from our house. Louise resumed work on her new novel, *Tracks*, and I taught a full load of college courses, often rising at 5 A.M. to find a quiet time in which to plow through recently published research and to start to write this book.

The Beet Queen, and then six months later *A Yellow Raft in Blue Water*, met with favorable reviews.

I found myself inundated with information on all aspects of fetal alcohol syndrome. I had amassed an overwhelming number of articles, monographs, professional papers, and unpublished theses dealing with a variety of related topics: Indian drinking patterns, addiction, pregnancy, public health, special education. In addition, I had gathered hundreds of pages of notes, transcriptions of taped interviews, and bibliographic entries that had to be retrieved.

My year in the Midwest had yielded more data than I could reasonably assimilate and, I soon realized, it had also steered my investigation on a rather arbitrary path. Because Adam was an Indian, because we were Indians, because reservations were the main locus of my research, I had come to unconsciously regard FAS and FAE as primarily Native American concerns. It was indisputable, of course, that alcohol, in all its manifestations, was historically and presently a major problem for American Indians. But after I had attended three national conventions of the Research Society on Alcoholism (RSA) and paid my dues to the Fetal Alcohol Study Group, it became clear that FAS and FAE knew no ethnic boundaries.

Problems analogous to those that I had observed and heard about on Pine Ridge and Rosebud were on the increase in cities throughout the country, were recorded for all economic and social groups, and were matters of serious concern in Europe, Asia, and Latin America. It indeed seemed that cultures with a laissez-faire attitude toward male drinking were especially susceptible when a change took place in adult women's behavior—and that dynamic covered a lot of territory in the 1980s. FAS laboratory and long-term human subject studies were ongoing in Scandinavia, France, and West Germany. Damaging maternal use of alcohol was reputed to exist in epidemic proportions in the Soviet Union, Poland, and Hungary.

My colleague in the anthropology department, Dr. Kirk Endicott, brought me reports of the problem in Malaysia, and Maori friends from New Zealand wrote that it was a major cause of birth defects among their relatives, as well as among Aborigines in Australia. Drinking alcohol, in many parts of the world, was a venerable part of social culture—for men. Women, especially young women, were often traditionally discouraged from the practice by formal taboos or by insistent peer pressure, but both these barriers now seemed everywhere to be falling. Statistics in nation after nation suggested that "modern" women, regardless of their class or ethnic background, were adopting habits of drinking, as well as of smoking, in a higher proportion than were men of the same age.

The frequent gathering place—two national conventions have been held there within four years—of the Research Society on Alcoholism (RSA) is a resort called Wild Dunes, located north along the Atlantic coast from Charleston, South Carolina. Nested among lanes of condominiums, tennis courts, and palmy trails, it is a conference center that offers every convenience. Air-conditioned at midday but open in the morning to receive the sounds of crashing surf only a few hundred feet away, the Wild Dunes facility is a four-star contrast to the ramshackle Project Recovery building where Jeaneen counsels pregnant Lakota women. It is a far cry from the linked, weather-beaten mobile homes of Project Phoenix, from Brenda Demery's Rosebud hospital, from the cinderblock classrooms of Little Wound School.

No one starved at Wild Dunes—crab and shrimp were offered buffet style in an open-air cabana every lunchtime, and charter buses transported the attending biochemists, obstetricians, psychologists, and hospital administrators to reserved seats at the annual Spoleto Festival, whose dates matched those of each meeting.

The only FAS or FAE victims at Wild Dunes were those there via photographs—as examples, illustrations of points, artifacts of field-work. They were subjects frequently discussed with a cavalier vocabulary. The self-conscious authorities were free to make light of the classic phenotypical markers of the syndrome because—this was implicit—they were veterans so intimately involved in its examination. "Funny-looking" or "FARKS" were the designations of choice in discussing FAS victims, perhaps because the terms sounded so nontechnical, so down to earth, so without the usual pretension.

"It would be okay if alcohol only made them *ugly*," one nationally recognized officer of the Study Group joked to the full assembly. "But they're *stupid* as well." That got a big laugh, as did his later quip: "If my mom hadn't drunk during her pregnancy . . ." he paused, his timing honed to perfection, "I might have been an *internist* instead of an OB/GYN."

I sat in the back of the room taking notes, my tape recorder going as usual, and looked at the smiling faces. It was unsettling to be the only parent of a fetal alcohol child, the spy in the midst of experts at play. At every session I attended, I had made an effort to introduce myself to presenters, as well as to scholars whose monographs and reports I had read. I led with my strong suit, my academic affiliation—Dartmouth was a respectable reference point. But as I continued to summarize my reasons for being interested—anthropology, Indians, a book, a son—I had the strong impression that I lost credibility with every successive identification.

The FAS Study Group was, at its founding core, a tight clique, a rarefied network that was its own best and most trusted audience. Its charter members had associated with each other for years, had reacted in print to the minutiae of each others' research, had polished each others' finest points. In the endless game of snagging federal funding, Study Group members alternately endorsed and evaluated each others' proposals. As if to accentuate and preserve its exclusivity, past and present Poobahs communicated among themselves with a specialized idiom, as replete with bandied acronyms as any Bureau of Indian Affairs subcommittee. Like a petty fiefdom that celebrated its own identity by issuing unnecessarily odd postage stamps or mandating an idiosyncratic salute, the FAS Study Group seemed both jealous and contemptuous of less select entities. Theirs was a small pond whose residents had come to consider themselves very large frogs indeed.

With the notable exception of Ann Streissguth, who was accessible, generous with her time, interested in American Indian material, and open-minded, I too often found the mavens of the fetal alcohol establishment to be arrogant, proprietary about their research, hard to approach, myopic, and self-congratulatory.

The lines of discussion seemed firmly defined by a preset index of topics officiously deemed worthwhile. Outsiders without known qualifications were not welcomed into the debate. When Eva Smith, the only American Indian physician in attendance, introduced material from her experience as head of the fetal alcohol program on the reservation where she practiced, no one responded or even asked for further explanation. When I had the temerity to pose a complex question that arose from my conversations in the Dakotas—about incarceration of drinking pregnant women who had borne FAS babies, for instance, or concerning the gray diagnostic area of "bad

judgment"—I encountered sneering evasion or condescending platitudes. I was framing the issues incorrectly, I was instructed by one
self-described "prenatal Republican." The very concept of intrauterine child abuse was a "disaster." Mothers' rights *always* superseded
fetal rights.

Most of the Study Group officers—save for the University of
Washington contingent—were loathe to attempt to identify adult
FAS or FAE victims because they were "dysmorphologically" harder
to label than infants or young children. After all, as one revered sage
put it, "Just because you identify someone with FAS doesn't mean
you can do anything with them." And as for Indians, they were simply
too complicated—all those messy intangibles and no constants or
control groups! It was much cleaner to gather data in urban teaching
hospitals where clients could be properly screened and monitored.

Many of the papers presented were highly technical and specialized. I have notebooks filled with information about such lab rat
esoterica as a "nose poking operant with two poke holes" and Dr.
Schlumpf of Zurich's "tail flick test." Another Germanic scientist,
introduced as "the most cited man in methol mercury literature,"
spoke at length on how to measure the avoidance of foot shock, the
first step of which was to "put animals in a box and forget them for
several days."

At each subsequent annual meeting I tried to project a more
palatable persona for myself. Anyone who has taught, especially at
the university level, has had a brush with intellectual snobbery. The
sanctum sanctorum of the elect, be they professional anthropologists,
English professors, or creative writers, is by definition an exclusive
club with easy scorn and a ready label for the amateur dilettante. But
why was I being perceived in such a manner? What preempted me
from the right to a receptive hearing? I came equipped with recorded
testimony that was fresh from the field, and with my book contract I
made available a vehicle for a wide dissemination of information.

There may have been a lot of reasons that I was repeatedly
snubbed, many that were probably my fault. But I suspect that one of
my major liabilities was a refusal to hide the degree to which I was
personally involved in the issue. Humorless and single-minded, I was
the antithesis of cool. I made and responded to no wisecracks. I had
not been initiated into a pose of professional superiority. FAS was not
a job for me, not a project, not a source of funding or of professional

advancement. It was the definition of my son's existence. And in that monomaniacal stance, I was overanxious, seeking in my approach to the assembled scientists to replicate that moment of fusion between question and answer that had so elevated and liberated my discussions with those who worked with FAS children in the West. Perhaps this attitude more than any other barred me from parity, from engaging as an equal contributor in discourse. It branded me as surely as if I had worn a sign around my neck that said FAS WAS BROUGHT BY ALIENS.

So I did what I could. I maneuvered to lunch next to the authors of papers I had found valuable or controversial. I cornered program participants with one or two questions before they could escape to the admiring circles of colleagues who shared the same assumptions. I raised my hand in the Q & A sessions at the end of each day's meeting.

But mostly I kept my mouth shut, fresh batteries in my tape recorder and an extra pen in my pocket. I did not abandon my questions, but the order in which they would be addressed, if they were addressed at all, was out of my hands. And there was, of course, much I had to learn. For all the boorishness of some of the presenters, these *were* among the most knowledgeable men and women in the world on the most crucial subject I had ever researched. They, not I, had uncovered and defined FAS, and they, not I, were the real hope of understanding and eradicating the problem.

The facts and figures that spewed from the podium were astounding for two reasons: first, because unlike all the accounts I had collected, these statistics had nothing particularly to do with Indians; this was a *national* profile, and it was ultimately as scary as the picture that arose from Rosebud or Pine Ridge. Though the percentages within given populations were smaller, the absolute numbers of children born with alcohol-induced impairments were far greater. The chances of a woman who had already given birth to one FAS child were 771/1000 that she would bear another. Approximately 7,542 FAS babies were born in the United States each year, and that didn't include borderline or FAE cases. Their mean birth weight was around five pounds, and only 66 percent had been carried to term. The brain, one speaker observed, was one of the first organs to be developed and one of the last to be completed; it was consequently at risk for a long period during gestation.

The tentative results of some studies hit me like a Mack truck.

Any son of an alcoholic biological father—whether raised by his natural parents or adopted—was three times more likely to himself become an abusive drinker than the birth son of a father who practiced sobriety. Where did that leave Adam? My other son? Study after scientific study weighted "nature" as more important than "nurture" in predicting not just a person's physical makeup but his or her behavior as well—a conclusion I had frequently read echoed in the daily newspaper columns of Ann Landers and Abigail Van Buren. Some early research suggested the horrible prospect that either females *or males* who were drunk at the time of conception could have a negative impact on a fetus, and that longtime women alcoholics, even if they abstained during their pregnancy, might *still* give birth to children who suffered some ethanol-derived impairment.

As I listened to these grim observations, antithetical to my erstwhile idealistic surety that each child was a "blank slate," I was reminded of scattered, corroborating evidence I had come across in my research. Communication with a national organization of single adoptive parents, in which I was once an officer, suggested that a disproportionate number of men and women who had adopted children from troubled backgrounds—alcohol or drug abuse, especially—and who had raised them in all variety of environments— religious, agnostic, urban, rural, only child, large families, rich, middle class—were experiencing a uniform set of problems as their children got older. Often these parents found themselves applying in desperation to the same special education boarding schools, searching the same self-help books for answers. In Los Angeles there was a "warm line" switchboard that adoptive parents whose children were unmanageable could call for support, pooled advice on programs, or the names of psychologists who had proven helpful. I had heard of several cases where adoptive parents discovered after the fact that their sons or daughters were victims of FAS or FAE and then sued the placement agency for not warning them what to expect. Few if any sought to undo their act of parenthood, but all resented the years of self-incrimination, confusion, and misdirected effort they had expended in ignorance on a condition that was neither their fault nor within their power to solve.

In at least one much publicized case in southern California, a whole family—religious to the core—literally went into hiding from their FAS teenager, who had turned hostile, abusive, and violent toward them.

Jeaneen had mentioned that as the Lakota community learned more about the permanent import of FAS and FAE, it had become increasingly difficult to find adoptive homes for abandoned children, even with members of their own extended families. Yet in his presidential campaign opposition to legalized abortion, George Bush had advocated the mass adoption of all unwanted babies. Did he not realize that many of these potential children, blighted before birth by maternal use of alcohol or cocaine or crack, might be hard to place?

My attention was drawn to another Study Group speaker who outlined why no one could predict with absolute accuracy which women would bear a fully symptomatic FAS or FAE child, regardless of her drinking behavior. Although alcohol reached the fetus of any drinking pregnant woman in just a few minutes, there were a number of mediating variables: dosage, gestational stage and idiosyncratic genetic sensitivity of the fetus, maternal metabolism, maternal nutrition, and parity (the children a woman had later in her life were more at risk than those she had earlier, all other things being equal).

Cause and effect was hard to measure for social reasons as well. In Sweden, for instance, it was estimated that 11 percent of women were drinking at a risk level during their pregnancy, but an unusually large number aborted their pregnancies. Yet, from every country, from every study, the same unambiguous warnings rang forth to women:

IF YOU THINK YOU MIGHT GET PREGNANT, DON'T DRINK *ANY* BEER, WINE, WINE COOLERS, OR LIQUOR. IF YOU *ARE* PREGNANT OR IF YOU ARE A NURSING MOTHER, DON'T DRINK *ANYTHING* THAT CONTAINS ALCOHOL, AND IF YOU HAVE BEEN DRINKING, *STOP*—REGARDLESS OF THE STAGE OF YOUR PREGNANCY—OR *CUT DOWN* IF YOU CAN'T STOP. EACH DOSE OF ALCOHOL YOU DON'T IMBIBE INCREASES YOUR CHANCES OF A HEALTHY BABY. EVEN DELIVERY IS SAFER WHEN YOU'RE SOBER. IT IS *NEVER* TOO LATE FROM A THERAPEUTIC STANDPOINT TO STOP DRINKING DURING PREGNANCY.

Furthermore, on a purely practical level, the economic costs of the problem were staggering; the pervasive incidence of low birth weight alone predicted a cumulative annual cost of $82 million for hospital and doctors' fees. One anatomy professor from the University of Iowa outlined a convoluted but persuasive formula by which a dollar amount could be pegged onto prenatal drinking. He plugged in the most conservative estimates—between one and two FAS victims per thousand births—then calculated the totals from census reports, yielding a minimum of thousands of clearly diagnosable children each year.

He then flashed on the display screen a list of the most common physical ailments associated with FAS—impairments of the heart and spine, of vision and hearing, of bone structure, and of internal organ formation—and estimated the average medical bills for the treatment of each one, multiplying a cautious fraction of that amount by the aggregate affected population he had previously determined. And, of course, that was just the beginning. He then factored in $113 million per annum for such low IQ-related intangibles as psychological counseling, special education, group homes, social services. There was no way to even guess at the price tag for the most obvious and yet the most subtle drain of all: the collective lifetime income *lost* because FAS victims could not hold regular jobs.

By even the most miserly estimate, using the lowest numbers, the minimum percentages, bargain-basement prices, fetal alcohol syndrome unambiguously cost the United States government hundreds of millions of dollars each year. Applied across the board to all age groups (not just to the newborn), it might challenge the budget deficit, it might rival the annual defense allotment.

This presentation reminded me of a 1987 article on the economic impact of FAS by Ernest L. Abel and Robert J. Sokol which I had read only that morning, and had stuck into my notebook because it was so pertinent. I took it out, turned to the last page, and read that "at the Federal level, the National Institute on Alcohol Abuse and Alcoholism spent $2.9 million on FAS research in 1985 (B. Turner, pers. commun). This is less than one-hundredth of our cost estimate for readily identifiable FAS-related outcomes. At this level of funding fetal alcohol research could go on for a century for the cost of 1 year of treatment, and . . . our estimates are very conservative. We have not even included disorders related to partial fetal alcohol syndrome which affect about three to five times more individuals than FAS."[1] If an education program aimed at prevention cost as much as thousands of dollars *per child spared*, it still made prudent financial sense. FAS was not just a personal tragedy or a social embarrassment, it was a fiscal disaster. Prevention not only saved lives, it saved a lot of money.

The Study Group's public agenda, over the next ten years, included more research, more lab work, but on a pragmatic level it called for a change in the attitudes of general practice physicians—the professionals who most frequently encountered pregnant women. First, the "credibility gap" of this group had to be eliminated. Many doctors, several speakers contended, did not believe the surgeon general's report that even a small amount of alcohol could be dangerous to a fetus. They had to be convinced. And second, they had to be educated as to how to counsel, in a nonthreatening, nonjudgmental way, pregnant women who came into their offices. Their approach should be calm, persistent, informative, and clear.

After the final session I took a long walk on the beach, collecting shells to bring home for our children. My mind could not perform the multiplications that the anatomy professor's formula would generate if fetal alcohol effects—all those amorphous, hard to diagnose traits that everyone knew existed but which, if they were not "full blown," never got included in the count—were added to the base of his calculations. How did one factor in the cost of prison operation, of goods lost to shoplifters, of the hours and hours of natural or adoptive parents' time as they toiled over shoelaces or hygiene or homework that created problems whose solutions were forever out of their children's reach? It is an article of faith that every human life is valuable, but we don't realize how very expensive it is until the cost of dependence is tabulated.

It was a hot, hazy day, and beyond the carefully tended beach of Wild Dunes, the tide had left a scattering of refuse: abandoned floats, driftwood, rusted cans, an assortment of indestructible plastic. Here and there the sunlight was caught in small ovals of glass that had been turned by the sea until all the rough edges had been burnished. These vivid specks of brown or green were set into the wet sand like stones cusped in a medieval crown. In my imagination I linked them to those glittering shards of muscatel bottles that littered the roads of Pine Ridge, the evidence of half-gallon jugs tossed from speeding cars in celebration or in disgust at their emptiness.

In the fall of 1988 there was yet another meeting on the subject of fetal alcohol syndrome, this one in Tucson, sponsored by the Indian Health Service. The daylong session took place in a neo-hacienda–style airport inn. Cacti and palm trees were displayed around a rectangular aqua pool, which in turn was bounded on all sides by three grill-railed stucco storys. Each Executive Suite afforded an obstructed view. The weather was mild for Tucson, no more than ninety degrees, as the invited participants congregated around a coffee urn at nine o'clock. We were a group selected by Eva Smith, coordinator of IHS alcohol programs—though she herself was in Los Angeles, awaiting the birth of a baby girl. Participants, who came from all regions of the country, had each grappled in one way or another with FAS.

Inside the air-conditioned Ranchero Room, the hotel's boxlike design was replicated by an arrangement of tables, but instead of chlorinated water the middle ground was dominated by a projector with an ominous number of slide trays stacked beside it. The agenda was simple: over the course of the next eight hours, each person would stand and briefly recount his or her insights and perspective on the topic at hand. I glanced down the list and checked the presentations to which I especially looked forward: I was sure Theda New Breast would speak ardently of the FAS programs that she had organized on the Blackfeet Reservation and in San Francisco. In those of her writings I had read, she attacked the problem as a feminist inspired by self-help philosophies and viewed maternal drinking as part of a larger legacy of sexism and exploitation. Kathy Masis, an energetic young physician who worked on the Navajo reservation, would describe the efficacy of the FAS education effort with which she had been involved—before its funding had expired. Ann Garneaux, a young woman in braids, promised to present an FAS coloring book that had been produced as an educational tool, and to speak of a "Dad's March Against Alcoholism" that she had recently organized in South Dakota. I had heard good things of her work from Jeaneen.

The first three speakers were assigned the task of bringing us up to date with a national overview of where things stood, and they were provided a longer time slot. Phil May, very much as I remembered him from my visit in Albuquerque two years previous, reiterated once again the results of his prevention studies, and Dr. J. M. Aase, the well-published dysmorphologist with whom Phil had closely collaborated, discussed the subtle means by which older FAS and FAE victims could be recognized: a forward jaw, recurrent behavioral problems ("a specific profile"), and certain particular physical problems, such as clubfoot and cleft palate, that recurred with disproportionate frequency.

Dr. Aase noted that many offspring of mothers who drank during their pregnancy appeared to be normal, but then asked the rhetorical question: *"Are they as normal as they might be?"* He pointed out that the most recent brain analysis of FAS victims showed aberrant cell migration and division, not merely a growth deficit, and that the hypothalmus—the part of the brain that controls learning, intellect, and performance—was almost always affected. After years of experience, he was not optimistic that what he called "passive education efforts" would sufficiently reduce prenatal drinking. "High-risk activity," he concluded, "is not just from lack of knowledge."

Ann Streissguth, recently back from a year of comparative research in France, stepped to the microphone. She was a small woman with a crown of prematurely white curls circling her face. Dressed in a stylish suit, she wore designer eyeglasses and low-heeled shoes. At first glance she was not easily identifiable as the foremost theoretician and psychological researcher on the subject of FAS, and yet no one was more deserving of the title. For twenty years she had, as much as anyone, defined the subject, made the intuitive leaps, interviewed the hundreds of patients. As she took a breath preparatory to addressing us, her eyes scanned the room, recognizing every face.

I had met Ann several times at RSA conventions and had often spoken to her on the phone. She had encouraged my Dakota study from the beginning and over the years had inquired about its progress. On a few occasions, but only a few, I had contacted her concerning aspects of Adam's development, and she had been forthcoming with good advice. I had read every word about fetal alcohol syndrome she had published, except for her latest study, prepared under contract with the Indian Health Service in conjunction with two University of Washington colleagues. Now I opened the blue cover of "A Manual on Adolescents and Adults with Fetal Alcohol Syndrome with Special Reference to American Indians" (1988),* ready to consult the pages as Ann followed its organizational outline in her presentation.

She began by describing the follow-up evaluations of the initial eleven FAS victims she and her colleagues had diagnosed in 1972, the group upon which the article that named the syndrome was based,

---

* A. P. Streissguth, Robin A. LaDue, and Sandra P. Randals, "A Manual on Adolescents and Adults with Fetal Alcohol Syndrome with Special Reference to American Indians" (Washington, DC: Indian Health Service, 1986, 1988). All quoted references in the following pages are taken from this source.

and then went on to extrapolate from the results of a larger, more comprehensive study of sixty-one adolescents and adults who had previously been diagnosed FAS (70 percent) or had FAE (30 percent). This latter group ranged in age from twelve to forty, with most under eighteen.

Ann seemed to me in this context more comfortable in asserting her opinions than she had been at the RSA meetings, and offered a number of cogent observations. The average IQ of the fifty-two patients for whom she had data was 68, ranging from a low of 20 (severely retarded) to a high of 105 (normal). Those designated as FAS had an average IQ of 66, compared to an average of 73 for those termed FAE. The group as a whole was functioning at the fourth-grade level for reading, the third-grade level for spelling, and the second-grade level for math, which was not good news. Math skills were known to be the best predictors for potential adult independence within a community—and as a result of their low achievement capability, "many patients have trouble making change at the store, let alone managing their finances. Poor arithmetic scores also reflect poor memory, poor abstract thinking, and difficulty with basic problem solving."[2]

What was more, even these minimal results might be too positively interpreted—actual reading *comprehension* was poorer than the simple word recognition the tests measured, and the gap increased with age. As Streissguth wrote, the alphabet was almost "overlearned" in childhood, and "the ability to generalize knowledge, both with language and numbers, requires a high level of abstraction" that went beyond rote. In addition, "careful penmanship and relatively good spelling skills give the impression that [patients] will be more functional than they actually are." The people in her study generally dealt with the world with the sophistication of a seven-and-a-half-year-old, though their median age was more than sixteen. Their IQs did not improve as they got older.

Around the room everyone took notes. Heads were bent low, and pens scribbled furiously to catch these rarest of gifts from a social scientist—straightforward statements, facts unqualified by "perhaps" or "usually." Ann Streissguth was in a position to speak with authority, and her candid words carried the weight of revelation. She was a synthesizer of diverse information, the magnifying glass that would clarify confusion to the extent that it was possible.

Government services, Ann pointed out, are normally available only for people with IQs of 70 or below, which meant that approximately 42 percent of those diagnosed in her study group were not eligible. Yet almost none of these people had lived with their birth mothers beyond their third year, if for that long, and, in fact, 69 percent of their biological mothers were known to be deceased.

There were some consistent common denominators that most members of the study group shared in both the physical and the behavioral arenas. Eighty-five percent of them had abnormalities of the philtrum, 80% had teeth problems, and a majority were unusual in regard to head shape, hirsutism, fingers, nose, ears, palms, back/neck/spine, and midface. Eighty-six percent had experienced neglect, 52 percent, abuse; 80 percent had "attention deficits," that is, they could not concentrate on a single task for an extended period of time; 73 percent had memory problems, 72 percent had been classified as hyperactive at some point in their development. A majority were characterized by willful or inadvertent disobedience and by school truancy. Ninety-five percent could not handle money on their own, regardless of sex, age, educational level, or background. None managed their own checking accounts. None were financially self-supporting. Only one held a full-time job. Ordinary duties like taking care of their own health, looking after their own clothes, saving money, and making purchases independently were accomplished by only four of the sixty-one patients in the sample—and *they* were diagnosed as FAE, with IQ scores of 75 and up. Only half of all those surveyed were able to care for all their hygienic needs.

Like Adam, these patients could dress themselves, even if it was slow and after considerable prompting; they could sweep or mop or do other household chores, if ordered to do so. They could use basic tools and could assist in the preparation of food. However, *none* of the patients over eighteen were fully independent, although ten had IQ scores over 85.[3]

As Ann continued to build a profile of the "typical" FAS or FAE victim, I listened like a visitor to a fortune-teller or a tarot reader, like a person who entered a seance skeptically, but whose doubts crumbled under an avalanche of precise information. If Ann had known Adam all his life and, disguising only his name, attempted to list his liabilities, she could not have been more on target.

Next to me an elderly social worker from a southwestern reservation had dozed off, her head slumped to one side. She had a soft nasal snore, inaudible, I suspected, to anyone but me, but I had to quash an impulse to shake her conscious. How dare she miss this? No matter how low the hum of the cooling machinery, no matter how lulling Ann's quiet voice, this room was filled with lightning. The words were undramatic, stones perfectly skipped one by one, and yet they were the distillations of ruined lives, the warning sirens of future catastrophes. Never before had statistics so come to life in my imagination, and yet, as I looked from face to face around the room, I saw that the numbers translated unequally. For some, like me, they resonated with personal knowledge, but for others they were only interesting, alarming enough to rate a line on yellow paper next to the doodle of a flower or a beadwork pattern.

Of the eleven patients from the 1973 study, Ann continued, two were dead—one had drowned in a bathtub. With the rush of a remembered nightmare I saw once again Adam's face submerged beneath the water, heard Sava's worried plea that Adam get up. Four patients were mentally retarded—these, Ann said, were the lucky ones because they *looked* as badly off as they were—and four were borderline, "bright enough to cause trouble."

The text of Ann's "Manual" expanded upon all she introduced. Neglect, abandonment, and abuse characterized the typical FAS/ FAE infancy: victims were slow to master motor milestones, slow to say or combine words. They often had poor appetites and had to be forced to eat regular portions of food. They were usually described as "very good," oriented toward people, and having no anxiety about strangers. I looked at Phil May. Did he recall his story to me about the little boys who ran up to him, unafraid, when he visited the Navajo reservation? His eyes were on Ann's face, and I saw him nod.

In early school years, Ann went on, "their needs for bodily contact seem insatiable. They may talk a lot and ask a lot of questions, but they often lack richness of speech, thought, and grammatical complexity. They can't sit still a minute."

I remembered Jeaneen's description of children bouncing off the walls of her office in Pine Ridge.

"They tend to wander away, need closer than usual supervision. Many caretakers find these children endearing during this period, and their slow development and poor performance is often excused on the basis of their small size. 'Oh, he'll outgrow it,' is a commonly expressed hope at this stage, and developmental delays are often not taken seriously by the family."

It was uncanny how her composite results paralleled my own experience, with my folders full of encouragements from Adam's early-grade teachers who maintained, every one, that he was simply young for his age. "School may be delayed a year with the idea that 'they'll catch up,' " Ann had written in her book, as if she could see into Adam's file. "The less handicapped children with FAS often continue in regular classrooms during their early school years. Reading and writing skills during the first two years may not be noticeably delayed, particularly for children who have repeated kindergarten. Arithmetic is usually more of a problem.[4] . . . Patients with FAS/FAE are often thought, on casual observation, to be brighter and more alert than the test scores indicate, causing both caretakers and teachers to perceive them as lazy, stubborn, and unwilling to learn, a faulty perception that frequently leads to frustration for all parties involved."

That was an understatement that brought to mind the Weekend of the Congressional Rules Committee!

"The academic functioning of FAS/FAE patients appears to peak at around age 12–15 years and grade 6–8. The majority of these patients have received many years of special education services without alleviation of the basic deficits. It is our clinical impression that parents and teachers often fixate on the academic development of the child, when, after a certain point, a more constructive focus would be on teaching vocational, survival, and daily living skills.

The Hartford High School program was squarely on the right track. The social worker next to me inclined too far, jolted awake. She blinked, picked up her pencil as if inspired to jot a note, then closed her eyes again. As she retreated into sleep her fingers gripped the blue pencil tightly, as if its upright posture would signal her alertness. It was a light left on in a dark house to ward off prowlers, but soon, as her breathing slowed, it strayed right and left like a metronome with every inhalation and expulsion.

"We asked teachers to tell us about their problems in working with these patients," Ann reported. "Concerns expressed included difficulty staying on task, distracting other children, poor use of language, inability to structure their work time, and a constant need for monitoring and attention. Stubbornness, immaturity, poor self-image, poor social attitude and difficulty dealing with change were frequently described problems. Interestingly enough, these complaints were almost verbatim to those expressed by parents and caretakers regarding the patient's behavior at home and in other social situations."

Almost identical to passages I had already recorded in a draft of this book. Details Ann mentioned in passing triggered one memory after another. "Some patients asked repetitive questions intrusively: 'Do you love me?' "

Just as Adam had done until he was nearly eight years old.

When one young male had performed an inappropriate behavior in a social situation, "he said he did it because 'the other kids told me to,' " Ann recounted, then explained that his "impulsiveness, lack of inhibition, and naïveté was common" among the patients she had seen, regardless of age or gender. It fit in with the expected behaviors of a much younger child, but it was complicated by the physical maturity of an adolescent or adult. A younger child was not expected to have good judgment or to have learned more abstract social rules, whereas a teenager or adult was.[5]

There seemed to be nothing Ann had noticed among her patients that didn't jibe with my personal observations. Through her research, she could sight unseen describe Adam, his strengths and weaknesses, as well as I could. Better. "The intellectually handicapped," she wrote, "have more difficulty conceptionalizing and verbalizing their experiences, and more difficulty, in general, in learning from their past experiences."[6]

I exchanged a mental look with Mona, Elaine, and Sharon, with Brenda Demery. They would understand. They could supply a million examples.

"These patients were commonly described as very 'people-oriented' and gregarious," Ann had written. "The outgoing, excessively friendly manner seen as positive in younger children with FAS became more and more of a problem as these people grew up. [It] is often combined with overly tactile behavior, again similar to what is seen in very young children. . . . But adolescents and adults who have little sense of personal space, are very 'touchy,' and have inappropriate and excessive curiosity are often disliked and shunned by their peer group." And even worse, FAS/FAE victims "are . . . easily influenced by others and seem to have difficulty comprehending social situations, remembering the appropriate behavior, and knowing when to say 'No.' "[7]

Ann provided a telling illustration of this point: "One of our adult male patients met a stranger at a bus stop and asked him to come home. The stranger went with our patient, stole all the patient's money, and then left. When asked why the patient had brought the stranger home, he replied, 'He wasn't a stranger, I met him at the bus stop.' "

I could hear the words in Adam's voice.

In terms of IQ scores, my son was almost a perfect match to the University of Washington group's averages on the Wechsler test: Verbal = 65 and Performance = 78. Similarly, the more concrete the task, the better both he and those in the study sample performed. Both faltered in areas calling for abstract thought. Patients functioned, according to the Socialization Scale of a Vineland test, at average intelligence of about six and a half years, though their mean age was nearly seventeen.

The pattern continued. About the middle school years she said, "During this time, academic achievement usually reaches the maximum point, with reading and spelling often being superior to arithmetic. . . . Good verbal skills, a superficially friendly social manner and good intentions often continue to mask the seriousness of the situation."[8] And then Ann used the very words that Louise and I, and others who knew and loved Adam, had always employed. "Despite their behavioral problems," she said, "most adolescents and adults with FAS/FAE remained 'sweet' in temperament and helpful and considerate in their interpersonal interactions as they matured. Thus many of the characteristics noted in the young children continued into adulthood."[9]

But adults were not children, not in this world. "The major changes seen from preadolescence to adolescence and adulthood are increasingly inappropriate sexual behavior; isolation; loneliness; depression; and inappropriate expectations for eventual work, schooling and independence,"[10] Ann concluded. The future she forecast was bleak, devoid of the deus ex machina that we human beings prefer to insert into the fairy tales we make up about ourselves. In Adam's story, he would never awake to the kiss of happily ever after.

✳

My turn to speak came late in the day, and in the company of so much expertise, so many years of devoted hard work, so many victories over despair and discouragement, so many thousands of patient contact-hours with drinking mothers or their impaired off-spring, I felt particularly presumptuous. For all my reading and interviewing and traveling I was first and foremost only an outraged parent looking for answers. Adam was my precipitating reason, the source of everything I knew as fact, the basis of my intuition, the instigator of my questions. I was not a doctor, not a social worker, not a clinical psychologist. My motives were selfish and narrow: more than for any altruistic reason, I cared about FAS because my kid suffered from it.

The confession of love renders us vulnerable. It admits prejudice, it stands us naked before the threat of rejection. I took a deep breath and told those smart, experienced professionals about how Adam shut the bathroom door on water running out of a broken pipe, how he bought a doughnut for ten dollars, how he didn't think to wear his coat when it was cold, and how, at twenty years of age, he couldn't tell time with any accuracy or real comprehension. I told about him going up the wrong staircase, day after day, at Stevens High School, and about him sleeping through his solo on Outward Bound. I recited a litany of anecdotes, some funny enough to elicit laughter, and made the claim that they added up to something very sad, very unfair, something that should not happen to a person before he had drawn his first breath of earth's air. I provided, as I do in this book, the lesson of just one boy. I offered a face to paste on all those pages of statistics. I told them Adam's name.

CHAPTER FOURTEEN

I showed these pages to Louise and she reminded me: Adam has the gift of loving, and that is better than arithmetic. His battered, deprived humanity has been somehow condensed into a core of unspoken connection with his family that is indissoluble, at one with his very being. He doesn't give credence to the possibility that love can end. He trusts his heart as impulsively as he approaches everything else.

How then do we cope with the decisions the doctors and counselors and teachers have advised us to make? How do we, in conscience, persuade Adam to have an operation that will make him sterile? How do we, in conscience, not do that? Though he's fully capable of giving life to a child, could he raise or support it? Of course not. Could he be trained to practice contraception? I wouldn't bet my next twenty years on it. But on the other hand, must he pass his life a celibate?

A by-product of living with Adam, of being responsible for him, of trying to grasp the world from his perspective, was an expanding definition on my part of the concept of "intelligence." All along I had argued—and still believed—that the standard IQ tests alone were an inadequate measurement. I had all the obvious reasons: these tools naturally contained an inherent cultural bias; their results were known to vary significantly for the same individual from one day to the next, suggesting that metabolic or emotional factors influenced results; most of them presupposed a standard core of skills for all participants. IQ tests could easily miss or fail to recognize such unspecific talents as artistic creativity, inventiveness, or manual dexterity.

The fact that Adam had consistently scored low did not in and of itself constitute a satisfactory geography of his mental capacity—but in all honesty, no one, no counselor, psychologist, or teacher, had ever claimed it did. Rather, they maintained that IQ tests were *indicators*, track lights illuminating the peaks and valleys of his capacity, which demanded closer analysis. And after years of witnessing Adam's behavior, the practical functioning of his mind, I came to the point of recognizing certain categories as essential to my own definition of intelligence.

The first was imagination—not so much the ability to make up a fictional story, but the basic act of *foreseeing* a possible consequence in one's own life. Most of us do it all the time: if I do x today, then y will occur tomorrow. If I work at a job, I will earn money. If I earn money, I can purchase more options for myself. If I go to sleep early, I will be rested when I wake up. If I eat my lunch at nine in the morning, I will be hungry at two. That kind of thing. And how do these associations work? By learning, I think, from previous experience, by inducing from empirical evidence, or by deducing from a theory incorporating examples gained from reading or from listening to snippets of general history or from close observation of other people. To imagine is in a way to believe in our power to predict, and therefore to affect, the future. Imagination hurdles us into an unknown scenario armed at least with the talisman of knowledge. It is, in the most general sense, a culture's collective way of self-perpetuation because, contrary to the popular belief that a person with great imagination is an iconoclast, a misfit, foresight is the normal channel through which elements of yesterday are introduced into the mechanics of tomorrow.

Adam, after exhaustive training, acquired routine, but not imagination. When functioning well, he repeated actions precisely in sequence, with no variation or fine tuning. Left to his own devices he would duplicate a pattern day after day, and if that habitual procedure included a subtle mistake—shoes on, laces tied, but tied backward—the error would not be corrected without the influence of some external intervention.

Louise and I were always reminded of this confusion on nights of winter ice storms, after the electricity in our house went out. When the power was restored, we had to reset all the clocks, especially

Adam's. If we forgot to reprogram his alarm, it would go off at odd, predawn hours. Then at 2 A.M., 3 A.M., we would be startled from sleep by the sounds of Adam fixing his sandwiches, eating his cereal, preparing to walk up the base of the hill and wait for his school bus. It didn't matter that there was no light in the sky, any more than it would have made a difference if the buzzer had rung at high noon. At its prod, Adam knew to rise, dress, and leave the house, unless we went downstairs and talked him into staying.

Knowledge, for Adam, was a repertoire of particular tried and true programs, analogous to Chinese writing, in which each word has a unique character. The process of his thinking often seemed to lack movable parts, building blocks that could be manipulated at will to form new constructions. Each unprecedented event was perceived as a wholly original situation, not as simply one within a flexible set of shifting possibilities.

And imagination, I came to understand, was crucial to motivation. Without a degree of prescience, there was no reason for effort. A squirrel that, on some instinctual abstract level, does not expect winter, does not gather and store nuts. A worker who does not comprehend the notion of passing years, of aging, does not provide for retirement income. And conversely, shoplifters who desire a stick of gum do not weigh the immediate pleasure they seek against the disproportionate consequences if they are apprehended. The idea to do, or not to do, something is revealed in the internal crystal ball that each of us constantly consults. In anthropological theory there is a concept called "the superorganic," which is based upon the premise that members of a culture derive their worldview from the same pool of historically generated assumptions. To live harmoniously in society, we must construe a roughly similar future.

Motivation fuels self-improvement, the completion of unsavory tasks, the wish to make a good social impression, the avoidance of crimes for which one is likely to be apprehended. Imagination informs a person of what he or she cannot directly perceive but only infer—for instance, that he is *visible* to other people and that how he looks to them will affect their behavior. This awareness, if he does not consciously rebel against it, may therefore cause him to maintain an affable or at least a nonthreatening expression on his face, to practice personal hygiene, to, at best, treat other people as he himself would want to be treated.

Louise and I have needed to say to our son hundreds and thousands of times: "Adam, people can *see* you; look in the mirror and be aware of what you look like." "Adam, don't scowl." "Adam, your shirt is buttoned crookedly (or, you have your shoes on the wrong feet, your pants are backward, your zipper is not zipped, your glasses are dirty)." "Adam, when people say hello to you, answer them." "Adam, don't push someone ahead of you out of the way."

Ann Streissguth's best and sometimes most challenging advice comes toward the end of her "Manual": "Perhaps the single most important coping skill in working with patients with FAS/FAE is a sense of humor." We endeavored to follow that prescription, but appreciated the fact that she had also included a section on coping with an adolescent or adult with FAS or FAE. Her conclusions reenforced our reluctant inclination to intrude ourselves in Adam's life.

"STRUCTURE! STRUCTURE! STRUCTURE!" Ann wrote. "Those caretakers who have established clear, consistent expectations and behavioral consequences are the ones who have the least problems and whose children appear to have done the best socially. . . . The use of immediate consequences, for both positive and negative behavior, is extremely important. Many FAS/FAE patients function on an intellectual level and social level of a seven to nine year old. Just as young children need constant monitoring and reminding to accomplish their chores and/or to stay out of trouble, so do many of these patients. . . . Setting clear, concrete limits is critical given the propensity for many of these patients to roam and to use very poor judgment."[1]

The story I told in Tucson, perhaps more than any other, unconsciously illustrated this point. On a warm night in the summer of 1986, Louise and I were invited to meet friends for dinner at a nearby inn. Sava was a mature fourteen, Madeline was eleven, Adam was eighteen. Our farm is quiet, far off the highway; our neighbors were at home, within shouting distance across the dirt road in case of emergencies. So, after much instruction and posting of phone numbers, for the first time we took the sleeping Persia and Pallas, then aged two and one, to their sitter and left the big children to themselves for three hours, from seven to ten. They could watch TV, play cards, and go to bed when they got tired.

We had a fine time. Our friends were just back from a trip to Asia and were loaded with exotic stories. The food was delicious. There was for us the rare and romantic sense of being out on a date.

When we returned to our house, most of the lights were off, and we paused for a moment at the back door to appreciate the spread of stars in the pitch-black sky. The mood ended, however, when we went inside. The kitchen floor was covered with several inches of water which, it appeared, was raining from the ceiling. We raced upstairs and found all the children peacefully asleep in their beds. Then, after opening the tightly closed door of the bathroom above the kitchen, we turned on the light and stared. A pipe connecting the sink to the wall had been pulled free and was gushing water that collected on the wooden plank floor and then seeped through. We exchanged a confused look, waiting for a logical explanation to occur to us. *Could* this have happened by itself? This was our bathroom, full of baby paraphernalia, officially off-limits to the older children, who were supposed to use the one on the first floor.

Sava and Madeline had heard us arrive and, still half asleep, came to investigate. They seemed as amazed at the situation as we were. I took off my shoes, waded into the mess, and easily fitted together the disconnected ends of the pipe. Immediately the flow ceased. There was nothing to it. Anybody could have fixed it.

I went back to Adam's room, at the far end of the house. He lay sprawled in his bed, on top of the sheets, partially covered with an unzipped sleeping bag. He had not put on his pajamas, and the radio was playing. I touched his shoulder and called his name until he woke.

"Adam, were you in our bathroom?"

"I didn't," he mumbled.

"Come on, Adam. Did you play in our bathroom?"

"Well," he said grudgingly, "I was just looking in the mirror."

"What else did you do?"

"Nothing."

"What about the water, Adam?"

"Well, it wasn't my fault."

"How did it happen?"

"Well, it fell off." He was irritated to be blamed for something that was clearly the pipe's mistake.

"Did you stand on it?"

"I didn't." His expression said he did.

"What did you do then?"

Adam knew what to say and was confident that he had followed the right course—The Bathroom Sequence we had drilled into him. "I turned off the light and closed the door."

And then he went to bed and fell asleep. The bad pipe could solve its own problems.

I fought to keep my temper. It would do no good to yell about the dangers of an electrical short circuit, about the costs of flood repair. To conceptualize these things required anticipation, and Adam had none. In the end I stuck to reenforcing an established rule: Adam was not supposed to go into that bathroom. *That* was his mistake, the focus of that night's harangue.

Louise and I spoke very little as we mopped the kitchen. The books and papers we had left on the table had been drenched and were ruined. The cries of frogs and peepers, the rumble of an occasional car passing on the road a quarter of a mile away, came through the open windows and mixed with the brush of sponges and rags against the floor. When we had repaired as much as possible, we turned out the lights and went in defeat, in grief, to sit outdoors on the granite stoop. We had lost one more confidence that, without realizing it, we had taken for granted. There suddenly loomed whole unimagined categories of things to worry about, pitfalls we couldn't anticipate before they had occurred. That was the time, I think, that we finally, completely accepted that Adam was never going to learn enough to survive on his own. There were simply too many contingencies, and we would never think to prepare him for them all.

One morning in the winter of 1987 I noticed a classified advertisement in *The Daily Dartmouth,* the campus newspaper. Interested parties were invited to contact the National Park Service about temporary summer jobs at St. Gaudens National Historic Site—in Cornish, ten minutes from our house. I telephoned immediately and asked for an application for the outdoor maintenance job; with supervision I was sure Adam could cut grass, weed gardens, pick up brambles. And, as federal government employment, it seemed probable that Adam would not be discriminated against in hiring because of his learning handicap.

Five months and many completed forms later, Adam and I drove one May afternoon to the estate where Augustus St. Gaudens had created many of his dramatic sculptures. St. Gaudens was the magnet of a celebrated artists' colony that had existed along the shores of the Connecticut River in the early twentieth century—an esoteric rural salon of painters, poets, and dilettantes who amazed the local citizenry by periodically staging public events which, to people other than themselves, seemed bizarre. There are sepia photographs of the colonists, dressed in pleated Greek tunics, standing frozen on the long lawns in poses imitative of ancient friezes and statues. Apparently these living tableaus would be maintained for hours at a time in homage to the classics that they mimicked.

The participants in these charades were long gone, but, thanks to the National Park Service, the estate grounds remained pristine, the original Victorian furniture protected behind velvet ropes in the main house. Every Sunday during the summer, visitors were invited to picnic on the veranda and listen to a free concert while they enjoyed the sweeping view far into the Green Mountains of Vermont. It was a breathtaking locale, a marvelous place to work outdoors, and the man in charge hired Adam almost immediately at the advertised, generous salary. The job would start each weekday at 7 A.M. and finish at 4 P.M., with a half hour free for lunch.

Louise and I were thrilled, though it meant some schedule adjustment on our part in order to drive Adam to work in the morning and pick him up in the afternoon. This opportunity was so unexpected, so perfectly tailored to our son's geographical range, so matching of the upper but possible limits of his skills, that we allowed ourselves to dream that it would go on indefinitely. In our fantasy Adam would enjoy the labor, make a good impression, form meaningful friendships with his associates, learn the self-motivating satisfaction of a task well done. When the summer ended he would hate to leave and his boss would be equally sorry to see him go. Over the course of the next school year, scheduled to be Adam's last, we would prevail upon the Park Service to upgrade the maintenance job from temporary to permanent, and then the following May, the new phase of Adam's life would begin—complete with a medical benefits package and civil service protection.

Looking ahead toward this rosy future, we ordered a full complement of uniforms—for cold as well as for warm weather. Adam was outfited in gray and green for any season, wet or dry. Our enthusiasm was contagious, and the whole family joined in its spirit. I dropped

Adam off at the gate that first morning with a manly handshake and a kiss on the cheek. If I had owned pom-poms, I would have tossed them in the air.

It didn't work out. The St. Gaudens staff was patient, instructive. Ken Kramberg, the Hartford vocational education teacher, did a full week's worth of on-the-job training. Adam's grandmothers, grandfather, aunts and our friends sent encouraging greeting cards and called at the end of his first week to hear a report. But it was the same old story—consistent with his school performance for twelve years, with his first job at the Pizza Hut in Northfield: if someone in authority stood over Adam and told him each thing to do, every day, he would follow instructions. The minute the person left, however, the minute he was on his own, he became distracted, wandered off, lost interest. Whenever unsupervised, he removed his eyeglasses and therefore was unable to cut accurately with the push-mower. His boss tried to help by each dawn spreading lime in long, straight lines, easy to follow even for one as nearsighted as Adam, but eyesight was not the stumbling block.

On more than one occasion Adam attempted to avoid a work assignment by hiding behind a tree. He refused to wear his hat, despite the fact that it was mandated by regulations and despite the fact that prolonged, unshaded exposure to direct summer sunlight could—and did—trigger minor seizures. Adam's biweekly paychecks were absolutely no incentive, either. There was nothing he wanted to purchase but candy and soft drinks. Yet late in the summer, by which time he had accumulated several hundred dollars—available to him for the asking from his bank account—Adam reverted to his old, intermittent habit of taking money from us.

We had battled over this practice for several years. If Louise's purse or my wallet was left unattended, odd amounts of cash occasionally disappeared and later turned up, when I did the laundry, in the pockets of Adam's pants or shirts. When asked *why* he stole it, he would reply, on the first round, "I didn't." When confronted with the evidence, he would say, "Well, I just wanted to."

"Is there something you wish to buy?" we always asked. "Something you need the money for?"

There never was, at least not that Adam could specify. And finally, either because we became more careful about concealing our loose change or because Adam forgot about carrying money, the problem seemed to abate. Then, late in September, when the temporary employment season was almost over, I received a call from the boss at St. Gaudens.

"I don't want to butt in," he said. "But I don't know if it's a good idea for Adam to have so much money."

"What do you mean?" I asked. "He only has three dollars."

"Well, I don't know about that. He has two twenties and a five. The reason I know is that he pins the bills up on the bulletin board every day under his work order. I'm afraid somebody's going to rip them off."

When Louise brought Adam home that day, I decided to approach the matter with relative calm. I had learned it made sense to confront Adam in the way that would upset us all the least.

"Adam," I said. "This can't keep happening. You have plenty of money. You just have to ask for it. You can't keep stealing from us. Stealing is a crime. If you do it to other people, you could get arrested and go to jail. You've got to understand this. Now why did you take the money from my wallet?"

"I didn't."

"You did, Adam. I cashed a check at the bank four days ago. I had two twenties and a five. I put the money in my wallet and came straight home, and I haven't been out of the house since. Now the bills are gone. Certainly, you took it."

"Well, I was just looking at it," he said.

We went a few more rounds, back and forth. Me pointlessly asking why, Adam not being able to answer. Finally I gave up, raised my voice, and was direct. "Adam, you cannot, *cannot,* steal. You cannot live here and do this. Now *think* about that." I stomped into the kitchen and slammed pots on the stove as I started to make dinner.

It was a chilly night, with the temperature predicted to drop into the low forties. Louise, who had been planting a few shrubs that afternoon, had gone to the grocery. After our talk Adam went outside and walked in the direction of where she had been working. Sometimes he helped by digging the holes, and I assumed that's what he was going to do.

At about six-thirty Louise came home with a trunk full of supplies, and while Madeline and Sava unloaded, I told her about my conversation with Adam.

"Where is he now?" she asked.

"I don't know. Upstairs? He was outside before." We called his name, looked in his room, in the bathroom, under the beds, in the basement, in the barn—his usual sulking places. No luck. It was dark by now, and I remembered that Adam had not been wearing a coat. We telephoned the neighbors, but nobody had seen him. Louise took a flashlight and walked around the property, calling his name. I got into the car and patrolled the road five miles in both directions, stopping often to shout "Adam." Louise and I arrived back at the house at the same time. There was no sign of him. I was overcome by guilt, by the sense that I had driven him into the night by my accusation. I pictured him lost, shivering, defenseless without his medicine or food. There's a bear in our woods, and in panic there is no thought too melodramatic.

"I'm calling the police," I said.

An officer was at the house in ten minutes, and we explained the situation. "Was there a fight of some kind?" the man inquired. "Something that would have made him run away?"

"Yes," I admitted. "Maybe." I felt like the worst father in the world, but the policeman did not comment.

"I'll put out a limited A.P.B.," he said. "He could have hitched a ride somewhere. Meantime I'll have a look around outside. You stay by the phone."

Louise sat at the kitchen table and I paced. We fed the little girls, then Sava and Madeline. "Forty-five dollars," I said. "Who cares about forty-five dollars if it makes him happy to pin it to a bulletin board." All I wanted was for Adam to be all right, to be conscious, not to have been picked up on the road by a maniac.

The back door opened. "Here's the wandering boy," the policeman said, and Adam appeared, head hung low, almost blue with cold. "He was just standing out behind the barn," the policeman reported. "Been there the whole time."

I stood and looked at Adam. "Didn't you hear us calling?"

"Yes."

"Why didn't you answer? Why did you worry us like that?"

"Well, you told me to think," he replied. "I was thinking."

Even with all his complications, Adam's co-workers were kind to him. Everyone agreed he had "grown in the job." He was invited to the end-of-the-season party, and his boss expansively assured me that Adam could have the same post next year, we could count on it. So in January I contacted St. Gaudens and asked for new summer work applications. We were sent two sets, one for the employment level Adam had held the previous summer, and another for a below-minimum-scale "assistant." I filled both of them out and attached a letter when I mailed them back. Adam had experience, I pleaded. He had hung in there. He was a minority and was handicapped, a double affirmative action bonus that I knew carried weight. Midway through the last summer, the St. Gaudens superintendent had received a letter of commendation from national headquarters of the Park Service congratulating him on not only hiring but *finding* an American Indian worker.

If Adam were ever going to be self-supporting, I pointed out, he needed to generate a living wage. He would save most of what he earned. He was twenty years old now, an adult. But if the only way he could be hired was in the reduced capacity, he had no choice but to accept it.

Months passed without a reply, and I assumed, because of the promises, that everything was in order, that it was only a question of which job Adam would be offered. When in late April I finally called to inquire, however, I was told that all positions were filled. Sorry.

It seemed damned unfair to me. I ranted and raved to Louise. Threatened to sue, to expose what seemed to me overt injustice. I was furious and indignant on an abstract level, and it was much easier to blame bad faith than it was to acknowledge the reality that, despite every effort on the part of the people at St. Gaudens, Adam had simply not worked out for them. Once he was gone, they must have realized how much of a burden he had been. They were not bad guys, just human. They did not have long-term responsibility for Adam's welfare. They had given him more second chances than most would have done. They should have called and said all this—legally speaking I felt sure they had an obligation to at least respond to the applications. I didn't like what they had done or how they had done it, but I couldn't pretend that I didn't understand. Ten years earlier, five years, I would have challenged their silence. I would have been on the phone to Washington, to the state office of equal opportunity, to advocacy organizations for Indians or handicapped people. I would have demanded justice. But this was now. No court order was going to make Adam wear his glasses, operate independently without the close scrutiny and encouragement of a supervisor, or be motivated by a desire for advancement. I could probably get him initially rehired for a season at St. Gaudens, but that wouldn't necessarily mean they would continue to employ him.

Adam moved out of our house in late spring of 1988. It was time, but the decision for him to go had not come easily. It was a choice made by default, a move we could rationalize as "for the best" but which was weighted with worry. Our farm was too remote for him to work at hours that lasted longer than the span of a school bus run. Moreover, he was in his final year at Hartford, the last period during which he would be eligible for employment training and placement assistance from the excellent staff. Adam had qualified as a client for the local social service agency, whose representative, Tony Gahn, found him a supervised boardinghouse in Hanover, near enough to public transportation that he could commute to and from a regular dishwashing job at a bowling alley. The manager liked Adam and was prepared to make allowances during what everyone rightly expected to be an erratic period of adjustment.

On a muddy Sunday in March we packed up the belongings Adam wanted to take with him to his new room. It was an odd collection of stuffed animals and paper dolls he had carefully cut out on the sly from a women's underwear catalogue and pasted on cardboard backing, a stack of *Minneapolis Star and Tribune* Sunday cartoons, a suitcase of clothing, a black-and-white television set, and a collection of family photographs and old birthday cards. He took his typewriter and the ongoing "Adam Dorris Story by Adam Dorris," and he brought the voluminous lists I had prepared—times and amounts of medication, sequence of actions to be followed each morning, emergency telephone numbers and instructions for using a pay phone.

He was to be one of several boarders in the home of a couple who bred hairless cats, but he didn't notice the distinctive pheromonal tang that permeated the residence. It was within a short walk of a grocery, a pharmacy, and a movie theater and only a twenty-mile drive from our farm. We were all very, very fortunate, and yet, as Adam walked without a backward glance from the house in which he had lived for almost sixteen years, I experienced a quiet weight of sorrow.

When things are the best they can be, you have no excuse to complain, but that doesn't mean you forgo regret. I had no right to want more for Adam than it's possible for him to have, no right to impose my aspirations on his life. If I were a better person, a wise and accepting person, I would have rejoiced without qualifications that he was agreeable and competent to make this step. Certainly that attitude was the tenor of the words I spoke as we drove to town, unloaded his possessions, and said good-bye. I was hearty in my congratulations and encouragements, proud in my praisings, full of upbeat confidence to Adam that this was the first rung on the ladder of his success.

But lurking within me as we drove away was a different reaction: its arms were folded tightly, its mouth was a compressed line, its shoulders were hunched in impotent fury. It demanded better for Adam. It demanded that he not be penalized for someone else's Original Sin, for a crime committed in ignorance or wanton carelessness before he was born.

Adam's departure was in many respects liberating for Louise and me; we were no longer responsible for arranging his schedule, for getting him places on time, for picking him up when he was done with an activity. It was no longer up to us to ensure that Adam took his medication, dressed in clean clothing, made his bed, did his chores. We soon became aware of just how much of our time had been automatically absorbed by rote instruction: Adam, sit up straight. Adam, say thank-you if someone does you a favor. Adam, that's too much potato on your fork. Adam, shut the door when you go out. Adam, don't wipe your runny nose on the wall. Adam, flush the toilet after you use it. Adam, your shirt is on backward. Adam, turn off the light and the radio when you go to bed.

After years of repetition, we eventually had uttered these sentences without adding verbal justifications. Direct commands were easier on all parties than tortuous, tedious, and ultimately wasted explanations. Appeals to logic had never worked with Adam. The question "Why?" had continued to stump him, no matter what the context, from early childhood. He would mouth the words he thought we wanted to hear. As often as not he guessed wrong, which would only increase the level of our frustration. We had become so used to thinking *for* Adam that the quiet of the house after he left was eerily luxurious, the silence of a painting or a book.

*

It was a good while before I visited Adam at his place of employment, and when I saw him, I knew why. I walked into the almost empty restaurant of the bowling alley—The Red Rooster—and caught a glimpse of my son through the open door that led into the kitchen. It was only the most fleeting look, snatched as he passed from view in the space of a few strides, but it was enough. He was a collection of repeated admonitions left unchecked, an impression he confirmed as, a few minutes later, he sat across from me in a booth.

I had determined in advance to under no circumstances be disapproving, so it was only to myself that I said: "Adam, where are your glasses? You can't see without them." I did not mention the fact that he had not shaved or washed his face in some time. I did not criticize his choice of clothing: a torn T-shirt in frigid November, a shabby pair of sweat pants, worn obviously without underwear, the ravaged running shoes I had begged him to discard weeks before. The nails on his fingers were long and jagged, his teeth not clean, his hair unbrushed. There was a spot of fresh blood on his lower lip, the result of his tendency for chapped skin in winter dryness. All through public school, from October through March, I would apply balm to his lips as my last act before he left the house. Today I controlled my urge to remind him.

Rather, I asked about his recent injury, a burn he had sustained on his forearm when he had stumbled into a hot stove. No one, least of all Adam, seemed sure how this accident had happened, but it was probable that on one of the many days he had neglected to take his midday medicine—or skipped lunch—he had suffered a minor seizure. That one was not a major attack, but those had occurred as well. In just a few months on the job, Adam had been sent in an ambulance to the emergency room at Mary Hitchcock Hospital on three separate occasions after collapsing. He had banged his head on the floor, bruised his leg, bloodied his nose, and each time it was later discovered that the convulsions had been released because the medication level in his bloodstream was too low.

When responsible for his own care, Adam sometimes became confused about his dosage, "remembering" he had taken his Dilantin or Tegretol but warping the time frame. After seventeen years of instruction he still mixed up breakfast and lunch, lunch and dinner, the hours intervening from one meal to the other evaporating in his memory. Or, conversely, the minutes seemed to him to multiply between the event of swallowing a pill and the event of sitting at the table; at those times he overdosed and became drowsy, lethargic. Every now and then, I was convinced, his failure to take his medicine was, to the extent Adam was capable of it, intentional—a nonact rising out of anger at his need, at routine, at infirmity. He got mad at the pills and spurned them, only to pay dearly later for his defiance.

Now he held up his arm for me to examine. A long red scar shaped like the blade of a sword extended from his wrist to his elbow. The doctor on the case had complained to me that Adam had not kept the bandages clean, had removed them often to examine the wound, and that as a consequence the healing process had been neither quick nor ideal. There would be more of a lasting disfigurement than there had to be.

But I didn't bring this up. "It looks much better," I said.

Adam, like me, is astigmatic—that is, without his glasses he has a "lazy eye." While one eye focuses, the other drifts. He seemed to be looking over my shoulder, even as he opened the clear plastic bag that held the food he had brought from his boarding home.

"What happened to your lunch box?" I asked, referring to the expensive contraption Louise had purchased for him when he started the job.

"The handle is loose," he said. "So to make sure, I don't use it." He unpacked three sandwiches, three hard-boiled eggs, and a banana and methodically began to eat. The blood on his lip was wiped with every bite, then reappeared as he worked his jaws. I wanted to reach across the table with my napkin and blot it. I wanted to run next door to the drugstore and buy Vaseline. I wanted to do a lot of things, but Adam would immediately discontinue doing them when I was gone.

Instead, I thought of all the school lunches I had fixed, early in the morning. There was a period of perhaps a year during which Adam consumed the entire contents of his lunch box on the school bus, minutes after he had eaten breakfast. At lunchtime he would have nothing to eat. Then there was another phase during which he didn't eat at all. One day I was looking for something in his closet and discovered a cache of decayed, moldy sandwiches, cookies, and fruit stuffed into a corner.

Today Adam's meal consisted of dry pieces of white bread framing thin slices of baloney. No mayonnaise or mustard. "I think they'd taste better if you jazzed them up a little bit," I offered. He labored to crack an egg, bending low over the table in his myopia and tapping the shell until a series of fissures appeared, then he peeled it, dropping each fragment, one at a time, into the plastic bag. When the surface of the egg was clear, he took a bite, and I couldn't stop myself. "Try just a bit of salt," I suggested. "It will bring out the flavor." He obliged me, prompting yet another memory as he virtually pressed the salt shaker against the egg skin. Years of instruction echoed in my brain: "Hold the ketchup away from the hot dog when you pour it, Adam." "Don't touch the potatoes with the pepper shaker, Adam." "Hold the milk carton above the glass, Adam."

He tried the salted egg and pronounced it an improvement, but as he progressed through the other two eggs, he forgot the salt. So did I. By all evidence Adam didn't take much notice of what he ate. Feeding, for him, seemed to be an act independent of sensation, of preference or enjoyment. He put what was before him into his mouth, chewed and swallowed it, and continued the exercise until there was nothing left. No matter what was served, one dish seemed indistinguishable from another to him. This impression had alternately irritated and depressed me; a well-prepared meal was one of life's small pleasures to which Adam was oblivious. It was a gift that a thoughtful host might serve a guest; but no matter what was offered, Adam reciprocated—unless he was prodded each time to do so—with not the slightest appreciation.

The conversation between my nearly twenty-one-year-old son and me consisted as usual of me asking questions and him answering.

"How's work going?"

"Good."

"Have you seen any movies?"

"I haven't gotten around to it yet."

I gestured to the wooden lanes visible through the interior windows. "Have you been bowling since you've worked here?"

"Not yet."

"What's your favorite program on TV these days?"

"I guess 'Mama's Family.' "

"What did you have for dinner last night?"

"A TV dinner."

"What kind?"

He paused in thought, searched his memory. "I can't say. Probably it was macaroni or turkey."

All this time he worked his way through the food he had brought like a beaver devouring a tree trunk.

"Don't you want something to drink?" I asked. "Some milk or a Coke?"

"No," he said. "I generally don't drink anything."

"You know, you've got a cracked lip. It's bleeding. Did you run out of the stuff you need this time of year?"

Adam touched his finger to the wound, then held it before him and examined the blood. "No," he said and turned his attention back to the egg.

"What's work been like today?"

This was a question he was equipped to handle, and he started with the beginning of the morning when he boarded the bus. He got off the bus at the bus stop. He came into the Red Rooster through the front door. He hung his jacket on the hook. He swept the floor with the broom. He stacked dishes from the dishwasher. He got his jacket and zipped it up. He went outside. He picked trash off the parking lot. A milk carton. A piece of newspaper. Two pop cans. Something else he couldn't remember. He came back inside. He took off his jacket and hung it on the hook.

I listened as Adam recounted, like a videocassette playback, the blow by blow of his day. The hours existed for him as a series of unrelated acts, connected neither by analysis nor by critical perspective, uncolored by like or dislike, undistinguished by incident. As I nodded, inviting him to continue, I yearned to put words in his mouth, to break through the barrier of his plodding progress, to find in him some spark of sarcasm or wit. "So Adam," I wanted to say. "Who are you going to vote for in the presidential election? What do you think of the new Soviet foreign policy? I just read this great mystery novel—you've got to try it."

This was my problem, not his. Where was the fine line between acceptance of a condition I could never change and despair or, worse, indifference? When did I stop wanting, demanding, feeling that Adam had been cheated? When did I let go, quell my passion to power his life, direct his interests, think his thoughts? I was not proud of my complaints; they had long since ceased to do Adam much good and, in fact, interfered with the rhythm of the father-son relationship that he would probably prefer. I tried to imagine this lunch through his perspective, and everything was perfectly satisfactory, better even than satisfactory: Dad had said he would come, and Dad came. No problem. No anxiety that the instructions had been remembered wrong. Adam had not forgotten his lunch. He had brought his medicine and taken it. He had not been criticized. He was on a turf with which he was familiar, at ease. He had not made a mistake. There were no questions he had to struggle to answer. There was no disruption of familiar pattern, and the rest of the day would proceed on schedule, no surprises.

I had no doubt that Adam was glad to see me, that my presence alone was for him a good thing. On an emotional level, he required no more of me than my tacit approval. He liked having the category "Dad" in his life—characters on TV had dads, and so did he. He liked having a person with whom he shared enough history to make some small talk. I confirmed his world, and that's all he wanted. The desire for more came only from me.

Adam's birthdays are, I think, the hardest anniversaries, even though as an adoptive father I was not present to hear Adam's first cry, to feel the aspirated warmth of his body meeting air for the first time. I was not present to count his fingers, to exclaim at the surprise of gender, to be comforted by the hope at the heart of his new existence.

From what I've learned, from the sum of gathered profiles divided by the tragedy of each case, the delivery of my premature son was unlikely to have been a joyous occasion. Most fetal alcohol babies emerge not in a tide, the facsimile of saline, primordial, life-granting sea, but instead enter this world tainted with stale wine. Their amniotic fluid literally reeks of Thunderbird or Ripple, and the whole operating theater stinks like the scene of a three-day party. Delivery room staff who have been witness time and again tell of undernourished babies thrown into delirium tremens when the cord that brought sustenance and poison is severed. Nurses close their eyes at the memory. An infant with the shakes, as cold turkey as a raving derelict deprived of the next fix, is hard to forget.

Compared to the ideal, Adam started far in the hole, differently from the child who began a march through the years without the scars of fetters on his ankles, with eyes and ears that worked, with nothing to carry except what he or she collected along the path.

Adam's birthdays are reminders for me. For each celebration commemorating that he was born, there is the pang, the rage, that he was not born whole. I grieve for what he might have, what he should have been. I magnify and sustain those looks of understanding or compassion or curiosity that fleet across his face, fast as a breeze, unexpected as the voice of God—the time he said to me in the car, the words arising from no context I could see, "Kansas is between Oklahoma and Texas." But when I turned in amazement, agreeing loudly, still ready after all these years to discover a buried talent or passion for geography, for anything, that possible person had disappeared.

"What made you say that?" I asked.

"Say what?" he answered. "I didn't say anything."

The sixteenth birthday, the eighteenth. The milestones. The driver's license, voting, the adult boundary-marker birthdays. The days I envisioned while watching the mails for the response to my first adoption application, the days that set forth like distant skyscrapers as I projected ahead through my years of fatherhood. I had given little specific consideration to what might come between, but of those outstanding days I had been sure. They were the pillars I followed, the oases of certainty. Alone in the cabin in Alaska or in the basement apartment near Franconia while I waited for the definition of the rest of my life to commence, I planned the elaborate cake decorations for those big birthdays, the significant presents I would save to buy. Odd as it may seem, the anticipation of the acts of letting Adam go began before I even knew his name. I looked forward to the proud days on which the world would recognize my son as progressively more his own man. Those were among the strongest hooks that bonded me to him in my imagination.

As each of these anniversaries finally came and went, nothing like I expected them to be, I doubly mourned. First, selfishly, for me, and second for Adam, because he didn't know what he was missing, what he had already missed, what he would miss. I wanted to burst through those birthdays like a speeding train blasts a weak gate, to get past them and back into the anonymous years for which I had made no models, where there were no obvious measurements, no cakes with candles that would never be lit.

It was a coincidence that Adam turned twenty-one as this book neared completion, but it seemed appropriate. On the morning of his birthday, I rose early and baked him a lemon cake, his favorite, and left the layers to cool while I drove to Hanover to pick him up. His gifts were wrapped and on the kitchen table—an electric shaver, clothes, a Garfield calendar. For his special dinner he had requested tacos, and as always I had reserved a magic candle—the kind that keeps reigniting no matter how often it is blown out—for the center of his cake.

I was greeted at Adam's house by the news that he had just had a seizure, a small one this time, but it had left him groggy. I helped him on with his coat, bent to tie his shoelace, all the while talking about the fun we would have during the day. He looked out the window. Only the week before he had been laid off from his dishwashing job. December had been a bad month for seizures, some due to his body's adjustment to a change in dosage and some occurring because Adam had skipped taking medicine altogether. The bowling alley's insurance carrier was concerned and that, combined with an after-Christmas slump in business, decided the issue. Now he was back at Hartford for a few weeks while Ken Kramberg and his associates sought a new work placement. I thought perhaps Adam was depressed about this turn of events, so I tried to cheer him up as we drove south on the familiar road to Cornish.

"So, Adam," I said, making conversation, summoning the conventional words, "do you feel any older? What's good about being twenty-one?"

He turned to me and grinned. There *was* something good.

"Well," he answered, "now the guys at work say I'm old enough to drink."

His unexpected words kicked me in the stomach. They crowded every thought from my brain.

"Adam, you can't," I protested. "I've told you about your birthmother, about your other father. Do you remember what happened to them?" I knew he did. I had told him the story several times, and we had gone over it together as he read, or I read to him, parts of this book.

Adam thought for a moment. "They were sick?" he offered finally. "That's why I have seizures?"

"No, they weren't sick. They died, Adam. They died from drinking. If you drank, it could happen to you." My memory played back all the statistics about sons of alcoholic fathers and their particular susceptibility to substance abuse. "It would not mix well with your medicine."

Adam sniffed, turned away, but not before I recognized the amused disbelief in his expression. He did not take death seriously, never had. It was an abstract concept out of his reach and therefore of no interest to him. Death was less real than Santa Claus—after all, Adam had in his album a photograph of himself seated on Santa Claus's lap. Death was no threat, no good reason to refuse his first drink.

My son will forever travel through a moonless night with only the roar of wind for company. Don't talk to him of mountains, of tropical beaches. Don't ask him to swoon at sunrises or marvel at the filter of light through leaves. He's never had time for such things, and he does not believe in them. He may pass by them close enough to touch on either side, but his hands are stretched forward, grasping for balance instead of pleasure. He doesn't wonder where he came from, where he's going. He doesn't ask who he is, or why. Questions are a luxury, the province of those at a distance from the periodic shock of rain. Gravity presses Adam so hard against reality that he doesn't feel the points at which he touches it. A drowning man is not separated from the lust for air by a bridge of thought—he is one with it—and my son, conceived and grown in an ethanol bath, lives each day in the act of drowning. For him there is no shore.

CHAPTER FIFTEEN

The Adam Dorris Story by Adam Dorris

The things that I can remember is when I was held at a foster home and I was on the floor playing with tracks and as I was playing a man came through the doorway and was standing right there I looked up and sure enough it was my father . I got up and went right to him . Then he took me home with him . He took me home and we lived in a white house with a man who lived right above us he was not a very nice man at all . We lived in sugar hill at that time . And when my father had to work I would go to a day care center and learn on how to do different kinds of things like on how to paint and on how to sing as well . and how to build things with blocks . Then my father would come and pick me up and we would head for home . Then we lived there for a while . Then after that we decided to move to a different house . At that time we moved to infield new hampshire . There was a big lake there the name of the lake was called mascoma lake . We lived in a little yellow house we had other neighbords to and they were much nicer than the people who we lived with . Sometimes father would tease me and he would say to me you wanna go down to the lake Adam you wanna go down to the lake this was when I was either playing or reading . And when he said that to me I would just cry because I didn't know that he was teasing me . I had a little orange bike that had tires that diden,t need pumping up because the tires were hard . The seat was hard as well . I would sometimes go over to see my neighbors and talk with them or just play with them . And at night when I went to bed my father would lock the door . In the morning before I got up I would have the bed all nice and sopping wet waiting for him bedcause I didn't know how to get his attention at first . Then he showed me on how I was sopose to get his attention . The way I was sopose to get his attention was to bang on the wall from my room and let him know that I had to go to the bathroom . But I never did tell him . All I did was wet the bed and just lie in the smelly urine . I would just lie there and wait for him to come in the room . When he came into my room I would be smelling like urine all over . Then he would give me a bath in my little tin tub . I use to have a little toy to play with in the tub . And that was the butcher the baker and the candelstick maker fro the nursery rhyme rub a dub dub . We diden,t have a bathtub in our house at that time . We only had a shower . I took my baths with mr bubble . He would sometimes get that at the store .

When we lived in enfeild new hampshire father would take me to the Norwich day care center wich is located right in Norwich Vermont . He would drop me off right there and then he would go right stight to work and I would spend my time at the Norwich day care center doing differant kinds of games and things like that . And I would take my naps there as well . I would also eat lunch there as well . Then when my day was over father would come and pick me up at the daycare center at the end of the day and we would head for home . Then it would be like any other day . Going in and out . When I was getting a little bigger I had my very first christmas with my grandparents in Louisville Kentucky . I flew to Louisville with my father on a big air plane . The thing that I liked about the plane was when we were getting ready to take off into the sky . I also liked it when the plane started to get faster as it was getting to take off from the airport . And as the plane was lifting off the ground I could see the wheels going into the wings of the airplane . Then we were high above the clouds . That was my first time I have been on an airplane . We were in the sky for some time . We ate on the plane when we were coming to Louisville . Then after a while the plane was getting ready to land . So I was watching closely to watch the wheels come down . First the back wheels would come down and then the wheels in the front would come down . When we were in the plane I could see houses and cars that looked like little minature toy cars and trucks . It was fasanating . Then finally our plane was about ready to land at the Louisville air port . When I got off the plane with my father I started running from one end of the airport to the other .

Until I was all outta breath . Then we got into grandma,s car and headed to her house .

The minute we got there I HAD this habit of going into my grandma,s kitchen and open the lid of her trash can with my foot . I have been doing that ever since I was little . I have never forgotten to do that ever since I was little . And while I was there I went to the zoo with grandma and with aunt marion for the first time . And while I was with them I rode on the train with them all the way around the zoo . And while we were riding on the train we saw all the animals that were at the Louisville zoo . Then we left the zoo and started to head home to grandma,s house . Then we got to grandma,s house we got out of the car and went inside . I would watch television and grandma would be making dinner for us . Then after we ate dinner we would have dessert . And then we would watch television for a little while and then we would all go right to bed . I had a little bed at the foot of grandma,s bed . And if I coulden,t sleep I would tell grandma that I coulden,t sleep at night . Somtimes I would snuggle with grandma in bed for awhile . And then we would get up and have breakfast . And while she was cleaning up the breakfast dishes I was in the livingroom playing with all my christmas toys that I had gotten from everybody . I had a little toy electic train that went around and around in circles . And I would sit right in the middle of the track and let the train go around me. And if I left the room I would let the train run off the track and ware down the batteries down . Then the train was no good anymore . I got taken out to lunch at Burger King for the first time when I was little . Then after we visited with grandma and aunt marion for a while we got ready to pack up and head for home .

Then when I was getting bigger I was taken to the Cornish school for the first time to meet my new teachers . I was pretty shy for the first time I was getting to know the teachers a little more better . And I also got to know the other kids there at the cornish school . Then when I was in the fifth grade I had a teacher who were strict about somethings . I did something at school that I shoulden,t have done and that was that I took a twenty five cents off her desk without asking her permission . This was when I got into trouble with one of my other teachers and that was with Miss Alexion . This is when the real trouble begins . I was taken into Mr. Hutchins office to have Miss Alexion call my father at work and tell him the bad news . And while miss Alexion was talking to my father on the telephone I was all in tears because I did somthing that I shoulden,t have done . Then after she talked to my father I would talk to him . It wasn,t very pleasant for either of us . Because that meant that he would be interupted in the middle of this classes and meetings .

Then after we lived in infeild for a while we moved to Cornish . And I went to school in cornish when we moved . That,s when I met all my new teachers there . And the new principal as well . I made some new firends there on my first day of school . Then during the summer we went all the way to New Zealand . We went to school there we had to walk to school from the house we were renting . One time I lost my way home and I was lost for good though . until I finally found my way back home . I had these little plastic lunchboxes that I had to carry with me everytime that I went to school I had to eat my lunch outside with my class . Because they diden,t have a cafeteria at the school . And also this school would not allow you to ware long pants . You were only allowed to ware shorts to this school only . It was kinda strange for me to have to ware shorts to this school that I was going to . Pluse I have never been to a school that wore shorts to school . At this school that had a lady principal instead of a man . I liked the school alot . I had a man teacher when I went to school there . And they had a school nurse as well I diden,t know they had a school nurse that worked on student,s teeth . I thought it was a nurse that helped student,s that were sick get better .

Then we visited Auckland for a while we went down to welling-ton . We went sailing with some peple who had a sailboat . And we went sailing with them out on a lake . We got into there dinghy that they were pulling along behind the sailboat . We stoped at a little beach like area and we got into the dinghy and we got rowed on over to me little beach for a while ro so . We ate a little while we were on there boat . Then after we stayed for awhile we went all the way back to Auckland New Zealand by train . We slept on the train all the way from Wellington to Auckland New Zealand . It was a very long train ride from Wellington all the way to Auckland New Zealand . As we were heading back to Auckland we were on the train all night long . It was a long train ride back .

Then after we returned back from Wellington we went back to our normal things . Then it was our last day to be in new zealand and to be at school as well . On my last day at school I stood in front of my class and told them what I thought about Auckland and how I liked the school . And things like that . And then when I got ready to leave the Auckland school I was handed a book from new zealand called AOTEAROA . And inside the book everyone had sighed there names on a piece of paper than glued the piece of paper that they had all sighed on the front page of the book that my teacher got for me . Then on my last day in New Zealand I told everyone in my class who I had that I enjoyed myself there a lot . And that I hope I can come again some other time . Then before I left the school everyone wanted to have my signature so that they could remember me . I signed my name on a little peice of paper for everyone at the school . Then after I said good by to everyone from the school I went on home and as I was heading on home I got lost and I coulden,t find my way back . Then finally found my way back to the house we were renting . I had to walk up a hill part way then there was this driveway which was surrounded by a steel fence . And I had to walk down this steep driveway and I lived in a brick house which had a big livingroom and a small kitchen and a bedroom with a big twinsize bed . We slept in the twinsize bed . And it had a downstairs with a office and a spare room with a big piano in the back corner of the room .

I had to take a plastic lunchbox with me to school every day . And I had to eat my lunch outside because the school diden,t have a cafeteria . And the other thing that I had to do at school was to ware shorts to school because the school woulden,t allow you to ware long pants to school . One day I diden,t have any shorts to ware to school so I ended up with wareing pants instead . Then on my last day of school I was asked to stand in front of the classroom and say a couple of thing . I said that I liked the school a lot and that I liked being there as well . Then before I left the school I was handed a book called ATOEAROA . Then when I went back to the house that we were renting I got myself lost and I coulden,t find my way back to the house that we were renting . Then finally I had to walk up the road a little ways then I finally found my way back to the house that we were renting while we were in New Zealand .

Then on our last day in New Zealand we got all our bags packed and headed on to the airport and we got back on the Air New Zealand D.C . ten and flew all the way back to California . And then from there I took a VERMONT TRANSIT all the way back to White river junction vermont . And when I got into White river junction Mr and Mrs green were there to greet me . I got all my luggage off the bus then after I got all my luggage I put it into Mr and Mrs green,s truck . Then I headed toward home after I got off the bus . I went straight to bed as soon as I got home from my trip .

Then one day jeffrey came along .* He was pretty cute when he first came to New Hampshire . He had this funny little smile that he would show to everyone . He would squint his eyes and smile at the same time . He had the biggest smile out of anyone . Plus when he opened his mouth real wide . He can still do it . As he was getting bigger he ws starting to look more like himself . He as nice to have as my very own brother when he was little . But as for now he is getting bigger and stronger . I can remember when he was little he would have these temper tantrums when ever he got into trouble and he would never stop crying . And if father would tell him to stop he would just keep right on crying . Plus he would scream for hours and never stop . And if he diden,t stop he would be sent straight to his room . And when he could stop crying he would be able to come back down stairs and joint the rest of the family . But not until then .

When he diden,t want to do anything and father told him to it father would get mad and yell at him until he did it . Then when jeffrey got into trouble he would cry for hours . And if jeffrey diden,t stop crying father would make him stop automatically . Jeffrey did not like going to bed at night . When he was little . And he also diden,t like taking naps either . When we were in Louisville jeffrey was taken to the zoo for the first time . This was when it was just me jeffrey grandma and Autn marion at the time . While we were we rode the train around the zoo and me and jeffrey rode on the ponies . But there was one thing that jeffrey did not want to and that was to get off the ponies neither did I . Also while were there we rode on a elephant The one thing that I diden,t like about the elephant was the noise that it made . I covered up both my ears when the elephant made that sound . But otherwise I liked the rest of the zoo . The one animal out of the whole entire zoo that we liked was the giraffes most of all . And while we were at the zoo we also went to the children zoo . Then after we visited with them for a little whiole longer we

---

* Sava's first name is Jeffrey, and Adam used this in his story .

started to head for home . And we were on our way back home we stop in new york city to visit Autn Ginny .

On Thanksgivingt day we go to new york city to see the Thanksgiving day parade . My aunt stays at her apartment and waches the parade and I watch the parade which is not to far from her apartment . I watch it all the way through from floats to hot air balloons . There is one thing that I like about the Thanksgiving day parade and that is the balloons . One time I was there one of the balloons was getting ready to come down this was snoopy who has having problems staying up . I guess snoopy diden,t have enough hot air inside him . Snoopy began to have problems staying up during the parade . He then started to lean toward where I was standing . Snoopy almost touched the ground . And plus he almost landed on top of me . But they finally got him back up there . Snoopy began to lean in all directions . Then after they got him on the right track he was okay . Snoopy probably diden,t have enough hot air inside him .

Then finally madeline came into the family . When she came into the family she had a very bad diaper rash . Father would take her outside on nice sunny days and let her lie in the sun naked without any clothes on . She had this diaper rash and father would take her outside on days that were nice . She diden,t like being outside . She had this little smile that she would show to every one . She always had on her sad little smile . When madeline was a little bit older she had this habit in stuffing her cheecks with food . Jeffrey also had the same habit as well . And when they stuffed there cheecks father would come up behind them and he push your cheecks together and madeline's food went across the table . Father explained to madeline not to stuff her cheecks but she did it any way . Then one day the only way for her to learn was to take bites when jeff did That's when she cought on . Jeff also had the exact problem as madeline . He also liked to stuff his cheecks as well . So they all had to learn from there mistakes .

When jeff went to a day care center he was playing and runing and at that time jeff was runing and he triped over another kid and he hit his head on a chair and there was a nail sticking out of the chair and he cut open his forhead . At that time blood was rushing out pretty fast . One of the teachers at the day care center notice that my brother was in pain . At that time jeff was taken to mary hitchcock memorial hospital in hanover . Father rushed him straight to the hospital as fast as possible . When they got there jeff was rushed right into the emergancy room When he got to the hospital he was sent stragith to the emergancy room . While he was there he got seven stiches where he cut opened his forhead . And from there on he has got the scare from where he got the cut . When that happened he triped over another kid by the name of paul . When that happened I was at school at the time .

My father and my sister and my brother were in a automobile accident at one time . As for my father he hit his ribs against the steering wheel . But as for my brother jeff and my sister madeline luckly for them they had on there safty belts on . It was the opel that they had the accident in . We had a Volkswagen stationwagen before we had the opel . Then after we had the opel we got a Mazda then on October 10th 1981 we got married right in the back of our house on our patio . Then after we had our ceremony we went out to a nice resturant in Claremont for dinner . And as we were having dinner we got our mazda covered with shaveing cream . We had these little pot pies trays tied on to our mazda . On the front hood of the car they wrote in big letters JUST MARRIED . They put all these little pot pies all over our car . Plus they put on the shaveing cream all over the car as well . We had to go home with the shaveing cream all over our car . Then the next day we got up and father asked us to wash the car and get all the shaveing cream off and also take off all the little pot pie trays off the car . At that moment as we were takeing off the shaveing cream off the mazda Father noticed that the paint of the mazda came off while we were taking of the shaveing cream off the car . The shaving cream was all over the mazda . And we also had those pie holders . They were also all over the mazda as well . They were on the windsheild wipers and on the trunk of the car as well . And there were some put on to the antenna of the mazda as well . We went home that night with shaving cream put all over our car . We went out to a nice resturant that night . Father put the little pot pie holders into the trunk of the car because he did not feel like having the pot pie holders drag around while he was driving home . And also he did not want to feel emmberssed while driving on his way home .

I can remember when I went to NORTH DAKOTA with mom for the first time . We packed up the yellow car with all our belongings in it . We were driving the yellow car along for quit some time and at

that time the car stalled on us . So we pulled over the side of the
interstate . Mom tried to start up the car but everytime she tried to
start it up the break light kept lighting up everytime she tried to start
it up . So we were stuck on the side of the high way for quit a long
time if I DON,T SAY so myself . I was sitting way up high on some
rocks . We waited for some help to come by . So then we waited and
waited for help to come by it was getting late then finally some help
came by . A tow truck pulled over and asked my mother what was the
matter and she told him . So then after Mom talked to him about the
car she took the car to a near by garage to be repaired on . Then after
we had the car repaired we got back on the road and tried to find a
motel . But instead we slept in these trailers instead . Mom went
inside to get our mony back but we could not get it back . So we
ended up in sleeping in these weird trailers .

But then we started out back on the road towad NORTH
DAKOTA to see gram and gramps . And also there little dog rascal .
Now rascal is a very very playful dog . He is the kind of dog that likes
to chase things like for instance a stick and maybe a ball . The one
thing that I like about rascal is the way he greets people when they
come to the house . And when I was there in North Dakota the
people next door had a swimming pool . And on very hot days I would
go over with grampa and he would sit in one of the chairs on the rim
of the pool and read a magazine or a book . While I was swimming in
the pool . I would only have about an hour to swim in the pool . By
then dinner would be ready by the time we got back inside the
house . In the morning we would get up and I would go for a run with
grampa . And then we would be back for breakfast . Then during the
day I would either go to a grocery store or on a bike ride with
grampa . On some days grampa and louise would sometimes they
would go play tennis on the days that were nice . And while they
were playing I would be helping gram out as much as I can . I helped
grampa out as much as I could while I was there . I was glad that I was
able to a little bit of help while I was there . I also liked meeting
louise,s grandparent,s .
I diden,t want to be such a hog of myself when she said he should
start to gain some weight . And while I was there she said that I
should eat as much food as I want . And I told her that I diden,t want
to make such a pig of myself while I was there visiting her but she said

that she diden,t mind at all . She said that I could help myself to as much good as I wanted and I told her that that was quite alright . But she made me eat more food . I diden,t want to disappoint her at all .

So then after I stayed with louise,s grandparents we headed on toward NORTH DAKOTA . And while I was there I went running with gramps in a feild which had a little running track in it . I would go running with him in the morning which was fun . I would run around the track with him in the feild which was just right behind the school . So I went running around the track about eight times and then I headed on back home with gramps . I one time went on a walk with them and I went over across the street and at that point I made gram go looking all over the place for me . I got home before they did . Then finally gram came through the door way at that moment and she found me sitting in the living room watching television and she thought that I had gotten lost . But what I had really done was that I had crossed the street without gram or gramps seeing me . I had gram worried for some time when I was at the house before they were .

Then after that we headed on toward home back to cornish . Then after that we did our usal things after I got back home . Like for instance I did the laundry dishes the trash and also the putting away my laundry . And mostly doing my own jobs around the house . Then when I got home I was pretty glad to be back home the next day . I started to unpack my suitcase and put away all the clothes that I had brought with me to NORTH DAKOTA . Then on one day mom decided to have the whole entire kitchen painted white . So she went into town and went to get some white paint . Then she painted the whole entire kitchen white . It made the whole entire kitchen look alot different . Then after that I started to go back to my own regular things like my story that Im working on right now . So as for now it has been taking me quit a long time for me to work on it . But so far I have been doing a pretty good job . It is pretty hard to remember all the things I did when I was little . When I started the whole thing I cought on very quickly . I can also remember when I was at school when time when my brother jeff my sister madeline and my father were in a very bad accident at that point . And what had happened was they they were heading on toward home and at that point they got into a pretty bad accident . . . .

One time my father had to lie flat on the floor in the living room because he twisted his back while doing his arobics class at that time he ended up lying on his back for quit some time . While that was happening the three of us were trying our best to be nice to father because of his bad back . And we did everyting that we could to help him out . It was really hard with just the four of us . And as for my father he needed all our help that he could get . The one thing that he needed help with was getting up off the floor . If he moved one single muscle it would hurt him very much . He did not enjoy lying on his back it was very uncomfortable for him . So if he had to go to the bathroom louise would have to help him get up very carefully and then she would help him back into the living room . And then she would help him back to the floor very carfuly . It was a very uncomfortable poion for father to lye in . Then in couple of days his back was feeling a little bit better each day . Then after his back was back to normal he was getting to the point when he could start doing more things . Then he started to get back to his normal stuff . Then a day later he was going to teach his arobics class and as he was going to his class he managed to go up a flight of stairs a little to fast and at that point he sprained his ankle it was his left ankle that he sprained . He came home that night limping on one foot . He had his left foot all bandaged up . That night he layed down on the couch with his sprained ankle hi up in the air . He put his left foot on a pillow and put some ice on it to keep the swelling down . He could get around okay it bothered him every so often now and then but he managed to get around placed without thinking about it .

Then after that happened I did a very stupid thing while my father and louise was out to dinner that very night . I went into my sister,s bedroom and fell asleep on her bed until my father and mother came home that very night . When they came up stairs to go to bed that night they both found me lyeing on madeline,s bed . And I got cought right there . My father asked me over and over and over what I was doing madeline,s room and I made up all these lies . Then finally my father had to answer my question for me which was very very emberssing for me . Then after he had to answer my qustion for me he pushed me out of madeline,s room and made me go face first into the wall . And at that moment I ended up with a lump on the head . I was really ashamed of myself then . From then on I was no longer allowed into my sister,s bedroom anymore . My father was really mad at me for what I had done . He was not pleased with me at all either . Then after that had happened he one time asked me to go into her room at one time and at that point I said to him that I was no longer allowed into her room then after I said that to him he said that I could go into her room and I said to him that I was not allowed into her bedroom anymore then he started to lose his pacients with me at that very moment . I was in very deep trouble at that moment .

Then one time when I was at my gandmother,s house in Louisville Kentucky I was watching television at that time and as I was doing that I got a severe sting on my left leg by a mud wasp . I was in severe pain at that point . When my grandmother saw that I was in severe pain she put some baking soda on it to keep the swelling down . Then after she put that on she put a bandage on to cover to baking soda . Thuis was when my father and mother went away for a couple of days . They took my aunts car when they left for there trip . And while they were away for a while we did some interesting things togegethr . The things that we did was like go to the zoo and go out to lunch to some kind of resturant .

When they would come up to new Hampshire we would go to burger king in Claremont . One time we went there there broiler I guess broken and they had to have there broiler fixed at that time . So we all got into grandmother,s car and we drove all the way into lebanon to kentucky fried chicken to have lounch . So this was the first time that we ever went to kentucky fried chicken in lebanon . We have been going to burger alot of times when they were both here . There was something else that I got a habit of doing and that habit was eating my school lunch on the school bus . And when my father asked me if I had eaten my lunch on the bus I would ending up saying yes toward my father . Then one day he said to me if you keep eating you lunch on the bus before you even get to school I'm going to have to staple your lunch together . So I said to him okay dad what ever you say so then I went to school the very next day . As usal I got onto the bus with my brother and sister . and at that point just before getting to school I had eaten my lounch on the bus . Then when lounch time came around I had no lunch with me at that time because I had eaten it on the school bus . Then when my father said that he was gettng tired of teling me the same thing over and over again he decided that he would staple my lunch bag all together so that I wouldn,t be able to get into it until lunch time .

Then after that was all done with My brother had this problem of getting good grades on his report card . And when father asked him if he had finished class work and passed it in he would always say yes about it then lie about it . Then get calls from his teachers . And at time he started to do very bad in school . Father told him if doesn,t start doing well in school he would not be able to play in any sports unless he started to show some improvment . And since then he started to do very poorly in school and he lied to our father AND HE GOT HIMSELF INTO alot of trouble then . After that happened he got his walkman taken away from him for a while . Until he could prove that he could start doing good in school .

Then after that was over with jeff started to take music lessons at school and every night when he came home he would practics on the organ every night . He would practice on the organ every night just before going to bed . Then after practicing on the organ for quit some time jeff decided to give up right away . Father was not pleased with jeff,s atatude at that time . Then a couple days later jeff got stung right under neath the right eye by a yellow jacket .

Then after a while father ordered a truck load of wood it came to us in logs . Then after we had our logs delivered to us we had mr storrs and the pattersons at our house cutting up our wood for us . And splitting it for us with there wood splitter and after a while some men came by in there pick up truck . and they stopped by to help out with the wood . And when I got home from school I would end up doing all the wood by stacking it all in the way back of the garage . And what we had for extra wood I would stack it on the right side of the garage . It took me a long time to stack all that wood . I might of not told you this before but stacking wood is one of my favorite hobbies . I don,t really mind stacking wood at all . And my other hobby is mowing lawns . I don,t have any other hobby besides those two right there . One time when I was stacking a row of wood I was almost finished stacking the very last row of wood when it came crashing down on top of me . Luckly for me my glasses were not broken . I WAS glad about that . After that had fallen I had to restack it all back up again . This time I made the stack of wood more stable than before . One time the roof of the garage caved in and father thought that the cars were going to be destroyed finally he got the cars out of the garage before the garage almost came crashing down on top of the cars . Luckly for us we finally got both cars out in time . Then after that father called up a company who could refix garages .

The very next day they came to see what had happened . They had this certain kind of jack which was only used for putting garages back to their normal position . After they got the garage back to where they wanted it they put these boards inside the roof of the garage to make it alot more stronger . This was when we had the CHEVY MALIBUE and the subaru .

Their was onle thing that my father did not like about this car well actully there was a couple of things that he didn,t like about this car and those were like when he went outside to try to start it up in the morning to go to work . He had problems with the yellow malibue . So then my father decided to trade in the car and get another one . We then traded in in the car for another car after we traded in the malibue . We got a seven passenger van after we traded in the Chevy Malibue . Then we got the van we were able to go places together more often . That way we woulden,t have to take two cars at once . Then after that my father would take the van to work with him more often than he would the subaru . It seems to me that my father has had more experience driving the van than mom has and it seems to me that mom has had more experience driving the subaru than father has . I,m not saying this to be disrespectful . I,m just saying that they are both very good drivers and that they both have different driving tecnects .

The other thing I can also remember is that one time during the summer time when my father asked for me to go all the way around the house and dig up all these bushes called a burlock bush . So then on that very same day my father came to me and said to me Adam starting this weekend I want you to start digging up all these burlock bushes so that there is no more to be seen . So then on that very weekend I started out by doing the burlocks up by the barn . Boy ho boy let me tell you that on that very day it was real hot . I worked myself to a sweat . After I finished doing the barn I started doing the back of the house . There was more in back of the house than there was up at the barn . Then after that was all over with I would end up putting the burlocks into garbage bags . Well actually I would put them all into a big pile . And then after I got all the burlocks into one big pile I would let them all dry out over night and then the very next morning I would take all the burlock bushes that were all dead and then put them all into hefty dudy garbage bags . Then after I was all done with the burlocks I ended up digging up more burlocks . It was a real pain in the neck digging up more and more burlocks each time but it had to be done anyway . I diden,t mind doing the job for my father . But there were times on those real hot days that I diden,t feel like digging up burlocks at all but they had to be dug up anyway . So then I had to get that job before I could do anything else . If I haden,t done that job for my father we would of ended up having all the burlocks growing around our house . And that would of been a catastrofe .

Readers who wish to make a contribution toward furthering research on fetal alcohol syndrome or fetal alcohol effect may send their (tax-deductible) donations to:

FETAL ALCOHOL SYNDROME
C/O THE SEATTLE FOUNDATION
WASHINGTON FEDERAL BUILDING
SUITE 510 • 425 PIKE STREET
SEATTLE, WASHINGTON 98101
(206) 622-2294

EPILOGUE

Since the publication of this book in August 1989, several new scientific discoveries have corroborated the dangers of prenatal alcohol use. The *New England Journal of Medicine* (8/17/89) reported that drinking during breastfeeding may cause "slight but significant" damage to an infant's motor development. Year-old children of women who had one or more drinks a day scored lower on psychomotor tests than children whose mothers had less than one drink per day.

On January 11, 1990, the same journal published an even more startling finding—that women as a gender process alcohol differently from men. Dr. Charles S. Lieber and his colleagues in the United States and Italy announced, according to Gina Kolata's front-page *New York Times* report: "Women become drunk more quickly than men because their stomachs are less able to neutralize alcohol. . . . The finding is even more pronounced among alcoholic women, because the stomach apparently stops digesting alcohol at all."

With less of the enzyme that breaks down alcohol, a proportionately greater part of what women drink enters the bloodstream as pure ethanol—30 percent more than for men of similar weight who drink the same amount. But men and women usually aren't the same weight, and therefore one drink for an average woman is roughly equivalent to two or more drinks for a man.

Laboratory researchers at Washington University in St. Louis, Missouri, had potentially disturbing news for alcoholic fathers as well. In January 1990 Dr. Theodore J. Cicero, a pharmacologist, described the results of an experiment in which "alcoholic" male rats were bred with healthy females. While their male offspring (the focus of the first study; female offspring will also be tested) had normal body weight at birth, they did not perform as well as their counterparts on memory tests in mazes. The study suggests that alcohol may damage the rat's sperm, thus passing on genetic defects in the same way as do other toxic substances.

Meanwhile, the number of drug-impaired babies continues to rise and preliminary research suggests that the long-term effects of illegal drugs, such as crack cocaine, on learning behavior are similar to those of ethanol. According to one recent survey, upwards of 11 percent of all infants born in the United States in 1988 tested positive for cocaine or alcohol the first time their blood was drawn. A New York City Health Department official estimated that births to drug-abusing mothers had increased there by about *3,000 percent* in the past ten years.

Why? Some causes are obvious. Only one residential treatment program (Odyssey House) for pregnant women exists in New York, where the State Assembly Committee on Alcoholism and Drug Abuse estimates that "twelve thousand babies will be born addicted in New York City in 1989, and the number of children in foster care has doubled in two years from twenty-seven thousand in 1987 to more than fifty thousand today, mainly because of parental drug abuse." Sixteen percent of all American women who give birth have had inadequate prenatal care—increasing to 33 percent for unmarried or teenage mothers, 30 percent for Hispanic women, and 27 percent for black women.

The effects of this neglect are by no means restricted to impoverished urban areas. *The Cardova* [Alaska] *Times* reported on August 3, 1989, that "Alaska has the highest estimated incidence of FAS babies in the nation, and certain portions of the state record the highest FAS rate among any population in the world."

Although the legislatures of Arizona, Illinois, Minnesota, Oregon, Pennsylvania, New Hampshire, and Florida have recently created study committees or passed laws aimed at addressing the needs both of pregnant alcohol and drug abusers *and* of their unborn babies, much more effort and funding are needed if an unprecedented national health crisis is to be averted. A drug-impaired baby is destined for, at best, an adult life of sorrow and deprivation, and at worst, for a fate governed by crime, victimization, and premature death. But fetal alcohol syndrome is preventable—it need not happen ever again. The future of society, in this instance more than in most, is in our hands. We can't claim ignorance any longer.

Michael Dorris
March 1990

NOTES

CHAPTER SIX

1. Lewis O. Saum, *The Fur Trade and the Indian* (Seattle: University of Washington Press, 1965), p. 50.
2. Beatrice Medicine, *An Ethnography of Drinking and Sobriety Among the Lakota Sioux*. Doctoral Dissertation, University of Wisconsin at Madison, p. 189.
3. Gerald Mohatt, "The Sacred Water: The Quest for Personal Power Through Drinking Among the Teton Sioux," in David D. McClelland et al., eds., pp. 261–275, *The Drinking Man* (New York: Free Press, 1972).
4. Wesley R. Hurt, "The Urbanization of the Yankton Sioux," *Human Organization* 20 (4): 226–231, 1961; Hurt and R. M. Brown, "Social Drinking Patterns of the Yankton Sioux," *Human Organization* 24: 157–169, 1965; Eileen Maynard, "Drinking As Part of an Adjustment Syndrome Among the Oglala Sioux," *Pine Ridge Research Bulletin* 9: 35–51, 1969; Luis S. Kemnitzer, "The Structure of Country Drinking Parties on the Pine Ridge Reservation, South Dakota," *Plains Anthropologist* 17: 134–142, 1972.
5. Washington, DC: GPO, 1977.
6. Omer C. Stewart, "Questions Regarding American Indian Criminality," *Human Organization* 23: 61–66, 1964.
7. J. O. Whittaker, "Alcohol and the Standing Rock Sioux Tribe: A Twenty-Year Follow-up Study" (unpublished manuscript, as quoted in Medicine 1983), Fort Yates, ND: Standing Rock Sioux Tribe, 1980.
8. Murray L. Wax, *Indian Americans: Unity and Diversity* (Englewood Cliffs, NJ: Prentice Hall, 1971).
9. 1962, p. 472.
10. Medicine, p. 97.
11. J. O. Whittaker, *Alcohol and the Standing Rock Sioux Tribe* (Fort Yates, ND: Commission on Alcohol, Standing Rock Sioux Tribe, 1961), p. 478.
12. Ibid., p. 197.
13. Ibid.; Maynard, 1969.
14. Whittaker, 1962; Medicine, p. 155.
15. Medicine, p. 103.
16. Kemnitzer, 1972, p. 139.
17. Maynard, p. 40.
18. Medicine, p. 162.
19. Whittaker, 1961, p. 477.
20. Medicine, p. 115.

21. Ibid., p. 116.
22. Ibid., p. 117.
23. Ibid., p. 153.
24. Ibid., p. 118.
25. Whittaker, 1980.
26. Clement Blakeslee, "Some Observations on the Indians of Crow Creek Reservation, South Dakota," *Plains Anthropologist* 5: 1955, p. 32.
27. Niels Winther Braroe, *Indian and White* (Stanford: Stanford University Press, 1975).
28. Whittaker, 1962.
29. Medicine, p. 133.
30. Ibid., p. 135.
31. Ibid., p. 170.
32. Ibid., p. 136.
33. Ibid., p. 160.
34. Ibid., p. 150.
35. Ibid., p. 158.
36. Gretchen Chesley Lang, "Survival Strategies of Chippewa Drinkers in Minneapolis," *Central Issues in Anthropology* 1 (2): 1979, p. 32.
37. Medicine, p. 226.
38. Ibid., p. 232.
39. Ibid., p. 148.
40. Ibid., p. 167.
41. Richard Cooley, "Alcoholism Programs," in Jack O. Waddell and Michael W. Everett, eds., *Drinking Behavior Among Southwestern Indians* (Tucson: University of Arizona Press, 1980); D. B. Heath and A. M. Cooper, *Alcohol Use and World Cultures: A Comprehensive Bibliography of Anthropological Sources* (Toronto: Addiction Research Foundation, 1981); Medicine, p. 156.
42. Medicine, p. 153.
43. Ibid., p. 160.
44. Ibid.
45. Ibid., p. 159.
46. Ibid., p. 215.
47. J. O. Whittaker, "Alcohol and the Standing Rock Sioux Tribe, II: Psychodynamic and Cultural Factors in Drinking," *Quarterly Journal of Studies on Alcohol* 24: 80–90, 1963.
48. Medicine, p. 164.
49. Ibid., p. 168.
50. Medicine, pp. 169–170.
51. Ibid., p. 170.
52. Thomas E. Mails, *Sundancing at Rosebud and Pine Ridge* (Sioux Falls, SD: Augustana College Press, 1978), p. 43, as cited in Medicine, p. 183.
53. Joseph G. Jorgenson, *The Sun Dance Religion: Power for the Powerless* (Chicago: University of Chicago Press, 1972), p. 7.
54. Medicine, p. 223.

CHAPTER NINE

1. W. C. Sullivan, "A Note on the Influence of Maternal Inebriety on Offspring," *Journal of Mental Science*, 45: 489–503, 1899. This and previous historical references are discussed at length in pp. 1–28 of Abel's *Fetal Alcohol Syndrome and Fetal Alcohol Effects* (1984, 1987).
2. K. L. Jones and D. W. Smith, "Recognition of the Fetal Alcohol Syndrome in Early Infancy," *Lancet* 2: 999–1001, 1973.
3. A. G. Gilman, Louis Goodman, et al. *The Pharmacological Basis of Therapeutics*, 5th ed. (New York: Macmillan, 1975).
4. Cortez F. Enloe, "How Alcohol Affects the Developing Fetus," *Nutrition Today* 15 (5): 1980, p. 15.
5. Ibid., p. 13.
6. Iain M. Murray-Lyon, "Alcohol and Foetal Damage," *Alcohol and Alcoholism*, 20 (2): 185–188, 1985.
7. Ronald Forbes, "Alcohol-related Birth Defects," *Public Health, London* 98: 1984, p. 240.
8. Frank L. Iber, "Fetal Alcohol Syndrome," *Nutrition Today* 15 (5): 1980, p. 7.
9. A. P. Streissguth and R. A. LaDue, "Psychological and Behavioral Effects in Children Prenatally Exposed to Alcohol," *Alcohol, Health, and Research World*. A publication of the National Clearinghouse for Alcohol Information, Rockville, MD, 1985.
10. Forbes, p. 239.

CHAPTER THIRTEEN

1. Ernest L. Abel and Robert J. Sokol, "Incidence of Fetal Alcohol Syndrome and Economic Impact of FAS-Related Anomalies," *Drug and Alcohol Dependence* 19:51–70, 1987.
2. Streissguth, LaDue, and Randals, "A Manual on Adolescents," p. 28.
3. p. 32.
4. p. 10.
5. p. 30.
6. p. 36.
7. p. 31.
8. p. 11.
9. p. 23.
10. p. 34.

CHAPTER FOURTEEN

1. Streissguth, LaDue, and Randals, "A Manual on Adolescents," pp. 37–38.

BIBLIOGRAPHY

Of the hundreds of books and articles consulted in preparing this book, four are most helpful in understanding particular aspects of the text.

Dr. Ernest L. Abel's comprehensive and authoritative *Fetal Alcohol Syndrome and Fetal Alcohol Effects* (New York: Plenum Press, 1984, 1987) provides by far the best overview of the scientific explanation for fetal alcohol syndrome and its manifestations. It is well written, superbly documented, and most erudite.

Dr. Ann Pytkowicz Streissguth's *A Manual on Adolescents and Adults with Fetal Alcohol Syndrome with Special Reference to American Indians* (Washington, DC: Indian Health Service, 1986, 1988) presents a clear and detailed summary of the known behavioral effects of prenatal alcohol impairment, and the best analysis of how parents and educators might cope with these problems.

Anastasia M. Shkilnyk's *A Poison Stronger Than Love* (New Haven: Yale University Press, 1985) is a graphic, moving ethnographic account of an Ontario American Indian community beset with the ravages of alcohol addiction. Although the story of Grassy Narrows, as this village is called, is particular and by no means typical, it portrays a true and terrible reality that informs the lives of men and women of every ethnic background and in every part of the world when they are victims of a cycle of chemical dependency.

Alcohol Health & World Research 10 (1) [Washington, DC: U.S. Department of Health and Human Services], Fall 1985, a special issue devoted to preventing alcohol-related birth defects, includes fourteen cogent and important articles by leading researchers. Together, they provide an excellent overview of the state of investigation and thinking on the subject of fetal alcohol syndrome in the mid-1980s. Each article is followed by a helpful bibliography.

A selected list of other sources follows:

Aase, Jon M. "The Fetal Alcohol Syndrome in American Indians: A High Risk Group. *Neurobehavioral Toxicology and Teratology* 3: 153–156, 1981.

Abel, E. L. "Characteristics of Mothers of Fetal Alcohol Syndrome Children" (editorial), *Neurobehavioral Toxicology* 4 (1): 3–4, 1982.

———. "Fetal Alcohol Effects: Advice to the Advisors" (editorial), *Alcohol and Alcoholism* 20 (2): 189–193, 1985.

———. "Fetal Alcohol Syndrome—Behavioral Teratology," *Psychology Bulletin* 87 (1): 29–50, 1980.

———. "Prenatal Effects of Alcohol," *Drug Alcohol Dependency* 14 (1): 1–10, 1984.

———, and C. Moore. "Effects of Paternal Alcohol Consumption in Mice," *Alcoholism: Clinical and Experimental Research* 11 (6): 533–535, 1987.

———, and J. A. Lee. "Paternal Alcohol Exposure Affects Offspring Behavior But Not Body or Organ Weights in Mice," *Alcoholism: Clinical and Experimental Research* 12 (3): 349–355, 1988.

———, and Robert J. Sokol. "Incidence of Fetal Alcohol Syndrome and Economic Impact of FAS-Related Anomalies," *Drug and Alcohol Dependence* 19: 51–70, 1987.

Ackerman, Robert J. *Children of Alcoholics: A Guidebook for Educators, Therapists, and Parents*, 2nd ed. (Holmes Beach, FL: Learning Publications, 1983).

Agarwal, D. P., S. Harada, et al. "Racial Differences in Biological Sensitivity to Ethanol: The Role of Alcohol Dehydrogenase and Aldehyde Dehydrogenase Isoenzymes," *Alcoholism Clin Exp Res* 5 (1): 12–16, 1981.

Alcohol and Pregnancy: Fetal Alcohol Syndrome, Drinking During Pregnancy, and Effects on Offspring. A Bibliography (Seattle: Alcohol and Drug Abuse Institute, University of Washington), September 1981.

American Indian Policy Review Commission Report (Washington, DC: GPO, 1977).

American Medical Association, Council on Scientific Affairs. "Fetal Effects of Maternal Alcohol Use," *Journal of the American Medical Association* 249 (18): 2517–2521, 1983.

———. *Report on Fetal Effects of Maternal Alcohol Use.* Adopted by AMA House of Delegates, June 1982 (Chicago: American Medical Association, 1982).

———. *Symposium on the Effects of Moderate Drinking:* San Antonio, TX, January 13, 1980 (Chicago: American Medical Association, 1980).

Anderson, S. C., and J. F. Grant. "Pregnant Women and Alcohol: Implications for Social Work," *Social Casework: The Journal of Contemporary Social Work*, pp. 3–10, January 1984.

Anonymous. "Mother's Experience with Fetal Alcohol Effects," *Lakota Times*, 3/12/86.

Aracona, James, and C. K. Lee. "Scoliosis in Fetal Alcohol Syndrome: A Case Report," *Orthopedics* 4 (1): 1141–1143, 1981.

Aronson, M., M. Kyllerman et al. "Children of Alcoholic Mothers: Developmental, Perceptual, and Behavioral Characteristics As Compared to Matched Controls," *Acta Pediatr Scandinavica* 74 (1): 27–35, 1985.

Asetoyer, Charon. "FAS/FAE: There Is a Difference," *Lakota Times*, 3/12/86.

Associated Press. "Study Finds Cards Stacked Against Indians," syndicated wire story, 10/17/87.

Bach, P. J., and P. H. Bornstein. "A Social Learning Rationale and Suggestions for Behavioral Treatment with American Indian Alcohol Abusers," *Addictive Behavior* 6 (1): 75–81, 1981.

Bacon, Margaret K., Herbert Barry III, and Irving L. Child. "A Cross-Cultural Study of Drinking: Relations to Other Features of Culture," *Quarterly Journal of Studies on Alcohol,* Supplement #3, pp. 29–48, 1982.

Barrison, I. G., E. J. Waterson, and Iain M. Murray-Lyon. "Adverse Effects of Alcohol in Pregnancy," *British Journal of Addiction* 80: 11–22, 1985.

Beauvais, F. S. LaBoueff. "Drug and Alcohol Abuse Intervention in American Indian Communities," *International Journal of Addiction* 20 (1): 139–171, 1986.

Bee, H. L., A. P. Streissguth, L. F. Van Egeren, F. Lawrence, M. S. Leckie, and B. A. Nyman. "Deficits and Value Judgments: A Comment on Dr. Sroufe's Critique," *Developmental Psychology* 2: 146–149, 1970.

Bennion, L. J., and T. K. Li. "Alcohol Metabolism in American Indians and Whites," *The New England Journal of Medicine* 294 (1): 9–13, 1976.

Bishop, Charles A. *The Northern Ojibwa and the Fur Trade: An Historical and Ecological Study* (Toronto: Holt, Rinehart and Winston of Canada, 1974).

Blakeslee, Clement. "Some Observations on the Indians of Crow Creek Reservation, South Dakota," *Plains Anthropologist* 5: 31–35, 1955.

Blum, K., ed. *Alcohol and Opiates: Neurochemical and Behavioral Mechanisms* (New York: Academic Press, 1977).

Braroe, Niels Winther. *Indian and White* (Stanford: Stanford University Press, 1975).

Braunstein, Susan. "Indian Women: Unending Battle for Better Health," *Lakota Times,* 9/11/85.

Brod, Rodney, P. A. May, and T. J. Stewart. "Recruitment and Retention of Federal Physicians on the Navajo Reservation," *The Social Science Journal* 19 (4): 47–66, 1982.

Brody, Jane E. "An Estimated 50,000 Babies Born Last Year Suffered from Prenatal Alcohol Exposure," *New York Times,* 1/15/86.

———. "Any Drink During Pregnancy May Be One Too Many, Latest Research into Fetal Alcohol Syndrome Shows," *Minneapolis Star Tribune,* 2/23/86.

———. "Widespread Abuse of Drugs by Pregnant Women," *New York Times,* 8/30/88.

Carroll, J. F. X., T. E. Malloy et al. "Personality Similarities and Differences in Four Diagnostic Groups of Women Alcoholics and Drug Addicts," *Journal of the Study of Alcohol* 42 (5): 432–440, 1981.

Center for Science in the Public Interest. "S. 2047, H.R. 4441. A Bill to Require Health Warning Labels on All Alcoholic Beverage Containers" [leaflet]. 1501 Sixteenth Street, NW, Washington, DC 20036.

Chambers, Marcia. "Are Fetal Rights Equal to Infants'?" *New York Times,* 11/16/86.

Chávez, Gilberto, José Cordero and José Becerra. "Leading Major Congenital Malformations Among Minority Groups in the United States, 1981–1986,"

Centers for Disease Control: Morbidity and Mortality Weekly Special Edition 37 (SS-3): 17–24, 1988.

Clarren, S. K. "Recognition of Fetal Alcohol Syndrome," *Journal of the American Medical Association* 245 (23): 2436–2439, 1981.

———, and R. J. Sokol. "Standards for Use of Terminology Describing the Impact of Prenatal Alcohol on the Offspring, a Policy Statement of the Fetal Alcohol Study Group of the Research Society on Alcoholism" [unpublished]. Prepared for the Fetal Alcohol Study Group of the Research Society on Alcoholism, June 1988.

———, E. C. Alvord, S. M. Sumi, and A. P. Streissguth. "Brain Malformations Related to Prenatal Exposure to Ethanol," *Journal of Pediatrics* 92: 64–67, 1978.

———, Ellsworth C. Alvord, Jr., S. Mark Sumi, A. P. Streissguth, and David W. Smith. "Brain Malformations Related to Prenatal Exposure to Ethanol," *Journal of Pediatrics*, vol. 92, no. 1, January 1978.

———, P. D. Sampson, J. Larsen, D. Connell, H. Barr, D. C. Martin, and A. P. Streissguth. "Facial Effects of Fetal Alcohol Exposure: Assessment by Photographs and Morphometric Analysis," *American Journal of Medical Genetics* 26 (3): 651–666, 1987.

Cloninger, C. Robert, and T. K. Li. *Alcoholism: An Inherited Disease* (Washington, DC: U.S. Department of Health and Human Services, Publication no. [ADM], 85–1426, 1985).

Cohen, F. G., R. D. Walker et al. "The Role of Anthropology in Interdisciplinary Research on Indian Alcoholism and Treatment Outcome," *Quarterly Journal of Studies on Alcohol* 42 (9): 836–845, 1981.

Cole, Robert J. "Alcohol Lawsuits and Stock Impact," *New York Times*, 7/26/88.

Coles, C. D., I. E. Smith, J. S. Lancaster, and A. Falek. "Persistence over the First Month of Neurobehavioral Differences in Infants Exposed to Alcohol Prenatally," *Infant Behavior and Development* 10 (1): 23–37, 1987.

Cooley, Richard. "Alcoholism Programs." In Jack O. Waddell and Michael W. Everett, eds., *Drinking Behavior Among Southwestern Indians* (Tucson: University of Arizona Press, 1980).

Cooper, S. "Fetal Alcohol Syndrome," *Journal of Child Psychology and Psychiatry and Allied Disciplines* 28 (2): 223–227, 1987.

Cordier, Rose. "Liquor Controversy at Rosebud Heats Up," *Lakota Times*, 9/12/84.

Daily Washington Law Reporter. "Parent and Child: Termination of Rights," pp. 1208–1209, 6/13/88.

Davis, Janet Haggerty, and W. A. Frost. "Fetal Alcohol Syndrome: A Challenge for the Community Health Nurse," *Journal of Community Health Nursing* 1 (2): 99–110, 1984.

Debo, Angie. *A History of the Indians of the United States* (Norman, OK: University of Oklahoma Press, 1970).

Department of the Interior. *Alcohol and Drug Abuse in BIA Schools* [unpublished] (Washington, DC: Bureau of Indian Affairs, June 1982).

Dorris, Michael. "The Grass Still Grows, the Rivers Still Flow: Contemporary Native

Americans," *Dædalus, Journal of the American Academy of Arts and Sciences* 110 (2): 43–69, 1981.

Dozier, E. P. "Problem Drinking Among American Indians: The Role of Socio-Cultural Deprivation," *Quarterly Journal of Alcohol Studies* 27: 72–87, 1966.

Eastman, Nicholas J., and Louis M. Hellman. *Williams Obstetrics,* 12th ed. (New York: Appleton-Century-Crofts, 1961).

Egan, Timothy. "Despairing Indians Looking to Tradition To Combat Suicide," *New York Times,* 3/19/88.

Elliot, David J., and Norbert Johnson. "Fetal Alcohol Syndrome: Implications and Counseling Considerations," *The Personnel and Guidance Journal,* pp. 67–69, October 1983.

Enloe, Cortez F. "How Alcohol Affects the Developing Fetus," *Nutrition Today* 15 (5): 12–15, 1980.

Ericson, Avis J. "What Is a Teratogen?" *Childbirth Educator,* pp. 44–49, Winter, 1986/87.

Ernhart, C. B., R. J. Sokol, S. Martier, P. Moron, D. Nadler, J. W. Ager, and A. Wolf. "Alcohol Teratogenicity in the Human: A Detailed Assessment of Specificity, Critical Period, and Threshold," *American Journal of Obstetrics and Gynaecology* 156 (1): 33–39, 1987.

Ervin, C. S., R. E. Little, A. P. Streissguth, and D. E. Beck. "Alcoholic Fathering and Its Relation to the Child's Intellectual Development: A Pilot Investigation," *Alcohol: Clinical Experimental Research* 8 (4): 362–365, 1984.

Escobar, Luis, D. Bixler et al. "Fetal Craniofacial Morphometrics: In Utero Evaluation at 16 Weeks' Gestation," *Obstetrics & Gynecology* 72 (X): 1–6, 1988.

Everett, M. W., J. O. Waddell, and D. B. Heath, eds. *Cross-Cultural Approaches to the Study of Alcohol* (The Hague: Mouton, 1976).

Forbes, Ronald. "Alcohol-related Birth Defects," *Public Health, London* 98: 231–241, 1984.

Fox, S. H., C. Brown, A. M. Koontz, and S. S. Kessel. "Perceptions of Risks of Smoking and Heavy Drinking During Pregnancy: 1985 NHIS Findings," *Public Health Reports* 102 (1): 73–79, 1987.

Frederick, C. *Suicide, Homicide, and Alcoholism Among American Indians* (Washington, DC: National Institute of Mental Health, 1973).

Frias, Jaime L., A. L. Wilson, and G. J. King. "A Cephalometric Study of Fetal Alcohol Syndrome," *Journal of Pediatrics* 101 (5): 870–873, 1982.

Fried, P. A., and C. M. O'Connell. "Comparison of the Effects of Prenatal Exposure to Tobacco, Alcohol, Cannabis, and Caffeine on Birth Size and Subsequent Growth," *Neurotoxicology and Teratology* 9 (2): 79–85, 1987.

Fuller, Jim. "Line Between Drunk, Sober Is Blurred," *Minneapolis Star Tribune,* 3/24/88.

Gilman, A. G., Louis Goodman et al. *The Pharmacological Basis of Therapeutics,* 5th ed. (New York: Macmillan, 1975).

Goleman, Daniel. "Lasting Costs for Child Are Found from a Few Early Drinks," *New York Times,* 2/16/89.

————. "Major Personality Study Finds That Traits Are Mostly Inherited," *New York Times*, 12/2/86.

Goodman, Louis M., and Alfred Gilman. *The Pharmacological Basis of Therapeutics*, 5th ed. (New York: Macmillan, 1975).

Grady, Ketron, B. Dath, and J. Weibel-Orlando. "The Directory of Indian Alcoholism Services [unpublished], The Indian Drinking Practices Project of The Neuropsychiatric Institute, UCLA, Los Angeles, June 1985.

Graham, J. M. "Alcohol Consumption and Pregnancy." In Marois, M., ed., *Prevention of Congenital Malformations* (New York: A. R. Liss, 1983).

Graves, Theodore D. "Acculturation, Access, and Alcoholism in a Tri-ethnic Community," *American Anthropologist* 69: 302–321, 1967.

Haggard, H. W., and E. M. Jelinek. *Alcohol Explored* (Garden City, NY: Doubleday, Doran, 1942).

Hall, R. L. "Distribution of the Sweat Lodge in Alcohol Treatment Programs," *Current Anthropology* 26 (1): 134–135, 1985.

————. "Alcohol Treatment in American Indian Populations: An Indigenous Treatment Modality Compared with Traditional Approaches," *Annals of the New York Academy of Sciences* 472: 168–178, 1986.

Halmesmaki, E., K. Autti, M. L. Granstrom, M. Heikinheimo, K. O. Raivio, and O. Ylikorkala. "Prediction of Fetal Alcohol Syndrome by Maternal Alpha Fetoprotein, Human Placental Lactogen, and Pregnancy Specific Beta 1-Glycoprotein," *Advances in Biomedical Alcohol Research: Third Congress of the International Society for Biomedical Research on Alcoholism. Alcohol and Alcoholism Supplement No. 1*, Helsinki: 8–13 June 1986, pp. 473–476.

————, K. O. Raivio, and O. Ylikorkala. "Patterns of Alcohol Consumption During Pregnancy," *Obstetrics & Gynecology* 69 (4): 594–597, 1987.

Hannigan, J. H., B. A. Blanchard, and E. P. Riley. "Altered Grooming Responses to Stress in Rats Exposed Prenatally to Ethanol," *Behavioral and Neural Biology* 47 (2): 173–185, 1987.

Hanson, J. W., A. P. Streissguth, and D. W. Smith. "The Effects of Moderate Alcohol Consumption During Pregnancy on Fetal Growth and Morphogenesis," *Journal of Pediatrics* 92: 457–460, 1978.

Harford, Thomas, and L. S. Gaines, eds. *Social Drinking Contexts, Research Monograph No. 7* (Rockville, MD: U.S. Department of Health and Human Services, 1979).

Heath, D. B. "Alcohol Use Among North American Indians: A Cross-Cultural Survey of Patterns and Problems." In Smart, R. G., F. B. Glaser et al., eds., pp. 343–396. *Research Advances in Alcohol and Drug Problems*, vol. 7 (New York: Plenum Press, 1983).

————, and A. M. Cooper. *Alcohol Use and World Cultures: A Comprehensive Bibliography of Anthropological Sources* (Toronto: Addiction Research Foundation, 1981).

Hellman, Louis M., and Jack Pritchard. *Williams Obstetrics*, 14th ed. (New York: Appleton-Century-Crofts, 1971).

Henderson, George I., Rashmi V. Patwardhan et al. "Fetal Alcohol Syndrome:

Overview of Pathogenesis," *Neurobehavioral Toxicology and Teratology* 3: 73–80, 1981.

Hirschfelder, A., M. G. Byler, and M. Dorris. *Guide to Research on North American Indians* (Chicago: American Library Association, 1983).

Hollstedt, C., L. Dahlgran, and U. Rydberg. "Outcome of Pregnancy in Women Treated at an Alcohol Clinic," *Acta Psychiatr Scand* 67: 236–248, 1983.

Hurt, Wesley R. "The Urbanization of the Yankton Sioux," *Human Organization* 20 (4): 226–231, 1961.

———, and R. M. Brown. "Social Drinking Patterns of the Yankton Sioux," *Human Organization* 24: 157–169, 1965.

Iber, Frank L. "Fetal Alcohol Syndrome," *Nutrition Today* 15 (5): 3–11, 1980.

Indian Health Service. "Illness Among Indians Report, Calendar Year 1977" (Aberdeen: IHS [unpublished], 1978).

———. *Listening Post* (special issue on FAS), vol. 5, no. 3 (Washington, DC: The Mental Health Programs of the Indian Health Service, 1985).

———. Task Force on Indian Alcoholism. *Alcoholism: A High Priority Health Problem* (Washington, DC: GPO, 1977).

Ioffe, A., R. Childiaeva, and V. Chernick. "Prolonged Effects of Maternal Alcohol Ingestion on the Neonatal Electroencephalogram," *Pediatrics* 74 (3): 330–335, 1984.

Iosub, S., M. Fuchs et al. "Incidence of Major Congenital Malformations in Offspring of Alcoholics and Polydrug Abusers," *Alcohol* 2: 521–523, 1985.

———. "Long-Term Follow-up of Three Siblings with Fetal Alcohol Syndrome," *Alcoholism Clin Exp Res* 5 (4): 523–527, 1981.

Jessup, M., and J. R. Green. "Treatment of the Pregnant Alcohol-Dependent Woman," *Journal of Psychoactive Drugs* 19 (2): 193–203, 1987.

Jones, K. L., and D. W. Smith. "Recognition of the Fetal Alcohol Syndrome in Early Infancy," *Lancet* 2: 999–1001, 1973.

———, D. W. Smith, A. P. Streissguth, and N. C. Myrianthopoulos. "Outcome in Offspring of Chronic Alcoholic Women," *Lancet* 1: 1076–1078, June 1, 1974.

———, D. W. Smith, C. N. Ulleland, and A. P. Streissguth. "Pattern of Malformation in the Offspring of Chronic Alcoholic Mothers." *Lancet* 1: 1267–1271, 1973.

———, and D. W. Smith. "The Fetal Alcohol Syndrome," *Teratology* 12: 1–10, 1975.

Jones-Saumty, D., L. Hochhaus et al. "Psychological Factors of Familial Alcoholism in American Indians and Caucasians," *Journal of Clinical Psychology* 39 (5): 783–790, 1983.

———, R. L. Dru et al. "Causal Attribution of Drinking Antecedents in American Indian and Caucasian Social Drinkers," *Advanced Alcohol Substance Abuse* 4 (1): 19–28, 1984.

Jorgenson, Joseph G. *The Sun Dance Religion: Power of the Powerless* (Chicago: University of Chicago Press, 1972).

Kaminski, M., M. Franc et al. "Moderate Alcohol Use and Pregnancy Outcome," *Neurobehavioral Toxicology and Teratology* 3: 173–181, 1981.

Kemnitzer, Luis S. "Structure, Content, and Cultural Meaning of Yuwipi: A Modern Lakota Healing Rite," *American Ethnologist* 3: 261–280, 1976.

———. "The Structure of Country Drinking Parties on the Pine Ridge Reservation, South Dakota," *Plains Anthropologist* 17: 134–142, 1972.

Kennedy, L. A. "The Pathogenesis of Brain Abnormalities in the Fetal Alcohol Syndrome: An Integrating Hypothesis," *Teratology* 29: 363–368, 1984.

Kindley, R. J., R. J. Curran et al., attorneys for the plaintiffs. Legal brief on case no. C87–1525D, United States District Court, Western Washington District at Seattle [unpublished], 3/29/88.

Klein, Dianne. "Dark Past Can Haunt Adoptions," *Los Angeles Times*, 5/29/88.

Kolata, Gina. "Alcoholism: The Judgment of Science Is Pending" (opinion/editorial), *New York Times*, 12/13/87.

Kuzma, Jan, and R. J. Sokol. "Maternal Drinking Behavior and Decreased Intra-uterine Growth," *Alcoholism: Clinical and Experimental Research* 6 (3): 396–402, 1982.

Kyllerman, M., M. Aronson et al. "Children of Alcoholic Mothers," *Acat Pædiatr Scand* 74: 20–26, 1985.

Lamanna, Michael. "Alcohol Related Birth Defects: Implications for Education," *Journal of Drug Education* 12 (2): 113–123, 1982.

Landers, Ann. "Disposition Largely a Matter of Genes?" syndicated column, May 1988.

———. "Mother Supports Genetic Theory," syndicated column, August 9, 1988.

Lang, Gretchen Chesley. "Survival Strategies of Chippewa Drinkers in Minneapolis," *Central Issues in Anthropology* 1 (2): 19–40, 1979.

Larsson, G. "Prevention of Fetal Alcohol Effects: An Antenatal Program for Early Detection of Pregnancies at Risk," *Acta Obstet Gynecol Scandinavica* 62 (2): 171–178, 1983.

Leland, Joy. *Firewater Myths,* monograph no. 11 (New Brunswick, NJ: Rutgers Center for Alcohol Studies, 1976).

———. "Native American Alcohol Use: A Review of the Literature." In Mail, Patricia D., and David R. McDonald, pp. 1–56, *Tulapai to Tokay* (New Haven: Human Relations Area Files Press, 1980).

Lele, Amol S. "Fetal Alcohol Syndrome: Other Effects of Alcohol on Pregnancy," *New York State Journal of Medicine*, pp. 1225–1227, July 1982.

Lemert, E. M. "Drinking Among American Indians." In Gomberg, E. L., H. R. White, and J. A. Carpenter, eds., pp. 80–95, *Sciences and Society Revisited* (Ann Arbor: University of Michigan Press, 1982).

Lemoine, P., H. Harousseau, J. P. Borteyru, and J. C. Menuet. "Les Enfants de Parents Alcooliques, Anomalies Observées," *Oest Medical* 21: 476–482, 1968.

Levy, Jerrold E., and Stephen Joshua Kunitz. "Indian Drinking: Problems of Data Collection and Interpretation." In M. Chafetz, ed., pp. 217–236, *Proceedings: First Annual Alcoholism Conference of NIAAA* (Washington, DC: National Institute of Alcohol Abuse and Alcoholism, 1971).

———. *Indian Drinking: Navajo Practices and Anglo-American Theories* (New York: Wiley, 1974).

Lewin, Tamar. "When Courts Take Charge of the Unborn," *New York Times*, 1/9/89.

Little, R. E., A Young et al., "Preventing Fetal Alcohol Effects: Effectiveness of a Demonstration Project," *CIBA Foundation Symposium* 105: 254–270, 1984.

Littman, Gerald. "Alcoholism, Illness, and Social Pathology Among American Indians in Transition," *American Journal of Public Health* 60: 1769–1787, 1970.

Lurie, Nancy O. "The World's Oldest Ongoing Protest Demonstration: North American Indian Drinking Patterns," *Pacific Historical Review* 40: 311–332, 1971.

MacAndrew, Craig, and Robert B. Edgerton. *Drunken Comportment* (Chicago: Aldine, 1969).

MacGregor, Gordon. *Warriors Without Weapons* (Chicago: University of Chicago Press, 1945).

Mail, P. D. "American Indian Drinking Behavior: Some Possible Causes and Solutions," *Journal of Alcohol and Drug Education* 26 (1): 28–39, 1980.

——, and David R. McDonald. "Native Americans and Alcohol: A Preliminary Annotated Bibliography," *Behavioral Science Research* 12 (3): 169–196, 1977.

Mails, Thomas E. *Sundancing at Rosebud and Pine Ridge* (Sioux Falls: Augustana College Press, 1978).

Marbury, Marian C., S. Linn, R. Monson et al. "The Association of Alcohol Consumption with Outcome of Pregnancy," *American Journal of Public Health* 73 (10): 1165–1168, 1983.

March of Dimes Foundation. "Will Drinking Hurt My Baby?" [pamphlet] (White Plains, NY: March of Dimes Birth Defects Foundation, 1986).

May, Lee. "Report Says Indians More Likely To Die Young," *Minneapolis Star and Tribune*, 5/1/86.

May, P. A. "Alcohol and Drug Misuse Prevention Program for American Indians: Needs and Opportunities," *Quarterly Journal of Studies on Alcohol* 47 (3): 187–195, 1986.

——. "Alcohol Beverage Control: A Survey of Tribal Alcohol Statutes," *American Indian Law Reporter* 5 (1): 217–228, 1977.

——. "Arrests, Alcohol, and Alcohol Legalization Among an American Indian Tribe," *Plains Anthropologist* 20 (68): 129–134, 1975.

——. "Contemporary Crime and the American Indian: A Survey and Analysis of the Literature," *Plains Anthropologist* 27 (97): 225–238, 1982.

——. "Explanations of Native American Drinking: A Literature Review," *Plains Anthropologist* 22 (77): 223–232, 1977.

——. "Substance Abuse and American Indians: Prevalence and Susceptibility," *International Journal of the Addictions* 17 (7): 1185–1209, 1982.

——. "Susceptibility to Substance Abuse Among American Indians: Variation Across Sociocultural Settings." In pp. 34–44, *NIDA: Problems of Drug Dependence*, NIDA Research Monograph, No. 41 (Washington, DC: Department of Health and Human Services, 1982).

May, P. A., and Karen J. Hymbaugh. "A Pilot Program on Fetal Alcohol Syndrome Among American Indians," *Alcohol Health and Research World*, vol. 7, no. 2, Winter 1982–83.

——, K. J. Hymbaugh, J. M. Aase, and J. M. Samet. "Epidemiology of Fetal

Alcohol Syndrome Among American Indians of the Southwest," *Social Biology* 30 (4): 374–387, 1983.

Maynard, Eileen. "Drinking As Part of an Adjustment Syndrome Among the Oglala Sioux," *Pine Ridge Research Bulletin* 9: 35–51, 1969.

———, and Gayla Twiss. *That These People Might Live: Conditions Among the Oglala Sioux on the Pine Ridge Reservation* (Washington, DC: GPO, DHEW Publication HSM 72-508, 1970).

McIntire, Shelley A. "Annotated Bibliography on Fetal Alcohol Syndrome (FAS)," [unpublished] (Minneapolis: Minnesota Indian Women's Resource Center [1900 Chicago Avenue South, Minneapolis, MN 55404], 1986).

———. "Bibliography on Children of Alcoholics," [unpublished] (Minneapolis: Minnesota Indian Women's Resource Center [1900 Chicago Avenue South, Minneapolis, MN 55404], 1986).

Medicine, Beatrice A. "An Ethnography of Drinking and Sobriety Among the Lakota Sioux." Unpublished doctoral dissertation, University of Wisconsin at Madison, 1983.

Mohatt, Gerald. "The Sacred Water: The Quest for Personal Power Through Drinking Among the Teton Sioux." In McClelland, David D., William N. Davis, Rudolph Kalin and Eric Wanner, eds., pp. 261–275, *The Drinking Man* (New York: Free Press, 1972).

Montagu, Ashley. *Life Before Birth* (New York: New American Library, 1964).

Morgan, Thomas. "Learning Disabilities and Crime: Struggle To Snap the Link," *New York Times*, 10/31/88.

Moss, F., E. D. Edwards et al. "Sobriety and American Indian Problem Drinkers," *Alcohol Treatment Quarterly* 2 (2): 81–96, 1985.

Murray-Lyon, I. M. "Alcohol and Foetal Damage," *Alcohol and Alcoholism,* 20 (2): 185–188, 1985.

Nadel, Meryl. "Offspring with Fetal Alcohol Effects: Identification and Intervention," *Alcoholism Treatment Quarterly* 2 (1): 105–116, 1985.

National Institute on Alcohol Abuse and Alcoholism. *Fifth Special Report to the U.S. Congress on Alcohol and Health from the Secretary of Health and Human Services, December 1983* (Washington, DC: GPO, 1983).

Neugut, R. H. "Epidemiological Appraisal of the Literature on the Fetal Alcohol Syndrome in Humans," *Early Human Development* 5 (4): 411–429, 1981.

New Breast, Theda. "Fetal Alcohol Syndrome" [unpublished]. Materials developed for the Blackfeet Community College Program on FAS. Browning, Montana.

New York Times. "Birth Defects from Alcohol Persisting," 9/10/85.

New York Times. "Mother Who Gives Birth to Drug Addict Faces Felony Charge," 12/17/88.

New York Times. "Reports of New York Infants Born with Drug Symptoms Up Sharply," 4/1/88.

O'Connor, M. J., N. J. Brill, and M. Sigman. "Alcohol Use in Primiparous Women Older Than 30 Years of Age: Relation to Infant Development," *Pediatrics* 78 (3): 444–450, 1987.

Oglala Sioux Tribal Council. "Ordinance to Amend Chapter 3B, Subchapter IX, Child Abuse Provisions of the Oglala Sioux Tribal Code" (undated).

————. "Resolution Recognizing January 12–18 as National Fetal Alcohol Syndrome Week by the Oglala Sioux Tribe," Resolution No. 86–03, January 14, 1986.

Oppenheimer, Ingebor. "The Civil Liberties of the Unborn" (letter to the editor), New York Times, 10/23/86.

Palmer, R. H. et al. "Congenital Malformations in Offspring of a Chronic Alcoholic Mother," Pediatrics 53: 490–494, 1974.

Petersen, L. P., G. Leonardson, R. I. Wingert et al. "Pregnancy Complications in Sioux Indians," Obstetrics & Gynecology 64 (4): 519–523, 1984.

Phelps, David. "Cuts Peril to Indian Health Progress," Minneapolis Star and Tribune, 6/1/86.

————. "Indian Adoption Issues Put Culture, Rights in Balance," Minneapolis Star and Tribune, 5/29/88.

Plant, M. L. "Alcohol Consumption During Pregnancy: Baseline Data from a Scottish Prospective Study," British Journal of Addiction 79 (2): 207–214, 1984.

————. Women, Drinking, and Pregnancy (New York: Methuen, 1986).

Powers, William K. Oglala Religion (Lincoln: University of Nebraska Press, 1977).

Pratt, O. E., and R. Doshi. "Range of Alcohol-Induced Damage in the Developing Central Nervous System," CIBA Foundation Symposium 105, pp. 142–156, 1984.

Project Cork. Alcohol Use and Its Medical Consequences: A Comprehensive Slide Teaching Program for Biomedical Education. Unit 5. Alcohol: Pregnancy and the Fetal Syndrome, by R. E. Little and A. P. Streissguth (Timonium, MD: Mitner-Fenwick, 1982).

Prugh, T. "FAS Among Native Americans," Alcohol Health Res World 10 (1): 36–37, 1985.

Query, J. M. N. "Comparative Admission and Follow-up Study of American Indians and Whites in a Youth Chemical Dependency Unit on the North Central Plains," International Journal of Addiction 20 (3): 489–502, 1985.

Reed, B. J., and P. A. May. "Inhalant Abuse and Juvenile Delinquency: A Control Study in Albuquerque, New Mexico," International Journal of the Addictions 19 (7): 789–803, 1984.

Rex, D. K., W. F. Bosron et al. "Alcohol and Aldehyde Dehydroigenase. Isoenzymes in North American Indians," Alcoholism [NY] 9 (2): 147–152, 1985.

Rice, Matilda. "Fetal Alcohol Syndrome: A Clinical Study," Journal of the American Medical Women's Association 40 (1): 23–27, 1985.

Rosett, H. L., and L. Weiner. Alcohol and the Fetus: A Clinical Perspective. (New York: Oxford University Press, 1984).

————, et al. "Patterns of Alcohol Consumption and Fetal Development," Obstetric Gynecology 61 (5): 539–546, 1983.

Russell, M., C. Henderson et al. Children of Alcoholics: A Review of the Literature (New York: Children of Alcoholics Foundation, 1985).

————, G. E. Kang et al. "Evaluation of an Educational Program on the Fetal Alcohol Syndrome for Health-Professionals," Journal of Alcohol and Drug Education 29 (1): 48–61, 1983.

Sandor, G. G. S., D. F. Smith et al. "Cardiac Malformations in the Fetal Alcohol Syndrome," *Journal of Pediatrics* 98 (5): 771–773, 1981.

Saum, Lewis O. *The Fur Trade and the Indian* (Seattle: University of Washington Press, 1965).

Schuckit, M. A., and J. Duby. "Alcohol-related Flushing and the Risk for Alcoholism in Sons of Alcoholics," *Journal of Clinical Psychiatry* 43 (10): 415–418, 1982.

Schusky, Ernest L. *The Forgotten Sioux* (Chicago: Nelson-Hall, 1975).

Schwarz, R. H., and S. J. Yaffe. "Drugs and Chemical Risks to the Fetus and Newborn," *Proceedings of a Symposium Presented by the State University of New York, Downstate Medical Center* (New York: Liss, 1980).

Seattle Times. "Washington's Indians," A series of articles appearing from December 15 to December 20, 1985.

Seixas, F. A., G. S. Omenn, and E. D. Burk, eds. "Nature and Nurture in Alcoholism," *Annals of the New York Academy of Sciences* 197: 167–169, 1972.

Shaywitz, S. E., B. K. Caparuto et al. "Developmental Language Disability as a Consequence of Prenatal Exposure to Ethanol," *Pediatrics* 68: 850, 1981.

———, D. J. Cohen et al. "Behavior and Learning Difficulties in Children of Normal Intelligence Born to Alcoholic Mothers," *Journal of Pediatrics* 96 (6): 978–982, 1980.

Shore, J. H., and B. Von Fumetti. "Three Alcohol Programs for American Indians," *American Journal of Psychiatry* 28: 1450–1454, 1972.

Smith, D. F., G. G. Sandor, et al. "Intrinsic Defects in the Fetal Alcohol Syndrome: Studies on 76 Cases from British Columbia and the Yukon Territory," *Neurobehavioral Toxicology* 3 (2): 145–152, 1981.

Sokol, R. J. "Alcohol and Abnormal Outcomes of Pregnancy," *Canadian Medical Association Journal* 125 (2): 143–148, 1981.

Sorkin, Alan L. *The Urban American Indian* (Lexington, MA: Heath, 1978).

Spohr, H. L., and H. C. Steinhausen. "Follow-up Studies of Children with Fetal Alcohol Syndrome," *Neuropediatrics* 18 (1): 13–17, 1987.

———. "Clinical, Psychopathological, and Developmental Aspects in Children with the Fetal Alcohol Syndrome: A Four Year Follow-up Study," *CIBA Foundation Symposium* 105: 197–211, 1984.

Spradley, James P. *You Owe Yourself a Drunk: An Ethnography of Urban Nomads* (Boston: Little, Brown, 1970).

Stanage, W. F., J. B. Gregg, and L. J. Massa. "Fetal Alcohol Syndrome— Intrauterine Child Abuse," *South Dakota Journal of Medicine* 36 (10), 1983.

State of South Dakota. "House Bill 1310: For an Act To Require Alcoholic Beverage Licensees to Display Certain Health Warnings," 61st Session, Legislative Assembly, Pierre, SD, 1986.

Stein, Gary C. "A Fearful Drunkenness: The Liquor Trade to the Western Indians As Seen by European Travellers in America, 1800–1860. *Red River Valley Historical Review,* pp. 109–121 (Summer 1974).

Steinhausen, H. C., and H. L. Spohr. "Fetal Alcohol Syndrome." In B. B. Lahey and A. E. Kazdin, eds., *Advances in Clinical Child Psychology,* vol. 9 (New York: Plenum, 1986).

————, and D. Gobel. "Psychopathology in the Offspring of Alcoholic Parents," *Journal of the American Academy of Child Psychiatry* 23 (4): 465–471, 1984.

Stephens, C. J. "Effects of Social Support on Alcohol Consumption During Pregnancy: Situational and Ethnic/Cultural Considerations," *International Journal of the Addictions* 22 (7): 609–619, 1987.

Stewart, Omer C. "Questions Regarding American Indian Criminality," *Human Organization* 23: 61–66, 1964.

Streissguth, A. P. "Alcoholism and Pregnancy: An Overview and Update," *Journal of Substance and Alcohol Actions/Misuse* 4: 149–173, 1983.

————. "The Behavioral Teratology of Alcohol: Performance, Behavioral, and Intellectual Deficits in Prenatally Exposed Children—A Review of the Literature." In J. R. West, ed., pp. 3–44, *Alcohol and Brain Development* (London: Oxford University Press, 1986).

————. "Maternal Alcoholism and the Outcome of Pregnancy." In Milton Greenblatt and Marc Schuckit, eds., pp. 251–274. *Alcohol Problems in Women and Children.* (New York: Grune and Stratton, 1976).

————. "Maternal Drinking and the Outcome of Pregnancy: Implications for Child Mental Health," *American Journal of Orthopsychiatry* 47: 422–431, 1977.

————. *Papers from the Pregnancy and Health Study and the Pregnancy and Health Program* (Seattle: Alcoholism and Drug Abuse Institute, September 1984).

————. "Psychological Handicaps in Children with Fetal Alcohol Syndrome," *Annals of the New York Academy of Sciences,* 1976, 273: 140–145.

————. "Smoking and Drinking During Pregnancy and Offspring Learning Disabilities: A Review of the Literature and Development of Research Strategy." In Michael Lewis, ed., pp. 28–67, *Learning Disabilities and Prenatal Risk* (Urbana-Champaign, IL: University of Illinois Press, 1986).

————, and R. A. LaDue. "Fetal Alcohol: Teratogenic Causes of Developmental Disabilities." In S. Schroeder, ed., pp. 1–32, *Toxic Substances and Mental Retardation* (Washington, DC: American Association on Mental Deficiency, 1987).

————. "Psychological and Behavioral Effects in Children Prenatally Exposed to Alcohol," *Alcohol, Health, and Research World.* A publication of the National Clearinghouse for Alcohol Information, Rockville, MD, 1985.

————, and J. C. Martin. "Prenatal Effects of Alcohol Abuse in Humans and Laboratory Animals." In B. Kissin & H. Begleiter, eds., pp. 539–589, *The Pathogenesis of Alcoholism,* vol. 7 (New York: Plenum, 1983).

————, and S. P. Randals. "A Report to the Indian Health Service on the Physical, Intellectual, Academic, and Psychosocial Manifestations of Fetal Alcohol Syndrome and Fetal Alcohol Effects in Adolescence and Adulthood" [unpublished], December 1, 1987.

————, S. K. Clarren, and K. L. Jones. "Natural History of the Fetal Alcohol Syndrome: A 10 Year Follow-up of the Initial Eleven Patients." *Lancet* II: 85–96, 1985.

————, James W. Hanson, and David W. Smith. "The Effects of Moderate Alcohol

Consumption During Pregnancy on Fetal Growth and Morphogenesis," *Journal of Pediatrics*, vol. 92, no. 3, March 1978.

————, C. S. Herman, and D. W. Smith. "Intelligence, Behavior, and Dysmorphogenesis in the Fetal Alcohol Syndrome: A Report on 20 Patients," *Journal of Pediatrics* 92 (3): 363–367, 1978.

————. "Stability of Intelligence in the Fetal Alcohol Syndrome: A Preliminary Report," *Alcoholism: Clinical and Experimental Research*, vol. 2, no. 2, April 1978.

————, R. A. LaDue, and Sandra P. Randals, "A Manual on Adolescents and Adults with Fetal Alcohol Syndrome with Special Reference to American Indians" (Washington, DC: Indian Health Service, 1986, 1988).

————, S. Landesman-Dwyer, J. C. Martin, and D. W. Smith. "Teratogenic Effects of Alcohol in Humans and Animals," *Science* 209: 353–361, 1980.

————, D. C. Martin, J. C. Martin, and H. M. Barr. "A Longitudinal Prospective Study on the Effects of Intrauterine Alcohol Exposure in Humans." In S. Mednick and M. Harway, eds., pp. 448–469, *Handbook of Longitudinal Research*, vol. 1: Birth and Childhood Cohorts, 1984.

————, H. M. Barr et al. "Attention, Distraction, and Reaction Time at Age 7 Years and Prenatal Alcohol Exposure," *Neurobehavioral Toxicology and Teratology* 8: 717–725, 1986.

————, H. M. Barr et al. "Maternal Alcohol Use and Neonatal Habituation Assessed with the Brazelton Scale," *Child Development* 54 (5): 1109–1118, 1983.

————, C. S. Herman et al. "Intelligence, Behavior, and Dysmorphogenesis in Fetal Alcohol Syndrome—Report on 20 Patients," *Journal of Pediatrics* 92 (3): 363–367, 1978.

————, R. A. LaDue et al. "Indian Adolescents and Adults with Fetal Alcohol Syndrome: Findings and Recommendations," *IHS Primary Care Provider*, vol. 12, no. 11 (Phoenix, AZ: The IHS Clinical Support Center, 1987).

Sullivan, W. C. "A Note on the Influence of Maternal Inebriety on Offspring, *Journal of Mental Science*, 45: 489–503, 1899.

Taylor, Patricia. "It's Time To Put Warnings on Alcohol" (editorial), *New York Times*, 3/20/88.

Thomas, R. K. "The History of North American Indian Alcohol Use As a Community-based Phenomenon," *Journal of Studies on Alcohol*, Suppl. no. 9: 29–39, 1981.

Trimble, J. E., and B. Medicine. "Development of Theoretical Models and Levels of Interpretation." In Joseph Estermeyer, ed., pp. 161–200, *Anthropology and Mental Health* (The Hague: Mouton Publishers, 1976).

U.S. Department of Health and Human Services. Food and Drug Administration. "Surgeon General's Advisory on Alcohol and Pregnancy," *FDA Drug Bulletin* 11 (2): 1–2, 1981.

U.S. Department of the Treasury and the U.S. Department of Health and Human Services. *Health Hazards Associated with Alcohol and Methods To Inform the General Public of These Hazards. Report to the President and the Congress* (Washington, DC: GPO, 1980).

U.S.A. Today. "Mom Accused of Fetus Neglect," 10/1/86.

U.S. News & World Report. "Alcohol, Poverty—The Killing Fields of Rosebud," pp. 52–53, 9/2/85.

U.S. News & World Report. "America's Richest, Poorest Counties," 93 (16): 18, 1982.

Vietz, M., G. Koranyi et al. "A Semiquantitative Score System for Epidemiologic Studies of Fetal Alcohol Syndrome," *American Journal of Epidemiology* 119 (3): 301–308, 1984.

Waddell, J. O. "The Alcoholic Patient as an Ethnographic Domain: The Anthropologist's Role in the Therapeutic Process," *Quarterly Journal of Studies on Alcohol* 42 (9): 846–854, 1981.

Warner, P. H., and H. L. Roset, "Effects of Drinking on Offspring," *Quarterly Journal of Studies on Alcohol,* 36 (11): 1395–1420, 1975.

Wax, Murray L. *Indian Americans: Unity and Diversity* (Englewood Cliffs, NJ: Prentice-Hall, 1971).

Weibel-Orlando, J. "Substance Abuse Among American Indian Youth: A Continuing Crisis," *Journal of Drug Issues,* pp. 313–335, Spring 1984.

Weiser, Ben. "Inside a Sioux Reservation: Villages of Despair" (series), *Washington Post,* 9/9/84–9/11/84.

Weisner, Thomas, J. C. Weibel-Orlando, and John Long. " 'Serious Drinking,' 'White Man's Drinking' and 'Teetotaling': Drinking Levels and Styles in an Urban American Indian Population," *Journal of Studies on Alcohol* 45 (3): 237–250, 1984.

West, J. R. "Fetal Alcohol-induced Brain Damage and the Problem of Determining Temporal Vulnerability: A Review," *Alcohol and Drug Research* 7(5/6): 423–441, 1987.

Westermeyer, J. "Depressing Symptoms Among Native American Alcoholics at the Time of a 10-Year Follow-up," *Alcoholism: Clinical and Experimental Research* 8 (5): 429–434, 1984.

———. "The Drunken Indian: Myths and Realities," *Pyschiatric Annals* 4 (11): 29–36, 1974.

———. E. Peake. "A 10-Year Follow-up of Alcoholic Native Americans in Minnesota," *American Journal of Psychiatry* 140 (2): 189–194, 1983.

———, and J. Neider. "Predicting Treatment Outcome After 10 Years Among American Indian Alcoholics," *Alcoholism* [NY] 8 (2): 179–184, 1984.

Whittaker, J. O. "Alcohol and Standing Rock Sioux Tribe: A 20-Year Follow-up Study," *Quarterly Journal of Studies on Alcohol,* 43 (3): 191–200, 1982.

———. "Alcohol and the Standing Rock Sioux Tribe: A Twenty-Year Follow-up Study" (unpublished manuscript, as quoted in Medicine). Fort Yates, ND: Standing Rock Sioux Tribe, 1980.

———. "Alcohol and Standing Rock Sioux, I: The Pattern of Drinking, *Quarterly Journal of Studies on Alcohol* 24: 80–90, 1962.

———. "Alcohol and the Standing Rock Sioux Tribe, II: Psychodynamic and Cultural Factors in Drinking," *Quarterly Journal of Studies on Alcohol* 24: 80–90, 1963.

———. *Alcohol and the Standing Rock Sioux Tribe* (Fort Yates, ND: Commission on Alcohol, Standing Rock Sioux Tribe, 1961).

———. "The Problem of Alcoholism Among American Reservation Indians," *Alcoholism* 2: 141–146, 1966.

Wilson, Paula J., R. V. Scott, F. H. Briggs et al. "Characteristics of Parental Response to Fetal Alcohol Syndrome," *Birth Defects: Original Article Series* 20 (6): 187–191, 1984.

Winfree, L. T., H. E. Theis et al. "Drug Use in Rural America: A Cross-Cultural Examination of Complementary Social Deviance Theories," *Youth Society* 12 (4): 465–489, 1981.

Winkler, Allen M. "Drinking on the American Frontier," *Quarterly Journal of Studies on Alcohol*, 413–445, June 1968.

Wisniewski, K., M. Dambska et al. "A Clinical Neuropathological Study of the Fetal Alcohol Syndrome," *Neuropediatrics* 14 (4): 197–201, 1983.

Wright, J. T., I. Barrison et al. "Alcohol Consumption, Pregnancy, and Low Birth Weight," *Lancet* 1 (8326): 663–665, 1983.

———, K. D. McCrae, I. G. Barrison, and E. J. Waterson. "Effects of Moderate Alcohol Consumption and Smoking on Fetal Outcome," *CIBA Foundation Symposium* 105, pp. 240–253, 1984.

Yellin, A. M. "The Study of Brain Function Impairment in Fetal Alcohol Syndrome: Some Fruitful Directions for Research," *Neuroscience and Behavioral Reviews* 8: 1–4, 1984.

Films

Honour of All. 1985. 56-minute videotape. Phil Lucas Productions, Inc., P.O. Box 1218, Issaquah, WA 98027.

One for My Baby. 1982. WHA Television Segment. 30 minutes, color. Friends of WHA Television, 821 University Avenue, Madison, WI 53706.

Pregnancy on the Rocks: The Fetal Alcohol Syndrome. 1982. 26 minutes, color. Peter Glaws Productions, 138 B. Avenue / Coronado, CA 92118.